New Sweden
in America

For Ann and Chuck —

This is how we spend our time.

Lorraine and Richard

New Sweden in America

Edited by
Carol E. Hoffecker, Richard Waldron,
Lorraine E. Williams, and
Barbara E. Benson

DELAWARE

Newark: University of Delaware Press
London: Associated University Presses

Associated University Presses
440 Forsgate Drive
Cranbury, NJ 08512

Associated University Presses
25 Sicilian Avenue
London WC1A 2QH, England

Associated University Presses
P.O. Box 338, Port Credit
Mississauga, Ontario
Canada L5G 4L8

The paper used in this publication meets the requirements
of the American National Standard for Permanence of Paper
for Printed Library Materials Z39.48-1984.

Library of Congress Cataloging-in-Publication Data

New Sweden in America / edited by Carol E. Hoffecker ... [et al.].
    p.   cm.
    Includes index.
    ISBN 0-87413-520-6 (alk. paper)
    1. New Sweden—History.   2. Delaware—History—Colonial period.
ca. 1600–1775.   3. Delaware River Valley (N.Y.-Del. and N.J.)—
History.   I. Hoffecker, Carol E.
F167.N49   1995
974.9′02—dc20   94-36142
                                                                   CIP

This volume is dedicated to the memory of Amandus Johnson, the pioneering scholar of the New Sweden Colony, on whose painstaking and prolific work all subsequent studies of the Scandinavian colonial venture must rest.

Contents

7

Part IV: The Forest Finns and the American Frontier

Part V: Sources and Questions for Further Study

Acknowledgments

At every stage of the organization of the New Sweden conference and the editing of this volume of proceedings, the editors have drawn upon the assistance of many individuals and organizations. In addition to the University of Delaware, support for the conference was provided by the New Jersey Historical Commission, the Delaware Humanities Forum, the Winterthur Museum, the Institute of Migration of Finland, and the Swedish National Committee for New Sweden for '88. Much of the credit for the smooth operation of the conference belongs to the careful behind-the-scenes work of Mary Kay Sterrett, Marie Perrone, and the staff of the University of Delaware's History Department.

The editorial process for this volume has been fraught with innumerable problems because the papers were presented in a variety of formats. In the effort to define a consistent style for this volume, the editors relied upon the assistance of several people, including Dorothy Hall of the University of Delaware Writing Center and Mary R. Murrin and Lee R. Parks, both of the New Jersey Historical Commission, all of whom provided numerous consultations regarding style and editorial policy. We also thank Patricia Thomas and Cassandra John of the New Jersey Historical Commission, Gina Giambrone of the New Jersey State Museum, and Dianna DiLorenzo of the University of Delaware Office of Graduate Studies, who collectively retyped the manuscript.

Introduction

CAROL E. HOFFECKER

The New Sweden Colony was the first permanent European settlement in the Delaware River valley. Established in 1638 along the west bank of the Delaware River, the colony survived for less than two decades. In 1655 New Netherland conquered the Swedes, only to succumb to the still more powerful English in 1664. In spite of these disruptions, most of the Scandinavian colonists remained on the Delaware.

The significance of the Swedish settlement transcended its brief life as an independent colony. The colonists, mostly Swedish and Finnish peasants, adapted quickly to frontier conditions. Skilled at building simple, functional structures from wood, they introduced the log cabin to America. The Swedes were close observers of Native American life. They sent native artifacts back to their homeland, where these important specimens of mid-Atlantic coastal Indian material culture have been preserved.

The Dutch and English conquests did little to change the lives of the Swedish-Finnish settlers. Under the liberal policies of the Quaker proprietor William Penn, the Swedes were encouraged to maintain their Lutheran faith. Pastors sent from Sweden helped to sustain the group's original language and ethnic identity for several generations until the era of the American Revolution. Today thousands of Americans trace their ancestry to those hardy souls who left their Scandinavian homes to establish farms among the forests of America.

To mark the 350th anniversary of the New Sweden colony's founding, the University of Delaware sponsored an international conference entitled "New Sweden In America: Scandinavian Pioneers and Their Legacy." The conference, which met from 3 to 5 March 1988, brought together a group of twenty-eight scholars from Sweden, Finland, and the United States that represented several fields including history, anthropology, and geography. Because they live in different countries and work in different disciplines, many of these scholars had previously known one another only through their writings. Their diversity of training and perspective generated stimulating and lively discussions of questions of mutual interest about the colony's creation, existence, and enduring significance. In addition to the University of Delaware, other major sponsors of the conference included the Delaware Humanities Forum, the New Jersey Historical Commission, the Winterthur Museum, the Historical Society of Delaware, Finland's Institute of Migration, and the Swedish National Committee for New Sweden '88.

The anniversary provided the appropriate occasion for the first modern examination of Sweden's short-lived colony in North America. New Sweden has long been ignored by American colonial historians; no one has written a comprehensive history of the colony since Amandus Johnson published his monumental two-volume work, *The Swedish Settlements on the Delaware* (Philadelphia: Swedish Colonial Society, 1911). Great though Amandus Johnson's achievement was, his work was constrained by the limited information available to him and by the nature of his generation's intellectual agenda. In common with other early twentieth-century American colonial historians, notably G. L. Beer, H. L. Osgood, and C. M. Andrews, Johnson focused on the role of government and official leaders in making history. The documents that he used, the instructions issued to the governors of the colony and the governors' official correspondence with officials at home, shaped his historical perspective and interpretation.

In the decades since Johnson published his work, the writing of history has undergone significant transformation. Long, narrative descriptions of the actions of kings, generals, and government ministers have given way to historical inquiries that are more broadly based. Drawing on new types of evidence and on methods borrowed from other disciplines, especially the social sciences, historians have extended their perspective beyond formal political life to embrace the study of the economic and social life of past populations. These studies have heightened our appreciation for the interconnectedness of a wide variety of influences upon history.

In the case of the New Sweden colony, scholars can now draw upon a variety of sources that were overlooked or unavailable half a century ago. These sources include the work of ethnographers and archaeologists who have uncovered, studied, and interpreted evidence of the life of Native Americans in the Delaware River valley and of the natives' interaction with the colonists. In addition, scholars are using such seemingly mundane colonial records as tax lists and parish membership lists, together with remaining examples of the settlers' material culture, to fashion a more complete picture of colonists' lives. Meanwhile, in Scandinavia, Swedish historians are asking new questions about the causes and effects of Sweden's Age of Greatness in the seventeenth century, and Finnish scholars are exploring the outward migration of Finnish agrarian populations into Sweden and New Sweden during that same period.

The papers presented at the New Sweden conference and published in this volume reflect these trends in modern scholarship. Taken together they constitute the most recent interpretation of the history of the Delaware River valley during the early colonial period. The papers are arranged into five sections that progress from an examination of the European environment out which the colonial venture came, through the colonists' relations with the Native Americans to the Swedish and Finnish settlers' adaptation to colonial life; the last section concludes with suggestions for further study in as yet unexplored sources.

The papers in the first section, which is entitled "Colonial Enterprise in Sweden's Age of Greatness," describe seventeenth-century Sweden as it emerged from its traditional life and isolation into the dynamic world of western European politics and trade.

In her paper, "The Making of a Civilized Nation: Nation-Building, Aristocratic Culture and Social Change," Margareta Revera, of the Department of History, Uppsala University, argues that imperial ambition led Sweden into its "century of greatness" but also caused the country's uneven social and economic development during that period. Sweden tried to do too much too fast and its ambition soon outran the modest population and underdeveloped economic base. To maintain their expensive military apparatus, kings and ministers embarked on a crash program to modernize the economy, not unlike the broad-based efforts observable in many third-world nations in the twentieth century. Among the strategies employed in this enterprise were the deliberate encouragement of conspicuous consumption among the nobility and the creation of trading companies and colonies to stimulate commerce beyond the home country. Revera concludes that because of its incessant wars Sweden lacked the economic and population resources necessary to fulfill its ambition to become a colonial power.

Stellan Dahlgren, Revera's colleague at Uppsala, illustrates in his paper, "The Crown of Sweden and the New Sweden Company," an important aspect of Sweden's self-conscious economic policy. Johan Rising, who is best known in America as the New Sweden colony's last governor, was also the economic theorist who helped to spread mercantilistic ideas into Sweden. Rising's goal was to wrest commercial control of the Baltic region from the Dutch. Toward that end he urged the Swedish government and private citizens to replicate Dutch commercial institutions such as trading companies and colonies. In the case of the New Sweden Company this policy was unsuccessful. In 1658, twenty years after the colony was established and three years following its conquest by the Dutch, the company drew up a final balance sheet which showed that the colony had failed dismally to repay its investors. Professor Dahlgren concludes that although the rich and noble investors lost money, the peasant settlers, whom the company's creators viewed as mere tools in their game of international commerce, ultimately gained the most, for they acquired good farmlands and built new lives for themselves and their families in a new land.

Charles T. Gehring, director of the New Netherland Project at the New York State Library, concludes this section with a discussion of Dutch-Swedish relations in the New World. Gehring notes that the Swedish colony builders relied heavily upon the more technically advanced and better-financed Dutch to supply the money and technology upon which the Swedes constructed their colony. The rivalry between the two nations for control of the Delaware River valley was never conducted by equals. As soon as international affairs permitted, the Dutch seized control of the weaker colony. Gehring also emphasizes the importance of the Swedish colonists' relations with England's North American colonies and with the Native Americans as counterbalancing factors that helped to keep New Sweden alive for nearly two decades in the face of superior Dutch power.

Part 2, "The Colonists and the Native Americans," focuses on the trade relationships that evolved among the Swedes, Dutch, the Susquehannock Indians, and the Lenni Lenape. The principal items exchanged in this trade were European-made goods (including metal objects, guns, and liquor), fur pelts, and wampum made from special kinds of seashells, corn, and tobacco. In the mid-seventeenth century the middle Atlantic region was populated by relatively weak rival European settlements and by Native Americans who were eager to trade with the Europeans as long as the terms of contact did not fundamentally compromise their way of life. Because of this balance of power, the Europeans and Native Americans coexisted in the Delaware River valley for half a century.

Karen Kupperman, professor of history at the University of Connecticut, examines the means by which the underfinanced Swedish colony carved out a role for itself within the trade networks that bound North America to Europe. She notes that Peter Minuit, the colony's first governor, shrewdly planted the colony astride a major convergence point in Indian-European trade. The Swedes overcame their lack of trade goods from home by becoming brokers in a complex system of trade that involved the Susquehannocks, the Dutch, and merchants from the English New Haven colony. Their chief trading partners, the Susquehannocks, were also intermediaries who traded furs for wampum, which they in turn exchanged with Indians further inland. Like the Swedes, the Susquehannocks were a relatively small group poised precariously among more powerful Indian nations, yet for about two decades they traded with the Europeans on their own terms. In the early 1650s wars between the Susquehannocks and the Iroquois and between the Dutch and English signaled the end of the particular conditions that had sustained Swedish-

Susquehannock trade and set the scene for the Dutch conquest of New Sweden in 1655.

Where Karen Kupperman concentrates on the relations between the Swedes and Susquehannocks, Lorraine Williams, curator of archaeology and ethnology at the New Jersey State Museum, studies the relationship that evolved between the Swedish colonists and the Lenni Lenape, or Delaware Indians, who occupied the Delaware River valley. The Swedes, pressed to make profits for the company, concentrated on tobacco cultivation for the home market and bought their major food, maize, from the Delaware Indians. Unlike the English colonists, who pushed the coastal Indians of Virginia and New England into the interior, the Swedes and the Delaware Indians lived in close proximity for many decades. These culturally different peoples coexisted in the same area not only thanks to their trade relations but also because conservative Scandinavian land use practices preserved Indian hunting grounds. Marshall Becker, professor of anthropology at West Chester State University, further elaborates the theme of the Swedish-Indian maize trade. In a paper entitled "Lenape Maize Sales to the Swedish Colonists: Cultural Stability during the Early Colonial Period," Becker contends that the Indians increased their production of maize to satisfy the Swedish market without abandoning their traditional pattern of seminomadic foraging.

In his paper entitled "The Delaware Jargon" Ives Goddard, curator of the department of anthropology at the Smithsonian Institution, analyzes the language in which the Europeans and Indians conducted trade in the Delaware Valley. A jargon is a stripped-down version of an existing language that is used for limited communication, such as that needed to conduct commercial transactions. When the Swedes established their colony in 1638 they discovered that the Dutch and Indians were already using the Delaware jargon. Goddard calls the jargon "a remarkable example of a colonist-era pidgin based on a local native language rather than on the language of the Europeans." The jargon thus represented the Indians' equality in their relations with the Dutch and Swedes. Following the English conquest, pidgin based on English superseded the Indian language as the medium of communication between Europeans and Native Americans. Ironically, William Penn thought the Indians were simple people because he assumed that the Delaware jargon was the Indians' real language.

The final paper in this section deals with the Native American artifacts that reside in the collections of several Scandinavian museums. Staffan Brunius, curator of the Americas at Stockholm's Folkens Museum, describes these objects and their provenance. He explains that European noblemen collected specimens of Native American handicrafts for their curiosity cabinets. Indian artifacts in Scandinavia include two elaborately made ceremonial tomahawks that may have had symbolic significance in the relations between the Swedes and the Lenape. Further study of these unusual objects may help us to understand the Indians' culture and their attitude towards the settlers.

Part 3, "The Swedish Colonists and Their Culture," concerns the processes of immigration adaptations and the persistence of culture in the new environment. Sten Carlsson, professor of history at Uppsala University (now deceased), discusses the geographical and social origins of the colonists and deals with the problem of defining settlers as Swedish or Finnish, based upon their place of origin, ethnicity, and culture. Using the surviving passenger lists from the Swedish-sponsored voyages to America, Professor Carlsson identifies the places of origin and social backgrounds of many of the settlers. He argues that since most of the Finnish immigrants had lived in the Swedish province of Värmland before they immigrated to America, they had became more Swedish than Finnish in both language and culture by the time they reached the colony.

Hans Norman, also of the department of history at Uppsala University, reviews the Swedish colonists in both the seventeenth and eighteenth centuries in "The New Sweden Colony and the Continued Existence of Swedish and Finnish Ethnicity," focusing on ethnically related remnants of Swedish culture among descendants of the colony. He notes that the number of Finnish immigrants increased toward the end of the colony's existence and that two shiploads of Finnish settlers arrived after the Dutch had taken command of New Sweden. Following the practice of contemporary Sweden, the Lutheran ministers who came to the former colony in the eighteenth century kept careful census records of their flocks. From these records Norman concludes that most of the descendants continued to be peasant farmers and that their numbers increased rapidly due to early marriages, large families, and long lives. The ministers' records also document the declining use of the Swedish language in the middle and late eighteenth century as English culture became overwhelmingly predominant throughout the Delaware Valley.

Picking up from this discussion of the persistence of Swedish culture, Peter Wacker, professor of geography at Rutgers University, locates Swedish and Finnish farm settlements in colonial New Jersey. The Scandinavian colonists initially settled on the west side of the Delaware River in presentday northern Delaware and southeastern Maryland and on the east side of the river in southern New Jersey. The Swedes and Finns of the latter colony preferred the southwestern portion of New Jersey because the soils in that region were superior to those of the colony's central and eastern sections. Drawing on information from colonial tax lists, Professor Wacker concludes that the Scandinavian farmers retained their cultural distinctions well into the eighteenth century. Where English farmers in New Jersey preferred open fields and raised sheep among their farm animals, the Swedes and Finns chose to live in forested areas where they could practice lumbering, and they did not list sheep among their farm stock.

Frank Blomfelt's paper, "The Lutheran Churches and Their Pastors in New Sweden, 1638–1655," offers yet another perspective on the colonists' lives, beliefs, and culture. In the seventeenth century Sweden was one of the leading Lutheran nations of Europe. Because the Lutheran church was the state church in Sweden, church authorities in the home country dictated policies designed to regulate the church life, liturgy, and religious behavior of the people in the colony. Blomfelt's survey of parish life in New Sweden includes information about the religious books used there and the backgrounds and experiences of the Lutheran clergymen who served the colony while it was under Swedish rule.

The Swedes were a water-oriented people. The Finns, by contrast, were forest-lovers. Part 4, "The Forest Finns and the American Frontier," addresses the importance of this small but significant ethnic group in shaping the adaptation of later Americans to frontier life. The Finnish settlers' idiosyncratic way of life forms a recurring theme that runs throughout the history of New Sweden. In the seventeenth century Finland was a province of Sweden. The Finnish settlers in the New Sweden colony were of two types: some came directly from Finland; others had already migrated to Sweden before coming to America. The papers in this section discuss the migration of the forest Finns from the most remote sections of Finland to other parts of Scandinavia and finally to America.

Per Martin Tvengsberg's paper, "Finns in Seventeenth-Century Sweden and Their Contributions to the New Sweden Colony," describes the origins of Finnish cultivation practices in the Scandinavian spruce forests. The forest Finns were seminomads used to living in isolated family groups that foraged in their remote forests and raised rye as their principal cereal crop. They developed a method of intensive agriculture based on burning a section of forest and planting seed in the fertile ashes. When the soil began to lose its fertility they moved on to another forest location to repeat the practice.

Professor Juha Pentikäinen of the University of Helsinki discusses the transmission of Finnish forest culture from the Savo region in Finland to Sweden and finally to the Delaware Valley. He traces the migratory patterns of the forest Finns and demonstrates the persistence of their culture, including their use of a distinct dialect of the Finnish language that has lasted until recent times. The theme of cultural persistence is also underscored by Terry Jordan, a geographer at the University of Texas, in his discussion of the significance of Finnish agriculture and building techniques in the American context. The forest Finns excelled in using the axe to make simple but durable structures. This skill, together with their practice of open-range herding and plowless slash-and-burn cultivation, was ideally suited to the backwoods settlements in the forests of eastern America. In a process that Jordan calls "cultural ecology," Finnish traits survived in America in spite of the group's small numbers because their practices were suited to the environment.

The final section, "Sources and Questions for Further Study," requires little comment. Richard Waldron describes a joint undertaking by the New Jersey State Museum and the New Jersey Historical Commission to publish a complete inventory of Swedish and American manuscript collections dealing with all aspects of the New Sweden Colony. Mr. Waldron challenges scholars and archivists in both countries to make these materials more accessible by translating them into English since few American colonial historians know the Swedish language. He also proposes that the New Jersey-sponsored survey be expanded to include other European countries that were involved in the New Sweden colony.

Borje Westlund, keeper of manuscripts at the Swedish Royal Library (Kungliga Biblioteket) in Stockholm, and Olavi Koivukangas, director of the Institute of Migration in Finland, discuss the relevant archival and library holdings in their respective countries. Westlund explains the functional differences between Sweden's two major government depositories, the Royal Library and the National Archives. Koivukangas describes potential sources of materials relating to early Finnish migration in Finland and urges scholars to pursue still-unanswered questions concerning the settlement of Finns in colonial America.

The last speaker at the conference was Clinton A. Weslager, who places the proceedings into the context of previous scholarship and points to areas ripe for future research. He suggests that Swedish relations with the Native Americans, which have often been romanticized, should be studied more thoroughly and objectively. The comparative contributions of Swedes and Finns to the evolution of frontier culture in America, a subject of dispute among scholars, are another area that he singles out for further scholarship. Weslager's most important plea is for the establishment of closer ties among scholars interested in the Swedish colony on both sides of the Atlantic Ocean, a collaboration that he said was greatly enhanced by the conference at the University of Delaware.

Considered as a totality, the papers presented at the conference on New Sweden in America and published in this volume present a new perspective on the beginnings of American history and point to the important role that the Swedish colony played in the settlement of the middle

Atlantic region. The colony's history sheds new light on important aspects in the evolution of the nations of northern Europe. In the seventeenth century the Swedes unquestionably trailed the Dutch and English in their development of commercial institutions and in their adoption of those forms of social and political organization that were necessary to support economic development. As a result, the Swedish colonial enterprise depended on foreigners and was underfinanced, underpopulated, and undersupported by its home government. That the colony lasted as long as it did testifies to the tenacity of its leaders and adaptability of its people.

The colony's failure should not suggest, however, that nothing is to be learned from its history. To the contrary, Sweden's very weakness required the country to become involved in the complexities of international finance and trade to an unusual degree, thereby illuminating the interconnection of the commercial world in seventeenth-century Europe. Too often the American colonies are studied in isolation from one another, each colony being shown as interacting only with its home country. This model, which is based on the experience of the major colonial powers England, France, and Spain, was impossible for the Swedes. To finance their colony and support its trade the Swedes had no recourse but to interact with an international trading network that included the Dutch, English, and others.

Another significant difference that separates the Swedish colonial experience from that of the major colonial nations was the settlers' relations with the Indians. Several of the papers illustrate how and why the Swedes and Finns were better able to live peacefully with the Native Americans than were the English colonists in New England and Virginia. The Swedes did not treat the Indians as helpless children, nor did they alter the Indians' way of life. Instead the native people adapted to the new economic environment created by contact with Europeans by making choices of their own based on their cultural predispositions and upon their recognition of new opportunities.

Finally there is the theme of the colonists' own survival strategies. In spite of their small numbers, especially compared to the British settlers who came into the Delaware Valley following the establishment of Penn's Quaker colony in 1681, the Swedes maintained their ethnic identity, their language, and their religion at least until the era of the American Revolution.

New Sweden
in America

Part I
Colonial Enterprise in Sweden's Age of Greatness

The Making of a Civilized Nation: Nation-Building, Aristocratic Culture, and Social Change

MARGARETA REVERA

The ostentatious extravagance of the seventeenth-century Swedish aristocracy is in many ways a highly charged story. It always has been so, for from the outset a definite purpose underlay the luxurious living that characterized the social elite in the Swedish Age of Greatness. I shall try to show why this luxury can still be enthralling by describing the transformation of Sweden from a relatively backward agrarian society on the fringe of Europe into a civilized nation.

The new aristocratic lifestyle was, like so much else in seventeenth-century Sweden, an import. With its origins in the European courtly culture of the late Renaissance it was intimately associated with the growth of the strong new nation states of early modern Europe, and when it belatedly took root in Sweden it did so in the context of the country's newly attained great-power status and the nation-building that was taking place initially under the energetic leadership of Gustavus Adolphus and Axel Oxenstierna. This building of a nation, against the background of the overshadowing dictates of military policy and war-financing and in an underpopulated country with a comparatively undeveloped economy, has been described and analyzed by Sven A. Nilsson in *The Age of New Sweden*, in which this essay also first appeared. The intellectual backwardness of Sweden has been thought-provokingly underlined by Gunnar Eriksson, who notes the absence in Sweden of the kinds of association that formed the centers of modern science elsewhere in Europe such as new academies or societies of representatives of commerce, engineering, and politics. Groups of this kind did not appear in Sweden until the first half of the eighteenth century, by which time Sweden had man-

Reprinted, in revised form, from *The Age of New Sweden*, published in 1988 by the Livrustkammaren, Stockholm, and edited by Arne Losman, Agneta Lundström, and Margareta Revera.

aged to cut back the lead of more advanced nations in other respects as
well. The most eye-catching change had been in the architectural environment, where after decades of intensive building activity the royal family and the aristocracy could now parade such residences as Drottningholm, the Palace of the Nobility in Stockholm, and Skokloster, while
many merchants had built "great houses of stone" of the kind that Gustavus Adolphus had wished to see replace their "little cabins," as he expressed it in a well-known address to Sweden's parliament, the *riksdag*, in
1630 before that country's entry into the German war. Furthermore, Sweden had by now developed from being very much an importer of both
scholarship and art to a level where the flow was also now going in the
other direction. By this time the period of great-power status had come
to an end, together with nearly forty years of monarchic absolutism, another European phenomenon that was late in reaching Sweden. And the
Age of Greatness had given way to the Era of Liberty.

Together with the role of the aristocratic life-style in this process, my
essay will also consider New Sweden, the 350th anniversary of whose
founding we celebrated in 1988. A Swedish professor of history observed
in connection with the tercentenary in 1938 that hardly any chapter of
Sweden's seventeenth-century history could have been so thoroughly investigated as the short-lived colonial venture in America and its background, a subject that, he nevertheless considered, had to be regarded
as somewhat peripheral to that century's main events. It is easy to agree
with his first assertion, bearing in mind the enormous literature on New
Sweden on both sides of the Atlantic, but today his second assumption
appears anything but accurate. The knowledge of seventeenth-century
Sweden that we now possess makes the New Sweden enterprise very interesting indeed, provided that it is put in its correct context. This is a
context that must also include the life-style of the aristocracy, however
unexpected this may sound.

MYTHS AND TRADITIONS

It may well seem that hardly any other epoch in Swedish history has
been so "thoroughly investigated" as the Age of Greatness, which is of
course no guarantee that its correct context has been brought to light.
The aristocratic life-style of the Age of Greatness and its place in the social transformation that took place at that time are, however, subjects
more cocooned in myth than investigated, ones that have entirely failed
to excite the interest of recent historians. One sure reason for this is that
the spendthrift excesses of the seventeenth-century nobility have been
regarded as having obstructed social progress. It is with this myth-envel-

oped and "reprehensible" extravagance that this essay is primarily concerned.

The myths surrounding this extravagance are old. On closer examination they are by no means uninteresting, but as they have gone unquestioned they have had an unfortunate influence on later research, leading to the decidedly misleading picture of the seventeenth-century aristocratic life-style that has been propagated in both serious and popular accounts. Among the hardiest of these myths is the claim that it was the young Count Magnus Gabriel De la Gardie who brought extravagant fashions to Sweden, which he is supposed to have done when he returned from his embassy to France in 1647. He is reported, for example, to have impressed his guests at a dazzling banquet by providing the cutlery for them all (the custom was for guests to bring their own), in a display of household affluence never before seen in Sweden.

De la Gardie's reputation as the main introducer of luxurious living is part of a critical tradition that pinpoints the reign of Christina as the time when ostentatious extravagance began to appear and that emphasizes its coincidence with the end of the Thirty Years' War, the donations of landed estates to the aristocracy, and, last but by no means least, the rise of a new generation within the aristocracy. With this younger generation of aristocrats—the newly rich successors of the war veterans of the 1630s—a new culture is supposed to have arrived, characterized by a new way of life that was also adopted by the remainder of the nobility as far as their means allowed. Uncouth habits were thus replaced by elegant manners, it has been said, and an important role in the rapid spread of the new life-style of the upper class was ascribed to Queen Christina— that of her hectic and expensive amusements, which was thought to have set the fashion. Also customary is the belief that the new mansions of the nobility were built with German money and filled with war booty. The most celebrated collection of war booty is also claimed to have opened Swedish eyes to the country's extreme cultural backwardness. This is a reference to the looting of Prague's fantastic literary and artistic riches, which were taken in the final stages of the Thirty Years' War in 1648. The Silver Bible from the imperial collection (now in the Uppsala University Library) and the bronze sculptures by Adriaen de Vries from the gardens of General Wallenstein's mansion (now in the gardens of Drottningholm Palace) are among the priceless treasures brought over to Sweden.

The idea of a change of generation is the most important strand in this tradition. It dates back to a nineteenth-century school of political and cultural historiography that was highly critical of the aristocratic regency for Karl XI from 1660 to 1672 (in which De la Gardie was chancellor) and depicted the nobility as uniformly degenerate or at least verging on deca-

dence. This decadence is taken to have contributed to the unhappy events
that ensued, such as the commission of inquiry into the regency, the reduction (repossession of landed estates by the Crown), the fall of the aristocracy constituting the council of the realm, and monarchic absolutism.
Nor did the strictest moralist doubt when and why the decline set in. The
cause was the foreign aristocratic culture—the luxury and the refinement—
imported by De la Gardie and others of his generation, whose life-style is
described as marked by prodigality, a craving for luxuries, and a general
"lack of public spirit." The whole period is sharply contrasted with the
simplicity of the previous regency (1632–44), and with the "first generation" of aristocrats in the Age of Greatness, normally represented by
Axel Oxenstierna and his political acumen, love of country, lack of self-
seeking and, of course, distaste for any form of luxury. Such a judgment
on the ills of the age was passed as early as 1675 by Per Brahe, the aging
steward of the realm who had been a member of both regencies.

In its present form the tradition has changed to the extent that the mor-
alizing has disappeared, and with it the condemnation of the extravagance, but the emphasis on a generation gap remains, and Magnus Gabriel De la Gardie is sometimes cited as evidence of its existence. This is
because, interestingly enough, the belief that it was De la Gardie who
brought the taste for extravagance to Sweden agrees with the chancellor's
own view of the matter, recorded for posterity by the Italian diplomat
Lorenzo Magalotti in his Swedish travel diaries of 1674.

While Magalotti was so impressed by the luxury of the Stockholm of
the 1670s that he portrayed the Swedish capital as a French colony, his
compatriot Marquis Alessandro Bichi saw no cause for similar eulogies
just over twenty years later. On the contrary, his travel journal, dated
1696, has been quoted as support for the widely held view that the luxurious living died out towards the end of the Age of Greatness, by which
time only vestiges of the old splendor survived. Underlying this view of
matters is the notion that the aristocracy was cursed by the upheavals of
the 1680s and that the men of the period of Caroline absolutism were for
the most part a crowd of uncultivated upstarts, a myth emanating originally from the opponents of the reduction and of absolutism among the
old titled nobility. As Bichi himself relates, his guide in Stockholm was
in fact a member of this latter group.

In other words, the tradition of a clearly demarcated age of luxury consumption rests on an unsure foundation. Many accounts contain contra-
dictions and it is evident that the theory of a change of generation has
tended to obscure, for example, the existence of luxurious housing in
and around the Stockholm of the 1630s, glimpses of which are seen in
the diary of Charles Ogier, the secretary of the French legation from
1634 to 1635. Prominence has instead been given to those settings that

did not find favor with the Frenchman, which have been used to justify talk of a still-prevailing simplicity. When we remember this we are no longer surprised at the contradictory nature of the contention that the trendsetter in luxury consumption, De la Gardie, appearing in his new French attire in Munnichhoven's portrait of the early 1650s, is displaying a singular contempt for all prohibitions of extravagance, by which is meant the sumptuary ordinances. In other words, there was already an awareness of an extravagance so widespread as to necessitate legislation for its restraint.

But there is not a lot about this in the literature, nor has the luxury of the final decades of the Age of Greatness been adequately researched. This is a result of the myths surrounding the subject, which must not of course be taken at their word. The interesting thing about them is, rather, what they imply about the function of the consumption of luxuries; that De la Gardie should have boasted to an impressed foreigner of having brought luxury to Sweden provokes a number of reflections. The striking interest of foreigners in Swedish homes, festivities, and mode of dress is an expression of their concern with one question: Sweden was indeed a great power, but was it also a civilized nation? And it is the foreigners who tell of the war booty, in reports that are not infrequently tendentious. As one of the more innocent examples, mention may be made of Bulstrode Whitelocke, Cromwell's ambassador to Sweden in 1653–54, who noted a particularly costly silver dish at a banquet given by Erik Oxenstierna and assumed it to be plunder from Germany, whereas it was in all probability a wedding present from Estonia, where Oxenstierna had been governor. That the Swedes did not lack insight into the function of a display of extravagance is clear from Per Brahe's attitude when he was criticized by his father for his expenditure while studying abroad in the years around 1620. Brahe defended his purchases of clothing on the grounds that it was not enough to have a roof over one's head if one was to keep up appearances among foreigners. In the story of luxury consumption, the new life-style, and aristocratic culture in Sweden this is a more telling episode than the same man's jeremiad, more than fifty years later, on the wastefulness of the younger generation.

Since the nineteenth-century denunciations of the extravagance of the Age of Greatness, the subject has hardly attracted the attention of any historian. One notable exception, however, is Eli Heckscher, the economic historian of international repute who made his classic attempt at a broad survey of Swedish seventeenth-century society in the 1930s. Heckscher, too, was critical of the extravagance, but for the reason that the enormous increase in expenditure on consumption prevented saving and productive investment. Being unimpressed by the change-of-generation theory, however, he put the start of the aristocracy's extravagance in the latter part of the sixteenth century. Other facts of the picture of an antiquated and nondynamic agrarian seventeenth-century society, as presented by Heckscher, are the emphasis on the payment of taxes in kind and the barter economy, and also the traditional belief that the rule of the aristocracy delayed agricultural development until the threat to peasant freedom had been removed by the great reduction. To this has to be added the drop in the living standards of the broad strata of the population, which in Heckscher's opinion occurred during the seventeenth century as a result of the great-power policy and the nobility's heavy taxation of the peasantry. What is more, since luxury goods such as wines and superior textiles for the exclusive enjoyment of the small elite were a significant part of the country's imports at the end of the seventeenth century, just as they had been at the beginning, Heckscher states that the seventeenth century "continued in all its essentials to rest on the foundations of the old economy."

In these circumstances it is understandable that the transformation of Swedish society is usually seen as having started in the eighteenth century. Foreign historians who have considered events in Sweden from an international perspective have also pointed out the slow pace of development, particularly by comparison with England. A similar attitude to the chronology of development (but only to its chronology) was expressed by one of Sweden's nineteenth-century cultural historians, who thought she saw in the enthusiasm of the early part of the Era of Liberty for industry and science—for the building of factories and the establishment of trading companies and for the Royal Swedish Academy of Sciences, which was founded in 1739—a counterpart of the "public spirit" of the days of Gustavus Adolphus, or the spirit that was supposed to have been buried shortly afterwards with Axel Oxenstierna and his generation.

As we have seen from Sven Nilsson's essay, however, new research has led to a reevaluation of the traditional view of the society of the great-power period; for example, the hoary myth that the freedom of the peasantry and the peasant economy were threatened by the transfer of lands to the nobility, a myth dating back to the quarrels between the Estates of the realm around 1650, has been laid to rest. New perspectives have shown different aspects of the period in a new light: it becomes difficult to imagine a worse time for the Swedish peasantry than the period of war during Gustavus Adolphus's reign, with its very heavy state taxation and frequent conscriptions. The figure of at least fifty thousand men lost between 1621 and 1632 (out of Sweden and Finland's combined total of just over a million inhabitants) is another indication of the severe depletion of the country's population during these extremely hard years. The traditional preoccupation with the rule of the aristocracy thus proves to be a cul-de-sac, whereas the military-state perspective has turned out to be much more rewarding as a key to an understanding of the society of the seventeenth century and the changes that took place then.

The extensive transfer of landed estates was therefore a consequence of the need of the military state to reward and pay its warriors and its creditors, while at the same time it bound the nobility to the state. This belatedly put a great deal of land in the hands of the Swedish nobility, which constituted less than half a percent of the total population, and especially in the hands of the higher nobility, or the aristocracy, who could also count on the potentially most lucrative posts in the state administration. The nobility thus came to possess very large resources until the "feudal era" was superseded roughly half a century later by the society of the reduction and the allotment system with its different method of remuneration, a system that was more reliable and did not entail the personal sacrifice required by the previous one.

It is here that the aristocratic life-style comes into the picture, not the least important aspect being the prodigality with resources, which also deserves consideration from a new angle, that of seventeenth-century Sweden's need for social, economic, and cultural development. In simple terms, the problem was not the old-fashioned nature of peasant agriculture so much as the fact that there was very little economic activity other than agriculture—in other words, little commerce, trade, and industry. This was also how the problem was quickly seen by the Swedish government, which was at the same time concerned at Sweden's unimpressive status as a civilized nation. In the shadow of the all-pervading problems of the war, a reform program, ambitious even if not immediately successful, was initiated with the object of modernizing the country. With this, great demands were made of the nobility by the regency council and by Axel Oxenstierna, who was the driving force behind the program and who even saw a beneficial connection between the extravagance of the new aristocratic culture and the economic advance of the country.

AN AGE OF AMBITION

In March 1638 the *Kalmar Nyckel* and the *Fågel Grip*, two small ships that had set sail from Sweden the previous autumn, reached the Bay of Delaware on the east coast of North America. The expedition was led by the experienced German-Dutchman Peter Minuit—better known as the founder of New Amsterdam on Manhattan—who immediately began to establish the colony of New Sweden, as instructed by Axel Oxenstierna. The first land was purchased from the Lenape Indians, Fort Christina began to rise on the site of present-day Wilmington, and fur trading began with the Indians known to the Swedes as the Minquas.

Backing these enterprises was a new trading company, the New Sweden
Company, with both Dutch and Swedish interests, the latter representing
the Swedish government. Tobacco, in which the company was also to
trade, was obtained on this occasion from St. Kitts (St. Christopher) in
the West Indies on the return journey to Sweden.

When this happened, a very important *riksdag* had just closed in Sweden. Chancellor Oxenstierna, whom we know from Nilsson's essay as the
leading organizer of the country's public administration and the man behind the Instrument of Government of 1634 (Sweden's first written constitution), had returned from Germany in the summer of 1636, but not
until the autumn of the following year was it decided to call the Estates
to a general *riksdag*. The delay testifies to the government's nervousness
lest the Estates, once they got together, should seize the opportunity to
demand relief from taxation, when the predicament of the country, both
internal and external, demanded continued sacrifice. And indeed it was
possible to accomplish a certain amount without the Estates' participation, such as the founding of the Board of Mines in 1637 and the planning of a Board of Commerce, both of which indicate the intensified efforts of those in power to develop the economy. But the need to raise
more soldiers, combined with the parlous state of the exchequer, finally
made the summoning of the *riksdag* inevitable.

The demands facing the Estates were therefore first and foremost for
personnel and funds for the war currently in progress, which was a familiar situation during the difficult initial period of the Age of Greatness, as
was the call for the nobility to renounce its tax privileges. The time also
appeared ripe to try to deal with a number of recurring questions concerning the nation's internal finances. These included the problems of
misappropriation of the little toll (the local market tolls) and of differences in weights and measures in different parts of the country, and also
the threat posed to the forests by new settlement and by burning, and to
the Crown parks by illegal felling and hunting. Another matter of business was the need to find ways of ensuring the settling of debts incurred
by private individuals, a question that primarily affected the burghers and
the nobility.

Cultural affairs were also discussed, but here the government addressed itself only to the Estate of the nobility, which was enjoined to
provide for the training of its younger generation in noble arts and exercises and to be responsible for financing the building of the Palace of the
Nobility. These questions, too, were not new ones. The building of a Palace of the Nobility had been approved in 1625 and those nobles who had
volunteered to contribute to its financing had already been asked at the
riksdagar of the 1620s to pay up so that the work could start. At the
same time the Estate had been urged to send its offspring to the planned

college for the sons of the nobility, for which a Dutch engineer had already been appointed by 1628. (As Arne Losman has pointed out, a mastery of the science of fortifications engineering was among the accomplishments expected of a man of the world or *gentilhomme*.) Despite this nothing had happened, which led Oxenstierna immediately on returning to Sweden to call attention to the need for a fencing school, a riding school, and a dancing school, and also to the importance of arranging the financing of the Palace of the Nobility. The outcome of deliberations at the *riksdag* of 1638 on the first of these questions was that the nobility asked to be allowed to use the teachers of languages, dancing, and riding, who had in any case to be maintained at the royal court. As far as the building of the Palace of the Nobility was concerned, a reluctant and divided nobility was prevailed upon—by the vigorous efforts of the chancellor—to agree to a personal contribution far in excess of what they considered they could afford. On the other hand, no sumptuary ordinance, such as the Estate of the nobility had called for some years previously and now called for again, was issued. Nevertheless, the government agreed that the ostentatious extravagance accompanying weddings and funerals was causing difficulty to the nobility—an extravagance in which the poorly off felt obliged to indulge "like the rich" in order not to be "disdained and despised."

At about this time, at Stockholm Castle, a performance of the French ballet *Des Plaisirs de la Vie des Enfants sans Soucy* took place for the entertainment of the young Queen Christina, still only eleven years old. The first recorded performance of a ballet in Sweden, it was produced by the French dancing and ballet master Antoine de Beaulieu, who had been recruited to Sweden the previous year. The dancers were the young gentlemen of the court, representatives of the "second generation" of the aristocracy. Among them could have been observed the fifteen-year-old Magnus Gabriel De la Gardie and also Lorentz von der Linde, nearly ten years his senior and strictly speaking not a member of the aristocracy at all, although a future baron, councillor of the realm, and field marshal. His father, who had recently died, was the prominent merchant Eric Larsson von der Linde, himself the son of an immigrant Dutch merchant. Eric Larsson had been involved in Holland in the extensive credit-raising operations, based on the security of Swedish copper, that were essential to Swedish participation in the war at this time, and he had himself advanced large sums to the Crown. He had been ennobled for these services in 1631 and part of his loans had been repaid in landed property. There were three things that this man was said never to be prepared to divulge: how much money he had put into his new house in Stockholm, what he had lost in damage sustained at sea, and what he had spent on his son Lorentz! Clearly it was an investment that had paid dividends.

These three seemingly very disparate events—the founding of a Swedish colony in America, the eventful *riksdag* of 1638, and the Swedish première of French courtly ballet—have more in common than their approximately simultaneous occurrence, which is in fact no coincidence. They not only indicate the government's intention to reform Sweden, an intention expressed more forcefully after the chancellor's return home. On closer inspection the events also illustrate the difficulties that needed to be overcome. A dire warning came in the serous disturbances that at once broke out among the peasantry in response to the new war burdens and the more efficient collection of tolls. Some projects failed very quickly, such as the New Sweden venture, to which I shall return, while others would take decades to carry out, such as the building of the Palace of the Nobility, which was not finally completed until the 1670s. Only the court ballet, which came to play an important part in courtly festivities and thus in the panegyric art of which Allan Ellenius has written, was an immediate success. In other words, the culture of the aristocracy could be modernized more quickly than the nation's economy.

The Swedes were not alone in seeking to copy foreign models; similar ambitions were a feature of the building of all the new nation-states. In the cultural sphere it was first Italy and later France that set the tone, while in the economic sphere it was first Holland, then England. The distinctive aspects of the Swedish situation were perhaps that everything had to be done at once and that the aristocracy was to lead the way in the work of modernization, which had begun under the strong direction of Gustavus Adolphus or in some cases even earlier.

The improvement of mining and the development of the towns, for instance, had been on Gustavus Adolphus's program, which envisaged the expansion of domestic industry for the purpose. The regency pursued the same policy, while at the same time the development of towns, manufactories, trade, and shipping—"following the example of others"—gradually came to be regarded as a means of bringing money into the country with the aid of a favorable balance of trade. This principle was clearly exemplified at an early date by the proposal to establish a Board of Commerce in 1637, and Oxenstierna has been described as one of the foremost introducers of mercantilism in Sweden. But customs policy was still shaped by the fiscal needs of the military state (protectionism belongs to a later era), and the development of shipping also had as an objective the strengthening of the navy. By granting special privileges for certain kinds of manufacture or trade it would be possible to attract foreigners with large capital resources to Sweden, and they would not infrequently lend money to the state. The most celebrated of them all arrived while Gustavus Adolphus was still on the throne. This was Louis De Geer, who came to be known as the father of Swedish industry. In addition specialist

skilled labor was also imported, and there is mention at one point of recruiting a company of flax weavers. But the object had to be to make the
country independent of foreigners by training Swedes. Such, at any rate,
was the attitude taken by Carl Bonde, councillor of the realm and president of the Board of Mines, when in 1640 he proudly announced that
Swedish carpenters could now make lock gates of wood that were as
good as those made of stone by imported Dutch lock builders.

The plea for a higher level of cultivation reflected even more clearly
the need for self-assertion. When Oxenstierna inspected Uppsala University in 1637, for example, it was decided that botanical gardens should be
laid out and an anatomical theater built, both of which projects, as we
have seen, were realized only in the time of Olof Rudbeck. The anatomical theater was to be provided with instruments, skeletons, and rarities
that would enable both Swedes and foreigners to observe in Sweden
what had hitherto been on view only overseas. The need for self-assertion is most plainly expressed in the plans of the regency council for the
nobility, which was to be the backbone of the new state. The reign of
Gustavus Adolphus was stated at the *riksdag* of 1638 to have marked
the beginning of a new period in the history of the nobility, which had
been oppressed and scorned abroad and had been unworthy of comparison with the nobility of other nations. The Palace of the Nobility was to
be a visible symbol of the nobility's new status, while at the same time the
nobles, before being sent on government service, needed to possess all
kinds of accomplishments, which ought first to be practiced at home, before being perfected in the course of study abroad. If we consider, for
example, the relatively impecunious Carl Bonde, we see how strongly—
and early—these ambitions were felt. In 1632 he is taking pleasure in his
sons' command of French (at the ages of twelve and ten); in 1634 he is
lamenting the fact that at the University of Uppsala they receive neither
instruction in "mores" nor training in noble exercises, and in 1638 we find
the sons being sent with their tutor to England, and from there to
Holland and France. Financial assistance was given initially by Axel
Oxenstierna and his banker, Peter Spiring, originally a Dutchman, now
a Swede.

Two very interesting discussions linking the financial and cultural
spheres took place in the council in the spring of 1641. In the first case
the point at issue was how to stop the outflow of Swedish coin and capital. Oxenstierna then rejected the sumptuary law, proposed, surprisingly,
by the burgomaster of Stockholm, giving three reasons for its rejection:
the difficulty of getting people to observe such a law, the fact that steps
were just being taken to "civilize the nation," and the importance of at-
tracting trade and commerce to the country. In the second case the discussion was complicated by the difficulty of resolving the question of the

disposal of landed estates to meet the state's critical financial problems, a subject that was especially delicate during the queen's minority. Discussion then moved to how Sweden could best emulate other countries' cultural standards in general. It was decided that this would be best done first by founding towns and promoting trade and manufacturing industry, which could be expected to yield large profits from town tolls and excise duties (implying the much-needed revenues in cash rather than in kind, it might have been added), and second by relying on the nobility to build up the country.

Oxenstierna's well-known program for the state finances is presented here as plainly as anyone could wish, as is the much less-noticed call for cultural renewal and transformation that accompanies it. The broad signification of "culture" should be noted, as should the strong expectation that the nobility will participate in the social transformation. Last but not least, Oxenstierna's realization of the importance of a real domestic demand in successfully bringing about the required changes ought to be observed.

Therefore there might be a desirable side to the spendthrift life-style of the social elite, a suggestion to which I shall return. But I must first refer to the possible connection between the New Sweden venture and the contemporary process of nation-building with its social background. There is reason to consider these matters in some detail, although without going into the full history of the enterprise.

THE CASE OF NEW SWEDEN

New Sweden was to enjoy an existence of only seventeen years. Consequently it never became the gleaming jewel in the Swedish crown which the Dutchman Willem Usselincx had predicted in the early 1630s that it could become and into which even the last governor, Johan Rising, believed New Sweden could still develop, if only supplies and colonists were sent without delay from home. Rising's opinion may be read in an optimistic report written in July 1654, soon after his arrival. But by September 1655 Rising was compelled to cede the colony to Peter Stuyvesant, the energetic governor of New Netherland, who was in turn forced, nine years later, to capitulate to the English.

With the exception of Rising, a few officers and soldiers, and a small number of other colonists, most of the Swedes chose to remain in America. Many of them had just arrived with the tenth expedition from their homeland, which had given a much-needed boost to the settlers' numbers. Previously the population of the colony had not only been small but also included remarkably few farmers, or freemen as they were known, which did not augur particularly well for the prospects of a colonial enterprise. At the time of the Dutch capture there were roughly four hundred Swedes in New Sweden in about 130 households, together with two hundred other colonists of other nationalities who had been allowed to settle there. The total number of Swedish voyagers to America in the mid-seventeenth century was probably at least twice as many, however, but not all of them reached New Sweden and some left the colony again to return home or settle elsewhere. Moreover there were a number who did not arrive until the Swedish era had already come to an end. Many were Finns who had come either from Sweden, some forest areas of which had quite a sizable Finnish population, or from Finland itself. There were also people of foreign origin, as in most Swedish contexts at this period. In any event the Swedes were never numerous, particularly by comparison with the total number of Europeans in the coastal colonies, from Virginia in the south to New England in the north, which was probably around one hundred thousand in the 1600s.

To many people in the tracts where the colony's institutions and the colonists' settlements once stood, in the states of Delaware, Pennsylvania, New Jersey, and Maryland, a lively interest in New Sweden is taken as a matter of course; people speak of the contribution of the New Sweden Swedes to American civilization and of "the Swedish heritage," which I can touch on only briefly here. The Swedes and their descendants, estimated in the second decade of the eighteenth century to number about one thousand and five hundred persons, existed as a distinct ethnic group for over a century. One reason for this was that for a long time pastors were sent over by Sweden to minister to the Swedish Lutheran congregations in the area, to which the survival of six old churches today bears witness. Of these, the Holy Trinity Church in Wilmington, consecrated in 1699, is the oldest church in America still standing on its original site and in use for services, while the Gloria Dei Church (now the Old Swedes' Church) in Philadelphia is the oldest church in Pennsylvania. Another Swedish influence is to be found in the field of housebuilding, where the Swedes' choice of timber as their building material, together with their special corner-timber technique, gave rise to the log cabin, which seems quickly to have become standard in all settlements of the wooded regions of North America. It has also been said that to some extent the later colonial style of the American settler had its roots in the Swedes' log cabin.

The leading chronicler of the New Sweden enterprise is the Swedish-American Amandus Johnson, whose *The Swedish Settlements on the Delaware 1638–1664* was published in 1911, but as was mentioned by way of introduction, a copious literature exists on New Sweden. As colonists Swedes have generally earned good ratings, whereas Sweden as a colonizing power has been portrayed in a less favorable light. The reason usually given for the initiation of the New Sweden venture is Oxenstierna's wish to find new markets for Swedish copper or the need for new sources of income after the loss of revenue from licenses to trade through the Prussian ports in 1635. The failure of the project has in turn been attributed to the inadequate support it received from Sweden as a result of the government's preoccupation with war and the alleged indifference of Queen Christina to affairs of state. The wreck of the *Kattan* in 1649, with the loss of the ninth expedition from Sweden and some seventy would-be colonists, has also been seen as very important, as have certain mistakes said to have been made by Governor Rising in the face of the threat from the Dutch. In addition it has recently been argued that the project was in any case doomed to failure as Peter Minuit applied to the founding of New Sweden the same set of assumptions as to New Amsterdam twelve years earlier and did not take into account Sweden's insufficiency of deep-sea tonnage.

One has to agree that the New Sweden enterprise had no hope of success, especially as both the Dutch and the English claimed the area at the mouth of the Delaware. And it is very true that the lack of vessels and, more particularly, of experienced seamen, was a problem. But the interesting point about the transport question is that this was in fact one of the main reasons for the Swedish interest in the enterprise. Time after time when New Sweden was discussed in council, a reason given for the government's involvement—in addition to the primary motive of an increase in trade—was that the nation would gain practice in navigation. This is how it was put in 1642, for example, when the reconstitution of the company was under consideration, and when shipping in the Atlantic was being discussed in 1646 Oxenstierna gave as reasons for the participation of the Crown's ships in trade with Portugal and Virginia "not profit alone" but also the fact that the people were "being trained" in navigation. On another occasion Oxenstierna said that with the aid of seafarers it would be possible to build up not only the fleet but also cities, thus augmenting the nation's income; here he was quoting Admiral Clas Fleming, who together with Oxenstierna was the venture's leading Swedish initiator. Trading companies were also considered to stimulate domestic shipbuilding, which was important if the expenditure on chartering and shipping charges was to remain in the country. The presence of oak forests in the colony and the possibility of building ships there, about which careful inquiries had been made, contributed to the decision in 1652 to make a renewed commitment to New Sweden, whereupon the direction of the company was entrusted to the Board of Commerce that had now come into being.

The New Sweden enterprise was thus a part of the reform program that was currently underway, or at least the section of it that was designed to develop trade and shipping and that required the assistance of foreign capital and mercantilist know-how. It is significant that the queen's first question to Louis De Geer, who had already settled in Sweden, when his charter for a company to trade in Africa, Asia, and America was being discussed in 1649, was whether foreigners too would be offered the chance to become part-owners, to which De Geer answered affirmatively, while her second was whether he intended to build ships.

That the New Sweden enterprise has to be seen in this context is confirmed by its prelude, which included the persistent wooing of the Swedish government by a group of Dutch entrepreneurs. A couple of these Dutchmen had been involved in the Dutch West India Company but, having become dissatisfied there, were offering their services to others. The first was the aforementioned Willem Usselincx, the founder of the Dutch West India Company, who was granted the Southern Company license by Gustavus Adolphus in the 1620s. The only mention that need be made here of this decidedly unsuccessful company is that large profits were predicted when the nobility was exhorted to subscribe to shares at the *riksdag* of 1627 and that the English and Dutch East and West India companies were pointed to as models. The last in the series of Dutchmen to lay out his stall was Minuit, who had been director-general of the Dutch West India Company and governor of New Netherland but lost his position after a dispute with his employers. Minuit joined his compatriots Samuel Blommaert and Peter Spiring, both active in Holland on Sweden's behalf, who were trying to interest the Swedish government in plans for a company trading in Africa, particularly the Guinea coast. The birth of the New Sweden Company, with five Swedish and six Dutch stockholders, appears to have been the result of Spiring's efforts—he was government adviser on customs matters and had become a Swedish nobleman in 1636. But it was undoubtedly Minuit's experience that led to the decision to make America and the Delaware the focus of the company's trading activities and to combine the company with a colonization project, and it was on the lines of his plan, as presented to Oxenstierna, that the venture was launched.

In these circumstances it must obviously have been a blow to the Swedes when the Dutch participants wanted to withdraw as soon as the first expedition arrived back home. The setback was surely all the more severe in view of the fact that Oxenstierna strongly favored a system that left trading to private enterprise and—unlike Gustavus Adolphus—was no friend of state-controlled trading companies. The reason for the Dutch wish to back out was probably that they did not want to or did not dare challenge the Dutch West India Company, in which they were also stockholders, particularly as the new company seemed to offer little hope of profit. Moreover Minuit had disappeared, in mysterious circumstances, on the journey home.

Therefore, the founding of New Sweden was not, as has sometimes been maintained, inspired by a dream of extending the Swedish empire to the New World. The enterprise was the result of an alliance between Dutchmen with short-term profit motives and representatives of the Swedish government who wanted to strengthen and consolidate the existing Swedish empire. The Swedish participants were, in addition to Oxenstierna and Fleming, two close relatives of Oxenstierna who were both members of the government, and Peter Spiring, ennobled as Silfvercrona. To the first four of these, partnership was not a demonstration of entrepreneurial spirit but a contribution comparable to the many "voluntary" efforts that had been made by the aristocracy in various contexts (including trading companies), and which councilors of the realm, in particular, were expected to make by way of a good example. The remarkable thing on this occasion is that so few contributed. "If all would contribute a few hundred *daler*, so that the country can be colonized," records a laconic minute of the meeting of the council in March 1639, when New Sweden was being discussed. And when the company was to be reorganized as a fully Swedish concern, a reason given for the Crown's entry as a partner was that private individuals lacked the capacity to operate the company on their own, which has been interpreted in the historiography of New Sweden as meaning that they lacked the capital. What has been overlooked is that the time was extremely poorly chosen for a venture of the kind planned by Minuit.

I am referring here to the condition of Sweden in the 1630s and first and foremost of its scanty population, which has led one historian to describe the country as "a land of soldiers' widows." The peasantry was in a state of unrest and large numbers of soldiers were deserting; nobles were complaining that labor was scarce and their farmsteads were lying desolate. In a debate on the problems of the towns by the council in 1636 it was agreed that without a larger population any attempt to build large cities in Sweden would be in vain. But Sweden was a thinly populated country even in normal times: as Per Brahe put it in 1645, Sweden had "few people and much land," whereas abroad there were "many people and little land." The time was hardly right for a colonization project.

When the company was reorganized in 1642, no attempt seems to have been made to increase the number of private stockholders. However, the company received an infusion of capital from the nearly dissolved South Ship Company and the Crown became a partner, confirming the character of the company as a state concern. That the intention was that "colonists in large numbers were to be sent over for the development of the country" has been assumed by Amandus Johnson and by other writers;

they have also concluded that it was the difficulty of obtaining sufficient willing emigrants in the early stages that made it necessary to resort to using New Sweden as a transportation colony for Finns from the mining areas of central Sweden—where their slash-and-burn methods of agriculture were regarded as a menace to the forests—and also for criminals of various kinds.

The fact is that nothing can be said with any degree of certainty about the intended number of colonists, but it is worth noting that it was the governors of certain counties in central Sweden, where tax-privileged land was virtually nonexistent, who were asked to recruit colonists. As conscription did not normally take place in these areas either, this also meant that disruption of the armed forces was kept to a minimum. Nevertheless, it was impossible to avoid a conflict of interest between the need for colonists and domestic considerations, as may have been experienced by the county governor who was ordered to build cities in his province and fill them with people, or by Carl Bonde, who used Finnish labor in the ironworks and on canal building. When in 1649 the queen was surprised to find that three hundred Finns wished to sail to New Sweden, as she thought there was surely enough land for settlement in Sweden, she was not revealing a lack of interest in affairs of state but expressing her view that domestic needs should be given priority, just as when a few months later she declared that the people who had been taken over to the colony were needed at home.

The government's dilemma—whether to colonize New Sweden or to attend to needs that had been declared to have higher priority—is evident from the use of the settlement as a transportation colony. While it might be desirable to induce Finns to emigrate rather than burn the forests, it would also be good if they could be persuaded to settle permanently in vacant homesteads. It should also be noted that the government showed itself well aware of the particular complications of the early stages of the colonization project. This is evident from what was said in 1639 when a country governor was ordered to pardon all married soldiers who were for any reason under sentence of death, provided that they departed for New Sweden with their families. It was pointed out that the matter had to be handled with a very sure touch, because even though it was important for sailing to New Sweden to continue and the colony to be populated with Swedes, it was even more urgent for Swedish subjects to be treated in such a manner as to discourage insurrection. The serious disturbances of 1638 were fresh in mind.

In the years that followed banishment to New Sweden was frequently proposed in connection with various felonies, but this method cannot actually have produced many colonists. Transportation was not a new form of punishment, however, which gives one cause to note an important dif-

ference between New Sweden and other colonized areas. In former times
both rebellious peasants and people guilty of damaging oak forests or of
illegal hunting had been banished to Ingria, which had been Swedish
since 1617; the aristocracy had received estates there and good care had
been taken to populate them. But the aristocracy had no landed estates in
New Sweden, and one of Sweden's largest landowners was highly indig-
nant when Oxenstierna suggested that she should pay the cost of crossing
to New Sweden for a thieving servant. Moreover the colony lay a long
way from the center of power and it is significant that no member of the
aristocracy ever visited it, although several of the untitled nobility served
there. A condemned and reprieved officer, Matthias Franke, who had in
1645 to be provided with a post—but not a "superior" post—was, however, the type of person that the council could contemplate sending to
New Sweden.

Sweden's performance as a colonizer in the New World has to be
judged in the light of the country's circumstances. Bearing in mind the
process of nation-building that was taking place and what the Swedes
hoped to accomplish from the New Sweden enterprise, it is easy to see
that a whole-hearted and successful commitment to colonization was
hardly to be expected from the Swedish government at this time and
that a trading station would have been more appropriate than a colony.
Once the colony was in existence, however, there was generally a wish
to preserve it—with the isolated exception of one occasion in 1649 when
the queen and certain councilors questioned the value of both the company and the colony. But an increased availability of willing colonists,
together with the establishment of the Board of Commerce, was undoubtedly one of the factors behind the decision in 1652 to invest further resources in the venture. There is a kind of logic in the fact that it was the
secretary of the Board of Commerce, Johan Rising, who was to be the
colony's last governor. Rising was also an economic theorist and a writer
of mercantilist views, and his optimistic plans for the colony, including the
founding of cities, manufactories, and extensive new plantations, meant
that the reshaping of commerce on Dutch lines that was proposed in Sweden was to be extended to the colony. That the plans were unrealistic
hardly needs stating. On the other hand it may be worthy of note that
Rising not only calls for craftsmen, essential supplies, and colonists to be
sent over from home but also Dutch colonists, which gives food for
thought. Slash-and-burn peasants were probably all right for breaking
new soil, but they were not the right kind of worker for the commercial
society that Rising was planning or for the growing of tobacco or the
planting of mulberry trees for silkworm farms or for sheep-farming, all
of which had been mentioned back in 1642 as urgent tasks for the colony.

The growing of tobacco in the colony would eliminate the need for the company to buy its tobacco from English and Dutch merchants in the area. The profits would go to the company, consistent with the mercantilist principle of obtaining the goods one needed from a primary source. As far as the company's trade is concerned, all that need be stated here is that most of the tobacco brought to Sweden in the company's ships was bought from merchants in America and Europe, not cultivated in the colony, and that the greater part of the merchandise needed for trade with the Indians, such as cloth, axes, adzes, knives, copper kettles, and so forth, had been purchased in Holland, not produced in Sweden. In other words, it was not only as a colonization project that New Sweden came at the wrong time. Finally there proved to be little demand in Sweden for the pelts (mostly beaver skins) that were a classic luxury article in other countries. For that reason Fleming wondered in 1642 whether the furs ought to be sent for sale in Holland, but Spiring did not agree and took the view that the merchants ought rather to come to Sweden—a logical attitude if the primary consideration was the interest of the Crown in form of increased customs revenues.

AN OVERLOOKED BOOM

For foreign merchants to come to Sweden (and preferably to settle there), their wares naturally had to be in demand. A domestic demand for goods and services was also essential if the cities that had been laid out and the manufactories that were planned were to have a chance of prospering. But a characteristic of Swedish society was of course the limited size of the market (or demand) and the predominance of the barter economy. This had to be changed before any investment could be more than a futile gesture. We shall now look at how the consumption patterns of the international elite life-style came to Sweden and how the new demand for luxuries helped in various ways to overcome the problem of the smallness of the market.

The need for a sumptuary ordinance to curb the extravagance of the nobility, which was in the air in 1638, suggests that something new was happening. The background was a process that had begun much earlier, at the time when Sweden embarked on an expansionist policy in the 1560s. Both Erik XIV and Johan III behaved like Renaissance princes, as may be seen from the palaces they built. The assimilation of the aristocracy in the courtly culture of Europe, on the other hand, was more problematical. There were several highly educated humanists and bibliophiles, and there was contact with the Italian Renaissance, but by European standards the Swedish aristocracy was impoverished. Moreover, it was long restrained by monarchic power, as demonstrated by the execution of several of its leaders in 1600. Not until the reign of Gustavus Adolphus did things change. The building of magnificent private mansions that was seen in the late Renaissance in Denmark, in England, and on the Continent thus has no counterpart in Sweden. The tardiness of developments in Sweden is also shown by the fact that noble sumptuary legislation was passed in Denmark in the 1570s, but not in Sweden until 1644. When the Swedish aristocracy really began to increase its consumption of luxuries, the peak had almost been reached in other countries.

The dramatic increase in consumption by the aristocracy in other countries has been seen as rising from the need of the new nation states for a representative public face and from the existence of a princely-aristocratic pattern of consumption, for which the royal courts set the standard. In Sweden, too, the monarchy led the way and the luxurious living of seventeenth-century Sweden started as a peaceful branch of great-power politics. The competition within the courtly society of absolutism, which resulted abroad in a battle in which consumption was a weapon, has, however, no equivalent in Sweden, where absolutism came later. On the other hand, local Swedish conditions did nothing to reduce competition, rather it was the reverse. In Sweden as abroad, what was important was conspicuous consumption, designed to serve as a status symbol (it should be noted that the concept tells us nothing about the quality of the luxuries consumed). Most of the main areas of consumption spotlighted by Lawrence Stone with reference to the English aristocracy were also favored in Sweden, namely the building of houses and their use for entertainment involving armies of servants and outrageously lavish festivities, costume, coaches (the Rolls-Royces of the day), and expensive funerals. The only exception was gambling, the great age of which comes later in Sweden.

If this kind of consumption was late in starting in Sweden, it made up for it by quickly reaching a very impressive level, which may be explained by a combination of the assertiveness of a new great power and domestic rivalry for influence, favor, and social prestige. By the 1630s competition was in full swing, Treasurer of the Realm Gabriel Bengtsson Oxenstierna having just built himself a country house said to be "the envy of the city" by Ogier, who at the same time praises the residences of Eric Larsson von der Linde, both in the capital and in the country. A few years later Axel Oxenstierna's Tidö was complete, work on it having begun in the 1620s, and the French architect Simon De la Vallée was engaged as architect to the aristocracy and the royal family.

The upswing of the 1630s is naturally linked to the fact that after the death of the king responsibility for the country's cultural image fell on the regency council and the aristocracy, to whom public and private spheres largely coincided. But an additional factor was the leading role that the nobility was expected to take in the building of the nation, a role that required training in noble arts and a courtly life-style. "In the past we have always kept our solemnities to ourselves," objected a member of the council (not altogether accurately), who feared that the shoddiness of the great-power façade would be revealed if emissaries from abroad were invited to the king's funeral. And when a few years later Jacob De la Gardie and his wife, Ebba Brahe, were expecting foreign visitors at Jakobsdal, the interior of the new country house was spruced up with the aid of furniture from their home in Stockholm—to demonstrate "that we live properly in this country, too." Rivalry for status within the aristocracy further raised the level of consumption, as did the fact that businessmen and officials who had not yet been, or only recently been ennobled indulged equally frenetically in conspicuous consumption. Von der Linde has already been mentioned, while Louis De Geer built the first Palladian mansion in Stockholm during 1646 to 1650, having on the same site already erected one in the German-Dutch Renaissance style that he now intended to demolish. Before long the point had been reached where an older Swedish aristocrat, Jacob De la Gardie, could have a staff of servants equal to that of the English aristocracy at the height of that country's excesses (his son Magnus Gabriel then doubled the number). Nor did the intended public relations effect fail to materialize: as early as 1649 a Spanish envoy was reporting that consumption of luxuries was greater in Sweden, in relation to resources, than in any other country.

In the 1650s the trend accelerated. The reason was keener competition, in conjunction with a change in taste and style that took place at that time, if not earlier. It should be noted that the Gallic predilections of the nobility were already evident in the 1630s, when Axel Oxenstierna was busy on a magnificent residence in the French style on his own account, and many, like Carl Gustav Wrangel, had already visited Paris. There are many testimonies to the fiercer rivalry that followed the conclusion of peace, such as that of the fortification officer Erik Dahlbergh (artist and architect and still a commoner, although a future count), who feared that his promotion would be delayed by the numerous sons of magnates in his way. He therefore accepted the offer of service as tutor and traveling companion to the newly created barons Cronstierna, thus joining the ranks of young men of limited means who found such a route to foreign study. It was also at this stage that the oft-mentioned new generation took over. In the course of a few years in the 1650s several older magnates died and the resulting intensification of rivalry may be clearly seen in the fantastic splendor of many of the funerals, at which fine processions also offered both a pretext and a stage for further struggles for precedence. To this has to be added the effect of two coronations in four years, those of Christina in 1650 and Karl X Gustav in 1654, producing mounting opulence in both dress and coaches.

While costs were rocketing, the previous steady growth in the nobility's income stopped as donation of lands came to a halt, a partial reduction (repossession of lands by the Crown) was ordered, and personal taxation was introduced. The increased luxury expenditure had, in other words, to be met from a reduced income. Moreover, the death of Karl X Gustav in 1660 restored to the aristocracy a kind of ultimate cultural responsibility, even though there was at this time a dazzling competitor in the shape of the dowager queen, Hedvig Eleonora, particularly when it came to building projects. The characteristic tendency throughout the remaining period until the upheavals of the 1680s was a quantitative and qualitative increase in luxurious living—nothing else was possible. Far too many had been inspired with the same spirit as Treasurer of the Realm Gustav Bonde, known as an opponent of De la Gardie and an advocate of thrift in the regency of Karl XI, but himself a great builder. Stockholm's first private mansion in the Parisian style, completed in the 1660s, was his achievement. Bonde's will stipulated that the new mansion had to remain in the family in perpetuity, as he had built it more for the glory of the family than for his own comfort. The aim of conspicuous consumption can scarcely be better formulated.

The new pattern of consumption was not therefore something to be adopted only according to one's means. It was *de rigueur* in all the leading circles of society, to which more and more people considered themselves to belong, and this accounts for its spread. It was also copied by ambitious groups outside the nobility. As far as dress is concerned, Katharina Wallenstedt, the wife of a civil servant of the untitled nobility in the Stockholm of the 1670s, fretted over the fact that people of her acquaintance adopted a finer style of dress even before they received their letter of ennoblement. And just as the aristocracy kept abreast of Paris fashion, so the provincial nobility kept itself informed of the fashions of the capital. It may be added that the obsession with status was less furious in the country than in Stockholm, where there were more people to indulge in it. But according to Katharina Wallenstedt, the capital was the place to be: although life there was much more expensive, it was nearer to the seats of power. The proud housebuilding bears witness to the ambitions of the merchant class, particularly in Stockholm, and in the 1660s sumptuary ordinances were extended to the clergy and the burghers, who were urged not to dress above their station and to refrain from extravagance at feasts and funerals. As usual in such cases, the prohibitions had no effect.

Neither commission of inquiry, reduction and absolutism, nor the wars of Karl XII put an end to the consumption of luxuries, although it assumes a different character in the final phase of the great-power period. What may at first seem to be a consequence of a radical deterioration in personal finances or of the monarch's disapproval of ostentatious consumption—as has been mentioned in connection with Karl XI—may also be attributable rather to new artistic impulses and international changes of fashion or even be an expression of a certain satiation. The importance of the monarch's attitude is reduced by the fact that many of the men of the new autocracy were at home with the elite life-style as a result of earlier service with the titled nobility or the royal family. Several had also had time to earn a reputation for luxurious living well before absolutism, and in Karl XII Sweden once more had a monarch with a liking for splendor and display, at least until war gave him other things to think about. At the king's prompting and with Nicodemus Tessin the Younger as the chief organizer there were several years of hectic entertainment, with theatricals, masquerades, balls, and pageants, very much in the spirit of the court of France.

In the field of building, the monarchy once again took over the initiative, even in the reign of Karl XI, whom Tessin had made aware of the opportunities for princely glorification afforded by the baroque. The fantastic building boom created by the projects of the nobility, which had lasted since the 1630s, thus died out in the 1680s. Very large private projects, such as Tessin's personal mansion, in close proximity to the royal palace, are the exception at the end of the century. The newly rich and the newly ennobled, when looking for homes appropriate to their social status, were in many cases able to move into existing mansions and manor houses, purchased, acquired by marriage, or leased. As work started on the building of the new palace, a price ceiling was imposed for bricks and a royal option declared on all lime and bricks produced in Sweden. In other cases it is the burghers who build in Stockholm in the eighteenth century, and the holders of civil and military allotments who build their dwellings elsewhere. At the same time a number of the old Stockholm residences, as if by design, became manufactories.

A decline in the building of private mansions necessarily implies that the level of ostentatious extravagance fell during the final period of the Age of Greatness. Against this, it seems that the demand for luxury goods became more widespread and that conspicuous consumption did not disappear. There were complaints that servants were too well dressed, and in the case of one of the nobility's finest status symbols—the coach—it was demanded early in the eighteenth century that only the nobility and the military command should have the right to use such vehicles, to maintain the difference between the Estates of the realm. Not only the nobility but also the *haute bourgeoisie* queued for the portrait painter Martin Mijtens, and among the buyers at the auction following the death of Maria Sophia De la Gardie in 1694 was not only the privy councillor Carl Piper but also the tapestry maker Gudmund Törnqvist, who bought an expensive mirror.

The tremendous increase in consumption among the seventeenth-century nobility had a devastating effect on the private finances of many of them. The building projects, which were the most expensive items, generally cost twice as much as at first estimated and tied up resources for a long time to come. When Field-Marshal Lennart Torstensson died in 1651 he left a number of uncompleted buildings, including a mansion in Stockholm that his son Anders was unable to move into until 1664. Similarly Gustav Bonde, who died in 1667, left the mansion that has already been mentioned unfinished and encumbered with enormous mortgages. Emerging worse off from inquiry into the administration of the regency and from the reduction, his widow was obliged to sell the mansion, although it was restored to the family when the son made a wealthy marriage.

The extravagance thus led inevitably to private debt that grew enormously; an equivalent to the deficit economy characteristic of the courtly society of absolutist France and of England a hundred years earlier was definitely not lacking in Sweden. Consider Claes Tott, a councillor of the realm, whose annual income from his landed estates and his offices totalled just over 23,000 silver daler, while his expenses were somewhere between 35,000 and 50,000 daler. The debts of the nobility led to legal actions and to changes of ownership of lands and farms, but the aristocracy in particular seems to have put off the day of liquidation. Many aristocrats therefore reached the upheavals of the 1680s with hopelessly undermined finances.

Although the circumstances have not been investigated with any great thoroughness, it is not difficult to see that parallel with this process there was a transfer of wealth in large and small portions to outside groups that supplied the nobility and the royal family with goods, services, and credit. The sections of the population doing this were in part those who assisted the military state, but only in part. One person who made himself rich on the demand for luxury goods was Claude Roquette, a merchant of French origin who was ennobled as Hägerstierna and soon owned his house in Stockholm, another just outside the capital, and estates elsewhere in the country. The shift of economic strength to certain parts of the bourgeoisie and to civil servants of the untitled nobility whose roots lay in this class, which we first see clearly towards the end of the century, must be the result of a process that had begun much earlier.

But luxury consumption not only required capital and credit, it also created employment and was labor-intensive, and to a large extent it demanded payment in ready money. This latter fact seems to have led to agreements between landowners and peasants, in those cases that have been studied, on permanent taxes payable in cash. Payment in cash instead of in kind transferred the onus of conversion to the taxpayers, resulting in a growth in the cash economy and in the incipient market integration of peasant agriculture. The rapidly rising demand for timber, stone, and other building materials and for meat and dairy products for entertaining also must have helped to bring about a reorientation of production. There were cases of builders competing for boards and planks, and rises in the prices paid for the peasant's timber were noted. Whom this benefited most, however—the peasants or the merchants—is uncertain.

The vigorous growth of the artisan class and the fact that a pattern of specialist trades now emerged that would survive until the nineteenth century were both directly and indirectly related to the new pattern of consumption. In purely luxury crafts, moreover, it seems that not only material but also labor costs were considerable. This may be why so many goldsmiths were able to lend money to nobility. A number of artists and architects enjoyed brilliant careers in society. There was also a remarkable increase in the number of servants, from butlers, tutors, and private chaplains to washerwomen. There were great differences in their remuneration, exaggerated by generous gifts to certain occupational categories.

But it is the labor required for building that is most striking. In return for exemption from other taxation many peasants did far more days' work than before. This work was largely done on the new building projects while the landlord's home farm (at the castle or manor house) barely kept going in the absence of adequate labor. Also employed were innumerable assorted laborers, female helpers and carriers, and soldiers, together with a large number of craftsmen of various kinds. In these dealings, too, wages were paid—at least partly—in cash, which together with the demand for transport of building materials, greatly increased the peasant's opportunity for subsidiary income. Finally, the unprecedentedly lavish funeral ceremonies gave ample scope for extra earnings for musicians, clergy, schoolboys, soldiers, and many others, and there were loud complaints when the funeral processions were abolished at the end of the century.

Seen from this perspective, and bearing in mind the specific need of seventeenth-century Swedish society for change, the luxury and the conspicuous consumption seem to have been the right medicine. Although there are many aspects of the topic that deserve more exhaustive research, the result was a long period of economic prosperity for many large and small merchants and for skilled craftsmen of all kinds, and also of high demand for certain agricultural products of the peasantry.

The necessary resources were largely found within the country: hardly anybody managed to build "with German money" and the significance of war booty has been wildly exaggerated. And even if there was an outflow of capital from Sweden for the purchase of foreign luxury goods and for the peregrinations of the young nobility, the majority must have benefited the home country. From this it follows that the consumption of luxuries must have resulted in a tremendous redistribution of wealth, which together with the growth of the cash economy and the emergence of new social strata unattached to agriculture, served to expand the domestic market.

AN AGE OF CHANGE

During 1715 to 1720, the final years of absolutism and the Age of Greatness, the French traveler Aubry de la Motraye visited Sweden. Taking an interest in manners and customs, in topography and in monuments and other sights worthy of note, La Motraye had traversed Europe and also been in Africa and Asia. At Bender, in Turkey, he had met Karl XII. He took a good look at Sweden, and some of his impressions are worth recalling as illustrations of the changes that had taken place.

The Stockholm of the second decade of the eighteenth century was described by La Motraye as one of northern Europe's most beautiful cities, with broad, straight streets, fine public buildings, stately residences, and large stone houses; it was a very different picture from that drawn by Ogier eighty years earlier, when the city still retained its medieval character. The Palace of the Nobility had then been in place for some time, adorned with sculpture and legend, even if its interior was still unfinished. Work on the new royal palace had been interrupted by the war, but Tessin's residence was complete—"an architectural gem" in the opinion of La Motraye—and Carl Gustav Wrangel's palace had become the home of the royal family. And in the center of Stockholm lay Kungsträdgården, a park of delightful flower beds, fountains, and a superb orangery. So Sweden now had the capital city and the appropriate setting for conducting the state's affairs that the government had called for when Sweden first emerged as a great power. In the meantime the city's population had grown explosively—from ten thousand in the 1620s to over forty thousand, a figure already reached by the 1670s.

Turning to country houses, La Motraye was amazed that Sweden could have "so many castles and gardens of such beauty and splendour," bearing in mind the rugged landscape and the harsh winters. Not expectedly, he was most impressed of all with Drottningholm—by the palace's architecture, which was the work of Tessin the Elder, by the gardens, which had been laid by Tessin the Younger, and by Ehrenstrahl's paintings. In Tessin the Younger, I should add, Sweden had an architect to whom foreign patrons, too, entrusted important commissions. The manor houses in other parts of the country were also praised by the Frenchman, notwithstanding the fact that they were generally of timber, which was regarded as a Swedish peculiarity. And even on the ironmasters' estates he found hothouses. It was, in other words, a striking architectural modernization that had belatedly taken place in Sweden.

At Uppsala La Motraye viewed the anatomical theater, the collection of curiosities and mathematical instruments and the magnificent curio cabinet with which Gustavus Adolphus had been presented by the city of Augsburg, and of course the Silver Bible. He particularly admired the fair-sized university library and its librarian, Eric Benzelius the younger. It may be worthy of mention—although La Motraye was unaware of it—that a few years earlier Benzelius, who was a humanist with a strong interest in science and mathematics, had founded Sweden's first learned society at the instigation of the celebrated mathematician, inventor, and industrial pioneer Christoffer Polhammar, later ennobled as Polhem. This was the first in a series of efforts to establish an academy that preceded the foundation of the Royal Swedish Academy of Sciences in 1739.

In the economic sphere La Motraye's interest was attracted primarily by the mines and the ironworks, whose prosperity in the seventeenth century was to a considerable degree the work of immigrants. Having started purely as a munitions industry, the ironworks had not been short of customers and Swedish iron-making had attracted the interest of other countries. But the iron manufactories did not only produce arms: La Motraye also mentions factories engaged in civil production, particularly the one founded by Polhem at Stjärnsund in 1699. Of the factory's many products he confines himself to the cups, plates, spoons, and other pieces of tinplate; these were made with the aid of a hydraulic machine that was operated by four people and did the work of thirty. The machine, which was the invention of Polhem, made a strong impression on the Frenchman.

Swedish production of artifacts of this type would have been inconceivable in the early years of the great-power period, given the country's undeveloped social and economic structure. But with the advent of the international aristocratic culture and the new luxury consumption a process of development began that entailed not only a dramatic increase in the demand for luxury goods in the strict sense but also an expansion of the domestic market generally. This had to happen before a domestic production of goods could come about. Another prerequisite was the transfer of wealth—a result of the luxury consumption—to bourgeois and newly ennobled circles with a more "modern" approach to the utilization of resources than that generally displayed by the nobility. The powerful merchant Roquette (Hägerstierna), for example, who was more aware than most of the size of demand, invested in brass and leather manufacture and in 1669 the descendants of Spiring (Silfvercrona), whom we recall from the New Sweden venture, were granted the monopoly to manufacture linen in the province of Halland. A change in the attitude of the nobility to investment of this kind would not be long in coming, as may be seen from the participation of various aristocrats in the Kungsholm Glassworks during the last decades of the seventeenth century and the involvement of the Estate of the nobility in a clothing factory early in the eighteenth.

The results of the extensive establishment of manufacturing industry that, encouraged and supported by the government, took place in the second half of the seventeenth century were not, of course, particularly impressive by comparison with what happened in the more developed countries of western Europe, where this type of production had a long history. Many of the projects had great difficulties to contend with, particularly the investment in the manufacture of silk, to which considerable resources were committed. But in relation to Swedish circumstances, and especially to the limited demand in the initial phase, the results were nonetheless remarkable.

These events formed the background to the founding in 1731 of the Swedish East India Company (initially almost an English business), which was successfully to trade Swedish ironware for tons of luxury goods such as tea, china, and silk. It also formed the background to Anders Johan von Höpken's choice of subject for his presidential address in 1740 to the newly formed Swedish Academy of Sciences, which was entitled "Om yppighets nytta" (On the benefits of luxury). With this address Höpken introduced to Sweden one of the most-discussed problems of the age. He argued that in considering the effects of vanity and abundance the economies of private households and individuals had to be distinguished from society's and the public good. While the demand for luxury goods could certainly bring personal ruin, there was no doubt that it constituted an important stimulus to handcrafts, industry, and science (including agricultural economics and navigation), and consequently to society as a whole. Höpken concluded by praising the way of life of the rich and self-indulgent Croesus, who squandered his inherited fortune on building and decorating houses, as well as on beautiful clothing, coaches, feasts, and gifts—an example that he probably drew from Voltaire. Even if the Swedish nobleman was not directly intended, his actions are not dissimilar from what many had tried to do. And to judge from the evidence, his life-style played an important role in the "civilizing" of Sweden.

BIBLIOGRAPHICAL NOTE
(Provided by Richard Waldron)

Readers who wish to learn more about the subjects of this essay should consult the following works:
A complete description of Swedish culture during the reign of Gustavus Adolphus is Michael Roberts, *Gustavus Adolphus: A History of Sweden, 1611–1632*, 2 vols. (London: Longmans, Green and Co., 1958). Volume 2 deals primarily with the king's military adventures in Poland and Prussia in the 1620s and in Germany during the Thirty Years' War. Volume 1 concentrates on cultural and political developments in sixteenth-century Sweden. It is especially provocative about the role of Gothicism—the intellectual fiction of the ancient Swedes as world-conquerors and saviors of European civilization—in the development of an upper class imperialist *mentalité* in the seventeenth century. For the seventeenth century after Gustavus's death, see Arne Losman, Agneta Lundström, and Margareta Revera, eds., *The Age of New Sweden*, trans. Bernard Vowles (Stockholm: Livrustkammaren, 1988). (This is the volume in which Professor Revera's essay was published originally.) See especially Sven A. Nilsson, "Imperial Sweden: Nation-Building, War and Social Change," 7–39. An interpretation of Swedish society as content with an increasingly absolutist political regime in the second half of the century is A. F. Upton, "Sweden," in John Miller, ed., *Absolutism in Seventeenth-Century Europe* (New York: St. Martin's Press, 1990). See also Michael Roberts, *The Early Vasas: A History of Sweden, 1523–1611* (Cambridge: Cambridge University Press, 1968), especially for the Swedish Reformation. Roberts edited a volume of essays about topics in Sweden's seventeenth-century history titled *Sweden's Age of Greatness, 1632–1718* (London: Macmillan & Co., 1973). Related to the subjects of this essay are Stellan Dahlgren, "Estates and Classes," 102–31, Göran Rystad, "Magnus Gabriel De la Gardie," 203–36, and Kurt Ågren, "The *reduktion*," 237–64. No institution was more important in Sweden in this era than the state church, and readers should consult Roberts's essay "The Swedish Church," 132–73. A complete treatment of King Karl X's *reduktion* of the 1660s, the precursor of the more devastating and comprehensive one of Karl XI, is Stellan Dahlgren, *Karl X Gustav och reduktionen* (Stockholm: Svenska Bokförlaget, 1964). An edition in English of significant documents of Sweden's "Age of Greatness" is Michael Roberts, ed., *Sweden as a Great Power, 1611–1697: Government, Society, Foreign Policy* (London: Edward Arnold, 1968).

The Crown of Sweden and the New Sweden Company

STELLAN DAHLGREN

THE IMPORTANCE OF TRADE

Sweden was one of the major powers in Europe in the seventeenth century. Through its military gains, especially in the Thirty Years' War, it had expanded its territory and come to dominate northern Europe politically, especially the Baltic area. In addition, the country had a strong military capability.[1]

Yet economically Sweden was rather weak and to maintain its position as a great power, Sweden had to develop its economy. In Immanuel Wallerstein's terms, Sweden had to advance from the semiperiphery in the world's economic system to the center, where Wallerstein placed such states as Spain, the Netherlands, and England.

The historical literature contains substantial discussion about the importance of trade in the development of the economy. Many scholars believe that international trade was the most important cause of the development of capitalism in Europe, while others maintain that changes in the production sector were primary. They also point out that commerce, especially that created by the trading companies, often played a conservative role and actually helped preserve existing production relations.[2]

In the seventeenth century, however, one of the leading principles of mercantilism—the economic doctrine of the time—was that trade was the great road to prosperity, not only for individuals, but also for whole countries: buy cheap and sell dear. We find this emphasis on the importance of trade in the works of the only prominent theoretical economist of Sweden at that time, Johan Claesson Rising, the last governor of New Sweden.

Rising's originality as a mercantilist thinker has been disputed, especially by Eli F. Heckscher. It is, however, probable that he significantly influenced the economic thinking of the politically important people in Sweden of his time.[3] In that context Rising's opinions will be referred to as typical of the thinking of the group that dominated Sweden economically and politically because his opinions generally correspond to what we know about the actions and opinions of the members of this group, foremost of all the famous chancellor of state, Axel Oxenstierna, who was the leading politician in Sweden, next to the regents, in 1611 to 1654. Additionally, Rising's two books on economic subjects were supported financially by the authorities in Sweden and printed with their permission.[4]

Like many other mercantilistic economists, Rising stressed that the development of trade strengthens the power of the state.[5] A country outrivaled in trade was a weak country. Thus, according to this theory, Sweden should strive for control of the trade in the Baltic, especially trade with the Russians and trade in grain.

The Swedish historian Ellen Fries has shown that Rising saw the Dutch as the great economic enemy of Sweden. As a young man Rising had spent a long time studying in the Netherlands and was envious of the Dutch. Moreover, his later experiences, especially in America, made him more and more hostile to them. According to him, the Dutch were taking all the trade profits from Sweden and on the Baltic, forcing the Swedes to buy dear and sell cheap. In this way the Dutch held the Swedes down.[6]

One of Rising's central ideas was that Sweden should connect trade in the Baltic with trade in the "Western Sea," the Atlantic. This trade should be carried out by subjects of the Swedish Crown so that the Dutch would lose their dominant position in international trade and economy. New Sweden should be the foothold in America for this trade, where Swedish ships could sell or store their cargoes for further transport and, in return, receive loads "of all sorts of West Indian wares." Preferably Sweden should also obtain a little island in the West Indies to use as an entrepôt trading center. With these measures, Sweden's long-sought *dominium maris Baltici* (the dominion of the Baltic) would become a reality and not "dead and waste," as Rising wrote after his return from New Sweden in a discussion of the reasons why Sweden should keep a North American colony.[7] In Rising's thinking, New Sweden was the cornerstone of Sweden's future economic prosperity.

WHY TRADING COMPANIES?

The great question for Rising and for the government was how Swedish trade should be developed. One of the most important means was the trading company. There were many reasons why states in the seventeenth century promoted these companies, but four reasons stand out as especially important.[8]

The first was that the strong feudal states of this period wanted to control trade, regulate economic life, and discipline society. Trading companies were one feature in that policy. The second reason was that the state found the companies to be a practical way to raise revenue from commerce. This was accomplished by sharetaking in the trade of the companies and by using the company to collect taxes on trade. The third reason was that the company could be used when the state wanted to expand, economically or politically, into areas outside Europe without directly involving the state. Last, the state's costs in protecting trade were internalized through a company and were more easily controlled and predicted.

There were also several reasons why private citizens wanted to invest in trading companies. In a trading company investors pooled capital for long and expensive commercial expeditions and shared the economic risks. A company's fusion of capital enabled it to compete with foreigners. Through a trading company it was also possible to monopolize trade for a specific commodity or with a specific area. And finally, through a trading company investors got the state's protection. For those who were members of or were well connected in the government, a company protected by the government was advantageous. It gave them opportunities to get into trade, to take advantage of privileges for self-gain, and to develop careers connected with a company.

Many varieties of trading companies existed in Sweden and in other European countries. Roughly speaking, there were four types of companies in Sweden in the seventeenth century.[9] One company, which was formed during the reign of Gustavus Adolphus (1611–32) was the Ships' Company, whose goal was to acquire ships to be used as trading vessels in peace and warships in war. Here the state interest was paramount. Other companies were established by the state in cooperation with particular merchants to promote the export of a specific domestic raw material, as in the cases of the Copper Company (1619–28, 1635–39) and the Tar Company (1648–82, 1689–1715). A third type of company was established to import commodities such as salt, sugar, and tobacco into Sweden. In these trading companies, the private and the state interest could be of varying importance. The fourth category included companies that also were used for political expansion. Characteristics of each of these four types of companies could be combined in any one company.

One particular characteristic of companies was very important for Johan Rising: companies could be either open or closed. In open companies anyone could subscribe for shares; if closed, the number of shareholders was restricted. Rising did not like closed companies because he thought that they interfered with the principle of free trade. He opposed trade monopolies for the same reason.[10]

THE NEW SWEDEN COMPANY: AIMS AND REALITY

How should the New Sweden Company be characterized, given this background? I will deal first with the aims of the company in theory and then with how the company turned out in the reality.

Looking at the company from the viewpoint of the Crown, all the aims that nation-states generally had in the seventeenth century for trading companies were valid for the New Sweden Company. The company fit with the desire to control trade and the Crown's wish to secure income from trade. In this case, it was tobacco, from the Swedish point of view, that was the most important product from America.[11] From the beginning, the Swedish Crown hoped to use the company for both economic and political expansion in America. And through the company, the Crown also regulated the costs of protecting its American trade and its colony.

In the case of the New Sweden Company, private interest must be seen as very much subordinated to that of the state. The Crown supported the first voyage to the Delaware region. At this time there was a strong mercantile interest in the company, represented by some Dutch merchants, who brought capital together for the expedition to America and thus divided the state's economic risks.[12] More important, the Crown's promotion of the company encouraged private participation by Swedes, who believed this would be a mutually beneficial private-state enterprise. Rising's characterization of companies would label the New Sweden Company a closed organization. There were, however, as will be seen later, signs that the authorities intended to make it an open one.

How did the New Sweden Company develop its relations with the Crown and private interests? First, we shall take a quick look at the company's affairs by considering a balance sheet found in its journal of accounts for 31 December 1658.[13] It is not the most appropriate source for our purposes since it is dated three years after New Sweden was lost and three years before the company was dissolved; nevertheless, I think it gives a correct overview of the general economy of the company.

The balance sheet shows that the company was very much a losing proposition. It owed money to its shareholders, who, with one exception, had not received any income from their invested capital. It also owed money to the people with whom it had done business. On the credit side it had the ship *Mercurius*, a real asset, and two other big claims, which would have balanced the remainder of the debts had it been possible to get the debtors to pay them. The claim on the Kingdom of Spain concerned a ship, the famous *Kattan*, which ran aground near the coast of Puerto Rico and was confiscated by the Spaniards. The claim on the Dutch

The Balance of the New Sweden Company

31 December 1658

In <u>daler silvermynt</u>

SHAREHOLDERS			
The Crown			
The Old Ships' Company			-46 212
The Crown directly	+39 629	-11 011	+28 618
Subtotal for the Crown			-17 594
Private Shareholders			
Axel Oxenstierna's heirs and Erik Oxenstierna			- 6 680
Gabriel Oxenstierna's heirs			- 2 925
Claes Fleming's heirs			- 2 022
Christer Bonde			- 4 210
P. Silfvercrona's heirs			- 4 618
H. Huyghen			- 3 000
H. Kramer			- 196
The burghers of Viborg			- 858
Subtotal for private shareholders			-24 509
Subtotal for all shareholders			-42 103
OTHER INTERESTED PARTIES			-16 313
CREDITS			
The ship <u>Mercurius</u> and cargo			+ 9 375
Claims on the Kingdom of Spain			+ 34 693
Claims on the Dutch West India Company			+241 134
BALANCE ("The Capital of the American Company")			+226 786

West India Company concerned New Sweden and all the ships, other assets, and articles that the Swedes had lost when the Dutch conquered the colony and in other related incidents. Both these claims were very doubtful and the Swedish Crown and the New Sweden Company never collected anything on them.[14] Economically, then, the company was a great failure for the Crown and its shareholders.

The Crown had given money to the New Sweden Company directly and also indirectly through the old Ships' Company, whose assets had long belonged to the Crown. In addition to what is noted in the balance sheet, the Crown had also supported the company with ships and much equipment.

The private shareholders number very few in the 1658 balance sheet: only seven persons or families are listed, in addition to the burghers of Viborg in Finland, near the Russian border. The Dutch shareholders had not only left the company in 1641, but had also gotten their capital back.[15] Two former Swedish shareholders had also taken out their shares: the former chancellor of the exchequer Gabriel Bengtsson Oxenstierna (September 1645) and the director of the New Sweden Company, Olof Strömsköld (November 1658) when he resigned from the directorship. Strömsköld is also the only participant who succeeded in getting interest (6 percent) on his capital in the company.[16]

That there were so few shareholders signifies that Sweden was a poor country with few economic resources. However, it also shows that the New Sweden Company was a closed company. The majority of the Swedish shareholders were members of the Council of State and belonged to the highest aristocracy in the country: these were the Oxenstierna, Fleming, and Bonde families. In addition there were one merchant (a Swedish agent in Amsterdam) of Dutch extraction, Peter Spiring Silfvercrona, three company officials, and the burghers of Viborg, who had special interests in the tobacco trade with Russia.[17]

A reorganization of the company was attempted in the winter of 1654–55. The impetus for the reorganization came from the new king, Karl Gustav (reigned 1654–60), and his councilors, who thought the company was ineffective. The reforms were to include increasing the company's capital by admitting new shareholders and increasing its independence with respect to the Crown. It was also renamed the American Company. But only a few new shareholders were recruited and the company was not opened up for general investment, perhaps because the Board of Commerce was waiting for a larger investment by the Crown.[18] The loss of New Sweden to the Dutch probably made acquiring new shareholders more difficult. We know that the burghers of Viborg took back most of their investment in the company when they got this information.[19]

Privileges were very important in the development of relations between the Crown and the company. Surprisingly, no regent gave a charter to the company.[20] The Chancellor of State and president of the Board of Commerce, Erik Oxenstierna, and his colleagues on the board made great efforts to get the king to sign a charter or letter of privileges for the company. Drafts of the privileges have been preserved showing that the company had the right to maintain its own soldiers and artillery. New Sweden and any other lands that the company might be able to obtain in

North America were declared to be its eternal possessions. The company was permitted to make its own treaties with the inhabitants of North America ánd to build forts, establish towns, and grant privileges. If the company had secured the privileges that emerge in these drafts, it might have gained an independent position similar to that of the Dutch West India Company. But it was all in vain. The king crossed out these statutes and did not confirm the privileges. The planned charter was never promulgated.[21]

It is interesting to note that in his big work, *A Treatise on Commerce*, Rising states that a trading company should be independent. He has a special section on the military forces of a company in which he says that a company should build forts for its defense and employ a general to direct its forces. The company should give the officers and the soldiers salaries, food, and ammunition. It should also make alliances with princes and other powers in the region where it is trading. As examples of well-arranged companies, Rising mentions the Dutch East and West India companies, whose charters he wanted to include in his treatise in a chapter on the trade with the Dutch.[22]

Most of the New Sweden Company's privileges concerned the tobacco trade.[23] It received its first monopoly on the import of tobacco into Sweden in 1641. The company was required to guarantee the Crown the income from the tax on tobacco. To hinder smuggling, which was considerable, in 1643 the Crown also gave the company a monopoly over the trade within the country. The company held this monopoly for some years, which should have been a good source of revenue. It is, however, difficult to establish who gained from this trade. The company's shareholders did not. Probably most of the profits remained with the people who collected taxes for the company. In any case, the company could not be a profitable concern as long as it was used to organize the expeditions to New Sweden.

Queen Christina had rescinded the company's privileges on tobacco in 1649. When the company was reorganized in 1654–55, the monopoly on importing tobacco was restored, as was, in 1658, in spite of the loss of New Sweden, the monopoly on the internal tobacco trade. It is interesting that this privilege was justified by two arguments: Swedish trade with America should be promoted and the colony of New Sweden and its inhabitants should be supported.[24] Behind this privilege was a hope that Swedish successes in the wars of Charles Gustavus would give the colony back to Sweden.

This hope dwindled, especially after the death of the king in February 1660. The company seems also to have functioned less and less well, and in fact was dissolved soon after.[25] It had too many old debts and obligations to be effective. Economically it was more profitable for the Crown to lease out the tobacco taxes and give the monopoly on the tobacco trade directly to individuals or to a company independent of the Crown that acted only according to business principles and was able to pay a good sum for the monopoly.

Did the Crown get what it wanted from the company? The hope of gaining a large share of the trade with the Americas clearly was not fulfilled. But this was not the fault of the company: Sweden was too weak economically and its shipping was too undeveloped to stand up to competition with England and the Netherlands. New Sweden was lost. With the stagnation of the Swedish empire after 1658, it was impossible to regain the colony.

THE RULE OF THE COUNTRY

The Crown exercised control over New Sweden through, and to some extent, outside the company. Rising received his instructions both from Queen Christina and from the Board of Commerce.[26] To some extent New Sweden was one of Sweden's provinces, and it may be instructive to compare New Sweden with the Swedish provinces on the European continent.

Some similarities can be seen. Like the European provinces, New Sweden had a governor appointed by and responsible to the Crown. The officials and soldiers in New Sweden were primarily in the service of the Crown, which also paid their salaries. Only when they managed or dealt with the property of the company were they servants of the company. This double position was, of course, different from that of the civil servants in the European provinces, who answered only to the government. Another difference between the governor of New Sweden and the governors of the European provinces was that the former had a lower status. In Sweden the governors belonged to the high aristocracy, but no Swedish aristocrats wanted the post of governor in New Sweden. Both Rising's predecessor, Johan Printz, and Rising himself were of lowly birth; Printz came to New Sweden to rehabilitate himself for bad behavior and disobedience in the Thirty Years' War, and Rising was a young man hoping to begin his career in New Sweden.

There has been some discussion in the historical literature about the difficulties that developed when the Swedish Crown tried to incorporate Sweden's provinces on the European continent into Sweden itself. Several of the former Baltic, German, and Danish provinces had their own laws, privileges, and systems of administration. The nobility, in particular, did not want to change and were often able to preserve the old laws and their privileges.[27]

Such problems did not exist in America. The Swedes introduced their language, their church, and their system of administration. New Sweden was to develop from a colony to an integrated part of the Swedish realm. The population could not influence this development. The Swedes and other Europeans thought that the Indians had to adapt to the European system or disappear in one way or another.

New Sweden's system of land distribution and tenure was feudal, as in Sweden itself. The system in America was modified in that no state existed before the Swedes arrived, nor was there a native aristocracy whose feudal rights needed to be recognized and confirmed. The land that the Swedish officials bought or that the Indians gave away belonged both to the company and to the Crown. According to a 1653 list, the company considered all land in New Sweden as company property with the exception of Printzhof, Johan Printz's estate.[28] In addition to Printz, Rising, Captain Sven Skute, and Captain Hans Amundsson received grants of land from the Crown.[29] Rising, however, prevented Skute and Hans Amundsson's son-in-law, Lieutenant Elias Gyllengren, from taking possession of their lands.[30] Some farms on the company's land were divided between the company and the peasants cn a share-cropping basis. The peasants cultivated the company's land with some help from the company, and the peasant and the company each took half of the crop.

The winter of 1654 to 1655 was very cold and much of what was sowed was lost. In addition, many colonists were newly arrived with Rising and were not able to produce enough to maintain themselves, even if the harvest had been good. Rising bought food to maintain the peasants and artisans but the company directors were not willing to pay the bill.[31] Rising probably thought that since the company owned the land it also had the duty to maintain the people who cultivated it, an opinion that the company directors did not share. It is interesting to note that in her December 1653 memorandum for Rising, Queen Christina stated that anyone who purchased land from the company or from the Indians in New Sweden would receive perpetual ownership of that land for himself and his heirs. That seems to imply that all non-Indian land in New Sweden belonged to the company.

Rising wrote in his report to the Board of Commerce in the summer of 1654 that the freemen who had lived for a time in New Sweden wanted to use these new rights to purchase new land.[32] His policy had been to pay them for clearing the land and then get new freemen to cultivate it for the company. Until this time, all the cultivated land was considered to be the property of the company, but freemen had begun to buy land from the Indians for themselves. The right to do that was also confirmed in Rising's ordinance, which stated that after three years' service the soldiers would receive land from the company "for an everlasting possession."[33]

The Board of Commerce instructed Rising to select a piece of good land as "a special property of the company." The surplus from this land should be sold on behalf of the company.[34] In 1654 Rising reported that grants of land by the Crown to individual persons were ratified by the governor or by the company so that there was no encroachment on the special property of the company or on the needs of the country.[35] He was no enemy to feudal grants in New Sweden; on the contrary, his writings emphasized the possibilities of making big fiefs in the Delaware area.[36]

Some of the peasants or freemen were not very pleased by the feudal grants. When Captain Skute demanded Passayunk and Kingsessing, which Queen Christina had given to him, the freemen protested that they had not come to the colony to become tenants. Evidently they wanted to become independent and own the land that they cultivated. Rising said that the matter would be referred to the authorities in Sweden and that in the future the governor would be able to give the colonists land on terms of perpetual ownership according to their merits.

Thus, during the last years of New Sweden, a land system was being developed similar to that in Sweden. Four features distinguished it. First, the land of New Sweden, in general, belonged to the New Sweden Company under the supremacy of the Swedish Crown. The peasants cultivated most of it as tenants, often on a sharecropping basis, which was the way Crown lands in Sweden were managed. The company was not a feudal lord; it represented the Crown in New Sweden and the Crown had shares in and fueled the company.

Second, one part of the land was to be used as "the special property of the company," or used for the needs of the Crown. This land was never to be granted to private persons. The company's own tobacco plantations and the forts of the Crown belonged to this category.

Third, there were pieces of land, granted by the Crown to noblemen, that were cultivated by tenants. At this time there were only two such grants: Printzhof, where Governor Printz's daughter Armegot (who was married to Printz's lieutenant, Johan Papegoja) ruled, and Timber Island, where Rising had a piece of land cultivated in the hope of having his previously mentioned grant of land declared valid for that area.

Finally, some pieces of land—in the 1640s probably very few—were owned by the peasants themselves. Rising planned that later on their taxes would help support churches and schools.[38]

THE CONSEQUENCES FOR THE COLONIES

The Swedish attempt at economic and political expansion in America was a failure. From the viewpoint of the Crown, the New Sweden Company and the whole New Sweden venture was also a failure. The company contributed nothing to the development of Swedish trade. Surely the trade in tobacco, which was the company's special task, would have developed without the company. The Crown would probably also have gotten its taxes just as effectively, even if the company had not existed.

The private shareholders received no profits from their involvement in the company. It was so closely ruled by the Crown that private business interests stood little chance of being satisfied. To a very limited extent the shareholders represented business interests. Most of their interest lay in various connections with the Crown. For the members of the Oxenstierna, Fleming, and Bonde families, their interest in the New Sweden Company was only one minor element of their interest in Sweden's total economic and political expansion. The activities of the company were of the greatest significance to the three groups of people the company sent to New Sweden: the officials, the peasants, and the servants, soldiers, and other working people.

It is very difficult, if not impossible, to speculate on what the New Sweden venture meant for the officials. It depended greatly on their individual character and gifts as well as on their personal circumstances. Printz succeeded in rehabilitating himself in spite of, or because of, his harshness and brutality, while Rising had no luck in his home country, probably because of the political situation and his bad health.

Hendrick von Elswick, the last factor of the New Sweden Company, seems to have met with success when he returned from New Sweden. Peter Lindeström, a very competent military engineer in the colony and author of a famous account of his journey to New Sweden, did not.[39]

As for the other groups of colonists one may say that in general they profited from the New Sweden venture. After serving three years the soldiers could get land from the company, which was a better opportunity than they would have found in Sweden. Likewise, the servants and farmhands, after they had paid their employers or the company for their transportation to New Sweden, ought to have been able to own their own farms. We know that one reason why people left Sweden was because farmland in central Sweden was scarce, especially for those who were using the slash-and-burn technique, which the authorities in Sweden discouraged.

For these colonists, as well as for those who were already peasants, the emigration should have improved their living conditions. Surely the first years in New Sweden were difficult, not only because of the need to clear new land, but also because Johan Printz drove the colonists hard. We should take seriously their complaints against him. The peasants and other working people in those days rarely won cases against persons in authority, so therefore did not complain without good reason.[40]

The period under the Dutch was very favorable for the freemen, as the

Swedes were privileged and had few obligations to the Dutch.[41] Perhaps times got harder for a while under English rule, after 1664, but the Swedish and Finnish people in the long run prospered.[42] In their 1693 letters to relatives in Sweden Peter Gunnarsson Rambo and Lars Persson Cock both emphasize that they were living "in plenty." Rambo had sent his sister money several times and said that the country was splendid and fruitful and that his children were well provided for.[43] This evidence of the good situation of the former Swedish colonists is confirmed by many other sources.

In summary, from the beginning the aim of the New Sweden Company was that the Swedish Crown should become rich and powerful and that the Crown, the company, the officials, and others who were engaged in the affairs of the company, should prosper. The idealism underlying these activities, especially in Johan Rising's thoughts and writings, mostly concerned how the company and New Sweden could become useful to the state of Sweden. The peasant colonists, the soldiers, and all other working people were seen as a means to reach that goal, an attitude typical of seventeenth-century Europe. It may be called a sort of historical irony that neither Crown nor company prospered from New Sweden and that in fact the people whose interests the leaders of the New Sweden Company cared so little about gained the most from the company's activities.

NOTES

1. Immanuel Wallerstein, *The Modern World System. Vol. 1. Capitalist Agriculture and the Origins of the European World Economy in the Sixteenth Century*, Studies in Social Discontinuity (New York: Academic Press, 1974), passim. See also Stellan Dahlgren, "New Sweden: The State, the Company and Johan Rising," in *The Rise and Fall of New Sweden: Governor Johan Risingh's Journal, 1654–1655, in Its Historical Context*, ed. Stellan Dahlgren and Hans Norman, vol. 27, Acta Bibliothecae R. Universitatis Upsaliensis (Stockholm: Almqvist & Wiksell Int., 1988), 1–2.
2. For this debate see Wallerstein, *The Modern World System*, passim; R. Hilton et al., *The Transition from Feudalism to Capitalism* (London: Verso, 1978); R. Brenner, "The Origins of Capitalist Development: A Critique of Neo-Smithian Marxism," *New Left Review* 104 (1977); and among others the different points of view in Fernand Braudel, *Civilization and Capitalism, 15th–18th Century*, trans. Sian Reynolds, 3 vols.; vol. 2, *The Wheels of Commerce* (New York: Harper & Row, 1982); and E. Fox-Genovese and E. D. Genovese, *Fruits of Merchant Capital* (New York: Oxford University Press, 1983), 3–25.
3. Dahlgren, "New Sweden," 27–30.
4. For Rising's printed books and the economic support he received, see ibid., 26–29.

5. Ibid., 14–15, 29.

6. E. Fries, "Johan Classon Risingh," *Svensk Historisk Tidskrift* (1896): 61–62, and Dahlgren, "New Sweden," 29–30 and n. 97.

7. A copy of this account, dated 3 June 1656, at Elbing in Prussia, is preserved in Palmiskiöldska samlingen, 322:272, Uppsala University Library, Uppsala, Sweden. On the entrepôt in the West Indies, see ibid., 268–70. Rising repeated this passage in a couple of accounts of New Sweden that are preserved in Handel och Sjöfart, vol. 196, Riksarkivet, Stockholm.

8. The articles in the anthology edited by L. Blussé and F. Gaastra, *Companies and Trade* (The Hague: Leiden University Press, 1981), provide excellent recent studies of seventeenth-century trading companies.

9. For an overview of the Swedish trading companies, see E. F. Heckscher, *Sveriges ekonomiska historia från Gustav Vasa*, 2 vols. (Stockholm: Albert Bonniers Förlag, 1936), 1:592–601. An economic liberal, Heckscher was very negative about the Swedish trading companies, which he thought did great economic damage and had no positive social value. But both the Crown and important private interests wanted these companies, which did fill important needs in Swedish society. For more recent views on trading companies, especially on the Swedish Africa Company, see G. Nováky, *Handels kompanier och kompanihandel: Svenska Afrikakompaniet 1649–1663, En studie i feodal handel*, Studia Historica Upsaliensia 159 (Uppsala: Uppsala University, 1990).

10. Rising's views on the importance of open trading companies are in his *Ett Uttåg om Köp-Handelen eller Commerciene* ... (Stockholm, 1669), 1, 19, 84–85. He expressed similar opinions in the manuscript of his major work, "En Tractat om Kiöp-Handelen," which was never published; see L121, Uppsala University, pt. 1, chap. 20, esp. 348.

11. In the seventeenth century the Swedes imported only tobacco in fairly large quantities from America. In New Sweden, on the other hand, furs and corn (maize) were the important items of trade. New Sweden (especially Johan Printz) exported an unknown quantity of furs to Europe, mostly to the Netherlands. See Amandus Johnson, *The Swedish Settlements on the Delaware: Their History and Relation to the Indians, Dutch and English, 1638–1664*, 2 vols. (Philadelphia: Swedish Colonial Society, 1911), 1:194, 317–19, 349–50, and Amandus Johnson, trans. and ed., *The Instruction for Johan Printz, Governor of New Sweden* (Philadelphia: Swedish Colonial Society, 1930), 40 n. 65.

12. Johnson, *Swedish Settlements*, 1:87–116; Dahlgren, "New Sweden," 4; and Hans Norman, "The Swedish Colonial Venture in North America 1638–1655," in *The Rise and Fall of New Sweden*, ed. Dahlgren and Norman, 46–47.

13. Johnson, *Swedish Settlements*. The photograph of the balance sheet is between 642–43 in vol. 2.

14. On the loss of *Kattan* and Sweden's unsuccessful efforts to gain compensation for the loss from Spain and the Netherlands, see Johnson, *Swedish Settlements*, 1:266–80, 2:648–56, and Dahlgren and Norman, eds., *The Rise and Fall of New Sweden*, 75, 143 n. 20, 224.

15. C. T. Odhner, "Kolonin Nya Sveriges grundläggning 1637–1642," *Historiskt Bibliothek* 3 (1877): 213–14; Johnson, *Swedish Settlements*, 1:131–32; and Dahlgren, "New Sweden," 7.

16. On Gabriel Bengtsson Oxenstierna's and Olof Strömsköld's investments in the company, see Dahlgren, "New Sweden," 8–9, nn. 23 and 24. In the au-

tumn of 1658 Strömsköld got his money back from the company; see the journal of the American Company in Handel och Sjöfart (KA:s series), vol. 44.

17. On these shareholders see Dahlgren, "New Sweden," 8–9, nn. 22–24. The burghers of Viborg invested two thousand riksdaler (or three thousand daler silvermynt, abbreviated d.s.) in the company via a bill of exchange. When they learned that the Dutch had conquered New Sweden they retrieved their investment by seizing the company's money and tobacco (valued at 2,142 d.s.) in Viborg. See the journal of the American Company, entry dated 26 January 1656, in Handel och Sjöfart (KA:s series), vol. 44. The sum of 858 d.s. in the balance sheet is thus the remainder of their investment.

18. With the exception of the burghers of Viborg, people who became shareholders at this time were already closely associated with the company: Olof Strömsköld, Hans Kramer, Christer Bonde, Hendrik Huyghen, and Erik Oxenstierna. The burghers' shares in the company were in payment for debts owed them from the tobacco trade to the Russian border. See Dahlgren, "New Sweden," 8–9.

19. See n. 17, above.

20. Dahlgren, "New Sweden," 4.

21. Ibid., 19–22.

22. See Rising, "En Tractat om Kiöp-Handelen," L121, pt. 1, chap. 20, 354–59, Uppsala University.

23. On the tobacco trade in Sweden, see Dahlgren, "New Sweden," 6, 16, 19 (including notes).

24. The privilege of 22 May 1658 is in A. A. von Stiernman, ed., *Samling Utav Kongl. Brev ... Angående Sveriges Rikes Commerce ...* (Stockholm, 1750), 2:875–76.

25. Johnson, *Swedish Settlements*, 2:637–40, 644.

26. Ibid., 727–33, 741–47 (Rising's instruction from the Board of Commerce "on behalf of the South Company"), and a memorandum for Rising from Queen Christina, 12 December 1653, Riksregistraturet, Riksarkivet, Stockholm.

27. J. Rosen has treated this problem in a famous article, "Statsledning och provinspolitik under Sveriges stormakstid," *Scandia* (1946): 224–70.

28. The journal of the American Company, Handel och Sjöfart (KA:s series), vol. 44, entry 1586, Riksarkivet, Stockholm. The entry portrays the situation in New Sweden at the time Johan Printz left the colony in the autumn of 1653. Hendrik Huyghen compiled the list.

29. Royal grants of land in New Sweden went to Johan Printz, 6 November 1643 (Johnson, *Swedish Settlements*, 1:317); Sven Skute and Hans Amundsson, 20 August 1653 (Riksregistraturet, Riksarkivet, Stockholm); and Johan Risingh, 12 December 1653 (ibid. and Samuel Hazard, *Annals of Pennsylvania from the Discovery of the Delaware, 1609–1682* [Philadelphia: Hazard and Mitchell, 1850], 145).

30. Dahlgren and Norman, eds., *The Rise and Fall of New Sweden*, 170, 202.

31. Ibid., 23, 233, 283.

32. Johan Rising, "Report of Governor Johan Rising, 1654," in *Narratives of Early Pennsylvania, West New Jersey and Delaware, 1630–1707*, ed. Albert Cook Myers (1912; reprint, New York: Barnes & Noble, 1967), 139.

33. The ordinance is in Peter Lindeström, *Geographia Americae, with an Account of the Delaware Indians, Based on Surveys and Notes Made in 1654–*

1656, trans. and ed. Amandus Johnson (Philadelphia: Swedish Colonial Society, 1925), 275–78.

34. Johnson, *Swedish Settlements*, 2:731, 745.

35. Rising, "Report, 1654," 148. On the Swedish term *immittera* (wrongly translated as "encourage" in this edition), see *The Rise and Fall of New Sweden*, ed. Dahlgren and Norman, 202 n. 82.

36. See for example his undated account of New Sweden in Handel och Sjöfart, vol. 196, last page.

37. Dahlgren and Norman, eds., *The Rise and Fall of New Sweden*, 170–71.

38. Rising, "Report, 1654," 146–50; Johan Rising, "Report of Governor Johan Rising, 1655," in *Narratives*, ed. Myers, 164–65.

39. Von Elswick became the Crown's accountant in Reval in 1659 and ended as "Assistenzrat" in the same town. (I am indebted to Richard H. Hulan for information about him.) On Lindeström's difficulties after he returned to Sweden from America in 1657, see Amandus Johnson's introduction to his translation of *Geographia Americae*, xxv–xxxiii.

40. On the complaints against Printz, see Johnson, *Instruction*, 37–41, and Dahlgren and Norman, eds., *The Rise and Fall of New Sweden*, 42, 172–75, 184–85 (including nn. 50 and 60).

41. J. A. Munroe, *Colonial Delaware, A History* (Millwood, N.Y.: KTO Press, 1978), 41–43; C. A. Weslager, *The Swedes and the Dutch at New Castle* (Wilmington, Del.: Middle Atlantic Press, 1988), 151–72.

42. On the Swedes under English rule, see C. A. Weslager, *The English on the Delaware* (New Brunswick, N.J.: Rutgers University Press, 1967), esp. 197; Munroe, *Colonial Delaware*, 66–68, 72–76; and Peter S. Craig, "The Stille Family in America, 1641–1772," *Swedish American Genealogist* 6 (1986): 152–53.

43. The letters from Peter Rambo, undated [1693], and L. Cock, 31 May 1693, are in Prästeståndets arkiv, ser. 4, vol. 5, R1100, Riksarkivet, Stockholm. I have quoted Richard H. Hulan's translation of them.

Hodie Mihi, Cras Tibi: Swedish-Dutch Relations in the Delaware Valley

CHARLES T. GEHRING

In the autumn of 1655, an event occurred on the Delaware River worthy of a painting. Picture Peter Stuyvesant, commander of the Dutch expeditionary force, negotiating with the Swedish representative, Hendrick von Elswick, about the surrender of Fort Trefaldighet and the status of the remaining Swedish possessions along the river. The scene is set in a clearing just beyond the walls of the forest. The Dutch force of seven ships has successfully landed three hundred troops north of the fort, cutting off communications with the Swedish administrative center at Fort Christina several miles upriver. After word reached the director of New Sweden that the Dutch had invaded his territory and were threatening his entire colony he sent his factor, Elswick, to inquire about Stuyvesant's intentions. Stuyvesant, in full battle dress and in sight of his siege cannon, responded that his orders were to recover all that belonged to his superiors, the honorable directors of the West India Company. Whereupon the Swede retorted, "Hodie mihi, cras tibi" (My turn today, yours tomorrow).[1] Truly a dramatic moment!

Nine years later Stuyvesant may have recalled this phrase, which at the time probably seemed nothing but an idle threat; however, when the English reduced the Dutch strongholds on the Delaware in 1664, Elswick's retort turned out to be prophetic, although upon closer examination we could say that it was a mere inevitability. For when one considers Swedish and Dutch relations on the Delaware, one cannot avoid the reality of the constant threat posed by the English colonies to the north and south. Elswick's remark merely articulated the outcome of inexorable English pressure for hegemony along the coast of North America. Although this paper naturally divides into two parts with the Swedes as competitors of the Dutch and the Dutch as conquerors of the Swedes, a common thread throughout belongs to England and its colonial interests in North America.

NEW SWEDEN

The first part begins in 1638 when Peter Minuit established the colony of New Sweden in a region of New Netherland called the Suyt Revier or South River by the Dutch. The Dutch claim to the Delaware River valley goes back to Hudson's exploratory movements in the entrance to the bay in 1609. His later explorations of the river named after him combined with the Delaware to form the axes of New Netherland. The Dutch considered both areas as their sphere of influence by right of exploration. As early as 1614 this territory between New England and the English tobacco colonies was referred to as New Netherland.[2] The area was soon exploited by a cartel of merchants licensed by the States General of the United Provinces under the name of the New Netherland Company. When the Twelve Year's Truce with Spain lapsed in 1621, the West India Company was formed to carry on the war with Spain in the Atlantic theater of operations. The company was also given exclusive rights to the trade in New Netherland.[3]

The directors of the West India Company initially issued instructions to form the administrative center for the colony in the Delaware region. When colonists were sent over in 1624 they were settled in the three major watersheds of New Netherland: at Fort Orange on the upper Hudson (or Noort Revier), at the mouth of the Connecticut (or Versche Revier), and on High Island (now Burlington Island) in the Delaware (or Suyt Revier). The directors had apparently received inaccurate information about the Delaware, which was painted as a tropical paradise. It probably did not take long for the first director, Willem Verhulst, to realize that the Delaware was also prone to unfavorable weather in the winter. Such information could have been supplied by Peter Minuit, who, as a "volunteer" attached to Verhulst, traveled from one end of the colony to the other; knowledge and experience that would prove useful to him in his future position with the Swedes. Although Verhulst formed his headquarters on Nut Island off the tip of Manhattan, a trading post was maintained on High Island in the Delaware for two years.[4]

Soon after Peter Minuit became director in 1626, he called in the outlying settlements because of unsettled relations with the Mohawks in the north. Although the small settlement and trading post on High Island was abandoned, Minuit maintained a Dutch presence in the Delaware by constructing a fortified trading post near present-day Gloucester called Fort Nassau. West India Company personnel staffed the fort during the summer trading season; however, for most of the year it was left to the elements and sometimes served as a shelter for local Indians during the winter months. This occasional occupation eventually attracted the attention of the English in Virginia. In 1635 Virginia sent a force of some fifteen men to occupy and hold the fort; however, they were soon taken prisoner and bundled off to New Amsterdam. When David Pietersz de Vries brought the prisoners back to Virginia aboard his yacht, he encountered another ship carrying twenty soldiers on its way to reinforce the English at Fort Nassau. When they discovered the fate of the initial probe, the mission was aborted.[5] Had the English succeeded in gaining a foothold in the Delaware Valley at this early date, the success of Minuit's venture into the Delaware might have been in doubt; indeed, Dutch claims to the area might have been jeopardized, as in the Connecticut Valley.

In addition to the settlement on High Island and the trading post at Fort Nassau the West India Company made one other attempt to demonstrate its interest in the Delaware region before the appearance of the Swedes. This settlement was the result of the resolution of a dispute between two factions of the company regarding the formation of settlements in New Netherland. From the very inception of the West India Company there arose a debate over whether the overseas territories should only be considered as sites for factories concerned with exploiting the natural resources from the region or open to colonists who would commit themselves to developing the region agriculturally. The first faction suspected that the colonists would be a drain on the company's profits through illegal competition and smuggling, while the other faction explained that an agricultural base was necessary to maintain the trading routes and discourage settlement by other foreign powers. In 1629 the faction favoring colonization won a concession called the "Freedoms and Exemptions."[6] In effect the question of colonization was turned over to the private sector. All the investors who filed for the right to become "patroons" in the New World were either directors of the West India Company or closely involved with its operations.[7]

In 1631 a settlement was formed on the Delaware near the present location of Lewes, Delaware, called Swanendael. The majority investor among those who registered their interest with the West India Company and invested their capital in the venture was Samuel Godijn, president of the Amsterdam chamber of the company. The colony began with a population of twenty-eight men who built a trading house surrounded by a palisade. Although the adjacent land was fertile enough for farming, the primary attraction in the area was the possibility of developing a trane oil works because of the numerous whales annually sighted in Delaware Bay. The seeds planted by Godijn, however, were not given a chance to bear fruit. In the following year a misunderstanding with the local Indians led to the massacre of all the settlers and the destruction of the trading house. Although the Dutch were denied a presence at the entrance to the bay, which allowed the English and Swedes to sail upriver unchallenged, the short-lived patroonship of Swanendael was responsible for the resolution of a border dispute between Pennsylvania and Maryland in the eighteenth century and the existence of the state of Delaware.[8]

High Island, Fort Nassau, and Swanendael, however, were all a prelude to the return of Peter Minuit and the establishment of New Sweden in 1638. For it was not until the Swedes appeared in the Delaware as a serious competitor in the fur trade that the Dutch attempted to maintain an annual presence in the region. When Minuit chose the location on the Minquas Kill (later Christina Kill) for his settlement, he probably did so from an awareness that it lay along the end of a major conduit bringing furs from the interior, and that it was in a region beyond the resources of the Dutch to contest; it is also possible that Minuit knew that ownership of the land was in question. In addition, the Swedish trading house and settlement at Fort Christina had the distinct advantage of being on the proper side of the river for involvement in the fur trade. The location of Fort Nassau on the east side of the river forced the Indians to cross this broad waterway after a long trip from the interior. The Swedish trading house obviated this final inconvenience and soon turned the Dutch post into an anachronism.[9]

Although such a confrontation between these two European powers may seem unusual to us today, Sweden and the Netherlands were hardly strangers in the seventeenth century. Dutch trading operations in the Baltic region, known as the "mother trade," brought merchants, financiers, skippers, and seamen into direct contact with Swedes; in fact, the trade was so critical for a Netherlands almost completely dependent on the Scandinavian countries and Poland for timber and grain that Dutch trading posts and associated settlements were scattered throughout the Baltic. According to Amandus Johnson:

> Of foreign nations, except the immediate neighbors, Holland stood in closest connection with Sweden. From Holland, Sweden received many of its best and most useful citizens, capitalists, merchants and warriors. Dutch soldiers served in Swedish armies and Dutch captains and skippers commanded Swedish ships; Swedish students went to Holland to study commerce and Swedish scholars gained inspiration from Dutch teachers; Dutch money helped Sweden to support its armies and found its commercial companies and Dutch brains developed the industries of the country, and from Holland came the first impulses of the transatlantic trade.[10]

In addition to these common bonds, the inspiration for a Dutch West India Company and the original Swedish South Company have a common source in the person of Willem Usselincx. Although Usselincx's plan was never implemented, his ideas were the inspiration for the company, which founded and promoted the establishment of New Sweden on the Delaware.[11] It should also be noted that the funding and workforce for the first expedition was half-Swedish and half-Dutch.[12] Thus in the beginning at least, the Swedish-sponsored venture to the New World was as much a binational cooperative venture designed to compete with the West India Company as it was strictly a Swedish affair. The confrontation on the Delaware represented, in effect, the maneuvering of two multinational corporations rather than the clash of colonial outposts defending the flags of competing European powers.

The establishment of New Sweden in 1638 coincides with the first year of the directorship of Willem Kieft on Manhattan. When word reached him of the arrival of the Swedes on the South River, Kieft was most likely unsure of his options and their possible international ramifications. As a new director with no previous experience to draw on in the region (unlike Minuit) he probably hesitated to react without instructions from the directors in Amsterdam. Instead he issued a formal protest, which Minuit ignored.[13] In addition to this cautious approach to the colony of a "friendly" power, Kieft soon found himself embroiled in a devastating war with the Indians near Manhattan. This protracted war, which was not resolved until 1645, left him few resources and little energy to devote to the South River. With regard to New Sweden, Kieft's attitude was one of accommodation, at least until clear instructions arrived from the Netherlands. Accommodation, however, developed into cooperation in 1641 when the Dutch and Swedes teamed up to thwart an attempt by some English from New Haven to settle in the Schuylkill. The settlers were returned to New Haven aboard a Dutch ship and their buildings burned. Constant vigilance against English incursions kept relations from becoming strained.[14] Mutual distress often creates unlikely partners.

Another New Haven settlement along the Varkens Kill below Fort Nassau (now Salem Creek near Salem, New Jersey) was left undisturbed by both the Dutch and the Swedes because of its apparently harmless location. However, when Johan Printz arrived as governor of New Sweden in 1643 he erected a fort called Elfsborg in this area, probably as much to monitor river traffic as to bring these English settlers under his control. Thus the state of relations between Printz and Kieft was cooperative, at least when faced with the mutual threat from New Haven. This amicable relationship soon changed when the commander at Fort Nassau was accused of fraud and replaced by Andries Hudde in 1645. The lack of friction on the Delaware during Kieft's Indian wars was probably the result of Jan Jansen van Ilpendam's attempt to maintain the status quo while the bulk of the colony's energies was being diverted elsewhere. However, this does not imply that Jan Jansen lacked any zeal in carrying out orders from New Amsterdam. Upon Kieft's order to remove the English from the Schuykill in 1642, he responded immediately and with resolution. Jan Jansen's failing may have been on the side of commission rather than omission; in his attempt to cooperate with Printz to repel the English he may also have worked out some personal arrangements with the Swedes in the fur trade.[15]

Hudde, on the other hand, was more aggressive in protecting and pursuing Dutch fur-trading interests in the Delaware and in preserving the territorial integrity of the West India Company. After his arrival Fort Nassau became an active trading post once again, rather than a mere outpost for maintaining the status quo. Although the Dutch located their post on the wrong side of the river for the trade coming from the west, they did have an important advantage over the Swedes—a constant supply of trade goods. Nothing annoyed the Indians more than to carry their heavy burden of furs for days over rough trails only to realize that their journey was in vain because the traders had no merchandise to consummate a deal.[16] The Dutch were able to bring more goods into the river on a regular basis than could the Swedes, assuring the Indians of a reward for their efforts. Thus under Hudde the cooperative atmosphere created by fear of English encroachment soon developed into competition for the fur trade.

Printz countered by strengthening his position as best he could. Lacking a steady flow of trade goods from Sweden, he reacted to Dutch competition in other ways. To neutralize the advantage in trade goods he began to spread rumors among the Indians about Dutch intentions along the river. One rumor told of Dutch plans to build a house near the falls (Trenton, New Jersey), and that two hundred fifty men would come from Manhattan to kill all the Indians in the valley.[17] Printz also attempted to impede Dutch expansion by contesting Dutch ownership of land in the Delaware and by threatening or actually destroying new construction beyond the fort, especially on the west bank of the river.[18] In addition to these methods of hindering Dutch trade, Printz also used his commanding position at Fort Elfsborg to control traffic in and out of the river. These draconian tactics kept the Dutch off balance in the Delaware until the appearance of Peter Stuyvesant.

When Stuyvesant became director-general of New Netherland in the spring of 1647, he assessed past and present relations with the Swedes on the Delaware and reacted in a calculated and single-minded manner.[19] Although Stuyvesant's instructions from his superiors in Amsterdam no longer exist, we do have the benefit of his instructions to Hudde in the spring of 1648. He instructed Hudde to be cautious in his dealings with the Swedes and to give no cause for complaints. However, he directed Hudde to build wherever Printz built to demonstrate the company's previous possession of such places.[20]

In the spring of 1648 Stuyvesant informed his commander on the Delaware that he was planning to come to the South River region to sort out matters in person. Hudde was probably ecstatic to hear of such concern and support for his area of responsibility, which had suffered from years of benign neglect. A private Dutch trader in the Delaware proclaimed in a letter to his superiors in Amsterdam that Stuyvesant was expected any day (so much for secrecy) and that matters would soon be straightened out.[21] Stuyvesant planned to march overland with thirty men and enough building materials necessary "to construct quickly a proper and strong house on the other side as a token of our ownership."[22]

The decision to construct another trading post on the Schuykill was prompted by reports that the Swedes were collecting building materials there during the winter of 1647 to 1648. Not only was Hudde concerned that the Swedes would attempt to control this major waterway into the interior, but he was even questioned by several sachems from the region as to why he also did not build there. As soon as Hudde began construction of a house on the Schuylkill, he attracted the attention of the Swedes. Upon Printz's orders Måns Kling, his lieutenant at Nya Korsholm at the mouth of the Schuylkill, marched to Fort Beversreede with twenty-four fully armed men. After a brief verbal exchange Kling and his men cut down the trees near the house and destroyed the fruit trees that Hudde had planted there. It was probably this action that prompted Stuyvesant to visit the area with a suitable force. For the Dutch strategy to succeed a place had to be carved out on the west side that would attract settlers. This would only happen in an environment of security. The Swedish counterstrategy seemed to be to isolate the Dutch house by driving away any attempts to establish a support community there.

Stuyvesant's plans to lead a force overland, however, were not carried out. Two attempts to reach the Delaware by sea also proved unsuccessful. Finally Stuyvesant informed Hudde that he was unable to come in person because of reports of an imminent attack by northern Indians. The council appointed Lubbert van Dincklagen and Jan de la Montagne, "trusted chief-officers and councilors," to go to the Delaware as Stuyvesant's representatives. Only a few days after their arrival in June they managed to meet with the proper sachems, who conveyed the land in the Schuylkill to the Dutch. Van Dincklagen and company then proceeded to Printz's residence on Tinnekonck to file a protest against his "illegal occupation of the Schuylkill." Before the Dutch commissioners were allowed in to see Printz, they were left standing in the rain for half an hour. Printz responded to the protest by promising a written reply before they left the Delaware, but he demonstrated his intentions by deeds rather than words. After the departure of the commissioners several Dutch settlers went to Beversreede to build a settlement to be called Nieu Hooven. As soon as construction was underway both men were confronted by a Swedish force, led by the son of Johan Printz. They ordered the settlers to tear down what they had built, and when they refused it was done for them. Violence to their constructions was accompanied by threats of violence to their persons if they persisted. Printz's tactics to isolate Beversreede by destroying any further construction in the Schuylkill were having the desired effect.

While Hudde was conferring with Stuyvesant on Manhattan over matters in the Delaware, Printz escalated the tension another notch. Alexander Boyer, Hudde's second-in-command, sent a messenger overland informing them that the Swedes had built a house directly in front of Fort Beversreede. It was so situated that the rear gable was only twelve feet from the fort's front gate. Boyer stated the obvious by speculating that Printz had done it more to mock the company than to gain profit from it. When Hudde returned to the Delaware, he was to find out that not only was the front gate to Beversreede obstructed by the Swedish construction but that it could barely be seen from the river. As one would expect, such proximity soon led to more tension and violence. One night a Swedish soldier tore through the palisades of the Dutch fort, displaying "insolence by words as well as deeds." Late in the fall several freemen made another attempt to build in the area. Printz made it clear that he intended no further development by the Dutch in the Schuylkill. Soon after construction began, a Swedish force tore it down, chopping the building material to pieces. Alexander Boyer's protest of the Swedish actions quickly developed into a shouting match, during which a fight broke out. With so many axes present miraculously no one was hurt, except for Boyer, who had his hair pulled by Sven Skute, the future commander of Fort Trefaldighet.

As low as Swedish-Dutch relations had sunk on the Delaware, Printz's confidence must have grown in proportion. He had prevented the Dutch from establishing a settlement on the Schuylkill and had effectively neutralized their only trading post on the west side of the river. Printz's strategy, however, was directed towards domination of the Indian trade.

For his colony to thrive he needed good relations with the Indians, who would supply him with a steady flow of furs that would convert into profits for his superiors and justify his existence. With this in mind, the summer and fall of 1648 was the high-water mark of Printz's administration; however, problems were soon to come. Not only had his last supply ship arrived in the beginning of 1648, something he would not realize until 1653, when he had to journey to New Amsterdam to catch a ship back to Europe, but he also had made an enemy of Peter Stuyvesant.

Although relations had deteriorated when the administrations of Printz and Stuyvesant coincided, policy on the Delaware was still being driven by apprehension of English designs on the area. In 1649 Stuyvesant informed Hudde that the English were preparing to seize control of the

Delaware. He feared that if the English were successful in settling there, they would not only steal the river "from us and the Swedes," but would also threaten the North River from behind, diverting the trade and separating the colony of Rensselaerswyck from Manhattan. Stuyvesant instructed Hudde to confer with Printz in this matter of mutual concern, but cautioned him not to reveal too much concerning their rights to the area. Stuyvesant needed Printz's cooperation in his attempt to keep the English out of the river. Although the Swedes lacked support from the homeland, they still outnumbered the Dutch on the river by about seven to one. The English threat from New Haven to seize the Delaware never materialized; however, two events were to occur that dramatically altered the balance of power on the river.

In the summer of 1649 the Swedish relief ship *Kattan* ran aground near Puerto Rico. All the goods and supplies aboard the ship were seized by the Spaniards; only a handful of the colonists and crew managed to make it back to Sweden, after almost a year of misery and hardship. Printz learned of the disaster in a letter from Stuyvesant dated 24 July 1650. Among other details, he informed Printz that the Spaniards had seized the ship and were detaining the governor and his family.[23] Printz's hopes for the future must have been dashed. Not only was the long-awaited relief ship lost, but his replacement was being held in Puerto Rico. The fact that he had to learn of this misfortune from his principal adversary also did not augur well for the future of the colony. Shortly after this news reached Stuyvesant, an agreement was reached at Hartford between New Netherland and the New England colonies concerning conflicting boundary claims. Stuyvesant's interpretation of one of the matters discussed at the conference was that any future attempts by New Haven to settle in the Delaware Valley would not have the approval of the other colonies of New England, and that New Haven would be left to its own devices if trouble should arise as a result.[24] This conjunction of events must have inspired Stuyvesant's next move in the Delaware.

Stuyvesant's fear of English encroachment in the Delaware had been reduced significantly. This, coupled with Printz's lack of relief from Sweden, allowed Stuyvesant to reconsider his strategy in the Delaware Valley. Rather than contend with the constricted situation at Fort Beversreede on the Schuylkill, Stuyvesant decided to relocate at a place both convenient to the Indian trade and militarily advantageous in his maneuvering against Printz. Without specific instructions from or notification to his superiors in Amsterdam, Stuyvesant led an impressive military force into the Delaware Valley. The plan was to enter the valley by two directions, meeting at Fort Nassau. Over one hundred men marched overland from Manhattan, while a fleet of eleven ships sailed up the river with drums beating on their decks. If Stuyvesant planned to impress the Swedes through a display of force and thus gain his objective without suffering casualties, he certainly succeeded.[25] With such a formidable force in the valley Stuyvesant could have done as he pleased, including the elimination of New Sweden. However, he was acting on his own in this matter. He had seen an opening and he took it. After making his presence felt throughout the valley, he proceeded to dismantle Fort Nassau and move what he could to the new site on the west side of the river.

Stuyvesant chose for the location of his new stronghold on the South River a point of land just a few miles south of Fort Christina. It was called Sant Hoeck by the Dutch and had never been occupied by either the Swedes or the Dutch. For Stuyvesant's purposes, it was an ideal location for a fort and trading post. It had a deep harbor, access to trade routes to the west, and commanded the river. Its location south of Fort Christina gave the Dutch an advantage over traffic sailing north, and effectively cut off Swedish access to Fort Elfsborg located just to the southeast on the opposite bank. Stuyvesant chose the name Fort Casimir, in memory of Ernst Casimir of the house of Orange-Nassau, a hero of his native province of Friesland. The directors in Amsterdam questioned his choice of name as well as his decision to demolish Fort Nassau. They admonished him to guard the new fort well. In a later communication the directors cautioned Stuyvesant not to give any cause for complaint or dissatisfaction among the Swedes because they did not want to add to the company's enemies.[26] These responses to Stuyvesant's actions on the South River came during the first naval war with England, which was a period when the war seemed likely to spill over into the colonies at any moment. Stuyvesant's preoccupation with guarding against possible invasion from New England made it necessary to maintain a peaceful posture in the south. Printz complained but was incapable of reacting with any force against Dutch initiatives.

By 1653 it had been almost five years since the Swedish governor had received a relief ship from Sweden. Printz longed for his homeland, and many of his colonists sought relief from the hardships of an unattended colony. Towards the end of the year Printz and his family traveled to New Amsterdam where they boarded a Dutch ship bound for the Netherlands. Accompanying the Printz family were about twenty-five soldiers and colonists. Left in command of New Sweden was Printz's son-in-law, Johan Papegoja. Printz promised to return soon, or at least send a relief ship. He did neither because the latter was already being equipped. By the spring of 1654 Stuyvesant had received instructions to permit resettlement of inhabitants of New Sweden within his jurisdiction. It seemed clear to the Dutch that the Swedish colony was finally succumbing to years of neglect. The directors pointed out that population increase was the life of the state and should be promoted by all means.[27] However, before any resettlement could take place, there was an unexpected turn of events on the South River.

While Printz was planning his return to Sweden after years of silence from his superiors, Queen Christina took a sudden interest in her American colony. Plans were made to send two ships to New Sweden. The *Örn* was to carry the new governor, Johan Rising, and over two hundred colonists directly to the Delaware; the *Gyllene Haj* was to be in the charge of the new commissary, Hendrick von Elswick, who was to proceed first to Puerto Rico. There he was instructed to settle matters concerning the wrecked ship *Kattan* before continuing on to New Sweden. Rising was instructed to attempt to remove the Dutch from Fort Casimir by argument and protest but without any display of hostility. If this was unsuccessful, Rising was to tolerate the Dutch rather than risk having "the same fort ... fall into the hands of the English as the strongest and consequently the most dangerous." If the latter tactic was necessary, then Rising was instructed to build a fort below Fort Casimir to render it ineffective and thus control the river.[28] Fear of the English continued to drive Dutch-Swedish relations in the Delaware.

After a stormy crossing Rising appeared before Fort Casimir on 30 May, Trinity Sunday, 1654. With a show of force and a good verbal bluff Rising was able to accomplish what must have seemed extremely idealistic in his instructions. Without firing a shot Rising had turned the Delaware once again into a Swedish river. Fort Casimir's defenses had been weakened in favor of strengthening Manhattan against a possible attack from New England during the first Anglo-Dutch war. The least of Stuyvesant's concerns during this troubled period was with New Sweden. However, the company's reservations about Stuyvesant's demolition of Fort Nassau three years earlier had been borne out. The Dutch were now left with no posts on the South River. Stuyvesant must have been extremely unhappy, but another twist of fate was soon to be played out. If Stuyvesant had ever witnessed an embodiment of just compensation, it must have occurred when the *Gyllene Haj* and Hendrick von Elswick sailed into the harbor at Manhattan. Following Rising by almost four months because of delays in Sweden and the mission to Puerto Rico, Elswick unfortunately had missed the entrance to Delaware Bay. Instead his ship sailed in behind Staten Island, where it was soon detected and confiscated by the Dutch.

Factor Elswick filed a strong protest with Stuyvesant, who responded by stating that the ship, crew, and cargo would be restored as soon as Fort Casimir was returned to its rightful owners. Stuyvesant offered Governor Rising a pass to travel to Manhattan to discuss the situation. The offer was not accepted. Elswick eventually made his way to New Sweden, leaving behind his ship and most of his crew and passengers, whom Stuyvesant was apparently able to convince to remain in New Amsterdam. The *Gyllene Haj* was renamed *Diemen* and put into service hauling salt from Curaçao. In 1659, overloaded with salt, it headed for New Netherland, never to be seen again.[29] Although Rising had lost a ship, he had gained an entire river. But forces were at work that would soon deprive him of everything.

Stuyvesant's superiors in Amsterdam reacted to the loss of the South River in no uncertain terms. They instructed him to do his "utmost to revenge this misfortune not only by restoring matters to their former condition, but also by driving the Swedes at the same time from the river, as they did us." Stuyvesant was also instructed to allow those inhabitants of New Sweden, who so desired, to remain in New Netherland; however, the directors preferred that the Swedes and Finns be resettled elsewhere within his jurisdiction, keeping the South River solely for their own Dutch subjects. They urged Stuyvesant to carry out the expedition before the Swedes were reinforced. The directors promised military support for the expedition and reminded Stuyvesant that he could use his troops on Manhattan more freely now that there was peace with England.[30] It was no longer necessary to handle New Sweden with kid gloves. Peace with England had given the Dutch an opening to eliminate their competition in the South River.

Hendrick von Elswick was unaware that within a year of his confrontation with Stuyvesant on Manhattan he would be facing him again in an even more tense situation on the Delaware. At the scene outside Fort Trefaldighet, Stuyvesant clearly had the upper hand and would be satisfied with no less than surrender of all Swedish possessions on the river. At Fort Christina on 25 September 1655, Governor Rising signed the surrender terms agreed upon with Stuyvesant, bringing to a close the seventeen-year history of New Sweden.

THE SWEDISH NATION

The articles of capitulation were very lenient. Stuyvesant was forced to rush his negotiations with Rising because of unfavorable news from Manhattan. Ten days after the Dutch expeditionary force had left Manhattan, a large confederation of Algonquin Indians from the lower Hudson, Long Island, and Raritan area attacked New Amsterdam. After being repelled from Manhattan they attacked the extensive agricultural communities in Pavonia and on Staten Island. Casualties were high during the so-called Peach War.[31] In a letter about the disaster to the directors in Amsterdam, Stuyvesant reported that twenty-eight farms had been destroyed, twelve thousand skipples of grain burned, forty Christians killed, and about one hundred captured, mostly women and children.[32] Reports from the council to Stuyvesant that all of Pavonia had been burned and everyone killed except for the family of Michiel Jansen must have alarmed the entire Dutch expeditionary force. Almost as distressing and ominous was the report that the chief of the Minquas had been among these Indians and that it was suspected that the Swedes had instructed this chief to bribe the Indians to attack the Dutch at this time.[33] This may explain the actions of the Dutch occupation force.

According to Governor Rising, the Dutch soldiers had run amok. In a protest to Stuyvesant a month after the surrender, Rising complained that the Dutch soldiers had plundered the colony "as if they were in the country of their archenemy." He goes on to describe how women were torn from their houses, animals slaughtered in large numbers, even horses wantonly shot, farms and provisions devastated and destroyed.[34] Such irrational behavior usually followed the frenzy caused by the storming of a fortress; however, hardly a shot had been fired in Stuyvesant's campaign against New Sweden. Therefore, it is quite possible that the fury unleashed against the Swedes and their possessions was precipitated by an emotional reaction to rumors of Swedish complicity in the Indian attacks at the heart of New Netherland.

The governing council on Manhattan, in their distress over the Indian attacks, advised Stuyvesant to level Fort Christina and expel all the Swedes from the South River. They reminded Stuyvesant that "a conquered or vanquished people are not to be trusted when the opportunity arises, as has been demonstrated in Brazil."[35] Stuyvesant was in no position to carry out such orders. His major concern was to return to Manhattan in all haste and hope that he was not too late.

The first years after the surrender of New Sweden were filled with tension. Rumors of Swedish plans to retake the colony caused the Dutch to view the "Swedish nation" with suspicion. When the Swedish relief ship *Mercurius* arrived in Delaware Bay in April 1656 it created quite a stir. Hendrick Huyghen van Cleef, its commander and nephew of Peter Minuit, claimed that he was unaware of the change. After lengthy negotiations in New Amsterdam, he was ordered to withdraw from the river and sail to Manhattan. Before Huyghen was able to return to the South River, however, some Swedes, Finns, and Indians boarded the ship and sailed it past Fort Casimir to New Gothenburg.[36] The *Mercurius* added more than a hundred new settlers (mostly Finns) to the upriver settlements, in addition to much-needed supplies.[37] After more lengthy discussions, the Swedish ship was eventually allowed to return to Europe with a cargo, while the new settlers were permitted to remain in their new homeland.

The peaceful resolution of the *Mercurius* affair must have had a cathartic effect on Swedish-Dutch relations. Although there certainly remained suspicions concerning the loyalty of the Swedes and Finns, by 1657 they had been allowed some form of local government. Stuyvesant had neither the resources nor the personnel to continue an occupation of their communities and rule them by military decree; he also needed to populate the region to discourage any attempts at encroachment by his neighbors in Maryland and New Haven. When Gregory van Dyck, the schout (a local official who combined the attributes of sheriff and prosecuting attorney) of the "Swedish nation," requested permission to form villages, his petition was not only approved but the council noted that it was considered necessary. His request for a court messenger and provost was also approved.[38] The following year Stuyvesant made an inspection trip to the South River. While upriver among the Swedes and Finns, he permitted more requests for local government, including power to apprehend anyone leaving his or her jurisdiction without permission, and access to the commander at Fort Altena (formerly Fort Christina) for assistance during emergencies. He also approved their request to be allowed to remain neutral should trouble arise between the Swedish Crown and the States General. Before administering an oath to those who had not already taken it, Stuyvesant referred to the people as "the Swedish nation, our good and faithful subjects, to whom we hereby assure and promise our favor and all possible assistance, as if they were our own nation."[39] Hardly any residue of suspicion remained on Stuyvesant's part. However, the same regard for these new subjects was not being shared in Amsterdam.

When the directors learned of Stuyvesant's actions on the South River, they bluntly objected to his appointment of Swedish officers, stating that they could not be relied on. They advised him to disarm the Swedes and scatter them among the Dutch so that they offered no threat; he should also not allow them to concentrate in their own settlements.[40] Stuyvesant retorted that he realized the Swedes had little affection for the country and that the Dutch would feel the same if they were conquered. However, he thought it proper to govern them leniently "to win their hearts and divert their thoughts from a hard and tyrannical form of government," which was rather enlightened thinking in an age that usually eliminated the nuisance of unwanted populations by displacement or death. Stuyvesant went on to explain that he had allowed the Swedes some officers to keep order against the Indians; he assured the directors that he had put nothing in writing and had not distributed any arms.[41] The directors continued to criticize Stuyvesant's Swedish policy, warning him that the English might attempt something against the South River under the Swedish flag and name. They persisted in their instructions to scatter the Swedes among the Dutch.[42] However, Stuyvesant continued to steer his own course when it concerned the "Swedish nation."

When war broke out with the Indians in the Esopus region (Kingston, New York), Stuyvesant attempted to recruit soldiers from the Swedish and Finnish communities. He also offered land in the Esopus for anyone desiring to relocate.[43] The response was unanimously negative. Stuyvesant was informed by his sources on the Delaware that "they have no inclination whatsoever. It seems that the leaders of their nation admonish and urge them not to disperse themselves, but to remain hereabouts."[44] The leaders of the upriver communities were apparently urging solidarity in anticipation of the day when they would all be returned to the Crown of Sweden. Rumors of an alliance between England and Sweden must have strengthened this notion. In fact, the desire was still strong enough some years later, after the English had taken New Netherland, that many of the most prominent inhabitants of the "Swedish nation" could be duped by an imposter who claimed that Swedish ships were off the coast and he had been sent to lead the revolt. The so-called Long Finn rebellion was quickly crushed, but references to the rebelliousness of the Swedes and Finns persisted for years.[45] This was strong testimony to the ability of the "Swedish nation" to remain intact through several changes of masters and much hardship.

When Hendrick von Elswick's "prophesy" "hodie mihi, cras tibi" returned to haunt Stuyvesant in the fall of 1664, the English commander, Sir Robert Carr, was given special instructions with regard to the former inhabitants of New Sweden: "To the Swedes you shall remonstrate their happy return under a monarchical government and his Majesties good inclination to that nation.... "[46] Thus ended the twenty-six-year relationship of Swedes as competitors and Dutch as conquerors in the Delaware Valley. In the end their mutual fear of English domination became a reality. But England's day would also come.

NOTES

1. Charles T. Gehring, trans. and ed., *New York Historical Manuscripts* (hereafter *NYHM*), vols. 18–19, *Delaware Papers* (Baltimore: Genealogical Publishing Co., 1981), 18:39.
2. See E. B. O'Callaghan and B. Fernow, eds., *Documents Relative to the Colonial History of the State of New York* (hereafter *NYCD*), 15 vols. (Albany, 1853–87), 1:10.
3. For a discussion of the formation of the Dutch West India Company, see Oliver A. Rink, *Holland on the Hudson: An Economic and Social History of Dutch New York* (Ithaca: Cornell University Press, 1986).
4. For the instructions to Willem Verhulst, see A. J. F. van Laer, trans. and

ed., *Documents Relating to New Netherland, 1624–1626, in the Henry E. Huntington Library* (San Marino, Calif.: Huntington Library, 1924).

5. Charles McKew Parr, *The Voyages of David De Vries, Navigator and Adventurer* (New York: Thomas Y. Crowell, 1969), 199, 247.

6. Under its terms, a patroon was allowed to negotiate with the natives for a tract of land upon which he was obligated to settle fifty colonists within four years at his own expense. The patroon was granted the rights of high, middle, and low jurisdictions, and held the land as a perpetual fief of inheritance, with the right to dispose of the colony by last will and testament.

7. For a detailed discussion of the establishment of patroonships, see Van Cleaf Bachman, *Peltries or Plantations: The Economic Policies of the Dutch West India Company in New Netherland, 1623–1639* (Baltimore: Johns Hopkins Press, 1969).

8. For the events relating to the patroonship of Swanendael, see C. A. Weslager, *Dutch Explorers, Traders and Settlers in the Delaware Valley, 1609–1664* (in collaboration with A. R. Dunlap) (Philadelphia: University of Pennsylvania Press, 1961), 83–104.

9. For the coming of Minuit and the establishment of New Sweden, see ibid., 159–83.

10. Amandus Johnson, *The Swedish Settlements on the Delaware: Their History and Relation to the Indians, Dutch and English, 1638–1664,* 2 vols. (Philadelphia: Swedish Colonial Society, 1911), 1:12–13.

11. Ibid., 87.

12. Ibid., 106, 112.

13. See *NYHM* 4:7 for Kieft's protest, which was drawn up in council on 6 May 1638, a month and a half after Minuit arrived.

14. For an extensive narrative of the New Haven ventures in the Delaware, see C. A. Weslager, *The English on the Delaware, 1610–1682* (New Brunswick, N.J.: Rutgers University Press, 1967), 89–106.

15. For documents concerning Jan Jansen van Ilpendam, see *NYCD,* 12:23–26.

16. Compare the complaint of an Iroquois chief during negotiations with the Dutch in 1635: "We have to travel so far with our pelts and when we arrive we often find no cloth, no sewant [wampum], no axes, kettles or anything else; and thus we have labored in vain. Then we have to go back a long way carrying our goods." Charles T. Gehring and William A. Starna, trans. and ed., *A Journey Into Mohawk and Oneida Country* (Syracuse, N.Y.: Syracuse University Press, 1988), 15.

17. See *NYHM* 18:5 for this reference, noted by Hudde in 1646.

18. See "Hudde report," *NYHM* 18:10, in which Hudde alludes to the destruction of a company's house in the Schuylkill preceding the construction of Fort Beversreede in 1648. Since Stuyvesant became director in 1647 and would have known about and reacted to such an event, it probably occurred in 1646 or earlier.

19. See "Hudde report" and the correspondence from Stuyvesant to Hudde in *NYHM* 18:22ff.

20. Ibid. 18:23.

21. Govert Loockermans to Gilles Verbrugge, 27 May 1648, Loockermans-Rutherford Collection, New-York Historical Society, New York, N.Y.

22. *NYHM* 18:24–25. My account of Swedish-Dutch relations is taken from this source, pp. 9–29.

23. Ibid. 18:362.

24. See *NYCD* 12:70 for Stuyvesant's letter of April 1651, informing the governor of Massachusetts that he had recently returned fifty colonists to Hartford who were bound for the Delaware River.
25. See C. A. Weslager, *The Swedes and Dutch at New Castle on the South River in New Netherland* (Wilmington, Del.: Middle Atlantic Press, 1988), 62, for a detailed description of Stuyvesant's military operation.
26. *NYCD* 12:72–73.
27. Ibid. 12:73.
28. Johnson, *Swedish Settlements*, 2:581.
29. Charles T. Gehring and J. A. Schiltkamp, trans. and eds., *New Netherland Documents, Curaçao Papers, 1640–1665* (Interlaken, N.Y.: Heart of the Lakes Publishing, 1987), 160.
30. *NYCD* 12:85–86. The first Anglo-Dutch War was ended by the Treaty of Westminster, July 1654.
31. The former fiscal, Hendrick van Dyck, had allegedly killed an Indian woman for stealing peaches from his orchard.
32. Extract of a letter from Stuyvesant to the directors, 30 October 1655, Bontemantel Collection, New Netherland Papers, New York Public Library, New York, N.Y.
33. *NYHM* 18:36.
34. Ibid. 18:44.
35. Ibid. 18:37.
36. Johnson, *Swedish Settlements*, 2:661. The Dutch renamed this place Kattenburgh. It was located on an island near the mouth of Tenakom Kill, or Darby Creek, according to Johnson.
37. Ibid., 634.
38. *NYCD* 12:190–91.
39. Ibid., 12:211.
40. Ibid., 12:232.
41. Ibid., 12:246–47.
42. Ibid., 12:271.
43. Ibid., 12:297–98.
44. *NYHM* 18:192.
45. Ibid., 20:93, 21:299, for such references in the years 1675 and 1680, respectively.
46. Ibid., 20:1.

Part II
The Colonists and
the Native Americans

Scandinavian Colonists
Confront the New World

KAREN ORDAHL KUPPERMAN

Swedish colonists were plagued by the same questions faced by all European settlers in America. Concerns centered on whether the new land offered rewards sufficient to compensate for the massive effort and sacrifice involved in colonization. Promoters and immigrants alike wondered whether their own society could successfully be transplanted and, more important, whether it would continue to be Swedish. Hopes for development, especially of commodities desired by European consumers, took priority in any colony because without them no venture could be planned, nor could support be attracted. New Sweden's 1638 founding date meant that promoters could take advantage of decades of Spanish, French, Dutch, and English experience. Thus the company appointed as governor Peter Minuit, an experienced colonial hand who, having earlier found the New Netherland colony in a crisis brought on by mismanagement, had acted quickly and vigorously to take control and save the settlements. His was clearly the type of character the colonial situation required. Moreover, the secret instructions issued to Minuit show evidence that the colony's backers had studied other North American settlements.

The company indicated clearly that its main expectations centered on the fur trade, which was to be initiated immediately. The ships carried cargoes designed for the tastes of the Indians the colonists would encounter. Minuit was urged to look for evidence of "ambergris ... as well as gold, silver, pearls, and other minerals," but adventurers in Europe knew very well that no North American settlement had yet found them. The settlers were well supplied with seeds and tools; planting was to begin immediately so the colonists could avoid the faltering beginnings and dependence on Indian charity that had characterized the early years of so many English colonies in the same regions.[1]

The company also knew that the best-laid colonial plans could go awry and the promised returns not materialize. Those colonies that folded did so because they failed to make a profit. This was not simply the result of rapaciousness on the part of backers. Enormous sums of money were required to establish and sustain a New World settlement; companies of private investors rarely could continue to supply such sums for long without returns. Therefore the New Sweden Company authorized Minuit to attack Spanish ships in and near the Caribbean to provide an immediate infusion of money into the company's coffers.

Privateering, government-authorized piracy, was practiced by many European nations. Its target was the great wealth Spain extracted from its empire. As Spain became ever more deeply embroiled in the Thirty Years' War, treasure from the Indies was increasingly crucial to its ability to continue. Therefore, to attack Spanish shipping in the Indies was to pursue the war on another front; Sweden joined the Dutch, French, and English, all of whom authorized their ships to prowl New World waters and weaken the enemy. New Sweden was founded as the European war entered its final phase and Spain's need for an uninterrupted flow of Indian treasure was at its greatest.[2] Though the Swedes, Dutch, and English might be in competition, they would unite to bring about "the discomfiture of our common enemy."[3] So closely intertwined were their fortunes in this conflict that the Massachusetts Bay Puritans greeted news of Gustavus Adolphus's defeat of Tilly by proclaiming a "day of thanksgiving at Boston for the good news of the prosperous success of the king of Sweden."[4]

Privateering was a dangerous game and the company warned Minuit not to risk his ships needlessly. At least in the early days, the Swedes were prepared to keep their activities on a very small scale, but Minuit hoped to recoup the inflated costs of the first voyage with "a good rich Spanish prize." The governor was given a detailed list of good locations from which isolated Spanish ships might be picked off. That such lists and instructions could be compiled indicates the intensive research the New Sweden backers put into planning their colony.

Oddly enough Minuit was also given instructions on how to participate in the complex international trade of the Caribbean.[5] Despite the relationship of enmity between Spain and other nations with New World empires, much illicit trading was carried on between Spanish colonists and ships from all over Europe. Spain, overextended in Europe and the Indies, no longer had the resources either to protect or to supply all parts of its empire; settlements remote from colonial centers were to a very great extent on their own. These settlers would trade with any and all ships that came by, sometimes after a mock show of resistance.[6] It was on such a trading mission that Minuit's life was lost in a sudden hurricane.[7]

Despite the dangers, Caribbean ventures, both peaceful trading and privateering, continued to figure in thinking about New Sweden. Governor Printz argued in the mid-1640s that trade with the West Indies could become the mainstay of support for New Sweden. Trade supplemented by legalized piracy would enrich Sweden as well as revivify the colony. Printz reminded the New Sweden Company that goods taken in privateering on the Spanish enemy were granted by God.[8]

Privateering was parasitic, and it preyed on an empire that was itself parasitizing Indian resources. The fur trade required continuous supplies of cargoes from Europe. True security, as Chancellor Oxenstierna wrote to Governor Printz in 1647, would come when the settlers could supply their own needs "through the cultivation of the land."[9] Once the colony was established the company hoped to add homegrown products to the plantation economy; commodities that could be produced entirely through the colonists' efforts and exported to Europe would make New Sweden's foundation secure.

Governor Johan Printz's instructions (1642) outlined the company's hopes for New Sweden; expectations were soberly drawn, emphasizing above all practical success. Printz was first commanded to make the colony self-sufficient in food; only in this way could the settlers' independence be guaranteed. One year's supply accompanied the ships; then, as Printz put it, "[if they wish to nourish themselves] the country indeed will feed them."[10] Other colonies had learned that not only was maize marvelously adapted to the North American environment, making it a grain of phenomenal fecundity, but European grains did poorly initially. Planters were urged to adjust their diets to this new grain.[11]

When subsistence was assured, then tobacco was to be the next object of colonist interest. Again the company showed its grasp of New World realities; adjacent English colonies had flourishing economies based on tobacco culture. Tobacco exports from the Chesapeake had reached a million pounds a year by the time of New Sweden's founding. Productivity advances had allowed planters to compensate for a steady decline in price. It was reasonable to assume that tobacco could also be New Sweden's gold.[12]

Once these basic commodities were established, Swedish planters could then begin to branch out and seek the products that would enrich them and the company. Wool production, timber and wood byproducts, and whale fishing sounded profitable, or so the company thought. Since New Sweden shared a latitude, and therefore by extrapolation a climate, with Portugal, settlers should be able to make salt naturally or with small additional labor by building fires to supplement the sun. Fish could then be preserved for sale in Europe. Printz was commanded to investigate winemaking to utilize the ubiquitous grapes of New Sweden. Support was promised if the governor thought silkworms could successfully be nourished and produce usable fiber.[13]

Other colonies had received similar instructions and had found them

unworkable; the North American climate exhibited extreme variation between heat and cold unknown in western Europe's maritime climate, and
winters were much colder than in comparable latitudes in Europe.[14]
What is striking about the New Sweden Company's instructions to Governor Printz is the modesty of the promoters' hopes. Though they mentioned the ever-present hope of minerals, the adventurers placed greatest emphasis on products that were already imported into Europe from
North America. Nor was there to be second-guessing from home. Printz
was spared the ill-informed interference that had plagued Virginia's early
years, where plans and strategies were commanded again and again by
armchair theorists in London. The governor was to use his own judgment "in the conservation of this land, New Sweden, with all possible
and feasible progress and commerce growing therefrom."[15]

Despite such modest plans, Governor Printz was forced to inform the
company in his 1644 report that the program was unworkable. Even the
first step, subsistence, was impossible for the short run. Food supplies
were "fearfully dear here" and the company had been misled on the
easy culture and natural increase of maize. Printz held out hope for European grains, but all that was for the future. Meanwhile, he had arranged
to buy maize from the Indians so that the colonists could spend their time
on tobacco culture. No time could be spared to look into "salt-making, oil
manufactories, whale-catching, minerals, or silk worms." Even hopes of
tobacco rested "on God and the weather." Nor could successfully completed cargoes awaiting transport back to Europe be counted on; nature,
in the form of vermin, attacked stockpiled goods and could ruin all the
planters' work.[16]

Governor Printz continued to paint a restrained picture of New Sweden's possibilities in a later report. In 1647 he wrote that the colonists
were in good health, largely because famine no longer threatened the settlements. Good harvests and great increase of cattle were supplemented
with supplies bought from neighboring English and Dutch planters, so
food was plentiful if expensive. Severe winters in 1645 and 1646, sometimes worse than those of northern Sweden, demonstrated conclusively
that while wine and whale fishing might prosper, salt and silkworm industries could not be developed.[17]

Moreover, no specialized products could be contemplated until the
company sent men skilled in their development. In sounding this theme,
Printz echoed the constant refrain of English colonists pressed by their
companies for American luxury goods: money must be spent to make
money. Colonists struggling to survive by working at all trades could not
be expected to possess specialized knowledge. There had been reports
even of gold and silver in the Delaware River region; for all Printz knew
they were true, but no one would ever know until mineralogists were sent

to New Sweden. Similarly, winemakers would have to select, tend, and process the grapes. Once skilled men were in the colony, many new economic avenues might be opened up. As Johan Papegoja wrote to Per Brahe: "If Her Royal Majesty would only take ahold with seriousness, the land would soon be fine."[18]

Peter Lindeström, the fortifications expert who accompanied Governor Johan Rising in 1654, was a trained observer, but his conclusions about New Sweden's environment were not much different from Printz's. He agreed that though summers were very hot, American winters were so sharply cold that no fruits requiring sustained heat to mature or a frost-free environment would grow there. More important, though he pictured the land as a new Canaan, "a land flowing with milk and honey," he, like Printz, argued that New Sweden required expert knowledge and the application of European technology to achieve its highest fruitfulness. So unruly was the land that species even broke down, crops of rye sometimes turning into barley and barley into rye.[19]

Lindeström believed in European technology. Once it was established in the new land, then the environment might be tamed and matured, becoming more like the Old World in comparable latitudes.[20] Certainly skilled vignerons could produce rich wines from the plentiful grapes. The engineer held out the prospect that even semitropical plants such as oranges and lemons, sugar cane, and bananas might yet grow along the Delaware, if Sweden were prepared to invest in their transplantation and care without counting the cost. Meanwhile North American nature supplied the beautiful, versatile, and miraculously productive maize to furnish the colonists' needs; and tobacco, studied and cultivated by planters, provided a cash crop so attractive to European consumers that poor beggars, according to Lindeström, would sooner deprive their families of bread than go without their tobacco.[21]

However good the land was, the gap between promise and reality was wide. Governor Rising's reports made no effort to disguise the fact that after a decade and a half the New Swedish could not feed themselves. He arrived in May to find much of the land uncleared and few crops in the ground. His ships provided the colonists with their first direct contact with home in almost six years.[22] Provisions, meanwhile, were carried in a regular trade with the English in New England. Rising wrote particularly of Richard Lord, merchant, of Hartford, Connecticut: "If he had not come to our rescue; we could not have subsisted with so many poor people in a desert country among so many enemies." Rising informed the company, as Printz had done before him, that only with sustained commitment in the form of regular supplies and expensive personnel could the promise of New Sweden be realized: "It would be possible now to do more with one or a half barrel of gold than could be done in the future with millions." With such support, a rich panoply of enterprises could be set up to enrich old and New Sweden and ensure permanent possession for the Swedish Crown; otherwise, "in the end it will all go to ruin."[23]

New Sweden did not become self-sufficient, nor did it produce commodities for the enrichment of Sweden and the company. But during its short life it solved the basic problems faced by all settlements in a unique way that makes this venture stand out among Europe's North American colonies. This special development can be seen as the conjunction of two basic facts of life in New Sweden. The first is relative lack of support from home. Most English colonies in North America relied on at least annual shipments of supplies and new settlers from home; Roanoke, abandoned by Sir Walter Raleigh for three years between 1587 and 1590, disappeared because it lacked support. By contrast, New Sweden went for as long as six years without any word directly from home; the planters were on their own, their survival in their own hands. Had they developed products in demand in Europe, those commodities might have sat for years before they ever became cargoes. If the colony was to survive, it would be through a creative response to an unprecedented situation.

The second fact is that New Sweden lay in a major North American trade center; Indian and European trade networks converged along the Delaware. The New Swedish forged a unique role for themselves in this trade nexus. Lacking trade goods from home, they could not participate in the Indian trade as other Europeans did, exchanging attractive manufactured tools, cloth, and other useful items for furs to be shipped across the Atlantic in the returning supply ships. Yet they had to participate in the trade; self-sufficiency was not possible for any group of planters in the seventeenth century.

New Sweden's masterstroke was to take up an intermediary role in the vital trade between Europeans and Indians. They took advantage of their central situation, buying trade goods from other European colonists, trading them to Indians with furs to sell, and reselling the furs for transport to European consumers. It was a difficult game, requiring continual fine-tuning as English and Dutch colonists tried to move in on New Sweden. Governors Printz and Rising constantly tried to regulate relations with Indian, Dutch, and English neighbors so as to keep them at arm's length while recognizing that the colony was dependent on all three. Clearly such a balancing act could not succeed forever, but while it lasted it was an experiment unique in the human relations laboratory of North America's east coast.

When New Sweden was settled in 1638, the colonists were guided to their intended location by Peter Minuit, former governor of New Netherland. The Dutch plantations were expansive, moving up the Hudson River to the site of Albany, up the Connecticut River to a location near modern Hartford, and into the Delaware River region. This expansion, always along the major rivers, had as its goal the control of the great fur trade of eastern North America. Minuit, who had organized the fur trade through Manhattan during his governorship there (1626–32), knew the advantages of the Delaware River site. Long before the Scandinavians arrived, Dutch traders had set up trading houses and plantations along the river.[24]

Fort Nassau was built in 1626 to prevent other European nations from controlling the Delaware and its lucrative trade. Though the Dutch West India Company considered making a Delaware River site the center of New Netherland, Fort Nassau rarely held more than a handful of settlers until the Swedes began to compete for control of the Delaware River trade. Peter Minuit had been sent to the area with the first Dutch settlers; his job then had been to reconnoiter the region's economic potential. Because of this prior experience Minuit clearly understood the centrality of the Delaware for the Indian trade.[25]

English colonists were also aware of the great advantages offered by the Delaware region. In 1634 Captain Thomas Yong sailed up the Delaware and claimed it for England; later sources asserted that he left settlers near the site of Fort Nassau to conduct a trade in furs for England. Virginians had their eyes on the Delaware region and sought to make good Yong's claim, but the English were soon removed by the Dutch. English settlers in Connecticut also had their eyes on this trade crossroads and would soon make moves to establish a presence there. The ultraconservative Puritan colony of New Haven sought to expand there in the early 1640s; its leaders envisioned a commercial empire whose center would ultimately be moved from the Connecticut shore to the Delaware.[26]

Because of English interest the Dutch moved to strengthen Fort Nassau; thus a renewed Dutch presence was being built just as New Sweden was founded in 1638. Peter Minuit, having lost his position with the Dutch West India Company, now served the New Sweden Company (formed with joint Swedish and Dutch backing) and led his colonists to the excellent spot he knew so well. As the company's secret instructions make clear, the plantation's conception was based on control of the fur trade. In spite of the "vast annoyance" of the Dutch, Minuit had his colonists build their Fort Christina athwart the access route to the Susquehannock Indians of the interior and the pelts they commanded.[27]

The Swedes and the Dutch saw grounds for cooperation at first; they both sought to keep out the English. The two colonies cooperated in efforts to keep settlers from New Haven and Massachusetts Bay out of the

Delaware. Only after the arrival of Governor Johan Printz in 1643 did New Sweden move vigorously to take control of the fur trade. To cut off the trade before it reached the Dutch, Printz built a new post, Fort Elfsborg, to control entrance to the river, and three others in the Schuylkill region. Not only was the trade preempted physically, but the Swedes undersold the Dutch and the English in valuable trade goods: "that said wild people may be withdrawn from them, and so much the more turn to our own [people]."[28] Throughout his governorship, Printz worked to protect the Swedish position of centrality in the fur trade of the Delaware region, and to fend off the encroachments of their "evil neighbors," the Dutch and English.[29]

The trade was conducted through the Susquehannocks, Iroquoian-speaking peoples who lived in fortified villages along the Susquehanna River in eastern Pennsylvania.[30] The Susquehannocks, known to the Swedes as the Minquas, were described by Captain John Smith in his book *A Map of Virginia* in 1612: "Such great and well-proportioned men, are seldom seen, for they seemed like Giants to the English, yea and to the Neighbors, yet seemed of an honest and simple disposition...." He described the largest as "the goodliest man that ever we beheld."[31] The Susquehannocks' command of the continental trade networks was clear to Smith and his exploring party before the two actually met. The English, involved in exploring the head of Chesapeake Bay in 1608, were surprised to find European trade goods, "hatchets, knives, and peeces [guns] of yron, and brasse," in the hands of Indians Smith called Tockwoghs. When questioned, the Tockwoghs said the goods came to them from the Susquehannocks.[32]

Smith expressed his desire to meet with the Susquehannocks, whom he described as living two days' journey north of the farthest point his boat could reach. The message was carried, and soon the explorers were approached by a party of sixty Susquehannocks. The Indians immediately demonstrated both their command of the trade and the terms on which they were willing to establish a relationship: they approached Captain Smith carrying "skins, Bowes, Arrows, Targets [shields], Beads, Swords, and Tobacco pipes for presents." The Susquehannocks were prepared to establish a connection with willing Europeans, but one whose ramifications they could control.[33]

Willingness to become trading partners did not imply acceptance of cultural imperialism. Governor Printz reported that the Indians firmly resisted any attempt to convert them to Christianity: "And when we speak to them about God they pay no attention, but they will let it be understood that they are a free people, subject to no one, but do what they please." European attempts to isolate captured Indians and convert them produced only implacable hatred. This relationship was to be a partnership, not a subjugation.[34]

The Susquehannocks were determined to maintain independence of action in the fur trade and to inspect and compare Swedish, Dutch, and English offerings of trade goods. They warned their trading partners that trade goods must be consistently available and in sufficient quantities. In 1648 Alexander Boyer, New Netherland's "Deputy-Commissary at the Delaware," reported the visit of the Susquehannock "General" (*velt-overste*), who came to inquire whether any Dutch ship had arrived with commodities. The Indian leader chastised the deputy-commissary, who reported: "They are also much dissatisfied, that this River is not steadily provided with cargoes by our people." Boyer indicated that with good supplies of trade goods, the Dutch might still beat the Swedes out of the Susquehannock trade.[35]

Archaeological work has recently demonstrated that the Susquehannocks, whom Governor Printz referred to as "the great traders," had assumed a key role in the inland trade north with members of the Iroquois League in the later sixteenth century. The trade was initially in Indian-produced commodities, but as European trade goods began to appear, they traveled the same Susquehannock-controlled routes. To master this trade, sometime after 1550 the Susquehannocks had moved three hundred kilometers down the Susquehanna River from their original lands on the North Branch. They had also changed their settlement pattern. Instead of living in scattered small villages, they built a single large fortified town. Through this relocation, they placed themselves closer to the sources of trade items and farther from the growing power of the Iroquois League. Thus they traveled to meet Captain John Smith as he explored the head of Chesapeake Bay in 1608 to offer the Virginia colonists a trading partnership and an alliance against the Five Nations. Their strategy was already cast in terms of European trade; they now sought Europeans as confederates. That their preparations required a fortress demonstrates the high stakes involved.[36]

The Algonquian-speaking Lenape Indians, whom we know as the Delawares, lived in the immediate vicinity of the Swedish settlements. Historians disagree on the nature of their relationship with the Susquehannocks. We know that the two had been at war before the settlement of New Sweden, but had made some sort of peaceful arrangement. Controversy centers on the nature of this arrangement. Some believe it was a clientage relationship, with the Susquehannocks having established a degree of overlordship over the strategically located Delawares, while others see it as a peace between equal and independent peoples.[37] A Susquehannock delegate was present, apparently as an interested observer,

at the Delawares' initial meeting with Peter Minuit and approved the
sale of land to the New Swedish, though the "Antient Swedes" interviewed in 1684 said that the Susquehannocks had actually sold the
land.[38] As soon as Governor Printz assessed the situation in the Delaware, he was anxious to reach beyond the Delaware Indians, the colonists' nearest neighbors, to form a firm trade alliance with the Susquehannocks, with their access to furs.[39]

The Susquehannocks, according to Printz, were "wise in trade and traffic."[40] They, like the New Swedish, realized the possibilities of the Delaware River as a great international trading depot. They became brokers
in the fur trade, ranging far into the interior in search of furs. They functioned as intermediaries in the trade of other Indians; the New Sweden
colony in turn took up that role in the trade between the Indians and
other Europeans. The Swedish settlers could not function in the trade as
other European colonists did, offering European goods in exchange for
furs, because, despite the promise of Chancellor Oxenstierna, cargo
ships were rarely sent out from Europe. Each year Governor Printz's la-
ment at the number of years since letters had been received from Sweden
grew more extreme.[41] So the New Swedish invented a new role for themselves. To a great extent the Susquehannocks and the New Sweden colonists became partners. Sharing one major advantage—location—the
Swedes and Indians made up for their drawbacks: lack of support from
Sweden and the Susquehannocks' fear of interference by the powerful
Iroquois League to the north.

To make the partnership work, the New Sweden colonists plentifully
supplied the Susquehannocks with European weapons, a practice followed by all European settlers to some extent, but officially deplored by
almost everyone. Lindeström argued that it was the Virginians who first
introduced guns into the Indian trade, and that the Swedes were thus simply reacting to an existing situation. Governor Printz had alleged that it
was the Dutch who had armed the Indians "against all Christian laws."[42]

No matter who initiated the practice in the Delaware Valley, the
Swedes apparently adopted it wholeheartedly. Only with these firearms
could the Susquehannocks compete effectively and maintain their independence.[43] According to an English report of 1648, the Swedes were
"striving to please and side with the Indians" to the extent of actually
"hiring out" soldiers to the Susquehannocks to teach the Indians "the
use of our arms and fights." Combined forces of Susquehannocks and
Swedes had confronted English troops from the colony of Maryland in
the field, with the Indians carrying out strategies planned by their Swedish advisors, according to the writer who signed himself Beauchamp Plantagenet.[44]

Beauchamp Plantagenet's tract, *A Description of the Province of New Albion*, written by or for Sir Edmund Plowden, who held a patent from the king of England for a colony there, called for a combined Virginia–New England effort to remove the Swedes and Dutch from the Delaware.[45] In fact the English not only did not wipe out the New Sweden settlements, but they supported them by providing the trade goods the Swedes could not get from home. English merchants played an essential role in the Swedish-Susquehannock alliance. Robert Evelin's eyewitness account of the region, reprinted in the *Description of New Albion*, emphasized the speed and ease of trade between either Virginia or New England and the Delaware: "And (which is a good comfort) in four and twenty houres you may send or goe by sea to New England or Virginia, with a fair winde...."[46] This ease of communication with the English colonies was the key that gave New Sweden the means to attract the Susquehannock partnership.

Officially the English and the Swedes were rivals; establishment of one meant defeat for the other. New Haven Colony, formed at the same time as New Sweden, had two purposes: strict observance of Puritan forms and trade. Its founders, upset at the religious conflict then raging in Massachusetts Bay, sought independence to follow their own stricter version of the New England way. The colony drew heavily on the London merchant community and it expected to base its economy on trade. When New Haven had proven a poor location for commerce, the New Haven-ites formed a company that purchased land and twice tried to establish settlements on the Delaware, with an eye to eventually moving their colony's center there: twice they were repelled, either by the Dutch or the Swedes.[47]

New Haven soon became a member of the New England Confederation; all Puritan New England stood behind it as it fought for rights to settle on the Delaware. But while combat proceeded on the official level, with charges and countercharges flying, on the individual plane mutually beneficial relations were the order of the day. As in the Caribbean, where sworn enemies traded peacefully for the goods they needed, so throughout America pacific trade between merchants and colonists of all nations transcended national boundaries and hatreds. Those on the front lines realized long before theorists in Europe that the entire Atlantic basin was a single world economy.

Benefits of this trade were not evenly distributed throughout the colonies. The New Haven Company lost heavily through its failure to make good its claims, but individual merchants there were big winners. Connecticut merchants, despite the official enmity between New England and New Sweden, early realized the rich possibilities opened up by the various participants' situations and got on with the trade. In fact Governor Printz, looking back over his American experience, asserted that the trade with English colonists had been the mainstay of New Sweden.[48]

Richard Malbon of New Haven was involved early in the trade network that developed between New England and New Sweden, sending the Swedes cargoes in 1644 and 1645. Malbon, a founder of the colony of New Haven, was captain of its prestigious artillery company. He had emigrated with the settlement's core group from St. Stephen's, Coleman Street, in London's commercial center, where he had been a leading member of the congregation.[49] Malbon was one of the eleven "visible saints" who became the first church members in New Haven, though his inclusion was protested by one who accused him of overcharging for grain when food was scarce, an infraction that Malbon had "confessed with griefe" and for which he had made restitution.[50] Despite these charges, Malbon, who had invested in the New Haven company organized to erect a colony on the Delaware, was a leading citizen until his return to England with the establishment of Puritan rule there in 1650.[51]

Probably the biggest operator in the New England–New Sweden trade was Isaac Allerton, another highly successful merchant accused of sharp practice in his business dealings. Allerton, the wealthiest and one of the highest-ranking people among the original Plymouth colonists, had come to America on the *Mayflower* and had become the Pilgrims' agent in their attempts to pay off their backers in London through the fur trade. Allerton and the London merchants apparently conspired to keep the Plymouth colonists in debt, mainly by overcharging for supplies they sent to the colony. Despite export of furs to the value of at least £10,000 in the 1630s, the "hoodwinked" Pilgrims' indebtedness remained at £1,200 in 1647.[52]

Allerton, whose trading operations covered the entire coast and the West Indies, moved to New Haven, where he built a "grand house ... with four Porches." He had a second establishment in New Amsterdam, where he also became an important citizen and office-holder, with all the rights that station implied. He first appeared in the Delaware Valley with cargoes for sale shortly after Governor Printz moved to control the fur trade, and his ships came regularly as long as New Sweden existed. His contacts made him invaluable to all parties; he often appears in the historical record as interpreter or courier as well as trader.[53]

Connecticut traders from Hartford also figured in the Delaware River trade. Connecticut Colony (which did not include New Haven at this time) regulated access to trade, both for furs and in foodstuffs. Those involved in the New Sweden trade had won trading privileges and the benefits they conferred on men with connections who were prepared to take risks. The possible profits were enormous, as estimated by Governor Printz.[54] The career of Captain Richard Lord, who "saved" the New Sweden colony according to Governor Rising, exemplifies two key aspects of the trade: the tremendous opportunities it offered and the resourcefulness required of its participants. Lord, son of Hartford's blacksmith, built the town's first warehouse, a facility he filled with merchandise of all sorts for English and Indian consumption. He got his start as partner of Thomas Stanton, who arrived in 1637 in time to serve in the Pequot War and who married Lord's sister. Stanton had Virginia connections, and Lord thus was launched into the multifaceted coastal trade.[55]

When Richard Lord died in 1662, after a distinguished career of office-holding, his estate was worth several thousand pounds; it included debts owed him from both sides of Long Island Sound as well as Newfoundland, Delaware Bay, Barbados, and England. His epitaph shows the regard in which he was held:

> To Marchantes as a Patterne he might stand
> Adventring Dangers new by Sea and Land

His son became an even grander merchant, worth £5,832.11.11 at his death.

William Whiting's name also appears frequently among traders to New Sweden before his death in 1647. He began as a much more prominent citizen of Hartford than Lord: his name, bearing the honorific "Mr.," appears near the top of Hartford's list of "such Inhabitants as have Right in undivided Lands." He held office at both the local and colonial level, repeatedly being reelected both assistant and treasurer of Connecticut Colony; his services and enterprise were rewarded by grants of rights to export corn and to trade in furs and whales. In 1644, control of the trade in corn was granted to Whiting and his fellow merchant, Governor Edward Hopkins, in part because the other New England colonies "looke uppon themselves as much prejudiced by our overfilling their marketts." Thus Connecticut was forced to find "some other way of trade for corne then hath bine hitherto attended," which helped propel its merchants into the coastal trade.[56]

Major Whiting, who was a judge of the quarterly sessions court, married his son to the daughter of John Pynchon, the great entrepreneur of the Connecticut River valley.[57] His estate inventory includes large amounts of trade goods including "hoes, hatchets, shoes, nails, pins, paper, shot, fish-hooks, blades, looking-glasses, pewter, bottles, brass ladles, brushes, bells, thimbles, boxes, knives, scissors, combs, 'Jewes harps,' brass kettles," and a wide variety of cloth, including the popular duffels. He also had a great deal of wampum and furs in store. His house and land in Hartford were worth £400 and those in Windsor a few miles up the Connecticut River were valued at £300. The total estate was the largest yet seen in Hartford.[58]

These traders entered Delaware Bay carrying wampum and grain: food supplies for the Swedish settlers and wampum for the Indian trade. In the early years, when the Swedes were still gathering goods for the expected supply ships from home, tobacco often appeared among the cargoes, but this commodity drops out of the later descriptions.[59] The New Englanders exchanged their grain and wampum for beaver pelts. Thus the New Sweden colonists functioned as intermediaries between the Susquehannocks and the English colonists. Their broker role overturned the usual relationship between colonists and American natives. Europeans liked to believe that they were accepted partly because Indians welcomed their alliance against traditional enemies; superior European arms thus were seen as covering Indian weakness. In New Sweden the roles were reversed since the colonists accepted the notion that the Susquehannocks were their "protectors."[60]

While the system functioned well, the English traders benefited from assured access to the rich fur resources available to the Susquehannocks. The Swedes, who never fully paid their bills, tied these influential New England traders to themselves; each ship that came to collect unpaid debts also brought a new cargo. Outstanding debts meant the colonists would never be forgotten.[61]

Recent work makes it possible to examine what benefit the Susquehannocks derived from their participation in this three-legged trade. Why was wampum a key trade item, rather than more apparently useful tools and duffels? Wampum (called *sewant* in the Swedish documents) had been exchanged between Indian communities before European contact, but had not functioned as a medium of exchange. Its significance in that context was spiritual and ceremonial; in certain circumstances it was thought to have healing power. Peter Lindeström's *Geographia Americae*, with its references to Indians wearing money in chains or bands and the practice of suspending one's personal totem from a "chain of money," shows ceremonial use of wampum. Governor Printz, called "Great Belly" by the Indians, was so well aware of the symbolic meaning of wampum that he had an entire suit made and decorated with "their money, which was very artistic, threaded and worked with all kinds of animals, which came to a few thousand florins."[62] He also sent a wampum belt to Queen Christina.[63] Wampum in small quantities was distributed all along the coast in precontact times. After European trade practices triumphed and wampum began to act as a medium of exchange, the volume rose dramatically and its form, as recovered in archaeological sites, changed.[64]

Wampum formed a key nexus in the international trade centered on European demand for American furs, and the shores of Long Island Sound, as the New Sweden Company's instructions for Peter Minuit acknowledged, was its major source.[65] The Dutch had first realized the possibility of converting the beads to a medium of exchange. They had introduced Plymouth Colony to the concept while Isaac Allerton was still associated with it, and together the English and Dutch had spread its use over their trade regions. Those Indians who had access to the shells from which the beads were made, notably the Pequots of Connecticut and the Narragansetts of Rhode Island, increasingly specialized in wampum production. The demand for ever-greater quantities was reinforced by the English colonists' practice of forcing the Indians to pay tribute or ransom in beads.[66]

The fur trade could not be carried on without wampum; Minuit was commanded to amass a supply of *sewant* before his arrival in the Delaware. As Governor Printz noted in 1644, at least a third, and more often half, of the cargoes for the Indians must be made up of the beads.[67] Lindeström unwittingly shed light on one possible reason why Indian traders insisted on wampum as a key item in the commerce: when furs were traded for wampum, Indians controlled the price; when trade goods were exchanged, the Swedes could and did cheat their trading partners.[68] The fur trade spread wampum all over the interior, where it was highly prized by Indians who had formerly had few sources of it. Tribes such as the Susquehannocks who had access both to the beads and to inland Indians with furs to sell thus enhanced their position; the partnership with the Swedes, and through them with the Connecticut merchants, gave the Susquehannocks great power.

The Hartford–New Haven connection was crucial since the Delaware region was poor in wampum: "Our Savages are poor, so that one can secure from them little and nowadays practically no *sewant* at all." Governor Printz flatly said that *sewant* was manufactured in New England and must be obtained from there, or through the Dutch, and he feared the Swedes were often charged exorbitant prices for it.[69] Access to the raw materials was necessary, but so was the skill and time to process the beads. Lynn Ceci confirms Peter Lindeström's estimate of the labor involved in wampum manufacture; she reckons that production of one fathom of wampum (360 beads) took a week to ten days. Increasingly English traders included in their trade-goods packages the tools to facilitate the labor. So difficult and painstaking was this manufacture that European attempts to duplicate the beads met with failure; Lindeström said Dutch-made *sewant* was immediately detected and rejected. Thomas Morton of Massachusetts noted that English colonists had tried to make their own "Wampampeak," but "none hath ever, as yet, attained to any perfection in the composure of them but that the Salvages [savages] have found a great difference to be in the one and the other." He said the Indians "doe slight" the "counterfett beads." William Wood observed that the Narragansetts were so skilled in wampum production that they had become the "Mint-masters" of New England.[70]

This trade relationship was always a fragile structure; as with so many relationships in the American colonies, it could be affected by apparently unconnected and faraway events. By the time Governor Printz left New Sweden in the fall of 1653, he believed the system was breaking down. Much of the blame, according to Printz, lay with the backers in Sweden who had failed to keep up regular shipments of cargoes. Though trade goods had been obtained from New Englanders and others, the price had always been high, at least double what the merchandise was worth. Not only were the prices exorbitant, but the Dutch and the English, particularly those around Chesapeake Bay, constantly worked to thrust themselves into a primary position in the trade. Printz said they pointed to the Swedes' abandonment to "stir up" the Indians against them. As he left, he warned that the renewal of cargoes from home was absolutely essential: "for if the Savages are compelled to seek elsewhere for cargoes, then the peace will have an end between them and us."[71]

Wars intervened to break up the established trading relationships. The Susquehannocks were increasingly beleaguered by other Indians. Printz reported that the flow of furs had been slowed dramatically by war between the Susquehannocks and the Arrigahaga, known to the Swedes as the Black Minquas for the black badges they wore. Modern research confirms rumors of a great battle between the Iroquois and the Susquehannocks in 1652, from which five to six hundred Susquehannock men were carried off as prisoners.[72] Meanwhile war had broken out between Holland and England; the Anglo-Dutch War disrupted the shipping between Connecticut and the Delaware River and knocked out the main support from under New Sweden.[73] Thus conflicts on both sides caused the system to fail; the Swedes, as always, were in the middle.

Despite Printz's pessimism, Governor Rising initially found some hope in the situation at his arrival in 1654. Since he had been promised that cargoes would now come regularly from Sweden, he looked to the wars to eliminate some of the competition. He pointed to rumors that the English would attack Manhattan, and he thought the disruption of both Dutch control and Indian trade routes might mean that, with sufficiently rich and reliable cargoes, the Swedes could establish trade contacts directly with members of the mighty Iroquois League.[74]

After a year's experience, Rising was less enthusiastic. The Delawares were establishing their own independent role in the fur trade and sought to break the Swedish-Susquehannock trade alliance. They even considered making war on the Swedes to achieve their goal, thereby challenging the protector role of the Susquehannocks. Furthermore, the Susquehannocks had made peace with Maryland; they could not sustain conflict with both the English to their south and the Iroquois to the north. Now the English from Chesapeake Bay were undercutting the Swedes' prices.[75]

Nonetheless the trade with the Susquehannocks was good, and the New England connection was reestablished on a firmer footing. The colonists still resented the high prices they paid for New England provisions and trade goods, but Captain Richard Lord was prepared to regularize his trade with New Sweden to the point of installing his brother as factor in the colony. Lord offered to function as a consultant, helping the settlers to develop the potential of their land. Because his ships regularly visited Europe, he also offered the first chance New Sweden ever had of frequent communication with home. Lacking resources, Rising paid for his first cargo from Lord with a draft drawn on the Royal Commercial College, the colony's sponsor, and prayed that it would be honored.[76]

Rising issued a ringing call to action in 1655: if even a modest investment were made in the colony at this crucial moment, the plantation could be set on a firm footing. If not, then millions could not repair the damage after other nations moved into the region. "If succor now is long delayed, then our affairs will have a short end and we shall all be ruined among so many jealous people and persecutors, for we sit here already as though we had hands and feet tied." The governor's next communication was his report of the colony's surrender to Dutch forces under Peter Stuyvesant.[77]

The Susquehannocks had continued their role as the colony's self-appointed protectors to the very end. Governor Rising wrote that forewarning of the projected Dutch attack had come to them from "the savages," which allowed the Swedes to rearm Fort Casimir to the best of their ability. Not only had Indians warned New Sweden, but, according to Peter Lindeström, the colony's Indian allies risked "death for their good friends," the Swedes. They attacked Manhattan "to exact revenge on our behalf." So devastating was this concerted attack by over nine hundred Indians, all coordinated by "the supreme chief of the Minquasas," that the governor's council in New Amsterdam begged Stuyvesant to leave the Delaware and return: "It seems to us better, to protect one's own house, than to gain one at a distance and lose the old property."[78]

The Susquehannocks had good reason to want to keep the Swedes free of threat from both Indian and European powers. Though many Swedes remained on the Delaware once it passed into Dutch control, and the Indians hoped the Swedes could continue to trade as before, the trade network was irrevocably broken.[79] Machinations of colonial governments, frontier violence, and competition from rival Indian confederations combined with the effects of devastating epidemics to drain Susquehannock power. The tribe, which had numbered over five thousand at the height of its power, was reduced to fewer than two hundred and fifty people at the end of the century. Many had been absorbed by the Iroquois and Delawares; the name *Susquehannock* was no longer used.[80]

The Susquehannock trade empire, like Sweden's North American empire, was an artifact of a particular time and place. Power came to those who were prepared to make the most of newly created circumstances; when the situation changed again, those opportunities vanished. But we cannot understand the nature of the early colonial experience if we confine our study to those colonies and peoples who went on to establish long-lasting entities; to do so would be to deny the reality of the founding period.[81] That reality was a mass of possibilities, with people of all sorts competing for them. We must recapture this sense of the manifold possibilities, the paths not taken or that turned into dead ends, and study why some succeeded where most failed if we are truly to understand the beginnings of American history.

NOTES

1. C. A. Weslager (in collaboration with A. R. Dunlap), *Dutch Explorers, Traders and Settlers in the Delaware Valley, 1609–1664* (Philadelphia: University of Pennsylvania Press, 1961), 173–74.
2. Carla Rahn Phillips, *Six Galleons for the King of Spain: Imperial Defense in the Early Seventeenth Century* (Baltimore: Johns Hopkins University Press, 1986), chap. 1, esp. 7–9.
3. Kiliaen van Rensselaer used this phrase in a letter asking Peter Minuit to carry settlers and supplies to his plantation in New Netherland, 25 December 1637, in *Van Rensselaer Bowier Manuscripts: Being the Letters of Kiliaen van Rensselaer, 1630–1643, and Other Documents Relating to the Colony of Rensselaerswyck*, ed. and trans., A. J. F. van Laer (Albany: University of the State of New York, 1908), 390. In the 1620s the Dutch States General had even briefly considered creating a combined English, French, and Dutch joint-stock company to engage in privateering and trade. See Oliver A. Rink, *Holland on the Hudson: An Economic and Social History of Dutch New York* (Ithaca: Cornell University Press, 1986), 72–73.
4. John Winthrop, *Winthrop's Journal: History of New England, 1630–1649*, 2 vols., ed. James K. Hosmer (1908; reprint, New York: Barnes & Noble, 1966), 1:92.
5. Weslager, *Dutch Explorers, Traders and Settlers*, 175–81; Amandus Johnson, *The Swedish Settlements on the Delaware: Their History and Relation to the Indians, Dutch and English, 1638–1664*, 2 vols. (Philadelphia: Swedish Colonial Society, 1911), 1:110–11, 116.
6. Phillips, *Six Galleons*, 14–15.
7. Weslager, *Dutch Explorers, Traders and Settlers*, 182–83.
8. Amandus Johnson, trans. and ed., *The Instruction for Johan Printz, Gover-*

nor of New Sweden (Philadelphia: Swedish Colonial Society, 1930), 125–26, 140, 153, 171. There was a price to be paid for such ventures: Printz was alarmed by reports that his replacement as governor had been captured by the Spaniards off Puerto Rico on his voyage to New Sweden: ibid., 175–76. Governor Rising also looked to Caribbean trade for New Sweden: Johan Rising, "Report of Governor Johan Rising, 1654," in Narratives of Early Pennsylvania, West New Jersey, and Delaware, 1630–1707, ed. Albert Cook Myers (1912; reprint, New York: Barnes & Noble, 1967), 141.

9. Johnson, Instruction, 169.
10. Ibid., 82–90, 150. The quotation is on 150.
11. For the similar experience of New England, see Karen Ordahl Kupperman, "Climate and Mastery of the Wilderness in Seventeenth-Century New England," in Seventeenth-Century New England, ed. David D. Hall and David G. Allen (Charlottesville: University Press of Virginia, 1985), 14–19.
12. Allan Kulikoff, Tobacco and Slaves: The Development of Southern Cultures in the Chesapeake, 1680–1800 (Chapel Hill: University of North Carolina Press, 1986), 31–32, and John J. McCusker and Russell R. Menard, The Economy of British America, 1607–1789 (Chapel Hill: University of North Carolina Press, 1985), 120–24.
13. Johnson, Instruction, 82–90.
14. See Karen Ordahl Kupperman, "The Puzzle of the American Climate in the Early Colonial Period," American Historical Review 87 (1982): 1262–89.
15. Johnson, Instruction, 88, 92.
16. Ibid., 105, 111–12, 122.
17. Ibid., 127–30, 135, 138–39, 177, 185–86.
18. Ibid., 129, 159.
19. Peter Lindeström, Geographia Americae, with an Account of the Delaware Indians, Based on Surveys and Notes Made in 1654–1656, trans. and ed. Amandus Johnson (Philadelphia: Swedish Colonial Society, 1925), 172–73, 175–77, 184. New England colonists reported similar experiences of grains changing their nature. See John Josselyn, "An Account of Two Voyages to New England," 2d ed. (1675), in Massachusetts Historical Society, Collections, 3d ser., 3 (Boston, 1833), 336; John Josselyn, New England's Rarities Discovered in Birds, Beasts, Fishes, Serpents, and Plants of That Country (London, 1672), 89–91.
20. This was a widespread belief. See Kupperman, "Puzzle of the American Climate," 1283–89.
21. Lindeström, Geographia Americae, 166, 181–84. See also Johnson, Swedish Settlements, 2:743.
22. Rising, "Report, 1654," 139, 149.
23. Ibid., 141–43; Johan Rising, "Report of Governor Johan Rising, 1655," in Narratives, ed. Myers, 160–62.
24. On Dutch activities in the Delaware, see Weslager, Dutch Explorers, Traders and Settlers.
25. A. J. F. van Laer, trans. and ed., Documents Relating to New Netherland, 1624–1626, in the Henry E. Huntington Library (San Marino, Calif.: Huntington Library, 1924), 44, 75.
26. On English aspirations and activities in the region, see C. A. Weslager, The English on the Delaware: 1610–1682 (New Brunswick, N.J.: Rutgers University Press, 1967).

27. Weslager, *Dutch Explorers, Traders and Settlers*, 134–37, 173–74. For the Dutch reaction, see Willem Kieft to West India Company Chamber at Amsterdam, n.d., in *Documents Relative to the Colonial History of New York*, ed. E. B. O'Callaghan and B. Fernow, 15 vols. (Albany, N.Y., 1853–87), 1:592 (hereafter *NYCD*).
28. Johnson, *Instruction*, 80.
29. Ibid., 131–33, 150, 165, 176–77. See also 255, 257–58, 260–61, 269–70.
30. On the Susquehannocks, see Francis Jennings, "Glory, Death, and Transfiguration: The Susquehannock Indians in the Seventeenth Century," in *Proceedings of the American Philosophical Society* 112 (1968): 15–53; Francis Jennings, "Susquehannock," in *Northeast*, vol. 15, ed. Bruce G. Trigger, *Handbook of North American Indians* (hereafter *HNAI*) (Washington, D.C.: Smithsonian Institution, 1978), 362–67; and Francis Jennings, *The Ambiguous Iroquois Empire: The Covenant Chain Confederation of Indian Tribes with English Colonies From Its Beginnings to the Lancaster Treaty of 1744* (New York: Norton, 1983), chap. 5, esp. 68–70, 98.
31. Philip L. Barbour, ed., *The Complete Works of Captain John Smith (1580–1631)*, 3 vols. (Chapel Hill: University of North Carolina Press, 1986), 1:149–50.
32. Ibid., 231. Francis Jennings argues that these trade goods were of French origin, in *Ambiguous Iroquois Empire*, 144.
33. Barbour, ed., *The Complete Works of John Smith* 1:148–50, 231.
34. Johnson, *Instruction*, 153, 164.
35. *NYCD* 12:43.
36. This paragraph is based on James W. Bradley, *Evolution of the Onondaga Iroquois: Accommodating Change, 1500–1655* (Syracuse: Syracuse University Press, 1987), 83, 90–99. Governor Printz's remark appears in Johnson, *Instruction*, 132. For the Susquehannocks' offer of an alliance to John Smith, see Barbour, ed., *Complete Works of Captain John Smith* 2:119. Smith confirmed that the Susquehannocks lived in palisaded towns (ibid. 2:106). James Bradley argues that the Massawomecks, of whom Smith writes, are the Five Nations Iroquois: *Evolution of Onondaga Iroquois*, 99.
37. C. A. Weslager argues for Susquehannock overlordship: see his *The Delaware Indians: A History* (New Brunswick, N.J.: Rutgers University Press, 1972), 98–99. Francis Jennings asserts Delaware independence: see his "Glory, Death, and Transfiguration," 17–20, 50–53.
38. "Affidavit of Four Men from the *Key of Calmar*," in *Narratives*, ed. Myers, 87; A. R. Dunlap and C. A. Weslager, eds., "More Missing Evidence: Two Depositions by Early Swedish Settlers," *Pennsylvania Magazine of History and Biography* 91 (1967): 38.
39. Johnson, *Instruction*, 117–18.
40. Ibid., 149. J. Frederick Fausz argues that it was the Susquehannocks who sought out the Swedes as trading partners when Captain William Claiborne, their contact in the Chesapeake, was expelled from that region; see "Merging and Emerging Worlds: Anglo-Indian Interest Groups and the Development of the Seventeenth-Century Chesapeake," in *Colonial Chesapeake Society*, ed. Lois Green Carr, Philip D. Morgan, and Jean B. Russo (Chapel Hill: University of North Carolina Press, 1988), 73.
41. Johnson, *Instruction*, 169. For Printz's constant reiteration of the need for a steady supply of trade goods and of the colonists' feelings of abandonment, see also 107, 127, 132, 135, 140, 175–76, 178, 183–85.
42. Charles I forbade the sale of guns to the Indians in New England in a pro-

clamation issued 24 November 1630. See W. Noel Sainsbury, ed., *Calendar of State Papers, Colonial Series, 1574–1660* (London, 1860), 122, 140. Orders prohibiting the sale of weapons to Indians by Dutch colonists acknowledged that such trade took place: "Ordinance of Director and Council of New Netherland, prohibiting the sale of firearms to Indians," 31 March 1639, and "Ordinance of the colony of Rensselaerswyck prohibiting the sale of powder, lead and firearms to Indians," 18 July 1641, in van Laer, ed., *Van Rensselaer Bowier Manuscripts*, 426, 565–66. For Lindström's continuation, see his *Geographia Americae*, 227. Printz's allegation occurred in his "Report" for 1647; See Johnson, *Instruction*, 133.

43. Jennings, *Ambiguous Iroquois Empire*, 102–3.

44. Beauchamp Plantagenet, *A Description of the Province of New Albion* (1648), in *Tracts and Other Papers Relating Principally to the Origin, Settlement and Progress of the Colonies in North America from the Discovery of the Country to the Year 1776*, comp. Peter Force, 4 vols. (Washington, D.C., 1836–46), 2:7, 18–20, 24.

45. Ibid., 19–20. See John Winthrop, *Winthrop's Journal* 2:342, for Plowden's visit to Boston.

46. Plantagenet, *Description*, 23.

47. On New Haven's founding and aspirations in the Delaware, see William Hubbard, *A General History of New England from the Discovery to 1680* (1682; reprint, Boston, 1815), 317–35, and Weslager, *English on the Delaware*, chaps. 7–10.

48. Johnson, *Instruction*, 188.

49. On Richard Malbon's career, see Isabel M. Calder, *The New Haven Colony* (New Haven: Yale University Press, 1934); and Bernard Bailyn, *The New England Merchants in the Seventeenth Century* (Cambridge: Harvard University Press, 1955), 36–37. For his trading voyages, see Johnson, *The Swedish Settlements*, 1:318–24.

50. Charles J. Hoadly, ed., *Records of the Colony and Plantation of New Haven, from 1638 to 1649* (Hartford, Conn., 1857), 16.

51. For Richard Malbon's trade expeditions to the Delaware, see Johnson, *The Swedish Settlements*, 1:318, 324n.

52. William Bradford, *Of Plymouth Plantation, 1620–1647*, ed. Samuel Eliot Morrison (New York: Knopf, 1952), 230–46, 250–52; Bailyn, *New England Merchants*, 24–25.

53. For Allerton's trade in the Delaware, see Johnson, *Swedish Settlements*, 1:316, 318, 323, 324, 330, 333, 339; 2:515–16, 530, 576, 579, 658–59. For his dual citizenship and consequent strains on his loyalty, see Calder, *New Haven Colony*, 165–66, 202. A sketch of his life appears in Walter S. Allerton, *A History of the Allerton Family* (New York, 1888), 21–47.

54. Johnson, *Instruction*, 138, 177.

55. On Richard Lord's trade in the Delaware Valley, see Johnson, *Swedish Settlements*, 1:311–12; 2:515, 525, 530–31, 570.

56. See the records of the General Courts of 11 December 1644 and 5 February 1644/5, in J. Hammond Trumbull and Charles J. Hoadly, eds., *The Public Records of the Colony of Connecticut*, 15 vols. (Hartford, 1850–90), 1:116–19.

57. On Pynchon's career, see Stephen Innes, *Labor in a New Land: Economy and Society in Seventeenth-Century Springfield* (Princeton: Princeton University Press, 1983).

58. On Whiting's Delaware trade, see Johnson, *Swedish Settlements*, 1:318,

324n, 327, 333. On Hartford's merchants, see William DeLoss Love, *The Colonial History of Hartford* (Hartford, Conn., 1914), 32–33, 124–25, 147, 277, 298–300, 331; Donald L. Jacobus, *List of Officials, Civil, Military, and Ecclesiastical, of Connecticut colony from March 1636 through 11 October 1677 and of New Haven Colony throughout its Separate Existence* (New Haven: Case, Lockwood & Brainard, 1935), 34, 62; Charles W. Manwaring, *A Digest of the Early Connecticut Probate Records*, 3 vols. (Hartford: R. S. Peck & Co., 1904–6), 1:136, 332–33; J. Hammond Trumbull, ed., *The Memorial History of Hartford County, Connecticut, 1633–1884*, 2 vols. (Boston, 1886), 1:249, 269–70; W. M. B. Hartley, ed., *Hartford in the Olden Time: Its First Thirty Years. By Scaeva* (Hartford, 1853), 153–60; and Glenn Weaver, *Hartford* (Woodland Hills, Calif.: Windsor Publications, 1982), 17.

59. In 1654, when the arrival of Governor Rising reopened direct contact with Sweden, the colonists were forced to buy a cargo of tobacco hurriedly from Isaac Allerton at a high price: see Rising, "Report, 1654," 145.

60. Rising, "Report, 1655," 159.

61. On the cargoes carried by New Englanders to Delaware Bay and the debt relationship, see Johnson, *Swedish Settlements*, 1:311–12, 316–33, 339; 2:515, 525–26, 576, 579, 638–39; and C. A. Weslager and Eva L. Butler, eds., "Thomas Doxey's Letter from the Delaware, 1651," *Delaware History* 8 (1958): 51–53.

62. Lindeström, *Geographia Americae*, 129, 195–200, 207, 222.

63. Johnson, *Instruction*, 166–67.

64. Bradley, *Evolution of the Onondaga Iroquois*, 89–90, 96, 178–80.

65. Weslager, *Dutch Explorers, Traders and Settlers*, 171. See also Neal Salisbury, "Toward the Covenant Chain: Iroquois and Southern New England Algonquians, 1637–1684," in *Beyond the Covenant Chain: The Iroquois and Their Neighbors in Indian North America, 1600–1800*, ed. Daniel K. Richter and James H. Merrell (Syracuse, N.Y.: Syracuse University Press, 1987), 62.

66. The trade revolution wrought by the changed use of wampum was noted early in New England, notably by William Bradford, governor of Plymouth Colony in his *Of Plymouth Plantation*, 203, and by William Wood of Massachusetts Bay in *New Englands Prospect* (London, 1634), 61–62. For modern studies, see Lynn Ceci, "The Effect of European Contact and Trade on the Settlement Pattern of Indians in Coastal New York, 1524–1665: The Archeological and Documentary Evidence" (Ph.D. diss., City University of New York, 1977), chap. 6, and Neal Salisbury, *Manitou and Providence: Indians, Europeans, and the Making of New England, 1500–1643* (New York: Oxford University Press, 1982), 148–52.

67. Weslager, *Dutch Explorers, Traders and Settlers*, 171; Johnson, *Instruction*, 118.

68. Lindeström, *Geographica Americae*, 223–32. Lindeström gives the prices of many goods both in wampum and in European currency and describes rates of exchange.

69. Johnson, *Instruction*, 118, 139. At first Printz believed New Sweden could station a man in New England who could trade more advantageously for wampum.

70. Lindeström, *Geographia Americae*, 229–32; Thomas Morton, *New English Canaan* (1637), in *Tracts*, comp. Force, 2:29–30; Wood, *New Englands Prospect*, 61–62; Ceci, "Effect of European Contact and Trade," 204, 206, 225, 245, 279.

71. Johnson, *Instruction*, 181–82, 184–85, 188–89, 192–93 (quote on 193).
72. Ibid., 188. The Arrigahaga have not been fully identified. They apparently lived in western Pennsylvania and possibly extended into the Ohio Valley. They may have been Iroquoian-speaking; some have identified them with the Eries. See Trigger, ed., *Northeast*, *HNAI* 15:412, 587, 588; and Johnson, *Swedish Settlements*, 1:189–91. On the 1652 battle with the Iroquois, see Jennings, "Susquehannock," 362–89.
73. Johnson, *Instruction*, 188–89.
74. Rising, "Report, 1654," 143.
75. Jennings, "Glory, Death, and Transfiguration," 20–25. Fausz, "Merging and Emerging Worlds," 76–83, discusses changes within the political structure of the English Chesapeake that made the Marylanders seek peace with the Susquehannocks.
76. Rising, "Report, 1655," 156–60, 162–63. In 1656 Lord's agent, Isaac Allen, successfully presented the draft for 2,196$\frac{1}{2}$ *riksdaler* to the Commercial College in Stockholm: Johnson, *Swedish Settlements*, 2:638–39.
77. Rising, "Report, 1655," 160, 170–76.
78. Ibid., 170; Lindeström, *Geographia Americae*, 235–36; and "Letter of the Gentlemen of the Council to General Petrus Stuyvesant at the South-River," 12 September 1655, in *NYCD*, ed. Fernow, 12:98–99. The Indians "offered great insult" to Isaac Allerton, who was resident in his Manhattan house at the time (98).
79. See Johnson, *Swedish Settlements*, 2:661, for hopes of continuing the trade.
80. On the fate of the Susquehannocks, see Jennings, "Glory, Death, and Transfiguration"; Jennings, "'Pennsylvania Indians' and the Iroquois," in *Beyond the Covenant Chain*, ed. Richter and Merrell, 75–91; and Weslager, *Delaware Indians*, 99–100.
81. New Sweden figures in Michael Roberts's *The Swedish Imperial Experience, 1560–1718* (Cambridge: Cambridge University Press, 1979) only in passing on the final page (156) as "the sad little enterprise on the Delaware."

Indians and Europeans in the Delaware Valley, 1620–1655

LORRAINE E. WILLIAMS

We have come to recognize a pattern in European-Indian relations along the Atlantic seaboard of North America during the sixteenth and seventeenth centuries. Europeans appeared in the rivers and bays with metal tools, guns, and ornaments to trade for Indian furs. The Indians at first moved toward the Europeans, anxious for the trade goods. But Native American trapping exhausted rapidly a nonrenewable resource. Once the fur-bearing mammals were depleted in their area, the Indians often attempted to stay in the trade by operating as brokers between the Europeans and Indians farther into the interior.

Eventually, however, the Europeans moved inland, bypassing the coastal Indian population, which then had only its land to sell to the ever-increasing numbers of settlers. Competition for resources produced conflict between members of the two groups, while sustained contact with Europeans exposed the Indians to diseases for which they had no resistance. Ultimately the Indians were faced with the choice of retreating westward to retain their traditional life-style or being absorbed into the evolving European-American society at the lowest socioeconomic level.

This scenario did not occur in the Delaware River valley in the seventeenth century. Decades after Henry Hudson's 1609 voyage opened the Delaware River and Bay to Europeans, the Delaware Indians (also known as the Lenape) had not been displaced by Dutch, Swedish, or English colonists. The Delaware were able to remain participants in the fur trade in the valley long after they depleted local fur-bearing mammals and Dutch and English traders were already in direct contact with the Susquehannnocks of Pennsylvania's interior. Theoretically this should have denied to the Delaware an intermediary position in the fur trade. Moreover, peaceful relations between Delaware Valley Indians and Europeans were the norm throughout the century. This is an intriguing divergence from the usual pattern of European-Indian contact. The reasons for this anomalous situation can be attributed to the somewhat peculiar circumstances of European settlement in the Delaware River valley.

Sustained European-Indian contact began with Dutch and then English ships appearing periodically in the river to trade for furs in the first four decades of the century. The Indians of the Delaware River whom we today call the Delaware were not one organized group, as current usage of the name implies. The Europeans called them the "River Indians" or "the Indians here in the river." The latter term is an accurate if cumbersome label.

As far as we can determine from the scanty ethnohistorical and archaeological records, the Indians lived in small bands, each occupying a drainage of the Delaware River.[1] Early maps, confirmed in part by archaeological evidence, indicate a differently named group on each major tributary of the Delaware River. On each branch the settlement pattern is that of larger sites on the main stream, with smaller camps at the headwaters and on feeder streams.[2] Each band seems to have been autonomous and consisted of at most two hundred persons.

For most of the year the Indians lived in unfortified settlements near their planting fields. After the communal hunts of the fall, they dispersed for the winter months into scattered campsites for hunting in small groups. They had, of course, a stone technology and met the European traders eager for guns and metal knives, hatchets, and hoes, as well as the glass beads and other trinkets the Europeans offered.

In 1623 the Dutch established Fort Nassau, a trading post between Big and Little Timber creeks on the New Jersey side of the Delaware, opposite present Philadelphia, where the Schuylkill River empties into the larger stream. They occupied the fort intermittently through the 1630s. In 1631 the Dutch founded Swanendael on the west bank of the Delaware, but conflict with the local Indians quickly led to an Indian attack in 1632 that killed all but one of the colonists. David De Vries established a modestly successful fishery at the Swanendael site in 1633 while he explored and traded up and down the Delaware, but Dutch attempts to found a permanent settlement in the valley ended with the abortive effort at Swanendael.[3]

During the next five years trade between Indians and Europeans in the valley continued with European vessels cruising the river and bay. In January 1633, De Vries found the Indians he called "Mantes" eager to trade and well stocked with beaver skins. The competition between English and Dutch traders on the river presumably provided the Indians with a good market for their furs. However, competition for trade was not only among the Europeans, for only a month later, while sailing the river in February, De Vries met three Armewamen Indians who were on the run from the Minquas Indians, who had attacked their village, plundered their corn, killed a number of the villagers, and burnt their houses.[4] De Vries also found in February 1633 a Minquas war party seeking Delaware Indians around Big Timber Creek.[5]

The Minquas, or the Susquehannocks, as the English of Virginia and Maryland called them, lived in the lower Susquehanna River valley. Archaeological evidence suggests that the Susquehannocks had moved downriver to that location toward the end of the sixteenth century.[6] They may have been forced downstream by Iroquois groups to the north that were better supplied with guns and metal tools by the French; or they may have moved closer to Chesapeake Bay of their own accord to have better access to European trading vessels. Iroquois speakers, the Susquehannocks were more numerous and organized into larger groups than the Delaware Indians.[7] From their fortified villages on the Susquehanna they sent large raiding parties against the Delaware. The party of Susquehannocks De Vries met numbered fifty and claimed that six hundred more were to follow.[8]

Competition continued among the Indian groups. In 1634 the Englishman Thomas Yong reported while trading in the river that the "River Indians" were at war with the Minquas, who had "killed many of them, destroyed their corne, and burned their houses."[9] That summer Yong found the Delaware Indians along the banks of the river fearful of the Minquas, who were boldly prowling the valley. One of the Delaware told him that his people—the Delaware—had "wholy left that side of the River [the western side], which was next to their enimies, and had retired themselves on the other side farre up into the woods, the better to secure themselves from their enimies."[10] By 1634 the Susquehannocks were clearly winning the competition for trade with Europeans in the valley.

It is worth noting that the Delaware-Susquehannock rivalry had depopulated the western bank of the Delaware River by 1634. When the New Sweden colonists arrived in 1638 they found an area open to settlement. They did not displace and antagonize local Indians because there were—temporarily—no local Indians.

That a brisk fur trade with the Susquehannocks and empty land on the west bank of the river were to be had in the Delaware River valley were certainly known to Peter Minuit, the former director-general of New Netherland and leader of the first Swedish expedition to the valley in March 1638. The Dutch were deeply involved in New Sweden from its very beginning as an idea in 1635 to its end as a Swedish possession with Peter Stuyvesant's conquest in 1655. Dutch interests led to the start of the colony and Dutch interests ended it.

Samuel Blommaert set in motion a train of events that led to the New Sweden Colony when he proposed to Axel Oxenstierna, chancellor of Sweden, the formation of a Swedish trading company backed by Dutch capital. Blommaert, a Dutchman, was a founding director of the Dutch West India Company and a former patroon of Swanendael. One wonders at this confusion of interests, which was evident from the beginning. In 1635 Oxenstierna seems to have been interested in finding New World markets for Swedish copper and iron.[11] The Dutch were interested in the New World fur trade. Once Peter Minuit entered the discussions in 1636, the Dutch interest in furs clearly began to steer Swedish plans for colonialism. Minuit, of course, was familiar with the Delaware Valley because the Dutch had explored it and established Fort Nassau by the time he served as governor of New Netherland from 1626 through 1631.

He and several of the stockholders of the Dutch West India Company, men such as Blommaert, were unhappy with the way New Netherland was being operated and sought a new and more profitable venture in which to invest. To them a Swedish colony in the Delaware Valley made good sense. Their "inside information" assured them that the location was ideal for trading with the Delaware and Susquehannock Indians for furs and that the Dutch at New Amsterdam would not be able to muster sufficent force to evict the Swedish settlers.

There were fewer advantages for the Swedes in the establishment of a colony in the Delaware Valley to trade for furs with the Indians and to grow tobacco. In the 1630s Sweden was basically an agrarian country. Unlike England and the Netherlands, it imported finished products and exported raw materials, largely to England and the Netherlands.[12] Since the Swedes had access to Scandinavian and Russian furs, the market for American furs in Sweden was a dubious prospect at best, and indeed most of the furs from the New Sweden colony were sold in Holland. There was a growing market for tobacco in Sweden, but during the life of the colony it remained a luxury item in a country with only a small urban population to provide a concentrated pool of buyers.

The problem that beset New Sweden throughout its history was that all of the goods for the Indian trade and most of the items needed to supply the settlers growing tobacco had to be secured in the Netherlands. In the early- to the mid-seventeenth century Sweden was not producing commodities for which a trading post in North America would provide a market. Sweden was also not in the market for the main products a North American colony could produce in the seventeenth century such as wood, furs, and grain, which the country produced for export itself.

The conflict of Dutch and Swedish interests was inherent in the beginning of New Sweden and the Swedish colony could not help but compete with Dutch interests in the New World. Thus the seeds of the colony's destruction—competition between Swedes and Dutch for the fur trade—were there at the start in 1638. Although Dutch backers were bought out of the New Sweden Company by 1641, Swedish reliance upon the Netherlands did not end either in the Old World or the New.[13] Swedish ships sent to the Delaware Valley continued throughout the colony's existence to be factored in the Netherlands. Lack of continuous supply from home could have turned New Sweden into another Roanoke except for the supplies the colonists were able to obtain from New Amsterdam. New Amsterdam was also the main source of news from Sweden and of wampum. This dependency is highlighted by the fact that when New Sweden's Governor Johan Printz left for Sweden in 1653 (disgusted at Sweden's lack of support), he had to sail for home in a Dutch ship.

Though the Swedes, the Dutch, and the English all claimed the Delaware River valley, none was able to control trade and/or settlement there before the English conquest of New Netherland in 1664. The Dutch in New Amsterdam, as I have noted, lacked sufficient strength to conquer New Sweden until 1655. Due to problems at home, Sweden was never able to supply its colony with enough people, arms, or capital to deny access to the valley to other colonial traders. Finally, the English, despite their abortive effort to plant a colony near the site of modern Salem, New Jersey, in 1641, were never able to muster sufficient support from New England to impose dominance themselves.

The result, despite efforts of New Sweden's governors and countermeasures of the Dutch governors at New Amsterdam to control trading access to the valley, was a brisk free trade involving Swedes, Dutch, and English, as well as the Susquehannock and Delaware River Indians. The blustering of the governors notwithstanding, the realities of this free-trade situation were evident by the fact that when Governor Printz called a court of inquiry at Fort Christina in July 1643 to look into rumors of the New Haven English plotting with the Indians against the Swedes, the court was composed of the English, Dutch, and Swedish trade commissaries in the valley.[14]

However much New Sweden's governors wished to carry out their orders to limit trade in the valley to the New Sweden Company, they were faced with the fact that because Swedish supply ships were rare, Dutch and English traders—the latter from both New England and the southern colonies of Maryland and Virginia—were a welcome source of supply to their own colonists and the New Sweden Company as well. The English traders brought European tools and wampum useful in the Indian trade and tobacco, which could be shipped back to Sweden. Throughout the colony's existence we find the commissaries traveling to New Amsterdam, Virginia, and New England to trade for food, draft animals, wampum, and tobacco. Currency was of course scarce, as it was along the Atlantic seaboard until after about 1660.[15] The real colonial currencies in this period were beaver skins and *sewant* (wampum).

By the mid-1640s it seems that most of New Sweden's fur trade was not producing furs for sale in Sweden, but to exchange with Dutch and English merchants for supplies needed to support its colonists and the New Sweden Company's employees. By the late 1640s, Swedish fur trading was producing more furs for the New Amsterdam market than for Sweden. Despite the lack of development of a viable fur market in Sweden, the colonists of New Sweden remained in the fur trade for their own survival. With furs they acquired from the Susquehannocks the settlers purchased supplies and goods to trade to the Delaware Indians for food. In another sense, this participation in the fur trade was a necessary survival mechanism—a lack of trade goods produced hostile Indians, a severe problem for small European groups such as the New Sweden colonists. Holm reported an Indian council of 1645 in which the Indians discussed the Swedes' lack of trade goods and considered killing these Europeans who had nothing to offer them.[16]

New Sweden's need to provide tobacco for Sweden and food for itself—and never producing the latter in sufficient quantity to support itself—enabled the Delaware Indians to remain active in the Indian-European trade long after their local fur supplies were exhausted. By at least 1644, when Printz reported the decline of the fur trade with the Delaware,[17] the fur-bearing mammal populations of the Delaware Valley had been trapped out. We would expect the Delaware to cease trading with the Europeans, except for selling land. This, however, did not occur because the Delaware Indians still had other commodities that the Europeans wanted such as corn, fish, and venison. The colonial administrators' interest in tobacco production increased the Delaware's opportunity to trade food to the Swedish colony. In 1644, Printz reported putting all of the company's lands into tobacco,[18] which he was able to do because corn was readily available from the "savages." The Delaware now had a new possibility for trade just as their fur supplies were exhausted, a rare occurrence in most Atlantic seaboard contact situations. The only equivalent of which I am aware was the intensified wampum production by some New England Indian groups that permitted them to remain active in European-Indian trade once local furs were no longer available.[19]

By the 1650s we can see from Governor Rising's report that the Delaware River Indians were making even more effective use of their trading opportunities.[20] Rising very testily described the way the Delaware were taking the trade goods they received from the Swedes, presumably for corn and venison, and intercepting the Susquehannock trading parties before the latter reached New Sweden. There the Delaware exchanged the trade goods for furs, which they in turn carried past New Sweden to New Amsterdam. There they received a better return for their furs since the Dutch were better supplied with trade goods (both European metal tools and wampum) than were the Swedes.

The mutually beneficial trade relationships that the New Sweden Company "enjoyed" with the Indians (to the despair of the governors) was an important factor contributing to the peace that prevailed throughout New Sweden's existence. From the data available we can also suggest other contributing influences. First, as previously mentioned, the New Sweden colony settlement on the west bank of the Delaware River did not displace any of the river's Indians, who had already been driven away by the Susquehannock. In fact, the Delaware River Indians may well have welcomed the colony as a buffer against continued Susquehannock raids, as well as a local and convenient source of trade goods. We find no reference to Susquehannock attacks on the River Indians after New Sweden began.

Another feature of New Sweden that undoubtedly contributed to peaceful coexistence with the Indians is that there were never more than a few hundred Swedes and Finns in the valley. Often their numbers were fewer than two hundred. This meant, in the first place, that there was enough land in the valley for both Indians and Europeans to pursue their life-styles. For example, as late as 1655, there were major Indian concentrations at the Schuylkill on prime land that would have been occupied by Europeans if the latter had arrived in great numbers.[21] Second, the small numbers of Swedes and Finns posed no threat to the Indian populations because the Swedish governors recognized that they lacked sufficient strength to attack the Indians.[22] Hence Printz, though he did not like the River Indians, did not allow individual incidents of violence between Swedes and Indians to precipitate the sort of massive countermeasures that the Dutch governors undertook in similar circumstances around New Amsterdam.

The infrequency of ships from Sweden—an obvious drawback, from the colonists' point of view—may also have contributed to peace. Disease frequently came to the New World on ships from Europe. Indian hostility towards Europeans quickly and understandably followed exposure to diseases for which they had no resistance. Aside from a reference by Governor John Winthrop of Massachusetts Bay Colony to reports of sickness among the Swedes on the Delaware[23] and the arrival of the *Örn* in 1654 with "a lot of sick and weak people" aboard,[24] we have no accounts of illness raging through the Delaware Valley among Europeans or Indians. Tellingly, Lindeström refers to increased tension with the River Indians following the spread of the illness in 1654.[25]

Another factor may have contributed to the peaceful relations between the Swedes and Finns and the Indians, one that is difficult to document but of great potential importance in understanding the dynamics of initial Indian-European contact. It is possible that the similar life-styles of the Indians and the Swedes and the Finns decreased the culture gap both experienced at first contact. Unlike the other Europeans who colonized North America, the Swedes and the Finns came from a wooded, riverine environment similar to that of the Delaware Valley. Like the Indians they were used to gaining their subsistence from a mixture of farming, hunting, and fishing. The settlers, particularly the Finns, practiced a method of farming very similar to that of the Indians—slash-and-burn horticulture—that would have seemed very normal to the Indians. More important, perhaps, this agricultural custom meant that the woodlands between the tilled plots were still open to Indians and Europeans for hunting, a very different type of land use by other European colonists, who cleared and fenced large areas of land and prohibited Indians from trespassing on it.

Other interesting similarities exist in the technologies of these two forest-adapted peoples. Both fished with nets and spears. The settlers were also used to hunting with crossbow and spear, another behavior that would have been familiar to the Indians. Given the meager historical sources available for the period, it is difficult to say how much these cultural similarities helped to reduce the potential for friction and fostered peaceful relations between the settlers and the Indians.

Even after the Dutch takeover of New Sweden in 1655, little changed in Indian-European relations in the valley. The Dutch West India Company was beset by its own difficulties and did not molest the Indians. The Swedish and Finnish colonists who remained in the valley enjoyed a sort of home rule under Sven Skute, the former commander of Fort Trinity. Thus when the English conquered New Netherland in 1664 they found a resident Indian population still in the valley more than fifty years after the onset of sustained European contact, an Indian population that greeted them in the hope of continued peace and moderate prosperity. Of course, such a continuation did not occur. By the mid-1680s great numbers of settlers arrived in the valley. Indians who sought to maintain a traditional life-style were displaced westward, while those who remained were forced to adapt as best they could to a new world.

NOTES

1. Dean R. Snow, "Late Prehistory of the East Coast," in *Northeast*, vol. 15, ed. Bruce G. Trigger, *Handbook of North American Indians* (hereafter *HNAI*) (Washington, D.C.: Smithsonian Institution, 1978); Ives Goddard, "Delaware," in *HNAI*; and Herbert C. Kraft, *The Lenape: Archaeology, History, and Ethnography* (Newark: New Jersey Historical Society, 1986).
2. Herbert C. Kraft and R. Alan Mounier, "The Late Woodland Period in New Jersey, ca. A.D. 1000–1600," in *New Jersey's Archaeological Resources from the Paleo-Indians to the Present* (Trenton: New Jersey Department of Environmental Protection, 1982).

3. David Pietersz De Vries, "Korte Historiael Ende Journaels Aenteycke-ninge" (1655), in *Narratives of Early Pennsylvania, West New Jersey, and Delaware, 1630–1707*, ed. Albert Cook Myers (1912; reprint, New York: Barnes & Noble, 1967), 9.

4. Ibid., 24.

5. Ibid., 22–23.

6. Barry C. Kent, *Susquehanna's Indians* (Harrisburg: Pennsylvania Historical and Museum Commission, 1984), 19.

7. William A. Hunter, "The Historic Role of the Susquehannocks," in *Susquehannock Miscellany*, ed. John C. Witthoft and W. Fred Kinsey III (Harrisburg: Pennsylvania Historical and Museum Commission, 1959); Francis Jennings, "Susquehannock," in *HNAI* 15; Kent, *Susquehanna's Indians*.

8. De Vries, "Korte Historiael," *HNAI* 15:22–23.

9. Thomas Yong, "A briefe Relation of a voyage lately made by me Captayne Thomas Yong, since my departure from Virginia, upon a discovery . . . ," in *Narratives*, ed. Myers, 38.

10. Ibid.

11. Amandus Johnson, *The Swedish Settlements on the Delaware: Their History and Relation to the Indians, Dutch, and English, 1638–1664*, 2 vols. (Philadelphia: Swedish Colonial Society, 1911), 1:92.

12. Amandus Johnson, *The Swedes on the Delaware, 1638–1664* (Philadelphia: Swedish Colonial Society, 1927), 47.

13. Johnson, *Swedish Settlements*, 1:132.

14. Ibid., 489.

15. Alden T. Vaughan, *New England Frontier: Puritans and Indians, 1620–1675* (Boston: Little, Brown, 1965), 224.

16. Thomas Campanius Holm, *Kort Beskrifning om Provincien Nya Sverige uti America* (Stockholm, 1702). Eng. ed.: *Description of the Province of New Sweden*, trans. Peter S. Du Ponceau, vol. 3, of Memoirs of the Historical Society of Pennsylvania (1834; reprint, Millwood, N.Y.: Kraus Reprint Co., 1975), 55.

17. Johan Printz, "Relation to the Noble West India Company in Old Sweden Sent Out of New Sweden on June 11, Anno 1644," in *Narratives*, ed. Myers, 103.

18. Ibid., 99.

19. Lorraine E. Williams, "A Study of Seventeenth-Century Culture Contact in the Long Island Sound Area" (Ph.D. diss., New York University, 1972), 225; Bert Salwen, "Indians of Southeastern New England and Long Island: Early Period," *HNAI* 15:166.

20. Johan Rising, "Report of Governor Johan Rising, 1655," in *Narratives*, ed. Myers, 156–57.

21. Peter Lindeström, *Geographia Americae, with an Account of the Delaware Indians, Based on Surveys and Notes Made in 1654–1656*, trans. Amandus Johnson (Philadelphia: Swedish Colonial Society, 1925), 170.

22. Printz, "Relation to the Noble West India Company," 103; Rising, "Report, 1655," 157.

23. John Winthrop, *Winthrop's Journal: History of New England, 1630–1649*, 2 vols., ed. James K. Hosmer (1908; reprint, Barnes & Noble, 1966), 2:70.

24. Johan Rising, "Report of Governor Rising, 1654," in *Narratives*, ed. Myers, 136.

25. Lindeström, *Geographia Americae*, 127–28, 130–31.

Lenape Maize Sales to the Swedish Colonists: Cultural Stability during the Early Colonial Period

MARSHALL JOSEPH BECKER

Interactions between some of the Lenape bands (also known as the Delaware Indians) and the Swedish colonists between 1640 and 1660 led to a temporary alteration in the residence pattern of some natives, but they did not produce changes in Lenape social structure or political organization. Lenape history during this period and later (early seventeenth century) is known from land deeds and references to their interactions with the colonists. These records document details of their band organization and dispersed residence pattern. However, from about 1640 until approximately 1660, several bands of these Lenape foragers clustered their summer encampments in the Passyunk region, where they grew maize for sale to the colonists. During this period these Lenape bands maintained traditional foraging patterns. After the collapse of the corn market, the participating Lenape bands returned to their traditional summer stations. Their social, political, and economic systems were unaltered by their temporary adjustment to secure trade goods over a period of nearly twenty years.

This unusual aggregation of foraging bands to grow maize as a cash crop has led several scholars to conclude that the Lenape foragers were sedentary horticulturalists or that contact with Europeans stimulated a transition to agriculture. Neither of these inferences is supported by the evidence, which indicates that aboriginal Lenape food procurement strategies, based on foraging, remained unchanged for two hundred years after the first direct contacts with Europeans in the 1620s.[1] Although Lenape technology rapidly incorporated many categories of European material culture, Lenape social organization and life-style remained almost entirely unaltered for more than two centuries. However, recent popular conceptions of the colonial-period Lenape often portray them as village-dwelling horticulturalists. This view largely derives from inferences based on evidence for horticulture among the Five Nations Iroquois and the

Susquehannock and on a lack of public awareness of the rich cultural diversity that was to be found among native Americans.

The documented production and sale of maize by the Lenape during the middle of the seventeenth century is often cited as evidence that these people were practicing horticulture. This paper reviews the recent literature to demonstrate that intensive maize gardening by the Lenape was a response to an unusual economic opportunity, rather than part of an agriculturally based economic system.

Lenape interactions with Europeans during the middle of the seventeenth century demonstrate Native American ability to maintain flexibility in the face of rapidly changing circumstances while sustaining their culture. Thus the Lenape, who traditionally gardened maize at their summer stations,[2] were easily able to increase maize production to trade with the Swedes. The Lenape received European trade goods without being burdened with the difficult task of storing this crop. This simple increase in the production of maize did not lead to the alteration of any other aspect of their culture.

By 1660 this cash-cropping of maize by the Lenape had ended. This short-lived intensification of production was not an attempt to increase or to stabilize food resources, but simply a means by which European goods could be secured by a people who had few furs to trade. In addition to securing trade goods, maize sales created an indirect food-storage system. Maize grown or purchased by the colonists could be secured by the Lenape during times of famine by reverse trade or through the social obligations created by the original sales of maize. Lenape purchases of alcoholic beverages at the time of the maize harvest also allowed them to amplify ritual behavior at the annual "renewal" ceremonies.[3] Due to increased grain production by the colonists, the cash-cropping of maize by the Lenape had ended by 1660. By that time the Lenape had become more active in the fur trade, largely due to the decline of the Susquehannock. Fur trading was a more efficient means to secure desired goods and also was better suited to their foraging culture.

LENAPE LIFE BEFORE 1623

Ethnohistorical[4] and archaeological[5] research demonstrates that Lenape subsistence systems during the Late and Terminal Woodland and the Early Historic periods were based on foraging. Lenape summer stations along the shores of the Delaware River were used for gathering fish resources,[6] as well as carbohydrates such as maize and chenopodium. The absence of storage pits at these sites reflects the absence of horticulture.

The presence of maize gardens at summer encampments of the coastal peoples of the Eastern Woodlands has led some scholars to infer horticultural activities, an error discussed by Lynn Ceci.[7] Ceci provides evidence for the absence of horticulture or a sedentary life-style in coastal New York using archaeological evidence similar to that which characterizes the entire region. Although horticulture may have been a Terminal Woodland (ca. 1400 A.D.) innovation in Iroquois and other interior areas, the Lenape and their coastal neighbors to the north continued to use foraging as their economic base.

After European contact, the limited number of furs produced by the foraging peoples of the Delaware Valley could secure only limited quantities of trade goods. By 1550 the fur trade was controlled by the Susquehannock of central Pennsylvania, who had outposts as far west as the upper Potomac in West Virginia.[8] The Susquehannock acted as brokers for furs coming from more westerly regions,[9] and after 1662 they shifted their outlets from the Chesapeake Bay to the Delaware (South) River. This shift in trade routes was made at the expense of the Lenape, whose limited fur resources were reduced by Susquehannock incursions.

EARLY DIRECT CONTACT, 1623–1640

The Lenape remained peripheral to the lucrative fur trade until the 1650s, when Susquehannock power was on the wane.[10] The Lenape developed alternative strategies to provide access to desired European goods such as performing tasks, carrying mail, bounty-hunting, and provisioning.[11] During this early period Dutch traders and Swedish settlers had difficulties in developing effective farming strategies and found it cheaper and more efficient to purchase food from the local people. Like the early European colonists in many parts of North America, their survival depended upon native food sales.[12]

Even before the Swedish colony was established (1638), the Dutch traders on the South River relied on native-produced maize for some part of their diet. David De Vries noted in his report for 1633 that the war between the Susquehannock and the Lenape prevented the Dutch from getting corn from the Indians.[13] To some extent, the more stable Dutch colony at New Amsterdam on the North (Hudson) River made up for these food deficits, but purchases of Lenape maize became increasingly vital to the economics of the Swedish settlement. After 1640 the gardens at the Lenape summer fishing stations appear to have increased in size, specifically to provide a cash crop. The products most in demand from the colonists were guns, tools, cloth, and decorative glass beads. However,

Lenape demand for these products rapidly leveled off since their population was small,[14] and they buried relatively few goods with their dead.[15]

When the saturation point in these goods was reached, the commodity preferred by the Lenape became alcohol. The intensification of maize production to exchange for liquor became part of the fall banqueting activities, stimulating expansion of native fields during the summer. This also led to the summer aggregation of several Lenape bands in the Passyunk region rather than at stations scattered along the Delaware River.

Johan Printz summarized the Swedish point of view when he noted that "the River Indians were poor and had nothing but maize to sell,"[16] but this simple commodity was a critical component in the survival of the European colonists. Although from a commercial viewpoint furs were the desired articles of native trade, foods such as maize, fish, beans, and venison were essential to the well-being of the early colonists. By the early 1640s, shortly after the Swedish colony was established, Lenape maize production was on the increase.

The precariously situated Swedish settlement around Fort Christina (now Wilmington, Delaware) dates from 1638. The colony's third governor, Johan Printz, arrived in 1643 with the intent of developing the potential of this distant outpost of the Swedish empire. Governor Printz's instructions from the Crown directed him to plant tobacco as an export crop so that the Swedes could avoid purchasing supplies from the English. Peter Ridder, his predecessor, advised Printz to plant corn in large quantities, noting that "one man's planting would produce enough corn for nine men's yearly food."[17]

Printz established his household (trading station) on Tinicum Island,[18] close to the Dutch trading post and to the Lenape summer station at Passyunk. When he arrived in New Sweden, Printz followed Ridder's advice, planting corn on most available plots and sowing very little tobacco.[19] However, Printz needed food to last until the harvest, and in May 1643 he traded "sewant [wampum] valued at 607 fl[orins] ... for 972 bushels of Indian corn."[20] The values noted in this document help to determine costs for grain in the spring, when stocks were depleted.[21] The following year Richard Malbon, a New Haven merchant, sold Printz 102.5 bushels of corn for 164 florins, half the rate previously paid by Printz. This suggests that the sale was made closer to harvest time.[22]

The Swedes lacked sufficient trade goods to make large purchases of furs, but diligence in growing tobacco provided them with a cash crop. By the spring of 1644, the Swedes did not bother to plant maize at all, preferring to buy it cheaply from the Lenape.[23] Swedish concentration on growing tobacco for export suggests that by 1644 the Lenape had amplified maize gardening to a level sufficient to meet Swedish needs. The maize trade between the Swedes and the Lenape was, however, not without problems.

In his report of 1644, Printz laments his own failure to produce enough grain. Referring to the Lenape and Jerseys, Printz enviously notes that he wished that he could break "the necks of all of them in the river, especially since we have no beaver trade with them but only the maize trade."[24] Printz reasoned that if the Swedes killed these people and took their cleared tracts of land, that each Swede could "feed and nourish himself unmolested with their maize, and also we could take possession of the places (which are the most fruitful) that the savages now possess; ...." This plan would also give the Swedes the "beaver trade with the black and white Minquas alone."[25] This suggests that by 1644 the Lenape not only were important producers of maize, but also that they had become at least partially involved in the fur trade.

Swedish difficulties in feeding themselves were accentuated by the failure of all their crops in 1646. By this time at least three bands of Lenape, previously summering at scattered stations along the Delaware River, were aggregating at Passyunk, where the Schuylkill enters the Delaware. This large, level area provided the Lenape with rich soil as well as proximity to the Swedes who were buying their maize.

The difficulties that the Swedes had in getting trade goods and provisions from Sweden reduced the viability of New Sweden, and the colonists increasingly turned their attentions to subsistence farming. Swedish efforts to feed themselves continued and in 1647 Printz purchased maize from New Amsterdam, three hundred bushels of *taru* (*tarw* = maize) for one hundred beavers. In August of that year he again bought maize from the Lenape and other grains from the English.[26]

The arrival of the *Swan* in January 1648 marked one of the few times when a Swedish ship actually supplied its distant colony and took home the goods produced there.[27] By April 1648, the Swedish-Dutch competition for furs led the Swedes to construct Fort Beversreede (Beaver Road) near the Lenape summer encampments at Passyunk.[28] This building secured better access to the Susquehannock fur trade and also provided a station at which maize could be purchased. The Swedes took advantage of the cleared space around this new structure to plant corn.[29] However, the continuing problems suffered by the Swedes in getting trade goods led the "Sachems of Passajonck" (on 24 April 1648) to ask the Dutch to build a trading house, like that of the Swedes, near these Lenape settlements at Passyunk.[30] This request reflects the Lenape desire to bring their European allies into a defensive network around their more dense, and therefore more vulnerable, summer settlements at Passyunk. Beversreede was abandoned in the summer of 1650,[31] for reasons still unclear, leaving the Lenape at Passyunk feeling exposed to attack by other native nations.

Although Johnson notes that in 1650 the freemen in New Sweden sold over one hundred barrels of surplus grain,[32] probably rye and barley, Swedish maize and meat purchases from the Lenape continued to be important as late as 1654. By 1650 alcohol had become the primary item that the Lenape wanted for their maize. Durable trade goods had reached a saturation point among these foragers. Lenape funeral rituals involved the redistribution of goods among the living, rather than burying them with the deceased.[33] Additional material goods would have burdened the living with more tangible resources than foragers can manage. Burial of more goods with the dead was not the Lenape way, as it was among the Susquehannock. The exchange of most of the maize crop for alcohol provided an ideal resource to enhance the fall celebrations just before Lenape dispersal for winter hunting.

The last years of Printz's activities in New Sweden are less clearly known. In 1652 heavy rains damaged the Swedish grain crops,[34] but on the whole the colonists' grain production continued to increase. The Swedes, numbering about two hundred at this time, noted the native population as increasingly "unruly," probably due to increased Lenape independence. Susquehannock hegemony was declining as Seneca incursions in central Pennsylvania were increasing in their devastation. This "unruly" behavior among the Lenape was not related to alcohol consumption, for the Swedes found no reason to limit the flow of this useful commodity, and no protests against liquor sales were made by the Lenape, as was commonly the case after 1680. In March 1653 Printz was able to buy much-needed trade material from the Dutchman Evert Cornelisen, including six *ankers* of Spanish wine and three of brandy (one *anker* in 1653 = 8.64 U.S. gallons).

THE END OF THE SWEDISH COLONY: 1655

Johan Rising, Printz's successor as governor, had little opportunity to develop the colony. In Rising's report for 1654 he notes not only problems in securing food but a lack of specialists to produce pottery, bricks, lime, and even furniture.[35] During New Sweden's final years and for some years after the Dutch conquest, Passyunk continued to be the summer area used by several bands of Lenape, even though most continued to use traditional summer stations.[36] On 5 June 1654 the Swedish engineer Peter Lindeström sailed up the Delaware to inspect tracts of land awarded by the queen to Sven Skute, "namely: Passajungh (where the principal Sachems, i.e., chiefs or rulers of the savages, *now* live), Kingsessing Mochorhuttingh and the land on both sides of the Schuylkill, all the way [down] to the [Delaware] River."[37] On 17 June, twelve sachems of the "Lenappi . . . living on our River, on the West Shore" assembled at Tennakonck (Tinicum Island). Eight came from "Passajung" and two each from Nittabakonck and Sipaessingh. Rising's report of 1654 notes that during this visit "they invited us to build a fort and houses at Pas-syunk (which is their main settlement and where most of them live) and stated that they would recognize all of our Land Purchases...."[38] Since Fort Beversreede had been abandoned four years previously, the Le-nape were concerned about their security and were constantly hoping that their European allies would provide some defense.

On 8 July 1654 these Lenape continued downriver to Christina to make formal sales of lands to the Swedes. Although Peminacka and Ahopa-meck were noted as being from Passyunk, the lands that they sold in-cluded large tracts at different points along the river,[39] indicating that they continued to hold rights to where their bands normally summered. Other lands, presumably including Passyunk, were reserved for Lenape use. Lindeström's description of the greater Passyunk area in 1654 sug-gests that it was the primary place along the river "where Lenape clus-ter."

> From Wickquakonick all the way to Nittabakonck, which is situated at the falls of the River Menejackse, the land is very fine.... This is occupied in greatest force by the most intelligent savages of several nations [bands] of savages, who own the River and dwell here. There they have their dwellings side by side one another, wherefore also this land is thereby being cleared and cultivated with great power. And six different places are settled, under six sachems or chiefs, each one commanding his tribe or people.... [40]

Lindeström also notes that these "nations" (bands) actually came from four separate places located further up the river. He then observed that the land at Passyunk is "being cleared," as if the work of field preparation (or expansion) were still in process. This, too, suggests continued expan-sion of old fields, although it simply may have been a normal relocation of a summer station at Passyunk. The clustering, land clearing, and maize gardening of these Lenape bands, so much like European styles of agri-culture in their superficial aspects, may have been the reason why Lindes-tröm identified these people (those at Passyunk?) as the "most intelli-gent" of all those living along the river.

In August 1654 the Lenape promised to gather hops as well as cultivate maize for sale. The Swedes sent a boat to collect the hops, but it returned with only a small quantity. Later the Swedes sent two boats upriver to negotiate the maize purchase. One returned from Passyunk with a small amount and the report that the Lenape were unfriendly. However, on 27 September 1654, Jacob Svensson, an accomplished trader, returned to Fort Christina in the large sloop with four hundred bushels of maize. Shortly after the Lenape elder Ahopameck came to Christina with a promise to sell large quantities of maize. Two sloops went up river and returned in four days with 960 bushels of maize and twenty of beans (probably gathered, not cultivated). The Lenape also sent Governor Rising an additional twenty bushels of maize as a gift.[41] These 1,400 bushels of grain would have been sufficient to provide the carbohydrate requirements of over two hundred colonists for the entire year.[42]

Johnson believes that by October 1654 agriculture and cattle production had become the primary activity of the Swedish colonists. However, Swedish grain production remained insufficient, and all of the freemen who arrived in the colony in 1654 were ordered to clear land and to plant wheat and maize.[43] At the end of the year (December 1654) Jacob Svensson negotiated the purchase of deer meat from the "savages" at Appoquenema,[44] at the southern end of Lenape territory (see fig. 1). This sale of meat, providing the Swedes with an inexpensive protein source, reinforces the belief that only a few of the Lenape bands were engaged in the maize trade, while others found different ways to negotiate for trade goods.

Johan Rising's reports to the Swedish Crown indicate that in 1654 the colonists would have lacked bread and provisions were it not for an English merchant from Hartford (now Connecticut) who sold goods on the South River.[45] Rising stated that in general the New Englanders "bring us our provisions, but we have had the disadvantage in this trade."[46] The more densely settled and productive English outposts were gaining economic power through both agriculture and trade, creating a threat to Rising and his tiny colony. Rising's report for 1655 also indicated that the Swedes had cleared more land along the Delaware (possibly by slash-and-burn techniques) and that the crops planted there were expected to be good. But a late frost spoiled these crops,[47] thus continuing the difficulties of the Swedes in maintaining their colony. Unfortunately the Swedes were not the only people in extreme difficulty during these turbulent years.

THE BEGINNING OF THE END

More than a century of warfare between the Seneca and the Susquehannock (White Minquas) created innumerable problems for both nations. Susquehannock power over the Lenape had long since ended, and a tacit alliance had emerged by 1650. Lenape increasingly traded with the Susquehannock and later even joined in their defense. On 5 July 1652 a peace treaty was signed between the Maryland colonists and the Susquehannock, with Iafer Peter as a witness for the Swedish governor.[48] Each nation in this region had vital interests in alliances being forged by the people around them, and this became evident only a few years later.

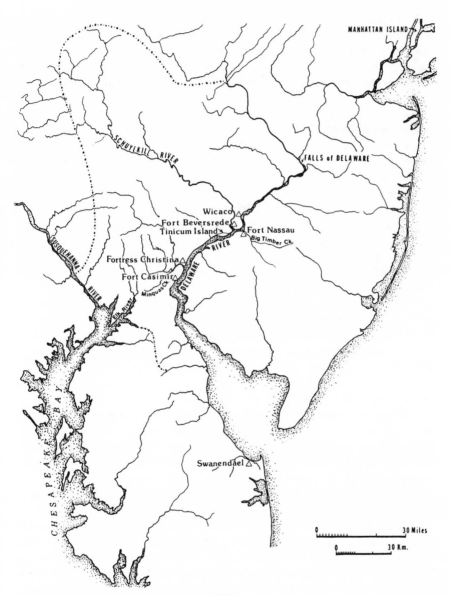

Fig. 1. Area occupied by the Lenape, 1600.

In his 1654 report Rising noted his desire to purchase all the lands that were in the area of New Sweden. Rising accurately noted that "... the savages now at this time and before this have often requested this of us...."[49] Continuing English expansion was encroaching on native lands to the north, and warfare in the Susquehanna Valley stimulated the Lenape to seek support from military allies.

By the middle of June 1655, the sachems of the White Minquas (Susquehannock) "and their united nations, the Tehaque, the Skonedidehoga, the Serasquacke, the true Minquas and the Lower Quarter of the Minquas" gathered at Fort Trinity (the Sandhook, now New Castle, Delaware) and collectively presented a large tract of land near their own heartland to the Swedes.[50] With this gift and affirmation of their alliance came offers for exclusive trade. But this proposal only reflected problems confronting the Susquehannock. The military pressures against them were mounting, and they wished to bring the Swedish colony closer to act as a buffer against encroachments by the English and Dutch. More significantly, the Susquehannock also wished the Swedes to serve as allies in their wars against the Seneca.

The Lenape, with their autonomy regained, were developing new opportunities to satisfy their appetite for trade goods. Their participation in the fur trade had grown through interactions with the declining Susquehannock, enabling the Lenape to gain advantage from trade with the Swedish colonists. Rising's 1655 report notes that "our neighbors the Renappi threaten not only to kill our people ... but also to destroy even the trade, both with the Minquas and the other savage nations...."[51] Rising also noted that the now-hostile Lenape would buy Swedish goods "half on credit, and then pay with difficulty. They run to the Minques [Susquehannock], and there they buy beavers and elk skins, etc., for our goods, and then they proceed before our eyes to Manathas [Manhattan], where the traders can pay more for them than we do, because more ships and more goods arrive there." Clearly the Lenape had learned how to profit from the fur trade.

The precariously balanced economy of the Swedish settlement could not support military resistance to its Dutch neighbors. Dutch tolerance of the Swedes ended as English power in the region increased and the fear of a Swedish-English alliance grew. In 1655, feeling the need to absorb New Sweden, the Dutch formally "conquered" the small Swedish colony. This failed to slow English expansion, which was related in part to the greater agricultural productivity of the English colonists. English agricultural output also reduced the value of the Lenape maize crop, but the fur trade was a much more profitable enterprise and culturally more suited to the foraging life-style of the Lenape.

Lenape cash cropping is an important example of cultural adaptation and is of interest to general theories of agricultural intensification. James Eder, examining the transition from foraging to agriculture, discusses the "mistaken idea" that a correlation exists between increasing reliance on food production (and storage) and increasing sedentism.[52] The belief that mobile foragers become increasingly sedentary as agricultural technology develops is contradicted by evidence gathered by Eder. The Lenape evidence, however, indicates that a population may amplify food production, but for reasons unrelated to storage or sedentism. Halstead and O'Shea indicate that the transformation from foraging to agriculture is a response to risk and uncertainty.[53] While food resources were uncertain among Native Americans in central areas of Pennsylvania and New York where horticulture did develop, this was never the case among the Lenape, who had available the abundant food resources of the Delaware River.

The evidence reviewed suggests that the Lenape and others were capable of generating and maintaining a wider range of variation within their "subsistence" activities than often is believed. Such variations,[54] however, need have no influence on overall cultural patterns. The naive and the ethnocentric, who believe that agriculture is "superior" to foraging, have difficulty in understanding why the Lenape did not become agriculturalists when they had abundant and rich land and European models for food production and storage techniques. Such views fail to understand the importance of "culture." Even cultures under long-term stress resist change, and the Lenape were never affected with the kinds of problems that were common among other coastal peoples to the south.

Lenape life-style and settlement pattern during and after nearly two decades of cash cropping maize remained unchanged. Traditional Lenape shelters (wigwams) continued in use, and winter hunting followed summer fishing in a pattern unaltered by their trade with Europeans. Maize production was intensified not to increase their own food resources, but to provide access to desired luxury goods. The relative clustering of a few Lenape summer settlements, so critical to the Swedish colonists, generated no significant alterations in native life-style during or after this interlude. Two decades of amplified food production, without use of food storage techniques, had no "enduring consequences for Lenape social or political structure."[55] This conclusion is clearly supported by the complete absence of Lenape agricultural activities over the next two centuries of their culture history.

Although Lenape fall banqueting may have been merrier and trade goods easier to come by during those years, Lenape sociopolitical organization and foraging patterns remained unchanged for over two hundred years. The Lenape continued to maintain their traditional life-style and language despite relocations that took them over a long and circuitous route throughout the heartland of the American continent.

NOTES

1. Marshall J. Becker, "A Summary of Lenape Socio-Political Organization and Settlement Pattern at the Time of European Contact: The Evidence for Collecting Bands," *Journal of Middle Atlantic Archaeology* 4 (1988): 79–83.
2. The term *gardening* describes a process familiar to contemporary suburbanites. Small crops are grown for immediate consumption, as distinct from horticultural and agricultural systems, which require storage for consumption over an extended period. The Lenape gardened maize and possibly tobacco. The "fields" in which these plants were grown, similar to the open areas fire-cleared by the Lenape, also yielded large quantities of *Chenopodium* ("goose foot"), which may have had caloric value equal in importance to the limited maize crops.
3. Anthony F. C. Wallace, "New Religions Among the Delaware Indians, 1600–1900," *Southwestern Journal of Anthropology* 12 (1956): 1–21; John Witthoft, *Green Corn Ceremonialism in the Eastern Woodlands* (Ann Arbor: University of Michigan Press, 1949).
4. Marshall J. Becker, "The Lenape Bands Prior to 1740 A.D.: The Identification of Boundaries and Processes of Culture Change Leading to the Formation of the Delaware," in *The Lenape Indians: A Symposium*, ed. Herbert C. Kraft (South Orange, N.J.: Archaeological Research Center, Seton Hall University, 1984), 19–32. See also Marshall J. Becker, "Cultural Diversity in the Lower Delaware River Valley: An Ethnohistorical Perspective," in *Late Woodland Cultures of the Middle Atlantic Region*, ed. Jay Custer (Newark: University of Delaware Press, 1986), 90–101, and Marshall J. Becker, "Lenape Population at the Time of European Contact: Estimating Native Numbers in the Lower Delaware Valley," *Proceedings of the American Philosophical Society* 133, no. 2 (1989): 112–22. See also Becker, "Lenape Socio-Political Organization."
5. Jay Custer, "The Prehistoric Archaeology of the Churchman Marsh Vicinity: An Introductory Analysis," *Bulletin of the Archaeological Society of Delaware* 13 (1982): 33.
6. Randall F. Schalk, "The Structure of an Anadromous Fish Resource," in *For Theory Building in Archaeology: Essays on Funeral Remains, Aquatic Resources, Spatial Analysis, and Systemic Modeling*, ed. Lewis R. Binford (New York: Academic Press, 1977), 207–49. See also Hetty Jo Brumbach, "Anadromous Fish and Fishing: A Synthesis of Data From the Hudson River Drainage," *Man in the Northeast* 32 (Fall 1986): 35–66.
7. Lynn Ceci, "Maize Cultivation in Coastal New York: The Archaeological, Agronomical, and Documentary Evidence," *North American Archaeologist* 1 (1979): 45–74, and "The Effect of European Contact and Trade on the Settlement Pattern of Indians in Coastal New York, 1524–1665: The Ar-

chaeological and Documentary Evidence" (Ph.D. diss., City University of New York, 1977).

8. Marshall J. Becker, "An Analysis of the Human Skeletons from 46HM73: A Susquehannock Population of the Mid-Sixteenth Century," *West Virginia Archaeology* 39, no. 2 (1987): 37–53.

9. Frederick J. Fausz, "The Historical Significance of the Chesapeake Bay Beaver Trade, 1620–1660," in *The Accokeek Creek Complex and the Emerging Maryland Colony* (Accokeek, Md.: Alice Ferguson Foundation, 1984), 23–31. Also see Barry C. Kent, *Susquehanna's Indians* (Harrisburg: Pennsylvania Historical and Museum Commission, 1984).

10. Elizabeth Tooker, "The Demise of the Susquehannocks: A 17th-Century Mystery," *Pennsylvania Archaeologist* 54, nos. 3–4 (1984): 1–10.

11. Marshall J. Becker, "The Okehocking Band of Lenape: Cultural Continuities and Accommodations to Colonial Expansion in Southeastern Pennsylvania in the Early 18th Century," in *Strategies for Survival: American Indians in the Eastern United States*, ed. Frank W. Porter III (Westport, Conn.: Greenwood Press, 1986), 43–83.

12. James R. Gibson, "European Dependence Upon American Natives: The Case of Russian America," *Ethnohistory* 25 (1978): 359–85.

13. David Pietersz De Vries, "Korte Historiael Ende Journaels Aenteyckeninge," (1655), in *Narratives of Early Pennsylvania, West New Jersey and Delaware*, ed. Albert Cook Myers (New York: Charles Scribner's Sons, 1912), 26.

14. Marshall J. Becker, "The Lenape and Other 'Delawarean' Peoples at the Time of European Contact: Population Estimates Derived from Archaeological and Historical Sources," in *Disease and Demography in the Americas: Changing Patterns Before and After 1492*, ed. Douglas H. Ubelaker and John H. Verano (Washington, D.C.: Smithsonian Institution Press, 1991).

15. Marshall J. Becker, "Lenape Mortuary Rites: A Survey of These Rituals Through Time Reflecting Cultural Stability Throughout the Post-Contact Period," paper presented at the Philadelphia Anthropological Society, 15 November 1985. The English term *feasting* is used by the modern Lenape in conjunction with the "feast of the dead." The term *banquet* does not have mortuary connotations and therefore is used here in the context of the fall celebration.

16. Amandus Johnson, "The Indians and Their Culture as Described in Swedish and Dutch Records From 1614 to 1664," *Proceedings of the 19th International Congress of Americanists* (Washington, D.C., 1917), 279.

17. Amandus Johnson, *The Swedish Settlements on the Delaware: Their History and Relation to the Indians, Dutch and English 1638–1664*, 2 vols. (Philadelphia: Swedish Colonial Society, 1911), 1:308–9.

18. Marshall J. Becker, "Ethnohistory and Archaeology in Search of the Printzhof: The 17th-Century Residence of Swedish Colonial Governor Johan Printz," *Ethnohistory* 26, no. 1 (1979): 15–44.

19. Johan Printz, "Relation to the Noble West India Company in Old Sweden Sent Out of New Sweden on June 11, Anno 1644," in *Narratives*, ed. Myers, 99.

20. Johnson, *Swedish Settlements*, 1:309.

21. F. G. Benedict and Morris Steggerda, *The Food of the Present-day Maya Indians of Yucatan*, Carnegie Publication 456 (Washington, D.C.: Carnegie Institution of Washington, 1936). These authors estimated that Yucatecan

Maya were consuming about 1.2 pounds (0.54 kg) of corn per day, which represented 75 to 85 percent of the caloric value of their diet. The additional information is provided by Morris Steggerda, *Maya Indians of Yucatan*, Carnegie Institution Publication 531 (Washington, D.C.: Carnegie Institution of Washington, 1941), 89, 123. These levels may be above the amount of maize the Swedish colonists needed, since they also had milk products as well as domestic and wild animals to supplement their diet. The foraging Lenape, and even the Five Nation horticulturalists, ate an even higher proportion of meat than did the Swedes, as indicated by Marshall J. Becker in "The Stature of a Susquehannock Population of the Mid-16th Century Based on Skeletal remains from 46HM73," *Pennsylvania Archaeologist* 61 (1991): 73–88.

A bushel of maize weighs 56 pounds (25.5 kg) and 1.6 pounds (0.73 kg) of maize per day is 100 percent of caloric needs (1 pound = 1,579 calories), following Beatrice K. Watt and Annabel L. Merrill, *Composition of Foods Raw, Processed, Prepared*, Agricultural Handbook No. 8 (Washington, D.C.: Agricultural Research Service, U.S. Department of Agriculture, 1963), 84–85. Thus the Swedish purchase of 1,380 bushels could feed at least 130 people for a year and perhaps as many as 260, depending on other foods consumed. We do not know if the Lenape or the colonials used lime or limewater to process maize in ways that would have increased the nutritive value of the grain.

The actual amount of maize purchased by the Swedish colonists may have been somewhat lower than indicated, depending on modern translations of old Swedish measures. The seventeenth-century Swedish term *skeppel* (or *skiepper*), generally translated as "bushel," may have been closer to the modern South African *schepel*, which is one-fourth of a *muid* or 0.77 bushels (U.S. Winchester bushel, which is 35.2361 liters). The modern Winchester bushel of maize weighs fifty-six pounds, while the equivalent volume of peas or wheat weighs sixty pounds.

22. Johnson, *Swedish Settlements*, 1:318, n. 63. Malbon also sold *sewant* to the Swedes.
23. Printz, "Relation, 1644," 99.
24. Marshall J. Becker, "The Moravian Mission in the Forks of the Delaware: Reconstructing the Migration and Settlement Patterns of the Jersey Lenape during the Eighteenth Century Through Documents in the Moravian Archives," *Unitas Fratrum* 8 (1987): 78–161. See also Marshall J. Becker, "The Forks of Delaware, Pennsylvania, during the First Half of the Eighteenth Century: The Migration of Some 'Jerseys' into a Former Shared Resource Area North of Lenape Territory and Its Implications for Cultural Boundaries and Identities," *Abhandlungen der Völkerkundliche Arbeitsgemeinschaft*, no. 55 (1987).
25. Printz, "Relation, 1644," 103.
26. Johnson, *Swedish Settlements*, 1:333.
27. Of note on the list of arriving cargo was the first large brewing kettle to reach New Sweden (Johnson, *Swedish Settlements*, 1:334). A beer-brewing kettle would suggest that a regular supply of grain was available to be converted for this use. However, Printz may have imported this kettle for sprouting grain as part of the baking process (see Printz, "Relation, 1644," 98), but he did have an ale house at his home on Tinicum Island; see Becker, "Ethnohistory and Archaeology."

28. Johnson, *Swedish Settlement*, 1:420.
29. Ibid., 335.
30. Charles T. Gehring, trans. and ed., *New York Historical Manuscripts*, vols. 18–19, *Delaware Papers* (Baltimore: Genealogical Publishing Co., 1981), 18:9; Johnson, *Swedish Settlements*, 1:419.
31. Johnson, *Swedish Settlements*, 1:433.
32. Ibid., 388.
33. Becker, "Lenape Mortuary Rites."
34. Johnson, *Swedish Settlements*, 1:341.
35. Johan Rising, "Report of Governor Johan Rising, 1654," in *Narratives*, ed. Myers, 142.
36. See Marshall J. Becker, "The Okehocking: A Remnant Band of Delaware Indians," *Pennsylvania Archaeologist* 46 (1976): 24–61.
37. Peter Lindeström, *Geographia Americae, with an Account of the Delaware Indians, Based on Surveys and Notes Made in 1654–1656*, trans. and ed. Amandus Johnson (Philadelphia: Swedish Colonial Society, 1925), 126–32 (emphasis added). Lindeström (179–80) also provides an accurate description of the way in which maize was grown in 1654, a procedure similar to modern garden techniques. In 1654 six or seven grains of maize were planted in each hill. The stalks grew more than two meters tall and bore six or seven ears each.
38. Johan Rising, "Een Kort Berattelse on Reesan till Nya Sverige, 1654–1655," General Collection E, Manuscript E 433, Uppsala University Library, Uppsala, Sweden. Translated by author.
39. Ibid.
40. Lindeström, *Geographia Americae*, 170.
41. Johnson, *Swedish Settlements*, 2:568.
42. Compare this with the calculations in n. 21.
43. Johnson, *Swedish Settlements*, 2:524.
44. Ibid., 568.
45. Johan Rising, "Report of Governor Johan Rising, 1655," in *Narratives*, ed. Myers, 162–63.
46. Ibid., 158.
47. Johnson, *Swedish Settlements*, 2:529.
48. William Hand Browne et al., eds., *Archives of Maryland*, 69 vols. (Baltimore: Maryland Historical Society, 1883–1961), vol. 3, *Proceedings of the Council of Maryland, 1636–1667*.
49. Rising, "Report, 1654," 140; Rising, "Report, 1655," 159.
50. Rising, "Een Kort Berattelse"; Rising, "Report, 1654," 140, and "Report, 1655," 159–60; Johnson, "The Indians and Their Culture," 278.
51. Rising, "Report, 1655," 156–57.
52. James F. Eder, "The Impact of Subsistence Change on Mobility and Settlement Pattern in a Tropical Forest Foraging Economy: Some Implications for Archaeology," *American Anthropologist* 86 (1984): 837–53.
53. Paul Halstead and John O'Shea, eds., *Bad Year Economics: Cultural Responses to Risk and Uncertainty* (New York: Cambridge University Press, 1989).
54. In addition to the historical evidence regarding Lenape maize gardening, an examination was made of the Lenape linguistic data relating to maize cultivation. The results suggest an absence of horticulture among the Lenape. August C. Mahr, in his "Eighteenth-Century Terminology of Dela-

ware Indian Cultivation and Use of Maize: A Semantic Analysis," *Ethnohistory* 2 (1955): 209–40, reviewed the two major "Delaware" word lists known from the eighteenth century, those of Daniel G. Brinton and Albert S. Anthonis, eds., *A Lenape-English Dictionary*, vol. 1 (Philadelphia: Historical Society of Pennsylvania, 1889), and David Zeisberger, *Zeisberger's Indian Dictionary: English, German, Iroquois—The Onondaga, and Algonquin—the Delaware*, ed. Eben Norton Horsford (Cambridge, Mass.: John Wilson & Son, University Press, 1887), seeking Lenape equivalents for English or German agricultural terms. No "Delaware" terms were identified for "storage" nor for other activities related to the processing of crops, nor for tools such as the pestle (pounder), except via the words used by the Onondaga. Although these absences may be no more than a coincidental series of minor omissions, they may be a significant piece of evidence.

55. J. F. Eder, personal communication to the author.

This research was supported by a research fellowship from the National Endowment for the Humanities while the author was a senior fellow in anthropology at the University of Pennsylvania. An earlier version of this paper was presented at the 1987 Archaeology and Anthropology Faculty Seminars, Department of Social Anthropology, University of Cambridge. My thanks are due to J. Colyer, Dr. Tom Davidson, Stephen Del Sordo, Dr. J. F. Eder, Dr. Mary Martin, P. Scheifele, Jean Smythe, L. Swartly, Dr. Lorraine E. Williams, and S. Wilmot for aid in various aspects of this research. This paper is dedicated to the late Lynn Ceci, whose suggestions regarding an earlier version are much appreciated. The ideas and interpretations presented are the responsibility of the author alone.

The Delaware Jargon

IVES GODDARD

When the Swedes arrived in New Sweden in 1638 they entered into dealings of various kinds with people now referred to in English as Delaware Indians. The Delaware, in this modern sense, lived throughout the Delaware River valley including its tributaries on both sides, in the lower Hudson River valley, and in the coastal area between. These Indians were not politically unified or culturally uniform, and in fact they spoke two sharply different though closely related languages. Since the eighteenth century linguists have called these two languages Munsee and Unami, using for each language the name applied to it by the speakers of the other language. Munsee was and is the more northerly of the two, once spoken in what is now the greater New York City area, in New Jersey north of the Raritan River, and in the Delaware Valley above the Delaware Water Gap. It continues to be spoken in the 1980s by a handful of Canadian Delawares. Unami, the more southerly language, was spoken in central and southern New Jersey and in the parts of Pennsylvania and Delaware opposite, from the Water Gap down. There was dialect diversity within each of these languages, and in particular there is good evidence for three distinct dialects of Unami, which can be referred to (in order from north to south) as Unalachtigo, Northern Unami, and Southern Unami.[1] Northern Unami was the dialect used by the Moravian missionaries in their extensive materials on the Delaware language, and Southern Unami is the variety spoken by the Delawares in the West, where a handful of speakers survive in Oklahoma. There is almost no data on the Unalachtigo dialect.

The Swedes, like other Europeans in America, made an effort to communicate with the Indians in the Indians' own language. The language they learned for dealing with the Indians was not, however, the local variety of Unami, but a pidgin form of Unami that scholars refer to as the Delaware Jargon. An examination and analysis of the Delaware Jargon materials illuminates life in New Sweden from a perhaps unexpected source. Pidgin languages are of intense interest to linguistic theoreticians for what they reveal about the nature of language, but this paper will, for the most part, ignore these aspects of the Delaware Jargon materials and

137

concentrate on historical, ethnographic, and antiquarian matters. First, however, some technical points regarding the term *pidgin* should be clarified. A pidgin is a greatly reduced form of a language, typically used between speakers of different languages who do not share a significant tradition of mutual bilingualism. The reduction is found in all areas of the language. Inflection is stripped away, the vocabulary is greatly diminished, and the pronunciation is simplified to eliminate sounds that are difficult for some users. Three stages of pidginization can be distinguished. Jargons (or trade jargons) have an extremely small vocabulary suitable for communicating about only a limited range of topics. Pidgins are jargons that have been fleshed out, by combining words into new expressions and by the wholesale importation of words from one or more of the languages of the users, to the extent that they can be used for communication on any topic. Creoles are pidgins that have become the native language of a speech community and have typically expanded the range of the grammatical and lexical concepts that they can express.[2]

There are a number of sources that document the use of the Delaware Jargon between Delawares and Europeans in the seventeenth century. The samples of Indian language given by William Penn in 1683[3] and Gabriel Thomas in 1698[4] are in fact jargon, as are most of the scattered Indian words that appear in early documents from New Netherland.[5] The most extensive attestations of the Delaware Jargon are a five-page English manuscript of 1684 or earlier called "The Indian Interpreter" (found among the early New Jersey land records in Trenton)[6] and the remarkable catechism and vocabulary compiled by the Swedish Lutheran minister Johannes Campanius (1601–83) during his service in New Sweden, 1642–48.[7] This catechism, which Campanius revised and completed back in Sweden, was published in 1696, after which it saw some, though apparently limited, use among the Indians for which it had been intended.[8]

This wide attestation of the Delaware Jargon reflects its widespread use among Europeans, and this in turn leads to the obvious explanation for why the Swedes adopted it. When the Swedes arrived the jargon was already firmly established as the medium of communication between the Indians and the Dutch throughout New Netherland. The Swedes most likely first learned the jargon from Dutchmen among them such as Andries Lucassen, who was the interpreter for Peter Minuit on the Swedish expedition of 1638.[9] In the same way, when the English arrived on the Delaware they would have learned the Delaware Jargon from Swedes like Lars Persson Cock, who was William Penn's interpreter.[10]

It is possible to say a certain amount about the likely origins of the Delaware Jargon among the Dutch. In this connection it is necessary first to determine which variety of Delaware was the basic source language for it. Somewhat unexpectedly, perhaps, it turns out that the Delaware Jar-

Table 1. The numbers from 'one' to 'ten'.

	Munsee Delaware	Unami Delaware	De Laet[12] (1633)	Campanius[13] (ca. 1645)	Interpreter[14] (1684?)	Thomas[15] (1698)
'one'	nkwǒtĭ	kwǒt·i	cotté	ciútte	Cutte	Kooty
'two'	nī·ša	nī·š·a	nyssé	nissa	Nisha	nisha
'three'	nxá	naxá	nacha	náha	Necca	nacha
'four'	né·wa	né·wa	wywe	næwo	Neuwa	neo
'five'	ná·lan	palé·naxk	parenagh	pareenach	Palenah	pelenach
'six'	nkwóta·š	kwót·a·š	cottash	ciuttas	Cuttas	Kootash
'seven'	nī·ša·š	nī·š·a·š	nyssas	nissas	Neshas	nishash
'eight'	(n)xá·š	xá·š	gechas	haas	Haas	choesh
'nine'	nó·li·	pé·škunk	pescon	paéschun	Pescunk	peskonk
'ten'	wī·mpat	télǝn	terren	thæræn	Tellen	telen

gon is based on Unami, the language of the middle and lower Delaware River, rather than on Munsee, the language of the Manhattan area. For example, three of the numbers from one to ten differ radically in the two Delaware languages ('five', 'nine', and 'ten'), and the Delaware Jargon has the Unami word in every case (see table 1).[11]

The presence of Unami features would be expected in the jargon attested in the four sources in table 1, since they are all from the Delaware River valley, where Unami was the local language. The crucial evidence that even the jargon used by the Dutch in New Netherland was based on Unami is among the few samples of Delaware Jargon that can be specifically localized to Manhattan and the Hudson River valley. For example, Isaack De Rasieres recalled an expression ⟨collatismarrenitten⟩ that evidently meant something like 'to observe the taboos imposed on a young girl between first menstruation and marriage'.[16] This expression is made up of two words, ⟨collatis⟩ (which bears the core meaning) and ⟨marrenitten⟩, the Delaware Jargon word for 'make' or 'do', which forms numerous phrases of this type; ⟨marrenitten⟩ is based on Unami *malǝni·to·-, the distinctive Unami verb 'to make', not found in Munsee.[17] Another such expression is ⟨rancontyn marinit⟩ (also spelled ⟨rancontyn marenit⟩), meaning 'to make peace', which David De Vries recalled as having been used by Indians both near Lewes, Delaware, in 1632 and near Rockaway, Long Island, in 1643.[18] Since De Rasieres makes it clear that while

on Manhattan he talked to local Indians but not to their enemies from the
Delaware River, his use of a Delaware Jargon expression containing a
Unami word shows that the language used between the Dutch and Indians in New Amsterdam was a jargon based not on the local language but
on Unami. Another jargon word that is distinctively Unami is ⟨cacheus⟩
'crazy, drunk', used by an Esopus sachem on the Hudson River in
1658;[19] ⟨cacheus⟩[20] is based on a form of Unami *kí·wsu* 'he is drunk',
which is entirely distinct from the Munsee equivalent *waní·sə̆məw*. Also,
there are many placenames in New Netherland that end with the distinctively Unami element ⟨hacky⟩ (or ⟨hackingh⟩) 'land';[21] these can be
understood as names that the Dutch learned through the medium of the
Delaware Jargon or, perhaps, reshaped or coined themselves in jargon
form. For example, ⟨Sewanhacky⟩ (or ⟨Sewanhacking⟩), a name used for
Long Island, is obviously a jargon expression for 'wampum land'.[22] In
this connection it is significant that the first mention of Hoboken, in
1630, refers to it as "the land by us called *Hobocan Hackingh*."[23] The
phrase ⟨Hobocan Hackingh⟩ appears to mean 'pipe place', though there
is no contemporary confirmation of this. Such a metaphorical description
of shape seems conceptually European, and although both words are distinctively Unami, the placename as it stands can only be Delaware Jargon.[24] It has the pattern of simple juxtaposition found in jargon colloca-
tions but lacks the modifications in shape required by Unami grammar,
when two nouns are put together into a single compound.

One aspect of the Delaware Jargon that directly reflects the way Delaware was adapted by Europeans is its phonology. For example, the Delaware sounds *š* (English *sh*) and *č* (English *ch*) gave Dutch and Swedish
speakers difficulty, apparently because they did not exist in the Dutch
and Swedish of the time.[25] In Campanius's recordings of Delaware Jargon there are renderings of Delaware *č* as ⟨s⟩ as well as ⟨tz⟩, ⟨si⟩, and ⟨ssi⟩,
and renderings of *š* as ⟨s⟩ and ⟨tz⟩ as well as ⟨si⟩ (see table 2).

The fact that some of these same substitutions are found in the Delaware Jargon as recorded by English speakers shows that the English
learned the jargon from the other Europeans, or from Indians who imi-
tated their imperfect pronunciation (see table 3). The English sources
also have words in which these sounds are present, indicating the reintroduction of the correct Delaware pronunciation from Delaware, or from
the jargon as pronounced by Delawares (see table 1 and table 4).

The grammatical simplification in the Delaware Jargon is readily seen
in the reduction of the categories of gender and number. Delaware has a
sharp distinction between animate and inanimate genders that affects the
form both of nouns and of the verbs that agree with them; seventeenth-
century Dutch, Swedish, and English had, to varying degrees, a distinct
neuter gender comparable in many ways to the Delaware inanimate. All

Table 2. Swedish renderings of Unami š̠ and č̠.

	Unami	Campanius[26]
'more'	č̠í·č̠	sijs (142)
'child'	nni·č̠·á·nəs[27]	nissiaanus (140)
'cold'	ntákɔhč̠i[28]	dakótze (137)
'but'	š̠úkw	suck (3)
'sun'	kí·š̠·o·x	chíssogh (136, 137)
'eel'	š̠ɔ́·x·ame·kw	tzáckamææs (146)[29]
'needle'	é·š̠ka·ns, é·š̠ka·nš	étzkans (142)
'shoot'	nəməš̠·ó·t·amən[30]	mosiuttamen (5-6)

Table 3. Reflections of Swedish pronunciations in English recordings.

	Unami	Campanius	Interpreter
'turkey'	č̠í·k·ənəm	síckenem (147)	sickenom
'shoes'	č̠ípahkɔ	síppack (140)	seppock
'hate'	nš̠inká·t·amən[31]	sinkáttan (8)	sinkoatum[32]
'fear'	nəwi·š̠·á·s·i[33]	hwisásse (23)	hwissase[34]

Table 4. Reintroduction of Unami pronunciations in English recordings.

	Unami	Campanius	Interpreter
'when'	č̠ínke	singa (4)	singa, chingo
'hog'	kwɔ́š̠kwəš̠	kѡskѡs (145)	kush-kush

of these languages made a sharp differentiation between singular and plural nouns. The jargon, however, makes no distinctions of gender or number (except for a possible contrast between the first-person pronouns 'I' and 'we' in "The Indian Interpreter"). As a result Campanius uses the pronoun ⟨jȭni⟩ (from Unami *yó·ni* 'this [inanimate singular]') for 'this' and 'these' of either Delaware gender, referring to people as well as things, and he uses ⟨kéko⟩ (Unami *kéku* 'something') for both 'someone' and 'something' (e.g. ⟨jȭni⟩ 'they [people]', 'these [command-ments]'; ⟨jȭni chéko⟩ 'those [people] who'; ⟨bakanta chéko⟩ 'hit some-one').[35] Delaware verb stems have two variants, each specialized for objects of one gender, or for subjects of one gender if intransitive, but the corresponding Delaware Jargon words have only a single form. As a result the jargon word ⟨orit⟩ 'good' (from an inanimate verb *wəlát* 'it is good') is used with animates (e.g. ⟨orit nietap⟩ 'good friend',[36] and jargon ⟨Makerick⟩ 'big' (from an animate participle *me·xkí·lək* 'he who is big') is used with inanimates (e.g. ⟨Makerick Kitton⟩ 'Delaware River', lit. 'big river';[37] ⟨mochijrick scháckhan⟩ 'hurricane', lit. 'big wind'[38]).

The early history of New Netherland provides an explanation for why the jargon the Dutch used was based on the language of the Delaware River. The first permanent Dutch settlements in the territory of any of the Delaware groups were on the Delaware, on Burlington Island (at Burlington, New Jersey) and at Fort Nassau (on the site of Gloucester). The first settlers arrived there in 1624, and they were all removed to Manhattan between November 1626 and October 1628.[39] When Johannes De Laet brought out the Latin edition of his book *The New World* in 1633, he added a section on the Indians of New Netherland that had not been present in the Dutch edition of 1630.[40] In this new section is the vocabulary that he specifically states to be from the Sankhikan Indians living on the upper Delaware River (that is, the falls area). Most of the words De Laet gives could be either true Unami or Delaware Jargon, but there is a complete lack of plural endings where the glosses call for them, which is a jargon feature. Distinctively jargon is the form of the word ⟨Renoes⟩ 'man'[41] and the pidgin phrase ⟨synquoy Mackyrggh⟩ '(mountain) lion', lit. 'big wildcat'.[42] Furthermore, the transcription shows the same phonetic simplifications found in the jargon versions of the Unami words. A Dutch settler from the Delaware must have been the ultimate source of De Laet's vocabulary, and it must have been settlers and traders who had been dealing with Delaware River Indians who introduced the Delaware Jargon to New Amsterdam.

It has been claimed on typological and theoretical linguistic grounds that the Delaware Jargon was in existence before European contact, having been originally used between Delawares and Iroquoians.[43] No historical evidence has been uncovered that would support this hypothesis, and in fact there is direct evidence that in the historical period neither the Mohawk nor the Susquehannock used the Delaware Jargon. Megapolensis emphasizes how difficult it was to communicate with the Mohawks, who had an entirely different language from the Mahicans;[44] Samuel Edsall, who must have been a speaker of Delaware Jargon to have served as an interpreter for Indians of Westchester County, western Long Island, and the Delaware River, could not understand the Susquehannocks.[45]

It is clear, in any case, that when the Swedes arrived in America they found the Delaware Jargon already in use by the Dutch and adopted it in their dealings with Indians. The nature of these dealings can be glimpsed from the vocabulary that Campanius compiled. The topics it covers include the environment, weather, and time; types of people and parts of the body; clothing and household goods; common activities and objects; animals, birds, and fishes; trees, fruit, and other types of vegetable food; and conversational phrases. Expressions appropriate for trading activities are found throughout. .

In several places it is clear that Campanius is not merely giving the jargon equivalents of Swedish words, but is giving Delaware Jargon expressions that he knew and explaining them in Swedish. For example, he gives us two expressions that mean 'I give this to you'. One is ⟨nijr pææt chijre jõni rankunti⟩, which word-for-word is something like 'I bring you this friendly', and the other is ⟨níjr pææt jõni nutskω⟩, word-for-word 'I bring this for nothing'.[46] Campanius explains that the first indicates that the recipient is expected to give something in return, while the second indicates that no reciprocal gift is expected. These two culturally distinct types of giving would obviously have been very important for the Swedes to keep straight. Typically for a jargon, the notion of giving has been decomposed into a base verb and a modifier; the base verb ⟨pææt⟩ is from the Delaware verb meaning 'to bring',[47] used in the jargon in a general sense to include all types of conveyance, and the modifying elements, one from a Delaware verb and the other from an adverbial particle, provide the further specification. The modifying element in the first expression, ⟨rankunti⟩, here glossed 'friendly', is the same word that is used with the verb 'to make' in the expression for 'to make peace'.[48] This pattern by which distinct expressions are built up out of simpler elements is highly characteristic of the way in which pidgins build up a full vocabulary from a reduced number of basic words. It also indicates that the pidgin was not simply broken Delaware cobbled together on the spur of the moment by imperfect speakers, but was in its own way an established conventional system of communication.

Campanius attests a number of other jargon verbs that consist of ⟨maranijto⟩ 'to make' plus another word. These include the expressions for 'to do wrong to' (⟨maranijto manúnckus⟩ literally 'do angry'), 'to sin'

(⟨mataétt maranijto⟩ 'do bad'), and 'to worship' or 'to pray' (⟨maranijto chíntika⟩ 'do holy'). In the expression for 'to worship' the word for 'holy' or 'prayer' is ⟨chíntika⟩. The combination of ⟨chíntika⟩ with ⟨manetto⟩ 'god, spirit' makes ⟨chintika manetto⟩ 'Holy Spirit'; ⟨chíntika⟩ plus ⟨saccheeman⟩ 'chief' gives ⟨chíntika saccheeman⟩ 'priest'; ⟨chíntika⟩ plus ⟨mamaræckhíckan⟩ 'book' gives ⟨chíntika mamaræckhíckan⟩ 'holy scriptures'. In origin the jargon word ⟨chíntika⟩ is from the Delaware word 'to dance'[49] and was applied to the religious dances of the Delawares. The building up of compound expressions like these is typical of how pidgins work, and these examples seem consistent with the grammar and style of the Delaware Jargon even if they evoke new concepts.

Some Delaware Jargon words have variants that might appear to attest different inflectional forms, but it is much more likely that such variants reflect the adoption of more than one inflectional or derivational form of the original Delaware words as separate invariant jargon words, as, for example, from the Unami verb $mi\cdot l$- 'to give to' the jargon has ⟨mijre⟩, ⟨kommijre⟩, ⟨mijrikon⟩, and ⟨skomerijne⟩.[50] All of these are used to mean 'to give in return' but they are frozen expressions not used in accordance with their original Delaware grammar. The phrase ⟨chéko nijr mijre⟩ 'what shall I give you in return', lit. 'what I give-in-return', has a form, ⟨mijre⟩, which probably reflects Unami $kəmí\cdot li$ 'you give to me'; ⟨chæǽk skomerijne⟩ 'I'll give you money (in payment)' consists of the word for 'wampum' or 'money' and a word ⟨skomerijne⟩ that probably reflects Unami Delaware $=\check{c}\ kəmí\cdot li\cdot n$[51] 'you will give it to me'. In both cases inflected Unami forms meaning 'you give to me' are used in the jargon in expressions that mean 'I give to you'. It is easy to understand how Delaware words learned in a trading context could have been generalized in this way, and as a consequence these words have become frozen as separate, specialized expressions. The pidgin speakers were not using the incorporated Delaware inflections as part of a productive grammar. Beside these simplified features, which are to be expected in a jargon, some aspects of Campanius's use of the jargon to attempt to explain Christian doctrine seem strained and artificial. The word order of complex sentences tends to conform to the word order of Swedish, and the occasional use of the possessive (or genitive-case) ending -s, following the model of Swedish, seems completely artificial.[52]

The fact that the Indian language that the Europeans learned was actually a pidgin form of the local speech provides an explanation for William Penn's description of the Indians' language as "in Signification full, like Short-hand in writing; one word serveth in the place of three, and the rest are supplied by the Understanding of the Hearer: Imperfect in their Tenses, wanting in their Moods, Participles, Adverbs, Conjunctions, Interjections."[53] Penn is obviously describing the Delaware Jargon, and like many Europeans he remained ignorant of the fact that there was also a real, full, and complex Indian language vastly different from the broken version of it that the Indians used with him, which he says he had learned to understand. One European who did remark on this fact was Jonas Michaëlius, who in 1628 clearly and somewhat acerbically described the language used between the Dutch and the Indians as a "made-up, childish language," greatly simplified from what the Indians spoke among themselves.[54]

The Delaware Jargon appears to have remained in use for some time. As late as 1785 the Delaware vocabulary recorded by Major Ebenezer Denny at Fort McIntosh in western Pennsylvania shows a number of Delaware Jargon features.[55] For example, in ⟨keigh willet lenew⟩ 'you [are] good men', lit. 'you good man', there is no plural indicated for the pronoun or noun, and ⟨willet⟩ 'good' continues the seventeenth-century jargon ⟨orit⟩, with the same generalization of an inanimate Delaware verb for use also with animates. Many new words and improved pronunciations had by this time been introduced or reintroduced from Unami proper, and Thomason concludes that "Denny's list does not represent the same language" as the Delaware Jargon.[56] More likely, however, Denny's vocabulary simply attests the well-recognized process of vocabulary replacement in pidgins called relexification.[57]

Eventually the Delaware Jargon was displaced by Indian Pidgin English and English, but in its time it was a remarkable example of a colonial-era pidgin based on a local native language rather than on the language of the Europeans.

NOTES

1. For example, Zeisberger attests three dialect variants of the Unami word for 'wolf': ⟨tumme⟩, ⟨tímmeu⟩, and ⟨mĕtümmeu⟩ (David Zeisberger, Zeisberger's Indian Dictionary, ed. Eben Norton Horsford [Cambridge, Mass.: John Wilson and Son, University Press, 1887], 234). The first of these is the Southern Unami form, attested in Oklahoma Delaware as *tə́me*. The third variant is presumably the Unalachtigo form; in phonemic transcription it would be *mətə́me·w*. It is also found in the vocabulary published by De Laet, where it appears as ⟨metumnu⟩ (Joannis De Laet, *Novus orbis seu descriptionis Indiae occidentalis. Libri XVIII* [Leiden: Elzevier, 1633], 75; there are some copying errors in the translation: "From the 'New World,' by Johan de Laet, 1625, 1630, 1633, 1640," in *Narratives of New Netherland, 1609–1664*, ed. J. Franklin Jameson [New York: Charles Scribner's Sons, 1909], 27–60); the final ⟨-nu⟩ is a copying error. De Laet's vocabulary was obtained from settlers who had learned the words among the Sankhikan band, who lived at the Falls of the Delaware (near Trenton), the same area from which the historically known Unalachtigo individuals came (William A. Hunter, "A Note on the Unalachtigo," in *A Delaware Indian*

Symposium, ed. Herbert C. Kraft, Anthropological Series no. 4 [Harrisburg: Pennsylvania Historical and Museum Commission, 1974], 147–52, esp. 150–51; William A. Hunter, "Documented Subdivisions of the Delaware Indians," *Bulletin of the Archaeological Society of New Jersey* 35 [1978]: 20–40, esp. 36–37). Zeisberger's second variant (phonemically *tə́me·w*) is clearly from a dialect intermediate between the other two, which would be Northern Unami.

2. Note, however, that the Delaware Jargon, despite its name, is in fact technically a pidgin rather than a jargon as here defined. In this it is like Chinook Jargon, the much better-known pidgin of the northern Pacific Coast.

3. *William Penn His Own Account of the Lenni Lenape or Delaware Indians, 1683,* ed. Albert Cook Myers (Moylan, Penn.: privately printed, 1937), 26–28.

4. Gabriel Thomas, *An Historical and Geographical Account of the Province and Country of Pensylvania; and of West-New-Jersey in America* (1698; facsimile reprint, New York: For Henry Austin Brady by Francis Michelin, 1848).

5. Ives Goddard, "The Ethnohistorical Implications of Early Delaware Linguistic Materials," *Man in the Northeast* 1 (1971): 14–26.

6. "The Indian Interpreter," Salem Surveys 2:64–68, New Jersey State Archives, Trenton; I am indebted to Lorraine Williams for a facsimile of the manuscript. There are copying errors in the editions: William Nelson, *The Indians of New Jersey* (Paterson, N.J.: The Press, 1894), 133–39; J. Dyneley Prince, "An Ancient New Jersey Indian Jargon," *American Anthropologist,* n.s. 14 (1912): 508–24.

7. [Johannes Campanius], *Lutheri Catechismus Öfwersatt på American-Virginiske Språket* (1696; facsimile reprint, *Martin Luther's Little Catechism Translated into Algonquian Indian by Johannes Campanius,* with notes by Isak Collijn, New Sweden Tercentenary Publications [Stockholm: Ivar Haeggström and Uppsala: Almqvist & Wiksell, 1937]); an English translation of the Swedish sections is furnished by Joh. Campanius, *Luther's Catechism Translated into the American-Virginian Language,* trans. Daniel Nystrom and E. W. Olson (New York: Swedish American Tercentenary Association, 1938).

8. Collijn, *Martin Luther's Little Catechism,* 16–17.

9. "Affidavit of Four Men from the *Key of Kalmar,* 1638," in Albert Cook Myers, ed., *Narratives of Early Pennsylvania, West New Jersey, and Delaware, 1630–1707* (New York: Charles Scribner's Sons, 1912), 86, 88; C. A. Weslager, in collaboration with A. R. Dunlap, *Dutch Explorers, Traders and Settlers in the Delaware Valley, 1609–1664* (Philadelphia: University of Pennsylvania Press, 1961), 151, 181; Collijn, *Martin Luther's Little Catechism,* 9.

10. Myers, ed., *William Penn,* 82.

11. The phonemic transcription of Munsee and Unami, which is indicated by the use of italics, basically uses consonants in their English values and vowels in their continental values. The values of other symbols are: ə (shwa) = the reduced vowel of English *c'mon*; ɔ (open *o*) = English *aw*; č (*c* hachek) = English *ch*; š (*s* hachek) = English *sh*; *x* = German *ch* in *ach*; (raised dot) = long vowel (like Latin *ā*) or long consonant (like Italian *tt*). Phonemic Delaware forms are from my field notes (1965–70). Delaware words cited in the original spelling of other sources are given in roman and, except in the tables, are set off by pointed brackets.

The Dutch spelling of the Delaware Jargon uses ⟨ch⟩, ⟨g⟩, and ⟨gh⟩ to write
x, but all these spellings are also used for *k*; the De Laet vocabulary also
attests ⟨ck⟩ for Delaware *x* and *xk*, ⟨chk⟩ for *xk* and *k·*, ⟨gech⟩ for *x* ('eight'
in table 1), ⟨r⟩ for *x*, ⟨ch⟩ for *š*, and ⟨ch⟩ for *č*. The ⟨sh⟩ in the word for 'six'
(table 1) has no significance as a combination in Dutch, but perhaps the
writer intended the English value. In the Swedish spelling ⟨c⟩ and ⟨ch⟩ represent *k*; *x* is written ⟨h⟩ or like *k*. Gabriel Thomas's use of ⟨ch⟩ for *x* may
reflect a knowledge of Welsh, German, or Dutch. Other aspects of the
transcriptions are discussed in the text.

The phoneme that is *l* in modern Delaware was generally recorded as ⟨r⟩
in the earliest seventeenth-century sources, with a gradual shift to ⟨l⟩ in later
sources; apparently there was a shift in pronunciation during this period.

12. De Laet, *Novus Orbis*, 75.
13. Campanius, *Lutheri Catechismus*, 154.
14. "The Indian Interpreter."
15. Thomas, *An Historical and Geographical Account*, [part 2], 12.
16. "Letter of Isaack de Rasieves to Samuel Blommaert, 1628 (?)," in *Narra-
    tives*, ed. Jameson, 107; "From the 'Korte Historiael eude Journaels Aen-
    teyckeninge,' by David Pietersz De Vries 1633–1643 (1655)," in *Narratives*,
    ed. Jameson, 218; Charles Wolley, *A Two Year's Journal in New York and
    Part of Its Territories in America*, ed. Edward Gaylord Bourne (1701; re-
    print, Cleveland: Burrows Brothers, 1902), 59–60.
17. In modern Unami this verb is *manni·to··*, with assimilation of *l(ə)n* to *nn*,
    but the earlier shape is attested by Zeisberger as ⟨mallenito⟩ (Zeisberger,
    Indian Dictionary, 119).
18. "Korte Historiael eude Journaels Aenteyckeninge," in *Narratives*, ed.
    Myers, 16, and *Narratives*, ed. Jameson, 230. De Vries's ⟨rancontyn⟩ corre-
    sponds to Unami *wəlankɔ́nti·n* 'peace is made, or exists (between two
    sides)'. A text about the first meeting of the Delawares with Europeans re-
    corded in the 1960s uses a fully inflected Unami equivalent of this Delaware
    Jargon expression: *kəmanni·tó·ne·n = č ktə́li- = č -ɔ·wəlankuntí·ne·n* 'we and
    you will make a lasting peace together'. (Enclitics are preceded by = [here
    in = *č*, the future enclitic], and discontinuous pieces of compound verb
    stems are indicated by hyphens; *k(t)–ne·n* is an inflection for first person
    plural inclusive ['we' including 'you']; the reduplication on the second verb
    [ɔ·-, representing |wa·-|] gives the notion of continuity here translated
    'lasting'; *ə́li* marks the second verb as the complement of the first.)
19. E. B. O'Callaghan and B. Fernow, eds., *Documents Relative to the Colonial
    History of the State of New York* (hereafter *NYCD*), 15 vols. (Albany,
    1853–87), 13:84.
20. Cf. ⟨cakeus⟩ 'drunk' in "The Indian Interpreter."
21. In these names ⟨hacky⟩ reflects Unami *hák·i* 'land' and ⟨hackingh⟩ reflects
    the corresponding locative form, Unami *hák·ink* 'in, at, on the land'; cf.
    Munsee *áhkəy* and *áhki·nk*, respectively.
22. William Wallace Tooker, *The Indian Place-Names on Long Island and Is-
    lands Adjacent, with Their Probable Significations*, ed. Alexander F. Cham-
    berlain (New York: G. P. Putnam's Sons, 1911), 232.
23. *NYCD* 13:1.
24. Unami *hupɔ́·k·an* 'pipe' (contrast Munsee *mătásən*); the spelling Hoboken
    conforms to that of a town in Belgium.
25. The pronunciation [š] of Swedish ⟨sj⟩ is supposed to have been already es-
    tablished by the seventeenth century, and the equivalent spelling (at that

time ⟨si⟩) was occasionally used by Campanius where Delaware has š. The pronunciations of ⟨sj⟩ in modern Swedish cover a considerable range, however, and Campanius's inconsistency in spelling this sound suggests that there were phonetic differences between the Swedish and Delaware sounds that caused him to fail to make this identification in most cases. (I am grateful to Börje Westlund and Einar Haugen for help with the Swedish facts.)

26. The numbers refer to the pages in Campanius, *Lutheri Catechismus*.

27. Diminutive of *nní·č·a·n* 'my child' (now especially 'my daughter').

28. 'I am cold'; cf. *tahkɔ́č·u* 'he is cold'.

29. The latter part has apparently been influenced by ⟨lamaéæs⟩ 'fish'.

30. 'I shoot it'.

31. 'I do not like it'.

32. 'I do not care, I will cast it away' (i.e., 'I do not care to, I dislike it'); the intransitive meaning is not idiomatic in modern Unami but is attested by ⟨schingattam⟩ 'to be unwilling, to dislike, to disapprove' (i.e., 'he is unwilling', etc.; Daniel G. Brinton and Albert S. Anthony, eds., *A Lenâpé-English Dictionary*, Pennsylvania Students' Series (Philadelphia: Historical Society of Pennsylvania, 1889), 1:129).

33. 'I am afraid'; cf. *wi·š·á·s·u* 'he is afraid'.

34. One of several words in "The Indian Interpreter" that suggest that its compiler had access to a written Swedish source that used spellings like those in Campanius's vocabulary (⟨hw⟩ is a Swedish spelling combination rather than an English one; the ⟨h⟩ is silent). Internal inconsistencies and variation in "The Indian Interpreter" and what appear to be copying errors further suggest that it was compiled from more than one source, at least some of them written, by someone with a poor command of the jargon. These aspects of "The Indian Interpreter" clearly have implications for its dating and origins.

35. Campanius, *Lutheri Catechismus*, 21, 153. Campanius's use of ⟨kéko⟩ (variant ⟨chéko⟩) as a relative pronoun 'who' and 'what' may be a calque of the Swedish relative pronoun *som*, as such pronouns are not an Algonquian feature.

36. *Collections of the New-York Historical Society for the year 1913*, John Watts de Peyster Publication Fund Series, no. 54 (New York: The Society), 125.

37. In a 1682 deed to William Penn in Myers, ed., *William Penn*, 77.

38. Campanius, *Lutheri Catechismus*, 136.

39. Jameson, ed., *Narratives*, 84, 88; some information on this move from 1626 is dated 1628 by Weslager and Dunlap, *Dutch Explorers*, 75.

40. Jameson, ed., *Narratives*, 57–60.

41. Cf. ⟨rheenus⟩, ⟨rhénus⟩ (Campanius, *Lutheri Catechismus*, 12, 19); ⟨renus⟩ ("Indian Interpreter"); contrast Unami *lə́nu* 'man'.

42. Cf. ⟨manúnckus mochijrick síngwəs⟩ '(mountain) lion', lit. 'angry bigcat' (Campanius, *Lutheri Catechismus*, 145).

43. Sarah Grey Thomason, "On Interpreting 'The Indian Interpreter,'" *Language in Society* 9 (1980): 182–86.

44. Johannes Megapolensis, Jr., "A Short Account of the Mohawk Indians,..." in *Narratives*, ed. Jameson, 172.

45. *NYCD* 12:523, 541; 13:494–95, 497; 14:704. Thomason discusses the fact that there is no evidence that the Delaware Jargon was used by any Indians other than Delawares, and hence no evidence that would directly sup-

port the possibility of pre-European use. Her hypothesis rests on theoretical arguments and typological parallels that suggest, for example, that a pidgin arising between Europeans and Indians would be based on the language of the Europeans. A discussion of these technical arguments would be out of place here, but given the tiny population of the first Dutch settlers and traders, especially on the Delaware River, accommodation to the Indians would not be surprising.

46. Campanius, *Lutheri Catechismus*, 153.
47. Unami *mpé·t·o·n* 'I bring it'.
48. See n. 18.
49. Unami *kə́ntke·w* 'he dances', *kə́ntka·n* 'there is a dance'.
50. Campanius, *Lutheri Catechismus*, 151–52.
51. Since the future enclitic $=č$ must follow another word, this sequence must have been extracted from a longer expression.
52. E.g., ⟨machaeaerick, mâchijrick saccheemans⟩ 'of the very great Lord', translating Swedish *then mächta stora HERrans* (Campanius, *Lutheri Catechismus*, 1).
53. Myers, ed., *William Penn*, 26.
54. "Letter of Reverend Jonas Michaëlius, 1628," in *Narratives*, ed., Jameson, 128.
55. "A Military Journal Kept by Major Ebenezer Denny," Memoirs of the Historical Society of Pennsylvania, vol. 7 (Philadelphia: The Society, 1860): 478–81.
56. Thomason, "On Interpreting," 189.
57. Ibid., 184.

Some Comments on Early Swedish Collections from the Northeast

STAFFAN BRUNIUS

Seventeenth-century Swedish narratives, reports, and letters that contain information about native Americans living in the area of the New Sweden colony (meaning the Delaware or Lenape, whom the Swedes called the "Renappi" or "River Indians," and to a lesser extent the more distant Susquehannock or "vita minkesser," the White Minquas), have been especially important in the study of the period of early contact between Indians and Europeans.[1] The information provided by Governors Johan Printz and Johan Rising has been helpful, but the observations of Peter Lindeström and Johan Campanius (Holm) have been the most useful for research about the Indian peoples who were in contact with the Swedish colonists.

Peter Lindeström's witty and informative, albeit biased, narrative is based on his visit to the colony from 1654 to 1655. It provides one of the very earliest accounts of the Lenape and is the first Swedish attempt to compile an ethnography of a Native American people.[2]

The minister Johan Campanius, who served with dedication in the colony between 1642 and 1648, translated Luther's catechism into a Lenape language.[3] During his time in the colony he compiled notes about Indian culture that were later used, together with other sources (such as Lindeström and Louis Hennepin), by his grandson, Thomas Campanius Holm, who in 1702 produced what I believe to be the first book about America written and printed in Swedish.[4] Even after the colony ceased to be under Swedish control, a substantial number of Swedish ministers served in the Swedish-speaking communities of Delaware, New Jersey, and Pennsylvania. Some of these men also gathered important information about relations between Indians and Europeans.[5] This ecclesiastical activity was to a great extent the result of the Swedish Bishop Jesper Swedberg's dedication to the Swedes living in the area of the former colony. Swedberg himself wrote a history of North America that focused on New Sweden and compiled other material about the New World.[6] Continued Swedish interest in the former colony is further indicated by Tobias Björck's 1731 disseration about Swedish churches in America. It also contains some information about the Lenape religion.[7]

The gradual European conquest and colonization of the New World contributed to the growing interest in Europe, especially among the ruling families and the nobility, in collecting and exchanging rare objects as personal and diplomatic gifts. These included "artificial curiosities" such as ethnographic objects. These collections of natural and artificial curiosities, known in Germany as *Kunst-und-Wunderkammern* were displayed in specially made cabinets or in particular rooms. Their owners meant them to be admired; they also served over time to inspire new questions about other cultures.[8]

The *Kunst-und-Wunderkammern* founded by Denmark's King Frederik III in Copenhagen and by Duke Friedrich III of Holstein-Gottorp in the mid-1600s (more or less contemporaneously with New Sweden) are just two examples of a phenomenon that was going on all over Europe. King Frederik III's *Kunstkammer* was very well managed. The collection was inventoried and similar objects (art, weapons, naturalia, and so forth) were displayed together. Also, as a result of the political development between Holstein-Gottorp and Denmark (Denmark's defeat of the duchy during the Great Northern War, 1700 to 1721), Duke Friedrich III's *Kunstkammer* was eventually transferred to Copenhagen,[9] which indicates the significance and value that was ascribed to the collections of natural and "artificial" rarities.

During the wars of the 1600s libraries and collections of art and scientific and cultural objects were often plundered.[10] In the turmoil of the seventeenth century, the Swedes too accumulated wealth in this way.[11] As elsewhere in Europe, the Swedes' interest in collections of natural and "artificial curiosities" in time reached social groups below the upper echelon of society. During the eighteenth century the collections were still of a quite unsystematic character, even though the collectors tended to prefer natural objects.[12]

The keen interest in empirical knowledge about nature and what could be of utility for humans, which we think of as typical of the eighteenth century, was already present in the Swedish government's instructions for Johan Printz. But in spite of this increasing interest in "artificial curiosities" it was still too early for a systematic and documented gathering of ethnographic collections. A more profound interest in these artifacts can be detected among several disciples of Carl von Linné who did fieldwork in the natural sciences during the eighteenth century. One such man was Anders Sparrman (1748–1820), who accompanied James Cook on his second voyage to explore the South Pacific and collected ethnographica, which he transferred to the Swedish Royal Academy of Sciences (founded in 1739). Sparrman was in charge of the Academy's cabinet of naturalia, which included ethnographic collections. Unfortunately early records of the collections are meager, perhaps because the scientific approach to studying ethnographic collections began much later. Hjalmar Stolpe (1841–1905), archaeologist and ethnographer, arranged a major ethnographic exhibition in Stockholm in 1878–79. In preparing his exhibition Stolpe was influenced by museological developments in Denmark, where an ethnographic department had been founded at the National Museum as early as 1841. In 1900 Stolpe was appointed director of the ethnographic section of the Museum of Natural History in Stockholm.[13]

Considering such factors as Lindström's ambition to describe Native American cultures, the trading contacts the colonists established with the Lenape and the Susquehannock, and the growing interest in *Kunst-und-Wunderkammern* during the 1600s, it is not too surprising that early ethnographic collections from northeastern America existed in Sweden. The collections I am referring to are at Skokloster Castle, some fifty kilometers north of Stockholm, and at the Folkens Museum, the National Museum of Ethnography in Stockholm.

The collection at Skokloster is located in Count Carl Gustaf Wrangel's (1613–76) armory, which resembles a *Kunst-und-Wunderkammer*.[14] It consists of eight artifacts. There are twined tumplines, slings formed by a strap slung over the forehead or chest and used to carry or to help support a pack on the back or to haul loads (perhaps also used to tie prisoners, as was done in the late eighteenth century),[15] and two ball-headed clubs. Furthermore, there are four red-dyed objects: a leather cord with pendants, a buckskin skull cap, an artificial wolf's head, and a more realistic wolf's head, "objects which are completely without known ethnological, archaeological, or historical parallels," according to Richard Manville and William Sturtevant.[16] Other researchers have suggested that these four red-dyed objects are the elements of a headdress.[17] Another interpretation is that the whole collection was once the personal property of two men, each one having a magical or ritual wolf bundle, headdress, tumpline, and club.[18]

Skokloster also houses an armory of the Brahe family that dates from 1702. Per Brahe the younger was a signer of Printz's instructions (1642), as was Herman Wrangel, Carl Gustaf Wrangel's father. One cannot exclude the possibility that Skokloster's Indian objects were once parts of the Brahe armory. However, given the symbolic value Swedish noble families attached to keeping their armories intact and the lack of documentation, it is safe to assume that this collection of Indian materials has maintained its original place in the Wrangel armory ever since it came to the castle.[19]

Traditionlly the collection has been considered a gift from Johan Printz to Carl Gustaf Wrangel.[20] However, no documents have been found to support this contention. It is even uncertain if Wrangel was the first

Fig. 1. Ball-headed club 6904. North American Indian collection at Skokloster Slott, 1661. Photo: Samuel Uhrdin.

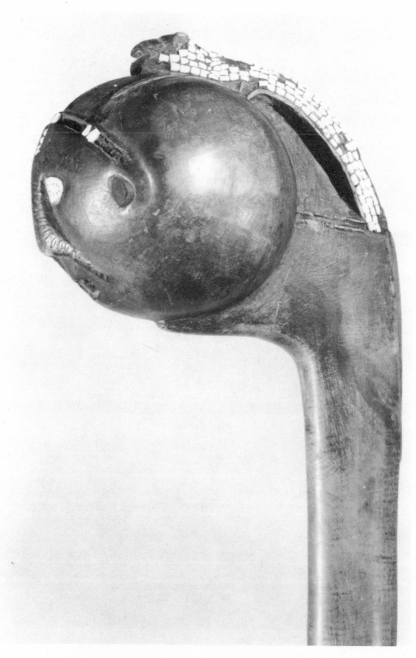

Fig. 2. Side view of club 6904. Photo: Samuel Uhrdin.

Fig. 3. Full view of 6904. Club is 64 cm long. Photo: Samuel Uhrdin.

Swedish owner of the objects. Even though one cannot rule out the possibility that the objects came from New Sweden, Wrangel may have bought them in Holland.[21] If this was the case, the objects may originally have come from New Netherland.

The collection at the Folkens Museum, which originally came from Livrustkammaren, the Royal Armory, in Stockholm, consists of a tomahawk/pickax and an exquisitely carved anthropomorphic ball-headed club that is practically identical to one of the ball-headed clubs at Skokloster. Of all the objects in these collections, these two clubs and the tomahawk/pickax have received particular attention.[22]

The origin of the tomahawk/pickax has variously been assigned to New Sweden, Delaware, New Netherland, or to the Iroquois.[23] Its haft has remnants of wampum, shell, and European glass or ceramic beads. A thong fastened through a hole on the lower part of the haft ends with a tassel of red-dyed deer hair. On top of the haft is an iron blade secured with leather thongs. If indeed this is the original and indigenous construction, it appears as an interesting adaptation of European material to a

Fig. 4. Ball-headed club, Livrustkammaren 1010, Folkens Museum Etnografiska/
The National Museum of Ethnography, Stockholm. Length 65 cm. Photo: Adolf
Hofer.

traditional type of haft. The shape of the postcontact blade is reminiscent
of the stone celts known from archaeological contexts.[24] This type of haft
with wampum decoration may be similar to what Robert Beverly referred
to in the beginning of the eighteenth century when he mentioned the
presence of tomahawks adorned with wampum in the region of Virginia.[25]

Curiously enough, there is a similar specimen at Etnografisk Samling
(the ethnographical museum) in Copenhagen. This specimen is somewhat bigger and has a heavier haft with some geometrical carvings and
more intact wampum decoration. More important, the blade is a finely
polished greenish stone celt with a small face on the upper terminal

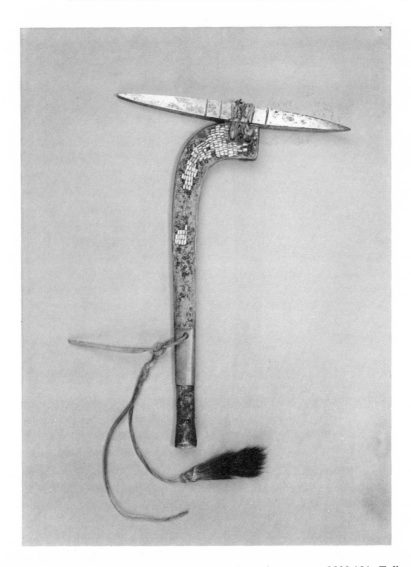

Fig. 5. Tomahawk/pickax with iron blade, Livrustkammaren 3932.131, Folkens Museum Etnografiska/The National Museum of Ethnography, Stockholm. Length of haft 44.5 cm, length of blade 33 cm. Photo: Adolf Hofer.

edge that is lacking on the Stockholm specimen.[26] Perhaps the Stockholm specimen also once had a kind of inlay on this edge. The earliest reference to the Copenhagen specimen is from 1725. It was once a part of Friedrich III's famous *Kunstkammer* in Gottorp. Its origin is uncertain, but it has been variously ascribed to New Sweden, New Netherland, Iroquoia, and the Virginia Algonquian.[27]

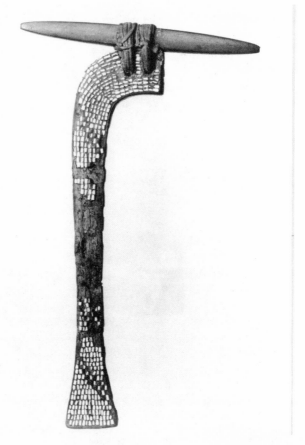

Fig. 6. Tomahawk/pickax with polished stone blade. Nationalmuseet Hb. 26, Etnografisk Samling, Copenhagen. Length of haft 47 cm, length of blade 29 cm. Photo: Lennart Larsen.

The earliest reference to the Stockholm specimen is from 1686. It then belonged to Sweden's King Karl XI (1655–97). His mother, Queen Hedvig Eleonora (1636–1715), was married to King Karl X Gustav of Sweden and was the daughter of Duke Friedrich III (during this time period Sweden had close political ties with Holstein-Gottorp). Thus there is a possibility that the Stockholm specimen also derives from Duke Friedrich III's *Kunstkammer*. However, the reverse situation, that the Holstein-Gottorp specimen may actually have been a Swedish gift to Duke Friedrich III, is also conceivable, which would support a possible origin of the two specimens in New Sweden.

These two tomahawk/pickaxs are unique pieces.[28] Their efficiency as striking weapons is questionable, considering the way the stone or iron blades have been secured to the tops of the hafts. Tomahawks and war clubs with iron blades and points are well known but the blades and points are usually fastened to the hafts more securely so that they could be used as weapons. A haft similar in shape to the Stockholm and Copenhagen specimens but with a small carved animal on the upper part is found on a particularly old Iowa tomahawk that has an apparently well-attached blade. Ethnographers have emphasized that the handle of this particular tomahawk or war hatchet "resembles closely that of many ball-headed war clubs."[29] Whatever their original form, function, and area of origin may have been, it seems certain that these two objects have a close and common historical relation.

There are, as previously mentioned, two ball-headed clubs at Skokloster. One is of a "plain" type, but with fine copper inlays in symmetrical patterns, including a parallel zigzag pattern ending in a bird, and a rhomboid figure with legs. The other club is of the same hard brown wood and is exquisitely carved into a striking human form. The ball is carved and decorated with wampum and shell or bone pieces so as to represent a human face. There are fine copper inlays, possibly native copper similar to the ones on the other club, that emphasize the nose and eyebrows. The handle is shaped into a human leg with a knee and a foot. A small four-legged animal with a long tail, possibly an otter, weasel, or lizard, is carved in a stretched-out position on top of the handle and ball/head. It is decorated with wampum and may represent a guardian animal. The earliest known reference to the club and the other Native American artifacts at the Skokloster armory is in a list that dates to 1710 and may be a copy or a part of an earlier inventory made at the death of Count Carl Gustaf Wrangel in 1676.

The club at the Folkens Museum, Stockholm, is almost identical to the anthropomorphic club at Skokloster. The main difference is that the small four-legged animal is decorated with flat bone or shell instead of the round wampum shells seen on the Skokloster club. This club has no copper inlays and its surface seems to have been treated differently. The club belonged to King Karl XV (1826–72) and its earliest reference is in an inventory of 1872 at the Royal Armory/Livrustkammaren, Stockholm. It is unclear how or when King Karl XV obtained the club but he had a profound interest in the arts and owned an extensive collection of weapons. The published inventory of his collection does not refer to the club.

Again, curiously enough, these two almost-identical clubs at Skokloster and at the Folkens Museum have a third counterpart at Ethnografisk Samling, Copenhagen. This club belonged to King Frederik VII (1808–63) of Denmark,[30] who was both a keen collector and a close friend of King Karl XV. Again, it is unclear how or when King Frederik VII ob-

Fig. 7. Ball-headed club Gb. 153, Etnografisk Samling, Copenhagen. Length 66 cm. Photo: Lennart Larsen.

tained the club. Like the specimen at the Folkens Museum, it has flat pieces of bone or shell covering the four-legged animal and lacks copper inlays.

It seems beyond doubt that these clubs, almost identical even in measurement, are somehow connected. It has, indeed, been pointed out that they were probably made by the same craftsman at the same time and place.[31] A closer examination of the clubs is needed to prove or disprove this possibility.

As mentioned previously, tradition has it that Governor Johan Printz gave the Skokloster collection to Count Carl Gustaf Wrangel. Amandus Johnson has pointed out that New Sweden's officials collected American Indian objects.[32] Had Printz an interest in ethnographica? It seems so. On 19 July 1644 Printz wrote to Per Brahe that he had a wampum belt and a pipe for Queen Christina.[33] We do not know the fate of these objects: perhaps they were among the personal belongings Christina retained after her abdication or perhaps they were destroyed in the fire that devastated Stockholm Castle in 1697, the same fire that destroyed Peter Lindeström's well-known map of the Delaware River.[34] In his letter Printz also mentioned that he had a pipe and an otter skin muff for Brahe. Printz's reference to these objects is the earliest mention of Indian artifacts from Delaware.[35]

Printz's instructions from Sweden ordered him to maintain good relations with the natives, but he was always ambivalent about and suspicious of them. According to Lindeström he was eccentric enough to have the Indians make him a dress or suit covered with wampum.[36] Considering Printz's great size, the suit must have been quite impressive. Printz had also gold rings and bracelets that an Indian brought him (he tried in vain to learn where the gold had come from).[37] At his death in 1663, his estate inventory included a wampum belt.[38] Apparently Johan Printz had an interest in native objects, and one can assume that this was also true of his successor, Johan Rising, as well as, of course, Peter Lindeström and Johan Campanius.

Considering the elaborate workmanship and execution of the three clubs, one can assume that they were intended to be more than ordinary war clubs. However, even plain war clubs could be finely carved, painted, and ornamented, at least among the later Iroquois.[39] The Iroquois apparently used special clubs in some of their ceremonial dances.[40] Early in the 1700s Robert Beverly saw in the region of Virginia some "tomahawks" of heavy wood "finely graved and painted" and wrapped in mats in a "house of religious worship."[41] Beverly is unclear whether the "tomahawks" were clubs. The term *tomahawk* was used rather vaguely in early sources.[42] Beverly's account does not say if the "tomahawks" he saw had special status because of particular iconographic features or if their status was "achieved," perhaps because they were war trophies.

The origin of the anthropomorphic clubs at Skokloster, Stockholm, and Copenhagen has been variously ascribed to the Iroquois or the Delaware or to the Delaware but with Iroquois influence.[43]

Considering the close contact the colonists had with some of the Lenape, probably mostly the Unami, or southern Delaware River Indians, and to a lesser extent with the more distant Susquehannock Indians of the Susquehanna River Valley, "the protectors of the Swedes," there were many situations in trading activities and more formal occasions when one can imagine that a club of this kind may have come into Swedish hands. The clubs' workmanship is in line with the statements of both Lindeström and Printz about native skill in arts and crafts. But there are no specific references to elaborately carved and ornamented clubs. If, indeed, a club of this kind was a gift to Printz, he did not have it at the time of his death, for it is not mentioned in his estate inventory.[44]

Clubs with carved faces can probably be seen as another expression of
the masking complex so typical of the northeastern Indians. This complex
was also important among the later Lenape and certainly among the Iroquois, as it is still today.[45] The presence of stone images with faces occurs
in archaeological contexts in the region and suggests that the masking
complex is quite ancient.[46] Descriptions of the masking complex of the
1600s are meager but the illustrations of John White indicate that the
North Carolina Algonquians used faces on poles at ceremonial dances in
the late 1500s. Presumably the masking complex was present to some extent among the Lenape. In 1766 Charles Beatty observed in a home of a
Lenape sachem the carved face of "a grave old man" on each door.[47]

From a sachem's point of view a club of this kind would be a suitable
personal or diplomatic gift for Printz's superiors, such as the "warrior
chief" Count Carl Gustaf Wrangel.[48] Perhaps Printz, eager to present a
forceful image of his people, informed the sachems about the count's
deeds during the Thirty Years' War. This would have been especially important since Swedish ships failed to arrive with trading goods. Perhaps
the human head on the club not only indicated supernatural power but
also brotherhood. This symbol was used at least once by a Lenape sachem in a meeting with Governor Johan Rising when the Swedes and
the Indians confirmed their friendship. According to Lindeström, the sachem said that the Indians and the colonists would be as one head, like a
calabash without cracks.[49] If the sachem was using a common metaphor,
how better could he use a gift to express respect on equal terms than
through a war club made of the hardest of woods? The four-legged animal perhaps represented his particular guardian animal or dream helper.
Be all this as it may, the club and the other artifacts of the Skokloster
collection certainly were suitable for any prestigious *Kunst-und-Wunderkammern*. The artifacts were perhaps even used occasionally when the
aristocrats at the Swedish court dressed up in exotic costumes.[50]

The origin of early, pre-1800 war clubs is uncertain. The description of
material culture in early sources and the documentation concerning acquisition of artifacts leave much to be desired. Late in the eighteenth century John Heckewelder pointed out that war clubs could be identified
with specific carriers and producers,[51] which probably applies for clubs
of earlier periods. As I have pointed out, a survey of known clubs of the
Eastern Woodlands may assist in defining the given fruitful area of distribution of native artifacts.[52]

A club quite similar to the "anthropomorphic" clubs described here
was discussed in a publication by Hans Dietschy.[53] This club has a
carved face and a similar four-legged animal with a long tail stretching
on top of the handle towards the ball/head. It has been suggested that it
may have been made in Iroquoia or in New France. The Swedes had little

to do with the Iroquois but had good relations with the Iroquoian-speaking Susquehannock. The Susquehannock had lost much of their once-powerful position by the end of the 1600s. It is not clear how closely they shared cultural traits with the Iroquois. It is difficult to relate ball-headed clubs with carved faces to a particular people or culture, but there is a possible relationship between ball-headed clubs with carved faces and certain symbolic aspects of lacrosse, which was played in cultures with higher-population densities such as the Iroquois.[54]

At Etnografisk Samling, Copenhagen, is yet another ball-headed club with a carved face, a Gottorp piece first mentioned in 1737. It may have been made by Mid-Atlantic or New England Algonquins during the first half of the eighteenth century.[55] The face on this club differs from those of the anthropomorphic clubs discused earlier. However, if it is of earlier date it may have an acquisition relationship with the Gottorp tomahawk/pickax and the similar tomahawk/pickax at the Folkens Museum.

Other objects that may be of New Sweden or Delaware Indian origin deserve mention. The Folkens Museum has a very well-preserved leather pouch, which in 1946 Frederick Douglas of the Denver Art Museum suggested was of New Sweden origin. If Douglas is correct it may be an object that Armegot Printz, the daughter of Johan Printz, owned.[56] Commenting that such pouches, called "notasser," were neatly made, Lindeström discussed their uses for keeping food, wampum, tobacco, and pipes.[57] We do not know how or from whom the museum acquired its pouch. Its tassels have red dye similar to that of the headdress at Skokloster.

The Royal Armory has a pair of leggings that Frederick Douglas suggested had been made in the eighteenth century in the Northeast, possibly by the Delaware Indians.[58] Its acquisition history is not known but the leggings were once kept at Gripsholm Castle, some forty kilometers west of Stockholm. Gripsholm was the residence of the dowager Queen Hedvig Eleonora. In spite of Douglas's suggested date of the leggings, one cannot rule out the possibility that they may have been part of Duke Friedrich III's *Kunst-und-Wunderkammern* and may have originated in New Sweden.

Some of the Lutheran pastors collecting naturalia and ethnographica who served in the area of the former colony were Israel Acrelius, Nils Collin, Andreas and Samuel Hesselius, and Carl Magnus Wrangel.[59]

Samuel Hesselius (1692–1753), who served in America between 1719 and 1731, had two brothers who would become famous: the minister Andreas Hesselius, who compiled information about the area of the former colony, and Gustavus Hesselius the "face painter," who painted portraits of the Lenape sachems Lapowinsa and Tishcohan. A third brother, Johan Hesselius, stayed in Sweden but occupied himself with Samuel Hesselius's collections and collecting Swedish soil samples and stones.[60] Folkens Museum has a document signed by Samuel Hesselius that lists "curious things ... collected in America" that he sent in 1736 to Carl Gyllenborg, chancellor for Lund and Uppsala universities, to be donated to Uppsala. The collection, which consisted of naturalia and ethnographica, apparently came to Lund. It may have been intended for the Museum Stobaeanum created by the medical doctor and natural scientist Kilian Stobaeus (1690–1742). Further research is needed to determine the fate of this collection.[61] The Stobaeus collections were famous but over time fell into neglect. In 1805 Lund University took over the collections, some of which are now at the university's Historical Museum/Institute of Archaeology.

In 1783 Carl Magnus Wrangel (1727–86), who was active in the Delaware River area between 1759 and 1768, presented five objects to the Royal Academy of Sciences: a pipe tomahawk given to him by Sir William Johnson, who had received it from the Seneca Chief Tagashata (it may have been used during negotiations leading to the Treaty of Easton in 1758); a small tomahawk; an Indian pouch decorated with wampum intended to hold cartridges and gunpowder; moccasins; and a headdress that may have belonged to the renowned Delaware chief Teedyuskung. The Wrangel collection became part of the cabinet of naturalia of the Academy, whose curator was, as we recall, Anders Sparrman. The collections of the cabinet eventually went to the Museum of Natural History. However, only the pipe tomahawk appears on an 1871 list of the museum's collections.

Documentation concerning artifacts and acquisition of collections of the 1600s is meager; it improves during the 1700s. Extensive archival research lies ahead, not necesarily only in Sweden, to present a fuller picture of the provenance and history of these interesting collections.[62]

NOTES

1. Ives Goddard, "Delaware," in *Northeast*, ed. Bruce G. Trigger, vol. 15, *Handbook of North American Indians* (Washington, D.C.: Smithsonian Institution, 1978), 213–39 (hereafter *HNAI*); Francis Jennings, "Susquehannock," *HNAI* 15:362–67; William W. Newcomb, *The Culture and Acculturation of the Delaware Indians* (Ann Arbor: University of Michigan Press, 1956); C. A. Weslager, *The Delaware Indians: A History* (New Brunswick, N.J.: Rutgers University Press, 1972).
2. Per Lindeström, *Resa till Nya Sverige*, ed. Alf Åberg (Stockholm: Natur och Kultur, 1962), and *Geographia Americae, with an Account of the Delaware Indians, Based on Surveys and Notes Made in 1654–1656*, trans. Amandus Johnson (Philadelphia: Swedish Colonial Society, 1925).

3. Johan Campanius, *Lutheri Catechismus, Öfwersatt på American-Virginiske Språket* (1696) (Stockholm: Almquist & Wiksell, 1937), and *Luther's Catechism*, ed. Daniel Nyström and W. W. Olson (New York: Swedish-American Tercentenary Association, 1938).
4. Thomas Campanius Holm, *Kort Beskrifning om Provincien Nya Sverige uti America* (Stockholm, 1702). Eng. ed. *Description of the Province of New Sweden* ..., trans. Peter S. Du Ponceau, vol. 3 of Memoirs of the Historical Society of Pennsylvania (Philadelphia: The Society, 1834). For a discussion of Holm's and Lindeström's contributions to North American Indian studies, see Åke Hultkrantz, "Swedish Contributions to North American Indian Studies," in *North American Indian Studies 2*, ed. P. Hovens (Göttingen: Edition Herodot, 1984), 16–35.
5. Israel Acrelius, *Beskrifning om de Swenska Församlingars Forna och Närvarande Tillstånd uti ... Nya Sverige* (Stockholm, 1759); English ed. *A History of New Sweden; or, The Settlements on the Delaware River*, trans. William M. Reynolds, vol. 11 of Memoirs of the Historical Society of Pennsylvania (Philadelphia: The Society, 1874); Andreas Hesselius, *Andreas Hesselii Anmärkningar om Amerika, 1711–1724*, ed. Nils Jacobsson (Stockholm and Uppsala: Almquist & Wiksell, 1938).
6. Jesper Swedberg, *America Illuminata: Skriven och utgiven av dess biskop ar 1732*, ed. Robert Murray (Stockholm: Proprius Forlag, 1985).
7. Goddard, "Delaware," *HNAI* 15:233; Tobias Eric Björck, *Dissertatio gradualis de plantatione ecclesiae suecanae in America* (Uppsala, 1825); English translation by Ira Oliver Nothstein, *The Planting of the Swedish Church in America*, Publication No. 19 (Rock Island, Ill.: Augustana College Library, 1943).
8. Margaret T. Hodgen, *Early Anthropology in the Sixteenth and Seventeenth Centuries* (Philadelphia: University of Pennsylvania Press, 1964), 162–206.
9. Bente Dam-Mikkelsen and Torben Lundbaek, *Etnografiske Genstande i Det Kongelige Danske Kunstkammer, 1650–1800* (Copenhagen: Nationalmuseet, 1980).
10. Arthur MacGregor, "Collectors and Collections of Rarities in the Sixteenth and Seventeenth Centuries," in *Tradescant's Rarities: Essays on the Foundation of the Ashmolean Museum, 1683, with a Catalogue of the Surviving Early Collections*, ed. Arthur MacGregor (Oxford: Clarendon Press, 1983).
11. Olof Granberg, *Svenska Konstsamlingars Historia*, vols. 2–3 (Stockholm: Gustaf Lindströms Boktryckeri, 1929–30).
12. Yngve Löwegren, *Naturaliekabinett i Sverige under 1700-talet* (Lund: Skånska Centraltryckeriet, 1952).
13. Rolf E. Du Rietz, "Hjalmar Stolpe och Etnografins Framväxt i Sverige," in *Resa med Vanadis* (Stockholm: Etnografiska Museet, 1984).
14. Arne Losman, "Skokloster—Europe and the World in a Swedish Castle," in *The Age of New Sweden*, ed. Arne Losman, Agneta Lundstrom, and Margareta Revera (Stockholm: Livrustkammaren, 1988), 100.
15. Goddard, "Delaware," *HNAI* 15:234.
16. Richard H. Manville and William C. Sturtevant, "Early Specimens of the Eastern Wolf *Canis Lupus lycaon*," *Chesapeake Science* 7 (1966): 219–20.
17. Stig Rydén, "Discovery in the Skokloster Collection of a 17th-Century Indian Headdress from Delaware," *Ethnos* 28 (1963): 107–21.
18. Manville and Sturtevant, "Early Specimens of the Eastern Wolf," 219.

19. Personal communication from Bengt Kyhlsberg, curator, Skoklosters Slott, Bàlsta, Sweden.
20. Rydén, "Discovery of an Indian Headdress," 107.
21. Losman, "Swedish Castle," 100.
22. Sigvald Linné, "Indian Weapons in the Ethnographical Museum of Sweden," *The Connoisseur* (1958): 34–36; "Drei Alte Waffen aus Nordamerika in Staatlichen Ethnographischen Museum in Stockholm," *Baessler-Archiv*, n.s., 3 (1958): 85–87; "Från Nya Sverige," in *Primitiv Konst: Konst och Konsthantverk hos primitiva folk*, ed. Sigvald Linné and Gosta Montell (Stockholm: Aktiebolaget Bokvark, 1947).
23. Linné, "Från Nya Sverige"; Ted J. Brasser, "Early Indian-European Contacts," *HNAI* 15:87; Kaj Birket-Smith, "Some Ancient Artifacts from the Eastern United States," *Journal de la Société des Americanistes de Paris* 12–13 (1920): 150; Goddard, "Delaware," *HNAI* 15:239.
24. Birket-Smith, "Some Ancient Artifacts," 149; Charles C. Willoughby, *Antiquities of the New England Indians* (Cambridge, Mass.: Peabody Museum of American Archaeology and Ethnology, 1935).
25. Robert Beverly, *The History of Virginia in Four Parts*, 2d ed. (London, 1722), 196.
26. Birket-Smith, "Some Ancient Artifacts," 146.
27. Dam-Mikkelsen and Lundbaek, *Etnografiske Genstande*, 31; Birket-Smith, "Some Ancient Artifacts," 153–54; Brasser, "Early Indian-European Contacts," *HNAI* 15:87.
28. For comparison with other Indian weapons of the same period see Christian F. Feest, "Tomahawk und Keule in Östlichen Nordamerika," *Archiv für Völkerkunde* 19 (1964–65): 39–84; Walter Krickeberg, "Ältere Ethnographica aus Nordamerika in Berliner Museum für Völkerkunde," *Baessler-Archiv*, n.s., 2 (1954); Harold L. Peterson, *American Indian Tomahawks* (New York: Museum of the American Indian—Heye Foundation, 1965).
29. Mark R. Harrington, *An Archaic Iowa Tomahawk*, Indian Notes and Monographs (New York: Museum of the American Indian—Heye Foundation, 1920), 56; Peterson, *American Indian Tomahawks*, 101.
30. Birket-Smith, "Some Ancient Artifacts," 160.
31. Linné, "Drei Alte Waffen aus Nordamerika," 87; "Indian Weapons in the Ethnographical Museum of Sweden," 36.
32. Amandus Johnson, "The Indians and Their Culture as Described in Swedish and Dutch Records from 1614 to 1664," *Proceedings of the 19th International Conference of Americanists* (Washington, D.C.: n.p., 1917), 277–82.
33. Amandus Johnson, ed., *The Instruction for Johan Printz, Governor of New Sweden* (Philadelphia: Swedish Colonial Society, 1930), 166–67.
34. Holm, *Description of the Province of New Sweden*, 54; Nils Jacobsson, *Svenska Öden vid Delaware, 1638–1831* (Stockholm: Svenska Tryckeriaktiebolaget, 1938), 120.
35. C. A. Weslager, *A Brief History of Archaeology in Delaware*, Transactions of the Delaware Academy of Science, 1974 and 1975 (Newark: Delaware Academy of Science, 1975), 11.
36. Lindeström, *Resa till Nya Sverige*, 128.
37. Ibid., 96–97.
38. Folke Elfving, *Kring Johan Björnsson Printz* (Mölndal: PR-Offset AB, 1986), 23.

39. Lewis Henry Morgan, *League of the Iroquois* (1851; reprint, Secaucus, N.J.: Citadel Press, 1972), 362–63.
40. Ibid., 266.
41. Beverly, *History of Virginia*, 166–67.
42. William H. Holmes, "The Tomahawk," *American Anthropologist* 10 (1908): 264–76; William R. Gerard, "The Term *Tomahawk*," *American Anthropologist* 10 (1908): 277–80.
43. Birket-Smith, "Some Ancient Artifacts," 160; Wolfgang Haberland, *Nordamerika: Kunst der Welt* (Baden-Baden: Holle Verlag, 1965), 181; Linné, "Drei Alte Waffen aus Nordamerika," 87, and "Indian Weapons in the Ethnographical Museum of Sweden," 35–36; Krickeberg, "Ältere Ethnographica aus Nordamerika," 183–84; Christian F. Feest, *Native Arts of North America* (London: Thames and Hudson, 1980), 11; Feest, "Tomahawk und Keule in Ostlichen Nordamerika"; Manville and Sturtevant, "Early Specimens of the Eastern Wolf," 219.
44. Elfving, *Kring Johan Björnsson Printz*, 22–24.
45. Mark R. Harrington, *Religion and Cermony of the Lenape*, Indian Notes and Monographs (New York: Museum of the American Indian—Heye Foundation, 1921); Rolf Krusche, "The Origin of the Mask Concept in the Eastern Woodlands of North America," *Man in the Northeast* 31 (1986): 1–47; Frank G. Speck, "Concerning Iconology and the Masking Complex in Eastern North America," *University Museum Bulletin* 15 (1950).
46. Krusche, "Origin of the Mask Concept," 4.
47. Charles Beatty, *The Journal of a Two-Months Tour; with a View of Promoting Religion among the Frontier Inhabitants of Pennsylvania* (1766; reprint, Ann Arbor, Mich.: Scholarly Press, 1972), 44.
48. Helmor Linderholm, *Nya Sveriges Historia; vårt Svenska Indianäventyr* (Stockholm: Tidens Förlag, 1976), 68.
49. Lindeström, *Resa till Nya Sverige*, 75–76; Holm, *Description of the Province of New Sweden*, 77; Amandus Johnson, *Den Första Svenska Kolonien i Amerika* (Stockholm: Gebers, 1923), 165.
50. Losman, "Swedish Castle," 97.
51. John Heckewelder, *History, Manners and Customs of the Indian Nations*, vol. 11 of Memoirs of the Historical Society of Pennsylvania (1876; reprint, New York: Arno Press, 1971), 1:54–56.
52. Marshall J. Becker, "A Ball-Headed Club from the Eastern Woodlands in the Collections of the Horniman Museum, London," *Pennsylvania Archaeologist* 50 (1980): 7.
53. Hans Dietschy, "Die Amerikanischen Keulen und Holzschwerter in Threr Beziehung zur Kulturgeschichte der Neuen Welt," *Internationalen Archiv für Ethnographie* 37 (1939): 125–26, 12a, Tafel II.
54. Marshall J. Becker, "Lacrosse: Political Organization as Reflected in Athletic Competiton," *Expedition* 27 (1985): 53–56.
55. Birket-Smith, "Some Ancient Artifacts," 159; Dam-Mikkelsen and Lundbaek, *Ethnografiske Genstande i Det Kongelige Danske Kunstkammer*, 32.
56. Elfving, *Kring Johan Björnsson Printz*, 33.
57. Lindeström, *Resa till Nya Sverige*, 112.
58. Frederick H. Douglas, "Some North American Indian Specimens," *Journal of the Royal Armoury* 4 (1948): 280–81.
59. Löwegren, *Naturaliekabinett i Sverige under 1700-talet*, 336–70.
60. Ibid.

61. Staffan Brunius, "Efterforskningar rörande piptomahawker, strid-ceremo-niklubba, Hesselius-samligen, släkten Hesselius," unpublished manuscript, Folkens Museum, Stockholm.
62. I would like to thank the following people for their assistance when I visited their institutions: Dr. Arne Losman, museum director of Skokloster Castle, and Bengt Kyhalsberg, curator of the armory at Skokloster; Dr. Berte Due, curator at Etnografisk Samling, Copenhagen; and Nils Dreiholt, senior curator at the Royal Armory, Stockholm. My thanks also go to Dr. William C. Sturtevant of the Smithsonian Institution, who chaired the session "The Colonists and Native Americans" in the conference "New Sweden in America" at the University of Delaware in which I presented this paper, and to the session's other speakers for their valuable comments. Finally I thank Dr. Karl Erik Larsson, former museum director of the Folkens Museum, Stockholm, and Dr. Ulla Wagner, the present museum director, for many helpful suggestions.

Part III
The Swedish Colonists
and Their Culture

The New Sweden Colonists, 1638–1656: Their Geographical and Social Background

STEN CARLSSON

In 1897 Amandus Johnson was matriculated at Gustavus Adolphus College in Minnesota. He had been born in Långasjö, Småland, in 1877 and had arrived in America in 1880 with his grandparents. His mother, single at the time, had emigrated in 1879. The father was unknown. Later Amandus was told that his father was a deceased nobleman who belonged to a family (probably Bonde) that had been active in Swedish politics when the colony of New Sweden was founded in 1638. Thus, Amandus Johnson, although poor himself, felt connected to Sweden's era as a great power.

At Gustavus Adolphus College he heard New Sweden discussed in a lecture by the famous Swedish-American journalist J. A. Enander. Some superficial knowledge of New Sweden probably had reached Johnson and his family before this, as, for instance, during the two hundred and fiftieth anniversary celebration in Minneapolis in 1888. Generally, however, Swedish immigrants in the Middle West at that time must have known or cared little about early Swedish-American history. Nevertheless, Enander's lecture became the starting point for Amandus Johnson's interest in the history of the colony and his research in that topic.[1] After doing research in both Swedish and American archives, in 1911 he published his magnum opus: *The Swedish Settlements on the Delaware: Their History and Relations to the Indians, Dutch and English, 1638–1664.*

Although Amandus Johnson's accomplishment is still the base of all later work on the history of New Sweden, we cannot be totally comfortable with his results. He was a man of his time and rather stubborn and self-conscious. An ardent Swedish-American patriot, he was very eager to teach his contemporaries about the Swedes' glorious past in America, what he called "Swedish contributions to American freedom." Johnson regarded the Swedes as pioneers in many different fields and even gave them a prominent place in the struggle against slavery, views that were more apparent in his later books. His New Sweden history of 1911 remained his most important work. Johnson's Swedish-American patriotism peaked in his small book, *Swedish Contributions to American Life 1638–1921*, published in 1921.

Like many of his contemporaries, Amandus Johnson wrote in a rather descriptive, chronological way, without attempting analysis. He did not, for example, show any real interest in the question that has engaged me for some time, the topic of this paper. While my research is based upon Amandus Johnson's account, it has been completed with many sources unknown to him.

The colonial enterprise was a part of Sweden's attempt to become a world power. One of its early high points was the 1629 armistice with Poland, when Livonia (northern Latvia) with its commercial center, Riga, was incorporated into the Swedish monarchy. At the same time Sweden was given control for six years over some Prussian ports, thus providing the Swedish Crown with customs income equaling about 30 percent of its national revenue. When the armistice expired in 1635, Sweden's position had been weakened by the death of Gustavus Adolphus in 1632 and setbacks in the Thirty Years' War, so the ports were returned. For Chancellor Axel Oxenstierna this was a great disappointment. Sweden had, as he dramatically pointed out, lost half of its power. It became important for him and his colleagues in the government, guardians of the young Queen Christina, to find other sources of income. The virgin territories on the banks of the Delaware in North America seemed full of promise because of potential trade in beaver pelts and tobacco.[2]

The enterprise was originally carried out with the cooperation of experienced Dutch merchants, but soon the colony became a purely Swedish undertaking, although the personnel on the ships remained mainly Dutch and, to some degree, German. Because Atlantic passages were fraught with hardship, the government had difficulty recruiting colonists. Some soldiers were ordered to go, and convicts who volunteered to settle in the colony had their sentences commuted to a fewer number of years, often six. Adultery, game poaching, and destruction of forests were typical crimes for which this commutation was offered. Finns coming to Värmland from Savolaks and Karelen, close to the Russian border, who had aroused the displeasure of the authorities and the mine owners because of their burn-beating agricultural practices, were encouraged to emigrate to "the precious and fertile" colony.[3]

From 1637 until 1655 twelve expeditions, carefully described by Johnson, were sent to New Sweden. Only seven of them had any importance for the recruitment of colonists, however. I am omitting the third expedition, which was a totally Dutch enterprise, the seventh and eighth expeditions, which brought very few colonists, and the eleventh expedition, which was sequestered in New Amsterdam.[4] I will discuss, however, the

ninth expedition, which was shipwrecked before arrival but which nevertheless has some importance for my topic.

The first expedition, of the *Kalmar Nyckel* and *Fågel Grip (Griffin)*, left
Stockholm in August 1637 and Göteborg in November of the same year;
it reached the Delaware River in March 1638. Johnson knew nothing
about the journey.[5] However, in 1903 a document was published in the
Virginia Historical Magazine that throws some light upon the first Swedish meeting with the New World. On 8 May 1638 the British treasurer of
Virginia, Jerome Hawley, reported to the British secretary of state, Sir
Francis Windebande, that a "Dutch" ship had arrived since his last report on 20 March with a commission from the young Queen of Sweden,
signed by eight of "the Chief Lords of Sweden," to have free trade in
tobacco to carry to Sweden. This commission was denied them. After
ten days this ship and another one sailed to the Delaware Bay, where
they planned to start a tobacco plantation, as the Dutch had already
done on the Hudson River. Hawley thought that the ships should be removed and others prevented from settling upon His Majesty's territories.[6] Clearly the Swedish presence in North America was never popular among the earlier colonial powers.

Information about the composition of the first expedition is fragmentary. The leader, Peter Minuit, had been in Dutch colonial service and
was of German or Walloon origin. The captain, the mate, and some of
the sailors were Dutch; the rest of the sailors and a group of soldiers
were Swedish. Only about a dozen colonists can be identified. Three sailors, whose widows lived in Stockholm in 1640, were reported as dead.[7]
The commanding officer, Måns Nilsson Kling, may be an officer named
Måns Nilsson who had served with Jönköping's regiment in Småland.[8]
One of the passengers was Clas Jansson (Jansen), possibly a Dutchman.[9] Some of the Dutch crew stayed in the colony, as did the Negro
slave, "Morian" Antonius from Angola, who may have been picked up
in the West Indies. He lived in New Sweden in 1654, by then probably a
freeman, and was called Swartz.[10]

The second expedition, consisting only of the *Kalmar Nyckel*, left Göteborg in September 1639 and reached the Delaware in April 1640.[11]
Only about twenty colonists can be connected with the expedition. Highest in rank was Peter Hollander Ridder, who served as New Sweden's
governor from 1640 until 1643. He obviously had a Dutch background,
but he wrote in German and had, according to Johnson, difficulty in
speaking Swedish. Recently, however, he has been connected with a Hollender family living in Ekenäs in southern Finland, an affiliation that may
be regarded as possible but far from certain.[12] Another member of this
expedition was the first clergyman in New Sweden—probably the first

Lutheran minister in North America—Torkillus Reorus or Reovius, called Ostrogothus, meaning that he came from the province of Östergötland.[13] Per Gunnarsson Rambo, an ancestor of a very large family, also arrived with this expedition. We know that he came from Hisingen, outside Göteborg. He married Brita Matsdotter of Vasa in Österbotten (Finland), who probably arrived with a later expedition.[14] A third passenger was Sven Gunnarsson, the ancestor of the well-known Virginia family Swanson, of Swansonville.[15] Per Gunnarsson's birthplace is unknown, and Amandus Johnson's suggestion that he was a brother of Per Gunnarsson Rambo is quite unlikely.[16] Anders Larsson Dalbo should also be mentioned. Amandus Johnson connects him with Dalbo on the island of Gotland, which did not, however, at that time (before 1645) belong to Sweden.[17] It is more likely that he came from the small province of Dalsland, close to Västergötland.[18]

The fourth expedition, the *Charitas* and *Kalmar Nyckel*, left Stockholm in May 1641 and Göteborg in July, arriving on the Delaware in November. Thanks to two lists, fifty-seven passengers are known; the total number may have been higher.[19] At least four Värmland Finns, coming from "Sund" Parish, probably Sunne, were on board. For burn-beating the forests they were sentenced to military service but were allowed to go to New Sweden instead.[20] One of them, Eskil Larsson, was a runaway soldier.[21] The bookkeeper Carl Johansson (Jansson), from Keksholm in eastern Finland, was punished for some crime and was also sentenced to military service. Later he was employed by Governor Printz as a bookkeeper.[22] Per Larsson Cock, a native of Bångsta in Södermanland,[23] had also been a prisoner at Smedjegården in Stockholm and was also sentenced to military service. He later became a respected member of the colony with many descendants. One of them was the first governor of Kentucky, Isaac Shelby.[24]

Olof Stille of Penningby in Roslagen, Uppland, also had a criminal past. In 1638 he was condemned to death by beheading for robbery. The sentence was then reduced to a fine.[25] There probably was no direct connection between this sentence and his emigration to North America. Once there he became a freeman and died in 1684, leaving numerous offspring.[26] Another member of the expedition was a young cavalry soldier of Ving parish, Västergötland (Skaraborg County), Hans Månsson, who had been convicted of cutting down six apple trees and two cherry trees, property of the Crown, in the garden of the old monastery church of Varnhem. The crime was considered serious because the church was a holy place. He was given two alternatives in April 1641: death by hanging or six years in New Sweden.[27] He preferred New Sweden, of course, and was first a laborer, then a freeman (farmer), and finally a captain. He left many descendants.[28]

The fifth expedition, on the *Swan* and the *Fama*, left Stockholm in August 1642 and Göteborg in November; they reached New Sweden in January 1643.[29] Lists of the crew, not the passengers, unknown to Amandus Johnson, have been found in Flottansarkiv (the Archives of the Navy) in Krigsarkivet (the Royal War Archives) in Stockholm. They contain seventy-six names, of whom sixty-seven can be localized: sixteen were from Stockholm, Uppland, and Södermanland, sixteen from Västergötland (including Göteborg), thirteen from Finland (mainly the southwestern Swedish-speaking areas), and eleven from the Netherlands and Germany, including members of the staff. Eight came from other Swedish provinces, two from Norway, and one from Danzig.[30] There is no known passenger list, but about fifty colonists can be identified.

The most prominent passenger was the new governor, Lieutenant Colonel Johan Printz, traveling with his German-born wife and four children.[31] He was the son of a vicar in Bottnaryd, Småland (Skara diocese), and had earlier served in Österbotten (Finland) and Germany. After his surrender of Chemnitz in 1641, he was partly in disgrace, and his command in New Sweden may be regarded as a sort of banishment.[32]

Two clergymen were also on board: Johan Campanius of Stockholm and Israel Holg Fluviander, a relative of Printz.[33] Other passengers were Lieutenant Sven Skute of Kronoby in Österbotten, Constable Elias Gyllengren of Västergötland, and Lieutenant Christer Boije of Nyland (Finland).[34] The soldier Jöran Snövit (Schneeweiss) was also on board. According to a contemporary account, he was a native of Saxony.[35] In America he was called Kyn, probably the German word *kühn*, "brave." The family name was soon changed to Keen.[36] Another soldier of foreign origin was Peter Joachimson of Schleswig-Holstein, who became a freeman and died in 1654 in New Amsterdam, where he had been sent on a mission by the new governor, Johan Rising. His family, still existing today, was later called Yocum or Yocom.[37]

Convicts were also on board. Per Michelsson of Hammarby, Uppland, was sentenced in 1642 to six years of deportation in New Sweden for spreading, without proof, "hard and rebellious words" about a sheriff.[38] He died in New Sweden in 1643.[39] Other criminals were the Finn Anders Andersson, serving as a soldier in Elfsborg in Västergötland, and the bookkeeper Johan Fransson of Viborg in eastern Finland.[40] The district court had sentenced two married men from Åland, not mentioned by name, to six years' deportation in New Sweden for adultery; one of them had, in addition, shot an elk without permission. It is not clear that they actually arrived in New Sweden, but one of them may be the peasant Lars Andersson of Åland, who died in the colony in 1643.[41]

The sixth expedition, the *Fama* and the *Kalmar Nyckel*, left Göteborg in December 1643 and reached New Sweden in March 1644. The *Kalmar*

Nyckel is said to have gone to the West Indies instead of New Sweden, but two of the passengers (Johan Papegoja and Walle Liur of Jönköping) did in fact arrive in New Sweden. So it seems clear that the ship paid a short visit there before going on to the West Indies.[42]

Some lists from this expedition, unknown to Amandus Johnson, have been preserved in Krigsarkivet. They show seventy crew members and eleven passengers and are probably complete. Sixty-five persons can be placed. The distribution is similar to that of the fifth expedition, with fourteen persons coming from Stockholm and Uppland, fourteen from Västergötland, seven from Åland, two from "Finland Proper" (Egentliga Finland), one from Finland (without specification), six from the Netherlands, mainly crew members, twelve from other Swedish provinces, and seven from foreign countries other than the Netherlands. Three men of noble birth were on board, Lieutenant Johan Papegoja of Västergötland, Christian Tott of Uppland, and Lieutenant Knut Lilliehöök of Västergötland. Knut and his brother Per, who also went to New Sweden, were illegitimate sons of a nobleman and did not consider themselves part of the aristocracy.[43]

Around two hundred colonists known by name had arrived in New Sweden by 1644. Some of them cannot be connected with any specific expedition. Only twenty-one of the colonists were women, and even if there was a terrible shortage of women in the colony (Papegoja and Printz complained very much about that[44]), it is clear that some females, as well as children, are missing from the sources. Even the documentation of adult men must be incomplete. We can assume that perhaps three hundred colonists reached New Sweden during these years, but not all were there at the same time. The mortality was high. During 1643 and 1644 at least twenty-five adult men died.[45] Some returned to Europe, at least ten in 1643.[46] Furthermore, some may have left for other places in North America. In 1647 Printz reported that the total number of men, women, and children was 183. The following year ten adult men returned to Sweden, yet by 1653 the total number had climbed to two hundred.[47]

Of the approximately two hundred known colonists arriving between 1638 and 1644, 130 can be localized geographically, in some cases with a degree of uncertainty. If one assumes that three of the ten listed as "Finns" came from Finland itself and from Värmland, the percentages for the five largest groups are as follows: eastern Svealand 34; Västergötland and Dalsland 15; the Finnish settlements in Värmland 10; Finland itself 12; the Netherlands and Germany 15; and all others 14. All percentages must be regarded as approximate.[48]

These statistics may be compared with a note by Professor Pehr Kalm, one of Linné's most famous pupils. During his visit to North America in 1749 to 1752, he made many observations concerning the Swedish settlements on the Delaware. He met Jacob Bengtsson, whose paternal grand-father, Anders Bengtsson, came from Fuxerna in Västergötland, whereas his mother was a daughter of Per Gunnarsson Rambo of Hisingen and Brita Matsdotter of Vasa. According to Bengtsson, the majority of the early colonists came from Göteborg—he meant via Göteborg—and were *västogötar*, while "a great deal" came from Uppland and "a multitude" from Finland. Other provinces were, as far as he knew, not represented among the "early Swedes."[49] This is a simplification, but not quite wrong because Jacob Bengtsson did not distinguish between Finns coming directly from Finland and the Värmland Finns. As a matter of fact, there was a considerable gap between these two groups.

The first group was dominated by people speaking Swedish and coming from regions with the same agriculture as Uppland or (to some degree) Norrland. The other group was Finnish-speaking and rooted in an eastern, burn-beating culture. All of them except the *ålänningar*—who belonged to Abo diocese—could be called Finns, regardless of their native tongue, and all of them were Swedish citizens. The term *Finn* in seventeenth-century sources has a regional rather than a national sense. So if we say that 20 to 25 percent of the early New Sweden colonists were "Finns," we should be careful to avoid an anachronistic interpretation.

From 1644 until his departure in 1653, Printz impatiently waited for additional colonists to arrive. As I indicated, two expeditions did arrive in 1647 and 1648, but few colonists were on board. One of them was a priest, Lars Carlsson Lock, a native of Lockerud, Västergötland.[50] In 1649 the Swedish government sent the *Katt* to New Sweden on the ninth expedition. It left Göteborg in July 1649 but in August was wrecked in the West Indies, where the crew and passengers were forced to abandon the ship. After a series of terrible events, most of them died and only a few made it back to Sweden. The crew consisted of six experienced hands and twenty-four farmhands and sailors. There were seventy passengers. The passenger list, preserved in the Riksarkivet in Stockholm, was ignored by Amandus Johnson, since none of the passengers reached New Sweden. Birthplaces are recorded for forty-nine passengers (all except some high-level or professional persons and their families). Twenty-eight were born in Västergötland, five in the still-Norwegian Bohuslän, close to Göteborg, five in Närke, two on the Isles of Åland, one in Österbotten, and eight in different Swedish provinces. The concentration of colonists from Västergötland and Bohuslän is striking.[51]

Consequently Printz was still isolated from his homeland. Furthermore, he became involved in a conflict with some of the leading colonists, who accused him of despotism. They wrote letters of protest and many of them moved to Maryland. Printz himself left the colony in 1653, taking some colonists with him. By May 1654 the number of inhabitants in New

Sweden dropped to approximately seventy due to deaths and the return of some colonists to Sweden.[52]

The situation changed, however, thanks to the tenth expedition, of the Örn, which left Stockholm in October 1653 and Göteborg in February 1654. While the colony had been regarded as a place not only for ordinary colonists but also for criminals, by 1649 there was a growing positive interest, especially among the Finns, who wished to cross the Atlantic in big groups of two or three hundred.[53] At the departure from Göteborg, about one hundred families were left behind. The number of passengers, at least 350, was the highest in New Sweden's history. Disease reduced the number considerably, so the arriving colonists numbered no more than 250 in May 1654.[54] About 170 of them, mostly men, can be identified.

The geographical information is very fragmentary, and only thirty-seven of the colonists can be localized. One came from Östergötland, namely the new governor, Johan Rising. Another was a nobleman from Stockholm, Per Lindeström, an engineer later famous for his report.[55] At least six other passengers were recruited in Stockholm in 1653 and 1654. Four of them were soldiers, one a tailor, and one a stonecutter.[56] Johnson also mentions sixteen men and twelve schoolboys hired in Stockholm for the Örn or for the Gyllene Haj, which left later and was sequestered in New Amsterdam.[57] The boys may have come from a secondary school founded in Stockholm in 1649.[58] No members of these groups can be identified among the New Sweden colonists.

A great deal of recruitment took place in Västerås.[59] While none of the colonists can be connected with this recruitment, one should note that Sven Skute, who had returned to Sweden in 1650 and who was making his second voyage to America (he is not included among the thirty-seven) had his wife, Anna Johansdotter of Dingtuna parish, Västmanland, with him on the Örn.[60] One of the passengers, the sawmill master Nils Matsson (Long) of Torshälla, Södermandland, was also on board, probably with his wife, and definitely with his son Anton Nilsson Long, who was listed as being born in Sweden.[61]

Two clergymen were among the passengers, Mathias Nertunius of Närtuna, Uppland, one of the survivors from the Katt, and Peter Hjort, a native of Hjorted, Småland. The packhouse clerk Jacob Junge of Göteborg is also mentioned, as well as the trumpeter Johan Schalbrick (Schalburger) of Reval, Estonia, a Swedish province.[62]

Nine of the thirty-seven passengers were foreigners. This does not mean, however, that more than 20 percent of all travelers had a foreign origin. Some cases are uncertain, and in any event one should note that a foreign background was often noted in particular. Börje Nilsson Jute must have been Danish.[63] Three Dutchmen are mentioned, with some doubt about their origin (in two cases) and their year of arrival in New Sweden (one case).[64] One German was on board, Markus Larsson of Holstein.[65] Simon Lane and Thomas Brown were Englishmen, probably coming on the *Örn*, and William Morris, who arrived in 1654, also had an English name.[66] Finally the Pole Paul Malich, mentioned in 1654, may have arrived with the *Örn*.[67]

Part of the recuiting took place in Värmland and Dalsland.[68] Among the passengers on board the *Örn* was Olof i Slobijen—that is, Slobyn in Mangskog parish in Värmland. In Maryland his son was labeled as a Finn.[69] Skate i Slobyen came from the same village and was probably a Finn, as well as Anders i Salungen, from the same parish, and Samuel Persson i Bogen, from western Värmland.[70] Six other passengers are explicitly called Finns and probably came from Värmland.[71] But there were also two Finns from Hälsingland on board, namely Pål Jönsson Mullika and his son Erik Mullika, coming from Mora Finnmark in Hälsingland, near the border of Dalarna.[72]

Finally, Mårten Mårtensson must be mentioned. When he died in Pennsylvania in 1706, he was believed to be around one hundred years old. According to the death register, he was born "in Finland in Sweden." He may have come directly from Finland, but it is somewhat more probable that he was a Värmland Finn, although born in Finland.[73] His wife, Helena, and son Mårten are said to have been born in Sweden.[74] That does not exclude Finland, but it seems more probable that they were born within Sweden's present boundaries. Mårten Mårtensson, Jr., had a famous grandson, John Morton of Philadelphia, who played an important role in Pennsylvania's acceptance of the Declaration of Independence in 1776.[75]

Information about the origins of the passengers on the *Örn* is fragmentary. Eleven of the passengers have been connected with eastern Svealand, three with Västergötland, Östergötland, and Småland, thirteen with Finland or the Finn districts in Värmland and Hälsingland, one with Estonia, and eight with various foreign countries. We cannot assume that this distribution reflects the exact proportion among the colonists arriving in 1654; it is likely that the foreign element is overrepresented. Since the recruitment took place in Stockholm, Västerås, or Värmland, it seems quite clear that there were two major contingents, one from eastern Svealand and one from the Finnish settlements in Värmland (and Hälsingland). Thus Västergötland and western Finland were not as important as in the period from 1638 to 1644, whereas the Värmland Finns became more important than before. Quite roughly, the Finnish element among the passengers on the *Örn* may have been around 40 percent and among all colonists arriving from 1638 until 1654 something like 30 percent.[76] But the name "Finne" was still a minority designation. In a population dominated by Finns, it is senseless to mark an individual as "Finn."

At this point the total number of inhabitants in New Sweden increased to 370.[77] Most of the increase was due to the arrival of the *Örn*, but Rising seems to have attracted other persons, too, especially those who had earlier left for Maryland.[78] For a time Rising was successful as governor, but in September 1655 the whole colony was lost to the Dutch.[79]

The twelfth and last expedition was organized when the colony was still believed to be Swedish. In November 1655 the *Mercurius* left Göteborg, and in March 1656 it reached the Delaware.[80] For the first time the migration had a real family character: husbands were accompanied by wives, children, and servants. A passenger list made in October 1655 registers 110 persons. Eleven had been in New Sweden before, but none of them can be identified from the earlier lists or other documents. At least ninety-two were Finns. Forty-nine came from Letstigen, an area near the border between Värmland and Närke, fifty-five came from Fryksdalen in Värmland, and six from Brunskog parish in Värmland.[81]

Very few of the passengers are known from other documents. Farmhand Markus Sigfridsson of Fryksdalen moved very soon to Maryland.[82] Henrik Jacobsson of Fryksdalen is probably a settler still alive in 1693. The same may be true for Johan Henriksson of Fryksdalen.[83] Ingeri Philips, born in Värmland and arriving with the *Mercurius*—a daughter of Olof Philipsson of Letstigen—married Erik Mullika (Mulleen) of Hälsingland, who had arrived in 1654. Their daughter Anna married the Englishman Richard Reynolds. Their son, Erik Rännilson, gave Kalm some information about their family history.[84] The vast majority of the Värmland Finns aboard the *Mercurius* probably settled the forests.

If we include the twelfth expedition and some individuals joining the colony in periods other than 1638 to 1644 and 1654 to 1656, the total number of colonists coming from Europe may be a little less than seven hundred.[85] Among them the Finnish element now seems to have been something like 270, around 40 percent.[86] The figure may be too high, since so many of the Finns included the term "Finn" in their names, which may have led to some overrepresentation. However, it may also be too low, since so many of the Värmland Finns, in particular, belonged to a rather anonymous group among the colonists. Regardless, the Finns were in the minority. But since so many colonists had died or left the colony before 1656, a large majority of them not Finnish, the Finnish element just after the arrival of the *Mercurius* must have been higher than 40 percent, possibly between 45 and 50.[87] Many Finns spoke Swedish as their native language and others were bilingual. Since all the clergymen spoke Swedish, their language also had an impact on the Finnish-speaking inhabitants, although some of them seem to have moved directly from

Finnish to English. At the beginning of the 1690s it was calculated that the inhabitants of the former colony needed fifty Swedish and twenty Finnish Bibles, and three or four hundred Swedish and two hundred Finnish hymn books.[88] By 1750 the Finnish language was almost forgotten, whereas the Swedish language survived for several decades in spite of English pressure.[89]

One should remember, when looking at the social background of the colonists, that around 95 percent of the population of Sweden were peasants or laborers. Only about 5 percent belonged to higher strata such as the nobility, clergy, officers, civil servants, and burghers.[90] Among the colonists, these upper classes were overrepresented. The noble families— Printz, Rising, Gyllengren, Boije, Papegoja, Lilliehöök—numbered about twenty persons; the clergy—Reovius, Campanius, Fluviander, Lock, Nertunius, Hjort, and a rather anonymous priest called Christopher—about ten; officers and higher civil servants—Skute and others—about twenty; noncommissioned officers, clerks, and other lower civil servants about twenty; and burghers (shippers, merchants, millers, artisans) about thirty.[91] The total of about one hundred corresponds to 14 percent of the colonists; the real percentage was probably higher. The small colonial community was thus more differentiated than was society at home, the result of the need for different types of qualified people. However, the majority of the colonists were peasants, soldiers, sailors, and laborers. While New Sweden started as a military colony, very soon it was dominated by agriculture, especially tobacco.

Convicts, whose numbers cannot be fixed, made up a special category. Only about twenty colonists were explicitly called criminals or convicts. Though the real number was much higher, this group was in the minority. According to Thomas Campanius Holm, who lived in Sweden but was familiar with New Sweden, thanks to notes by his grandfather Johan Campanius, the evil-doers among the colonists were regarded as slaves and kept from the other inhabitants.[92] This probably was only partly true since some former convicts attained responsible positions in New Sweden.

After several decades a small group of families became dominant in the area; many of them are still in existence today in different parts of the United States. Stille of Penningby and Homman of Sollentuna came from Uppland, Cock of Bångsta, Nilsson-Nelson (Long) of Torshälla, and Stålkofta-Stalcup of Strängnäs from Södermanland.[93] One of the places in New Sweden was called Upland. The Bonde-Boon family cannot be traced through the male line, but the ancestor's wife came from Nya Kopparberget, Västmanland.[94] Västergötland is represented by the families Rambo of Hisingen (the ancestor's wife coming from Österbotten), Lock of Lockerud, Jonasson-Jones of Skåning härad, Månsson-

Steelman of Skara, Bengtsson of Fuxerna, and Gustafsson-Justis of Kin-nekulle.[95] The influence from Västergötland is visible in the placenames of Fort Elfsborg, Mölndal, and Nya Göteborg. The small Norrland group is represented by the Stiddem-Steedham family, whose ancestor, one of the survivors from the *Katt*, was a barber-surgeon, probably a native of Medelpad.[96] The families Skute of Kronoby, Österbotten, Mattson of Borgå, Nyland, and Morton came from Finland.[97] The placenames Fin-land, Nya Korsholm, Nya Vasa, and Torne can also be mentioned. The Värmland Finns are more anonymous, but the Slooby family has been recorded.[98] The Mullika family of Mora Finnmark in Hälsingland played an important role in New Jersey, leaving placenames of Mullica (the township), Mullica Hill, and Mullica River.[99] The immigrant element in the old multinational Swedish society is represented by the families Joachimson-Yocom of Schleswig-Holstein, Kyn-Keen of Saxony, and Larsson-Huling-Hulan of Holstein.[100]

In 1697 Pastor Andreas Rudman at Wicacoa (Philadelphia), one of the first clergymen sent to New Sweden by the Church of Sweden, reported that there were twelve hundred inhabitants in the former colonial area speaking as pure a Swedish as anywhere in Sweden.[101] If we add the Swedish groups in Maryland and New York City, we can assume that ap-proximately two thousand inhabitants in the colonies, later united as an independent American republic, could be classified as Swedes, which amounts to about 0.7 percent of the total white population of three hun-dred thousand around 1700.[102] This figure should be compared to the statistics in 1900, when "the Swedish stock" (the immigrants and their children) totaled 1.1 million, or 1.5 percent of the total population.[103] In absolute numbers the difference between 1700 and 1900 is tremendous, in percentages it is not very great.

Today there are probably millions of Americans descended from the New Sweden colonists. While the vast majority of them do not know of this ancestry, a surprisingly large number are aware of it. Their ances-tors, arriving in New Sweden between 1638 and 1656, were few and their achievements limited, but in the long run their contributions have had some significance in the history of the North American continent.

NOTES

1. A. Widén, *Amandus Johnson, svenskamerikan: En levnadsteckning* (Stockholm: P. A. Norstedt & Söners Förlag, 1970), 48, 54f., 232f., 237f. The jubilee in Minneapolis is treated by D. Blanck in an unpublished pa-per, "Pomp and Circumstances in Swedish-America: The Role of Ceremo-nial for an Ethnic Group," Department of History, Uppsala University, 1988.

2. The connection with the armistice of 1635 is stressed by N. Ahnlund, *Nya Sverige: De historiska huvuddragen* (Stockholm: Svenska Kyrkans Diakonistyrelses Förlag, 1938), 14. Oxenstierna's disappointment is also mentioned by J. Rosén, *Svensk historia*, vol. 1, *Tiden fore 1718*, 4th ed. (Stockholm and Lund: Svenska Boktörlaget, 1978), 416.

3. Some documents concerning the propaganda for recruitment of colonists were printed as early as 1848 in *Historiska Handlingar rörande Skandinaviens historia* (Stockholm: Hörbergska Boktryckeriet, 1848), 29:213.

4. Amandus Johnson, *The Swedish Settlements on the Delaware*, 2 vols. (Philadelphia: Swedish Colonial Society, 1911), 1:135ff., 250ff.; 2:490ff., 758ff.

5. Ibid., 1:116f.

6. *Virginia Historical Magazine* 10 (1903): 424.

7. Johnson, *Swedish Settlements*, 1:109f., 2:758.

8. A. Åberg, *Folket i Nya Sverige: Vår koloni vid Delawarefloden 1638–1655* (Stockholm: Natur & Kultur, 1987), 12.

9. Johnson, *Swedish Settlements*, 2:700, 710.

10. Handel och Sjöfart, vol. 196, Riksarkivet (National Archives, Stockholm) ("ein Morian oder Angoler"); Johnson, *Swedish Settlements*, 2:699, 706, 710, 722.

11. Johnson, *Swedish Settlements*, 1:120ff., 2:759.

12. Ibid., 1;120ff., 2:691f., 759; lecture by O. Koivukanges at the 350th anniversary of the founding of New Sweden in Newark, Delaware, 5 March, 1988.

13. *Svenska Riksrådets Protokoll*, vol. 8: 1640–41, ed. S. Bergh (Stockholm: P. A. Norstedt & Söner, 1898), 130; T. Campanius Holm, *Kort Beskrifning om Provincien Nya Sverige uti America* (Stockholm, 1702), 16 (English ed. trans. Peter Du Ponceau, *Description of The Province of New Sweden*, vol. 3 of Memoirs of the Historical Society of Pennsylvania [Philadelphia: The Society, 1834]); Johnson, *Swedish Settlements*, 1:127, 129, 205, 2:697, 699, 707; N. Jakobsson, *Svenska öden vid Delaware, 1638–1931* (Stockholm: Svenska Kyrkans Drakonistyrelses Bokförlag, 1938), 53.

14. Pehr Kalm, *En resa till Norra Amerika*, ed. F. Elfving, 2 vols. (Helsinki: Mercators Tryckeri Aktiebolog, 1929), 4. Additional volume edited by F. Elfving, *Skrifter utg av Svenska Litteratursällskapet i Finland* (Helsinki, 1929), 182, 187, 199, 204, 206, 225.

15. Johnson, *Swedish Settlements*, 2:711; *The National Cyclopaedia of American Biography* (New York, 1945), 32:177; A. Kastrup, *The Swedish Heritage in America* (St. Paul, Minn.: Swedish Council of America, 1975), 112, 585; O. R. Landelius, *Swedish Place-Names in North America* (Carbondale: Southern Illinois University Press, 1985), 228.

16. Johnson, *Swedish Settlements*, 2:711; Landelius, *Swedish Place-Names*, 228.

17. Johnson, *Swedish Settlements*, 2:711.

18. Landelius, *Swedish Place-Names*, 160f.

19. Johnson, *Swedish Settlements*, 1:145ff., 151ff., 2:711f., 759.

20. *Svenska Riksrådets Protokoll, 1640–41*, 165, 640; Johnson, *Swedish Settlements*, 149f.

21. Johnson, *Swedish Settlements*, 1:153, 2:713, 718.

22. Ibid., 1:150, 152f., 409, 460f.

23. P. S. Craig and R. H. Hulan, "Membership of the Swedish Lutheran

Church at Raccoon and Penns Neck, N.J., 1771" (mimeographed paper, Wilmington, Del., 1985), 4.

24. Kalm, *En resa till Norra Amerika*, 204; Johnson, *Swedish Settlements*, 1:152, 2:712, 720; P. S. Craig and H. W. Yocom, "The Yocums of Aronamock in Philadelphia, 1648–1702," *National Genealogical Society Quarterly* 71 (1983): 258f., 269ff.; R. H. Hulan, "Historiska Minnen i Delaware," in *Det började vid Delaware: Om Svenska hembygder i Amerika*, ed. Gunilla Lindberg (Karlskrona: Riksförbundet för Hembyqdsvård, 1986), 45.

25. F. Nordström, "Olof Stille of New Sweden," *Swedish American Genealogist* (1986): 97ff.

26. Johnson, *Swedish Settlements*, 1:152, 2:712; Craig and Yocom, "The Yocums of Aronamock," 248, 251, 253.

27. *Handlingar rörande Skandivaniens historia* 29:217f., Valle härads dombok 31/5 1641, according to information by B. Hange-Persson.

28. Handel och Sjöfort, vol. 42, Riksarkivet; Johnson, *Swedish Settlements*, 2:596, 712, 720; R. W. Harper, "När Sverige skulle bli en världsmakt," in *Det började vid Delaware*, ed. Lindberg, 39.

29. Johnson, *Swedish Settlements*, 1:237ff.

30. S. Carlsson, "Three Swedish Expeditions to North America, 1642–1649," *Swedish American Genealogist* (1988): 3.

31. F. Elfving, *Kring Johan Bjornsson Printz*, vol. 1: *Familjen och ättlingarna* (Göteborg & Molndal: PR-Offset AB, 1986), 9.

32. Ahnlund, *Nya Sverige*, 26ff.

33. Holm, *Kort Beskrifning*, 108; I. Acrelius, *Beskrifning om de svenska församlingars forna och närvarande tillstånd, uti det sa kallade Nya Sverige* (Stockholm, 1759), 85, 105, 199 (translated by William M. Reynolds, *A History of New Sweden; or the Settlements on the Delaware River*, vol. 11 of Memoirs of the Historical Society of Pennsylvania [Philadelphia: The Society, 1874]); Kalm, *En Resa till Norra Amerika*, 93; Johnson, *Swedish Settlements*, 1:371ff., 510, 668, 678, 709f., 716; Craig and Yocom, "The Yocums of Aronamock," 244, 246f., 270, 273.

34. Johnson, *Swedish Settlements*, 1:238, 282f., 307, 310, 330, 407, 425; 2:477, 486, 623, 663f., 703, 705, 709f., 713, 716; G. Elgenstierna, *Den introducerade svenska adelns ättartavlor* (Stockholm: P. A. Norstedt and Söners Förlag, 1925), 1:482 and 3:264; M. Kerkkonen, "Finland and Colonial America," in *Old Friends—Strong Ties*, ed. V. Niitemaa et al. (Vaasa: Institute for Migration, 1976), 16; Craig and Yocom, "The Yocums of Aranamock," 272. See also *Svenska Riksrådets Protokoll*, 1651–53 (1920), 15:292.

35. Handel och Sjöfart, vol. 196, Riksarkivet.

36. G. B. Keen, *The Descendants of Jöran Kyn of New Sweden* (Philadelphia: Swedish Colonial Society, 1913).

37. Johnson, *Swedish Settlements*, 1:425, 439; 2:587f. 703, 714; Craig and Yocom, "The Yocums of Aronamock," 243ff.

38. R. Swedlund and O. Svenonius, *Svenska skriftprov 1464–1828* (Stockholm: Hugo Gebers Förlag, 1938), document X. Dr. Ann-Sofie Ohlander called my attention to this document.

39. Johnson, *Swedish Settlements*, 2:707.

40. Ibid., 1:239, 2:703, 714.

41. Ibid., 1:239. See also *Svenska Riksrådets Protokoll*, 1642 (1902), 9:200, 284, 404.

42. See also Åberg, *Folket i Nya Sverige*, 56.
43. S. Carlsson, "The Swedish Expeditions," 56.
44. Letter from J. Papegoja to Count P. Brahe, 15/7 1644, quoted in *New Sweden in Documents, 1638,* ed. K. Tarkiainen (Stockholm: Riksarkivet, 1988), 4; Amandus Johnson, *The Instruction for Johan Printz* (Philadelphia: Swedish Colonial Society, 1930), 129, 136, 177. The shortage of women is typical for a community of settlers. See H. Norman, "Från Bergslagen till Nordamerika," *Studia Historica Upsaliensia* 62 (1974): 240, 271ff.
45. Johnson, *Swedish Settlements*, 2:707.
46. Ibid., 700. One of them, Johan Papegoja, returned to the colony the same year.
47. Ibid., 1:259, 2:715; Johnson, *Instruction*, 130; Craig and Yocom, "The Yocums of Aronamock," 273.
48. One "discredited" soldier from Kajana, Österbotten, and two peasants from Satakunta, Finland, who were guilty of adultery are not included (Johnson, *Swedish Settlements*, 1:243). In 1643 they were all sentenced to go to New Sweden, but it is not clear that they really arrived there, and if they did, they may have been included among the already identified Finnish colonists.
49. Kalm, *En resa till Norra Amerika*, 187.
50. Johnson, *Swedish Settlements*, 1:260, 373; Hulan, "Historiska Minnen i Delaware," 44.
51. Handel och Sjöfart, vol. 196, Riksarkivet; Carlsson, "The Swedish Expeditions."
52. Johnson, *Swedish Settlements*, 1:462ff.; C. Sprinchorn, "Kolonien Nya Sveriges historia," in *Historiskt Bibliotek*, n.s., 3 (1878): 265; Craig and Yocom, "The Yocums of Aronamock," 269f.
53. *Svenska Riksrådets Protokoll*, 1647–48 (Stockholm, 1909), 12:176, 289, 293; 13:128; 15:73, 76, 300, 311, 326, 437; and 16:292, 300; Johnson, *Swedish Settlements*, 2:469.
54. Johnson, *Swedish Settlements*, 2:480ff., 716ff., 761.
55. A. Åberg in *Svenskt Biografiskt Lexikon* (Stockholm: Norstedts tryckeri, 1981), 23:485.
56. The soldier was Gösta Danielsson (see also F. Blomfelt, *Andreas Sandels dagbok, 1701–1743* [Stockholm: Erene Document, 1988], 121), the tailor Lars Esbjörnsson Skräddare, the stonecutter Hans Preutz Stenhuggare, the soldiers Påvel Nilsson Quist, Lars Jonsson Rudenius, and Nils Matsson Utter. See Johnson, *Swedish Settlements*, 2:718ff.
57. Johnson, *Swedish Settlements*, 2:472ff.
58. W. Sjöstrand, *Pedagogikens historia* (Stockholm: Lund & Malmö, 1958), 2:198f.
59. Johnson, *Swedish Settlements*, 2:472.
60. Ibid., 1:282; 2:477; Åberg, *Folket i Nya Sverige*, 48.
61. Johnson, *Swedish Settlements*, 2:720; Kalm, *En resa till Norra Amerika*, 190f., 206; Craig and Hulan, "Membership of the Swedish Lutheran Church," 6.
62. Handel och Sjöfart, vols. 43 and 44, Riksarkivet; Acrelius, *Beskrifning om de swenska*, 65; Johnson, *Swedish Settlements*, 2:475, 503, 682, 685, 693, 716ff., 724; J. A. Westerlund and J. A. Setterdahl, *Linköpings stifts herdaminne* (Linköping: Östogöta correspondentens boktrycheri, 1925), 4:2, 2:19.

63. Johnson, *Swedish Settlements*, 2:721.
64. Jan Jansson Bockhorn, first mate on the *Örn*, probably a Dutchman, stayed for some time in the colony (see Johnson, *Swedish Settlements*, 2:470, 761); the Dutch freeman Alexander Boijs, probably arriving in 1654 (ibid., 2:717); and Frans Lorensson or Lorans, probably a Dutchman (ibid., 720).
65. Ibid., 720; Blomfelt, *Andreas Sandels dagbok*, 125.
66. Johnson, *Swedish Settlements*, 2:720f.
67. Ibid., 547.
68. Ibid., 472.
69. Ibid., 721; Craig and Hulan, "Membership of Holy Trinity (Old Swedes) Church in Wilmington, Delaware (1764)" (mimeographed paper, Wilmington, Delaware), 4.
70. Johnson, *Swedish Settlements*, 2:717, 721f.
71. Anders Finne, Lars Andersson Finne, another with the same name, Hans Jansson Finne, Henrik Larsson Finne, and Henrik Matsson Finne (see Johnson, *Swedish Settlements*, 2:717ff).
72. Kalm, *En resa till Norra Amerika*, 185; H. D. Paxson, *Where Pennsylvania History Began* (Philadelphia: George H. Buchanan, 1926), 78; Landelius, *Swedish Place-Names in North America*, 172; Craig and Hulan, "Membership of Holy Trinity (Old Swedes) Church," 4, and "Membership of the Swedish Lutheran Church," 6; Blomfelt, *Andreas Sandels dagbok*, 108f.
73. Kalm, *En resa till Norra Amerika*, 206, 219; Johnson, *Swedish Settlements*, 2:721; Kerkkonen, "Finland and Colonial America," 27; R. Kero, "Värmlandsfinnar y Nya Sverige," in *Värmlandsfinnar*, ed. S. Huovinen (Stockholm: Kulturfonden för Sverige och Finland, 1986), 115.
74. Kalm, *En resa till Norra Amerika*, 219.
75. Kastrup, *The Swedish Heritage in America*, 94.
76. Sixty-five of three hundred, 1638–44, one hundred of 250, 1654. It must, of course, be stressed that the figures are very approximate.
77. Sprinchorn, "Kolonien Nya Sveriges historia," 265.
78. See Craig and Yocom, "The Yocums of Aronamock," 246, 270.
79. Johnson, *Swedish Settlements*, 2:581ff.
80. Ibid., 634, 761.
81. Ibid., 633, 724.
82. Ibid., 667.
83. Kalm, *En resa till Norra Amerika*, 205f.; Johnson, *Swedish Settlements*, 1:219; Craig and Hulan, "Membership of Holy Trinity (Old Swedes) Church," 3. A suggestion that Mattson Run in Delaware was named after Erik Mattson of Fryksdalen (A. R. Dunlap, *Dutch and Swedish Place-Names in Delaware* [Newark: University of Delaware Press, 1956], 40, and Landelius, *Swedish Place-Names in North America*, 44) must be regarded as very doubtful.
84. Kalm, *En resa till Norra Amerika*, 185; Johnson, *Swedish Settlements*, 1:219; Craig and Hulan, "Membership of the Swedish Lutheran Church," 6; Blomfelt, *Andreas Sandels dagsbok*, 120.
85. $300 + 250 + 110 = 660$. Some other colonists have to be included.
86. $65 + 100 + 92 = 257$. Some have to be added.
87. Of the approximately sixty-five early Finnish immigrants, something like twenty-five of the one hundred and ninety-two arriving in 1654 and 1656,

respectively, may have lived in the area in 1656. However, there may have been some Finns among the twenty persons leaving with Rising in 1655 (Johnson, *Swedish Settlements*, 2:724): $25 + 100 + 92 = 217$. After the arrival of the *Mercurius*, the total population seems to have been around 460 persons $(370 + 110 - 20)$. I should mention that some of the inhabitants were born in America.

88. *New Sweden in Documents, 1638.29.3*, 1988, p. 14.

89. Kalm, *En resa till Norra Amerika*, 187; H. Nelson, *The Swedes and the Swedish Settlements in North America* (Lund: Skrifter utg av Kungl Humanistiska Vetenskaps-Samfundet i Lund, 1943), 78.

90. Compare S. Carlsson, *Svensk historia*, 4th ed. (Stockholm and Lund: Esselte Studium, 1980), 56.

91. Christopher is mentioned by Johnson, *Swedish Settlements*, 1:153.

92. Holm, *Kort Beskrifning*, 66.

93. For Stille, Cock, and Nilsson (Long) see above; for Homman see Johnson, *Swedish Settlements*, 2:713, and Paxson, *Where Pennsylvania History Began*, 219, and Craig and Hulan, "Membership of the Swedish Lutheran Church," 5; for Stalcup see Hulan, "Historiska Minnen i Delaware," 45f.

94. Kalm, *En resa till Norra Amerika*, 219; Craig and Hulan, "Membership in the Swedish Lutheran Church," 5.

95. For Rambo, Lock, and Bengtsson, see above; for Johasson-Jones and Mansson-Steelman see Johnson, *Swedish Settlements*, 2:713, and Craig and Yocom, "The Yocums of Aronamock," 248ff.; for Gustafsson-Justis see Kalm, *En resa till Norra Amerika*, 208, Johnson, *Swedish Settlements*, 2:714, and Craig and Hulan, "Membership in the Swedish Lutheran Church," 5.

96. Johnson, *Swedish Settlements*, 1:248, 268; 2:667, 709, 716; Craig and Hulan, "Membership of Holy Trinity (Old Swedes) Church," 4; Blomfelt, *Andreas Sandels dagbok*, 129.

97. For Skute and Morton see above; for Mattson see Johnson, *Swedish Settlements*, 2:712, and Craig and Hulan, "Membership of the Swedish Lutheran Church," 6.

98. Craig and Hulan, "Membership of Holy Trinity (Old Swedes) Church," 4.

99. Landelius, *Swedish Place-Names in North America*, 172f.

100. For Keen and Yocom, see above; for Larsson-Huling see Blomfelt, *Andreas Sandels dagbok*, 125.

101. Nelson, *The Swedes and the Swedish Settlements*, 77.

102. *Rand McNally Atlas of World History*, ed. R. Palmer (Chicago, 1957), 193.

103. Nelson, *The Swedes and the Swedish Settlements*, 53; *Rand McNally Atlas*, 193.

The New Sweden Colony and the Continued Existence of Swedish and Finnish Ethnicity

HANS NORMAN

During Fredrika Bremer's well-known journey to America in the middle of the nineteenth century, the Swedish author visited the area of the New Sweden colony. In a letter of 25 June 1850 she tells about the last Swedish-born minister to have served in the former colony, Nils Collin, who had died at a very old age some years before. An American minister, Jehu Curtis Clay, was now in charge of the Swedish congregation and church in Wicacoa. He assembled as many descendants from the original colonists as possible for the visit, and Bremer comments: "It was a company of from fifty to sixty [people], and I shook hands with many agreeable persons, but they had nothing Swedish about them, excepting their family names, of which I recognized many. No traditions of their emigration hither remained; language, appearance, all, had entirely merged into that of the now-prevailing Anglo-Saxon race."[1]

That this was the case is hardly surprising. Almost two hundred years had passed since Sweden had lost its colony on the Delaware River, and by this time the Swedish language and other remnants of the Swedish ethnic heritage were long gone.

The small group of colonists from New Sweden who remained in the area after Sweden lost the colony in 1655 consisted of Swedes, Finns, some Dutch, and people from German-speaking areas in Europe who had enlisted in Swedish service. The great majority spoke Swedish, and a Swedish ethnicity, primarily rooted in the language and religion, was maintained in the area for a surprisingly long time.

The first part of this study determines the conditions among the former colonists and their descendants that helped maintain a sense of Swedish ethnicity. The second part addresses those factors that contributed to the longevity of the group's ethnicity, with special focus on religion and church life. The role of the ministers, sent to the former colony by the Swedish authorities, is also addressed, as are the reasons for sending them to America. I attempt to analyze the social and demographic structure of the members of the old Swedish congregations on the Delaware River, concluding with a discussion of the use of the Swedish language.

THE SIZE OF THE POPULATION FROM THE SWEDISH REALM ON THE DELAWARE RIVER

When Peter Minuit's expedition sailed into the Delaware River on the ships *Kalmar Nyckel* and *Griffin* in 1638, it included twenty soldiers, of whom half were Swedes and half Dutch. The soldiers eventually became the garrison at Fort Christina that was erected on the Minquas River (later renamed the Christina River). Minuit himself died during his return to Europe a few months later. Except for the soldiers, the only people left in the embryo of what was to become the colony of New Sweden were the commander, Lieutenant Måns Kling, the agent, Hendrick Huygen, who was responsible for trading with the Indians, and an interpreter.

During the next two years these were the only Europeans living in New Sweden. In April 1640 the *Kalmar Nyckel* returned, bringing the new director of the enterprise, Peter Hollander Ridder, soldiers to relieve the small New Sweden garrison, and some colonists. Over the next several years, twelve expeditions carrying soldiers and colonists were sent to New Sweden. Even though ten reached New Sweden, the population of the colony never exceeded a few hundred, of which few were women. (See table 1, which, however, only includes the male population.)

In 1647 Governor Johan Printz reported that there were 183 people in New Sweden. After the problems of the later years of Printz's tenure and

Table 1

The Number of Men in New Sweden in Various Years, According to Occupation

Occupation	1638	1640	1643	1648	1654
Officials/officers	3	8	20	10	26
Artisans	--	4	7	7	11
Farmers	1	7	5	15	61
Soldiers	21	6	26	24	42
Sailors	--	9	6	6	2
Laborers/Farmhands/ Unknown	--	34	29	21	62
Totals	25	68	93	83	204

Source: M. Svejebäck, "Värvning av kolonister och social struktur i kolonin Nya Sverige 1638-1655," unpublished paper, Department of History, Uppsala University, 1986, who compiled the information from Amandus Johnson, The Swedish Settlement on the Delaware. Their History and Religion to the Indians, Dutch and English 1683-1664, 2 vols. (Philadelphia: Swedish Colonial Society, 1911).

his return to Sweden, the population decreased significantly because of outmigration, primarily to Maryland but also to New Amsterdam.

By the time Johan Rising arrived on the *Örn* in 1654, there were only some seventy persons left in the colony. This expedition was the only Swedish attempt to bring substantial numbers of new people to the colony. The ship was filled to capacity with more than 350 persons on board, including the crew and the soldiers. Although about one hundred died either during the crossing of the Atlantic or shortly after arrival, Rising could still report to his principals in Sweden that the colony now numbered 368. This figure included approximately twenty Dutch who had sworn an oath of loyalty to the Swedish Crown and the New Sweden Company after the Swedes seized the Dutch Fort Casimir, which was located on the Delaware River.

As the immigration to New Sweden continued, the percentage of the colonists coming from Finland increased. There were, for example, a large number of Finnish families on board the *Örn*. This increase in Finnish immigration was rooted in the conditions of the homeland. In 1647, to save the forests for the important production of iron, the Swedish Crown prohibited slash-and-burn agriculture. The Finns, who had originally moved to forested areas in Bergslagen in Sweden to make their living from this now-prohibited agricultural technique, had heard about the possibilities of acquiring new land in the colony.[2] Thus it is possible to speak of an "American fever" and of the establishment of an emigration tradition in Sweden by the middle of the seventeenth century, although on a much smaller scale than the mass emigration that occurred some two hundred years later. As a matter of fact, when the *Örn* was ready to set sail in early 1654, about one hundred families had to be turned away from the quay in Götenborg, due to lack of space. Some of them were able to get on *Gyllene Hajen*, which departed in April of that same year. However, this ship went off course and was seized by the Dutch governor, Peter Stuyvesant, in the harbor of New Amsterdam.

More Finnish colonists arrived in the New Sweden area on two later crossings. The ship *Mercurius*, which had been fitted while Sweden still retained the colony but did not arrive until March 1656, six months after the colony was lost, carried about one hundred passengers, of whom ninety were Finns. In December 1663 thirty-two emigrants of Finnish descent arrived at the former colony. They came from the province of Medelpad in the woodlands in north central Sweden and had been enticed to cross the Atlantic by Israel Helm. Helm, himself an emigrant, lived on the Delaware and had been in Sweden to recruit emigrants on the initiative of the Dutch governor of a portion of the former New Sweden, Alexander D'Hinojossa. Although attempts were made by the Swedish authorities to stop them, the emigrants Helm recruited traveled from Christina in Norway via Amsterdam, reaching their destination successfully.[3]

Consequently, about three hundred Swedes and Finns stayed on the Delaware when the Dutch took over the colony in 1655. After the fall of Fort Trinity (Fort Casimir) some of the soldiers were forced to participate in the defense of New Amsterdam, which had come under attack from the Indians during Peter Stuyvesant's military expedition against New Sweden. Even though thirty-six people accompanied Rising on his return to Sweden, the population increased by approximately one hundred people, mostly of Finnish descent, when the ship *Mercurius* arrived. Later Helm's thirty-two people reached the former colony via Amsterdam. When the natural population increase is taken into account, the number of inhabitants from the Swedish realm on the Delaware at the time the English took control in 1664 ought to have been between five and six hundred.

During the Dutch period the population in the former Swedish colony was affected by the area's division into two administrative units separated by the Christina River. The area south of the river, centered around New Amstel (formerly Fort Casimir), was administered by the city of Amsterdam in repayment for its help during the Dutch attack on New Sweden. The area north of the river was controlled by New Amsterdam, and it centered on the old Fort Christina, which was renamed Fort Altena. There was a certain amount of migration between the two areas, especially when D'Hinojossa tried to attract people from the northern area to the city's colony, as the southern part was called. Some Finnish colonists from the *Mercurius* who had settled in the northern part, in the vicinity of Tinicum, had some difficulties establishing themselves there and moved to the city's colony.[4]

As a legacy from the earlier Swedish colonists, two centers for religious activities already existed in the area. One was situated at Fort Christina and the other at Tinicum, which had been the location of Printz's residence, Printzhof. The church at Tinicum was frequented by the inhabitants of the northern area, but gradually the timbered church at Wicacoa took the old church's place. In the southern part, where previously the church at Fort Christina had been used, a new timbered church was erected at Crane Hook in 1667. This church was more conveniently located for those who lived south of the Christina River, including the Dutch and the newly arrived Finns who had settled around New Amstel.[5]

When the English gained control over the area in 1664, their immigration increased, although initially rather slowly. A significant change occurred during the 1680s with a major immigration of Quakers under William Penn's leadership. There were also strong elements of Welsh and

Irish in this group. In 1700 the population of Pennsylvania consisted of roughly 68 percent English, 20 percent Welsh and Irish, and 5 percent Germans and Dutch. Of the remaining 7 percent many had Swedish or Finnish ancestry. Philadelphia, founded by Penn in 1683, quickly became a major city, dominating the area where the Schuylkill River joins the Delaware River, an area inhabited by Swedish colonists. After 1730, the German share of Pennsylvania's population increased significantly as a result of strong German immigration.[6]

There was no immigration to the Delaware area from Sweden during the last three decades of the seventeenth century. As time went on the descendants of the immigrants tended to marry non-Swedes. Depending on how the children of these mixed marriages are classified, it becomes very difficult to determine the size of the Swedish group in these later years. Based on Carl Springer's list of 1693 (mentioned later in this essay), which included 942 individuals, we can estimate that the total included slightly more than one thousand persons by 1700. By that time some Swedish colonists had also spread to other areas, including Maryland.[7]

Factors That Have Strengthened Ethnic Cohesiveness

Ethnicity is an elusive concept, with different meanings in different historical and social contexts. Many factors affect a group's sense of ethnic distinctness, and it is not always obvious which of these factors are most important.

In trying to define the phenomenon of ethnicity, one can use subjective or objective criteria. The subjective definition is based both on how the individuals of the ethnic group perceive their differences from the larger community and on how the larger community views the ethnic group. The objective definition uses more easily determined factors such as origin, religion, and, not least, language. Among the subjective criteria, a group's early arrival to an area and common cultural background are often emphasized as particularly important. Moreover, to establish itself successfully, the group cannot be too small. Additional factors that may affect the group's unity are outside pressures such as political, economic, and social changes in the surrounding society, all of which can strengthen the collective sentiments and identity of a minority group.[8]

When there are certain institutions within the ethnic group, they play the role of tradition bearers and thus focus and strengthen its consciousness. A religious organization with a church building for common worship services and general social interaction contributes to the maintenance of both religion and language, two of the objective criteria of ethnicity. On the other hand, marriages across ethnic boundaries gradually work to the detriment of ethnic cohesiveness.[9]

In the case of the ethnicity of the Delaware Swedes the fact that the overwhelming part of the group had their origins in the Swedish realm was of great significance. The majority of the population spoke Swedish, and there was a long tradition of conformity with the Lutheran religion.

Ethnic unity was strengthened by the fact that the Swedish immigrants were the first arrivals, and they constituted the majority among the various European ethnic groups in the Delaware region for at least two decades. Thus Swedish became a lingua franca in the area for several decades.[10]

The socioeconomic situation of the colonists also contributed to their ethnic consciousness. Many of them had improved their socioeconomic status by becoming freeholding peasants during the Swedish period. This was done partly through the acquisition of land directly from the New Sweden Company and partly as remuneration paid to the soldiers and civil servants after a certain time of service. In 1653 the Swedish government sought to encourage immigration to the colony by stipulating that every colonist could buy land directly from both the company and the Indians, even if purchase of Indian lands had to be confirmed by the governor. Based on this, Johan Rising drew up an ordinance that regulated various practical matters in the colony, including the purchase of land.[11]

The colonists experienced outside pressure both when Sweden ruled the colony and after it had been taken over first by the Dutch and later by the English. Although the Dutch and English threat to New Sweden was a problem primarily for military and political leaders, ordinary civil servants, soldiers, and residents probably saw this as a real threat as well. The threat was particularly strong when the Dutch attack on the colony in the late summer of 1655 resulted in occupation and plundering.

Most of the information available, though, indicates that the colonists remaining from the Swedish period adjusted well to the Dutch and later to the English rule and that they lived under relatively acceptable conditions. There are, however, clear instances of pressure from the outside to adjust to foreign ways during this period.

The Dutch governor, Peter Stuyvesant, demanded early on that all Swedes and Finns swear an oath of loyalty to the Dutch West India Company. Those who refused were to leave the Dutch colony within one year and six weeks. He also demanded that the Swedish and Finnish colonists leave their scattered settlements and consolidate in villages, where the Dutch could more easily supervise and administer them.

Through passive resistance, the former New Sweden colonists strengthened their position and sense of ethnic distinctiveness. Only a small number of the colonists swore the oath of loyalty to the Dutch. Those who refused to do so were able to go on living in the area with unaltered privi-leges.[12] Stuyvesant's closest associate in the Delaware area, Vice-Gover-nor Beekman, found it almost impossible to move the colonists into the proposed villages against their will since they were by then established in their places of residence.[13] In addition, the Swedish colonists had a counterweapon. When Alexander D'Hinojossa invited Swedish and Fin-nish colonists to settle in the proximity of New Amstel, many accepted his offer. Some of them also moved on to the Sassafras River in Maryland. Faced with the threat of losing important inhabitants in the colony, Stuy-vesant had to abandon his demands.[14]

One illustration of the degree of independence that the former Swedish and Finnish colonists retained under Dutch rule is the fact that Stuyves-ant granted "the Swedish nation" limited self-determination in certain internal matters in exchange for promises of loyalty. In 1658 a council was named consisting of Gregorius van Dijk, sheriff; Sven Skute, cap-tain; Anders Dalbo, lieutenant; Jacob Svensson, ensign; and magistrates Olof Stille, Mats Hansson, Peter Rambo, and Peter Cock.[15]

This special status that "the Swedish nation" acquired under Dutch rule made it possible for the former New Sweden colonists to continue to speak the language of their homeland and to retain their own reli-gion. They became a small but not insignificant population element in what is usually called "the Middle Colonies," which were a mosaic of eth-nic groups, religious preferences, and varied economic life-styles. In con-trast to other parts of the English colonies in North America, the Middle Colonies experienced a progressive but turbulent political development, and it was this area that fostered many of the ideas and actions that re-sulted in the later independence of the English colonies.[16]

One factor that meant increased outside pressure on the Swedish-speaking population was the large immigration of English Quakers and other ethnic groups that began in the 1680s. Gradually the Swedish-speakers became a minority in the area. At the same time the Swedes had to face new legal restrictions on land holdings that made it difficult to acquire large and well-situated tracts of land. In addition, Penn's new regime required deeds proving earlier land acquisitions. Finally, as the price of land increased, wealthy English immigrants dominated the land market.[17]

THE SWEDISH MINISTERS ON THE DELAWARE

In the late 1680s the ministers Lars Lock and Jacob Fabritius, who had served the Swedish congregations at Crane Hook and Wicacoa, respec-tively, could no longer continue their work, so the congregations made a few futile attempts to recruit Swedish ministers via Amsterdam, but not directly from Sweden.[19]

Not until 1691, when the postmaster in Göteborg, Johan Thelin, addressed the need for new Swedish ministers in America, did the Swedish government show any interest in its former colony. Thelin stated that he had met a man called Anders Printz in Stockholm who claimed that he had recently been to America and had visited the Delaware Swedes. He told Thelin about their need for ministers and religious literature in Swedish. Thelin (who earlier had been a secretary to Magnus Gabriel de la Gardie, Sweden's chancellor of state), and Lars Riddermarck, an official of the House of Nobility, wrote a letter to the royal chancellery based on Printz's information. In it they described the needs of Swedish immigrants on the Delaware River. King Charles XI became interested in them and asked the bishop of Turku, Johannes Gezelius, to arrange for a Finnish minister as well as Finnish Bibles and hymnals to be sent to America.[19]

An important question concerns Thelin and his active engagement in the matter. He states that he was "somewhat related" to the merchant Nils Printz, who, it was claimed, was Anders Printz's brother.[20] One could therefore ask if Thelin was influenced by those in trading circles in Göteborg to evaluate potential markets in America. At any rate there is a clear family interest involved. Both in his and in Riddermarck's letters to the chancellery and in a later letter to Secretary of State Samuel Akerhielm, Thelin proposes that his brother, Carl Thelin, a theology student in Turku, be given assistance until his studies were completed and then be sent to America to minister to the Swedish congregations there. This request was, however, turned down by Bishop Gezelius in Turku.[21]

The largest question, however, concerns the person supposedly called Anders Printz. It is unclear who he was or if he really had visited America around 1690. Thelin passed on some of the information about the conditions in Delaware that he said he had learned from Printz in his 1692 letter to Carl Springer, a well-educated layperson who assisted the Delaware congregations when they were without ministers. Some of the information was incorrect, which Springer noted. Springer mentioned a visit from Printz in his reply to Thelin in 1693, but he did it in a way that suggested he got that information from Thelin. Moreover, Thelin was more vague about Printz in his letter to the Delaware Swedes than he was in his letter to the royal chancellery. In the former he stated that it would be desirable if Printz could accompany the ministers who were to be sent to America as a guide, but that at the present, no one seemed to know where Printz was. Even more mysterious is that the three ministers claimed that he did accompany them as a guide, but disappeared after a stop in London.[22] According to Israel Acrelius, Anders Printz claimed to be a nephew of Johan Printz, the former governor of New Sweden. This does not seem possible. Johan Printz had only one brother, Sven Björnsson, who was married but childless.[23] Who Anders Printz really was and what his role was in connection with the dispatch of the Swedish ministers to Delaware thus remains to be investigated.[24]

With the king's encouragement Thelin wrote the letter mentioned above to the Delaware Swedes in November 1692, in which he mentioned his meeting with Printz. He asked them to describe their living conditions and to explain their need for ministers. He also stated that Sweden was willing to assist them.[25]

In May 1693 Thelin received a detailed answer from Carl Springer, which was also signed by a number of prominent Delaware Swedes. Springer wrote that the former colony needed two ministers.[26]

The Swedish government did not act on the issue until 1696, when Charles XI ordered the cathedral minister in Uppsala, Jesper Svedberg, to attend to the matter. Eventually Svedberg sent three ministers to America—Erik Björck, Andreas Rudman, and Jonas Aurén. Björck and Rudman took on congregations; Jonas Aurén was to gather information about the country and make a report to the king.[27] All three ministers made significant contributions to the Swedish mission on the Delaware.[28]

The start of these Swedish missionary activities took place forty years after Sweden had lost the colony. The question then arises if motives other than religious and idealistic ones prompted the Swedish government's action. Did the Swedish government expect any benefits from this undertaking? Since the hope of regaining New Sweden had been long given up, why would the Swedish government consider it advantageous to promote the maintenance of "Swedishness" among the population in the former colony?

The three ministers were greeted warmly when they arrived in Delaware. Björck took charge of the southern congregation at Christina and Rudman led the northern congregation at Wicacoa. Aurén, who had not been given any particular clerical responsibilities, did not return to Sweden with his report as he had been instructed to do. Instead he assumed responsibility for the Swedish and Finnish families who were living in northeastern Maryland and who attended the English Episcopal church, St. Mary Anne's. Later he became the minister of a new congregation on the New Jersey side of the Delaware near Raccoon and Penns Neck.

The first years seem to have been characterized by enthusiasm and many activities. In fact, new churches were soon erected at both Christina and Wicacoa. Both churches were made of stone, and the first, Holy Trinity, was located close to the old fortress at Christina. The other, Gloria Dei, stood at the same place as the old timber church at Wicacoa.[29] Later, new congregations were founded in Raccoon, Penns Neck, and Maurice River in New Jersey. In addition, Kingsessing, Upper Merion, and Manatawny were formed as annex congregations to Wicacoa. The latter two were located on the Schuylkill River.

Between 1696 and 1786 the Swedish church continued to support the former colonists and their descendants with a total of twenty-four ministers, as well as with Bibles, hymnals, catechisms, and other devotional material. The Swedish ministers were important tradition-bearers and preservers of their ethnic heritage. Swedish was the language of the Bible, the hymns, and the sermons. In addition, the church records were kept in Swedish for a long time.

The ministers were also important in strengthening the inner organizational life of the congregations. When Andreas Sandel succeeded Rudman at Wicacoa in 1702, a church council was instituted to supervise the church, the parsonage, and the morals of the members. It was the duty of the church wardens to collect money for the ministers' salaries, to handle the economic affairs of the congregation, and to care for the poor. Similarly, at Christina, where Andreas Hesselius replaced Björck when the latter returned to Sweden in 1713, the twelve-person church council was given authority over church discipline and related issues.[30]

Jesper Svedberg played a significant role in organizing the Swedish ministers in Delaware. For forty years (1695–1735), in addition to his regular duties as bishop of Skara, he served as superintendent of the religious work in Delaware. He maintained an ongoing correspondence with the ministers, served as a source of inspiration, and supplied them with material and resources as far as possible. Svedberg saw to it that the congregations received schoolmasters and even sent his own son (also called Jesper Svedberg) to Delaware, where he remained for nine years. In the long run, maintaining the schools proved difficult. There was no money for salaries and the quality of the teachers was low. It was also hard to find suitable schoolhouses. Finally, because the families lived far apart, it was difficult to gather the children together.

Economically, the ministers depended on the support of their congregations. To supplement their incomes, from time to time the ministers also served English and German congregations. It was not until 1740 that the Swedish government began paying salaries for one vicar and one assistant pastor at each congregation.[31] One significant difference between the ministers in Delaware and in Sweden was that Delaware ministers could not enforce the strict church discipline that was so characteristic of eighteenth-century Sweden. This was also a source of numerous complaints by the ministers in the former colony.[32]

In 1751, on the initiative of the archdiocese in Uppsala, the ministers were required to maintain records of their parishioners. In connection with this, the old Swedish tradition of dividing the congregations into subdistricts (*rotar*) was inaugurated.[33]

The Composition of the Swedish-Speaking Population After 1750

It is possible to describe the composition of the Swedish ethnic group during the second half of the eighteenth century by using the ministers' records of the congregations.[34] During Israel Acrelius's time as vicar (1749–56), membership records were drawn up for the congregations in Christina, Wicacoa, and Penns Neck. Of prime importance for the archdiocese in Uppsala were the number of members in the different congregations, how frequently they attended church services, and their knowledge of the Swedish language. Unfortunately these instructions were never supplemented with a standardized form of record keeping; therefore, the information varies and is not complete enough for exact demographic analyses. The most commonly noted entries include the parishioners' knowledge of Swedish, in which language they read the Bible, how well they knew Luther's catechism, and how often they took Holy Communion. In addition, entries include the members' occupations and sometimes their ages. The youngest household members are somewhat underrepresented.[35]

It is important to keep in mind that by this time quite a large proportion of the population of Swedish descent had married across ethnic boundaries, and many descendants of the original Swedish colonists were probably not members of the Swedish congregations. Conversely, a large number of people with no Swedish background had joined the congregations. Therefore, the Swedish ethnic group is defined as the members of the Swedish congregations, the majority of which still spoke Swedish in the decades following 1750. A calculation based on these congregations yields a total of 1,195 persons who spoke Swedish. If the members who spoke only English are included as well, the total exceeds 1,700.[36] Table 2 shows their distribution in the various congregations. The years in parentheses indicate the dates of the records.

It is hard to determine the number of colonists of Finnish descent. Some had come directly from present-day Finland, but the majority descended from immigrants who had immigrated to Sweden during the sixteenth and seventeenth centuries and had settled in the forest areas of Bergslagen in central Sweden or further north. The latter group had largely preserved their Finnish language and culture and were *svedjebönder* (slash-and-burn farmers) in Sweden. They became a significant ele-

Table 2

Swedish Lutheran Congregations in the Delaware Valley
Around the Middle of the Eighteenth Century:
Number of Members in Selected Years

Christina (1754)	490
Wicacoa (1754)	331
Kingsessing (1784)	186
Upper Merion (1784)	77
Manatawny (1760)	76
Raccoon and Penns Neck (1754)	429
Maurice River (1770)	140
Total	1,729

Source: Church registers, from Sture Eilertz, "Nova Svecia: Den svensk-
lutherska befolkningen i Delaware-omradet vid 1700-talets mitt,"
unpublished paper, Department of History, Uppsala University, 1986.

ment in the emigration to New Sweden during the colony's later years. At first the Finns settled between Fort Christina and Tinicum. Later many settled south of the Christina River, due to the relocation offers from the Dutch director of the city's colony. It seems likely that they started speaking Swedish, since none of the sources indicate anything to the contrary.

Many persons of Finnish descent also seem to have taken part in the settlement of the opposite side of the Delaware River, in present-day New Jersey. There was a strong Finnish settlement at Penns Neck, and as late as in the mid-eighteenth century Swedish minister Pehr Kalm reports that the older settlers there still spoke Finnish, whereas the younger people spoke English. No one seems to have spoken Swedish.[37]

As I have already mentioned, Sweden was prepared to send to the Delaware River both a Swedish and a Finnish minister, as well as books in Swedish and Finnish. The Finnish element was, however, largely ignored, primarily due to the letter from Carl Springer, which stated that since everybody in the former colony spoke Swedish, only Swedish-speaking ministers were needed.[38] Since Finland remained a part of the Swedish realm until 1809, and since it is likely that most Finnish colonists spoke Swedish (especially those who lived side by side with Swedes), in terms of ethnicity I will treat all colonists as Swedish, as of Swedish descent, or Swedish-speaking, whether their ancestry was Swedish or Finnish.

By analyzing the churches' membership records, one can get a picture of the social structure of the Swedish congregations. The analysis rests on

Table 3

The Social Structure of the Swedish Lutheran Congregations
in the Delaware Area, based on Occupational Notations
in the membership records

Occupation*	Christina 1754, 1764		Wicacoa & Kingsessing 1754, 1784, 1786		Raccoon & Penns Neck 1754, 1771	
	No.	%	No.	%	No.	%
Ministers, military, organists, judges	4	1.4	8	6.5	11	2.9
Freeholding peasants	202	69.9	77	62.6	250	67.0
Merchants, craftsmen, business owners	44	15.2	26	21.1	27	7.3
Workers, floaters	6	2.1	--	--	14	3.8
Servants (men and women)	33	11.4	12	9.8	71	19.0
Totals	289	100.0	123	100.0	373	100.0

*Men only unless noted.

Source: Church membership records, compiled by S. Eilertz, 1986 (see Table 2).
Figures for Wicacoa and Kingsessing in 1786 are from church council
records.

the occupational classifications noted by the ministers for male church
members and for female servants. Occupational classifications are available for Christina in 1756 and 1764, Wicacoa in 1754 and 1786 (the latter
year refers to the church council only), Kingsessing in 1784, Raccoon and
Penns Neck in 1754 and 1771.

Since the ministers did not use any set formulas, information varied
from place to place and from year to year. Even so it is possible to get a
fairly accurate picture of the social structure of the congregations. To
minimize inconsistencies, in each instance the figures for Christina, Raccoon, and Penns Neck reflect both years for the respective congregations.
I have included the two years from Kingsessing with the data for Wicacoa
because it served as an annex congregation and was located not far from
Wicacoa in the Philadelphia vicinity. As can be seen in table 3, five main
occupational groups have been identified, making possible a rough analysis of the social structure.

By the mid-eighteenth century two-thirds of the group still depended
on the agricultural sector. A relatively small percentage of the congregations were servants, indicating that there was not a great need for hired
hands on the different farms. There must have been a great number of
children in the households who could help in the work on the farms. It

can also be noted that the share of the population engaged in nonagricultural pursuits was greatest at Wicacoa in the Philadelphia vicinity.

DEMOGRAPHIC STRUCTURE

In several studies of the colonial period in North American history, the population's structure and reproductive capabilities have received attention. Based on various evidence, it seems clear that the Delaware Swedes had a high rate of reproduction.[39] In an often-quoted characterization, William Penn said about the Swedes that "as they are a people proper and strong of body, so they have fine children and almost every house is full. It is rare to find one of them without three or four boys, and as many girls; some six, seven or eight sons."[40]

Two of the early colonists illustrate this point (although they are hardly representative). Peter Gunnarsson Rambo wrote to his sister in Göteborg in the 1690s that he and his wife lived well in New Sweden and that they had four sons, four daughters, and as many as thirty-seven grandchildren. When Lars Persson Cock wrote to his relatives back in Södermanland in 1693, he told of his father, Peter Cock, who had thirteen children and seventy-one grandchildren. He himself had eleven children.[41]

In some cases it is possible to use the membership records from the Swedish congregations to study the populations' demographic structure and reproduction rate. The best records for these purposes are those by Johan Wicksell for Raccoon and Penns Neck in 1771. Here we get a fairly good picture of the size of each family and the number of its children at the time of the census. Figure 1 presents a population pyramid based on that information.

This age pyramid shows an equal age distribution for men and women. The only underrepresentation occurs in the lowest age groups because the notations deal largely with the population's church attendance and knowledge of the catechism and the Swedish language. The pyramid indicates that the population in Raccoon and Penns Neck had a rapid rate of reproduction, resulting in a significant number of children. There is a clear underrepresentation in the age group 0–4 years, but this group must have been larger than the age group 5–9 years. Even if a high rate of out-migration in the 15–29 age groups had occurred, it seems more plausible that the low figure indicates a high mortality rate in the 0–14 age groups.

For the kind of rough analysis used here, it can be instructive to use the topology of populations constructed by Swedish population statistician Gustav Sundbärg. Sundbärg identifies three groups: a progressive type with a strong natural population increase, a stationary type with virtually no natural population increase, and a regressive type where the popula-

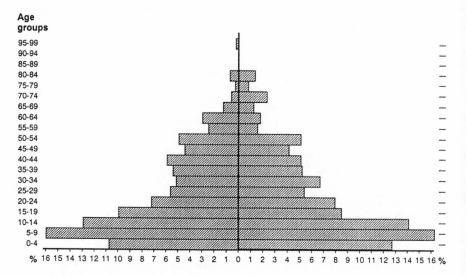

Fig. 1. Age structure of the members in the Swedish Lutheran congregations of Raccoon and Penns Neck, 1771. *Source*: Membership records of Raccoon and Penns Neck, 1991.

tion declines if no immigration takes place.[42] According to Sundbärg, the relationship between the three types of populations (per thousand people) can be expressed as in Table 4. A similar calculation based on the membership records from Raccoon and Penns Neck yields the results shown in table 5.

In other words, in a progressive population one hundred out of one thousand people will be age fifty or older, five hundred will be fifteen to forty-nine, and four hundred will be fourteen or younger. As can be seen, the results indicate a strongly progressive population structure where the share of children (0–14 years) is even greater than in Sundbärg's figures, in spite of the statistics' underrepresentation in the 0–4 age band seen in figure 1. Moreover, it should be noted that the reproductive portion of the population (15–49 years) is surprisingly small, which further points to the high rate of reproduction in the population. It is also interesting that the share of people over fifty is remarkably large. People in New Sweden grew quite old. Age statistics are based on individual statements and may not be entirely reliable, but it is worth noting that John Mullica was recorded as being ninety-seven years old and that Måns Keen, Sr., claimed to be 105.

One of the reasons for the high rate of reproduction was that many of the women married young. A calculation of the age of women when

Table 4

Three Types of Populations
by Age and Natural Population Growth

	Progressive	Stationary	Regressive
50+ years	100	230	300
15-49 years	500	505	500
0-14 years	400	265	200

Source: Gustav Sundbärg, Bevölkerungsstatistik Schwedens 1750-1900. Urval
Skriftserie utgiven av Statistika centralbyran nr 3 (Stockholm:
Statistiska centralbyran, 1970), 4.

Table 5

Members of the Swedish Lutheran Congregation
at Raccoon and Penns Neck, 1771
Age Structure Compared With Sundbärg's Ideal Progressive Population

	Ideal Progressive Population	Raccoon and Penns Neck (number/000)
50+ years	100	145
15-49 years	500	436
0-14 years	400	419

Source: Church membership records.

they had their first child shows that the majority were between nineteen
and twenty-three years old, which suggests a marriage age of eighteen to
twenty-two years. There are individual examples of younger mothers, but
also a fairly large share of first-time child-bearers between twenty-six and
twenty-eight years of age. One problem with this method of calculation is,
of course, that the firstborn child may have died or already moved away
from the family at the time of registration. The mean female age at marriage must have actually been somewhat lower than indicated above.

Men were considerably older than their wives. Of all marriages recorded in Raccoon and Penns Neck, almost half of the men (48 percent)
were five years older than their spouses and as many as 17 percent were
more than ten years older. In some instances, however, the situation was
the reverse.

The high marrying age for men may be related to the fact that at this
time new land was growing scarcer in this part of America. Studies have

shown that during the first phase of colonization, when there was an almost unlimited supply of land or when the fathers of the marrying men had large farms that could be divided, the marrying age for men tended to be low as well.[43]

This demographic pattern with a highly reproductive population fits well with results from other colonial areas such as New England and Canada.[44] Two factors seem to have been particularly important for explaining the high number of children during the earliest colonization phase. First, the supply of land was ample and all those who wished to marry could do so and start farming without waiting. A second, somewhat surprising, reason was that the sex distribution was skewed and there were fewer women than men. Men sought young wives who could have many children. It also meant that widows tended to remarry quickly.[45] The result was that the first generation of settlers in a newly colonized area had the highest number of children per family. This pattern is confirmed by Susan Klepp's studies of membership records in Wicacoa and by Philip Greven's study of colonial Andover, Massachusetts, during the seventeenth century.[46]

The Language Question

The transition from Swedish to English was decisive for Swedish religious activities and thus also for the church's role as carrier of Swedish ethnicity in the Delaware area.

Springer's letter of 1693 noted that most of the people in the area spoke Swedish. The conditions for the preservation of the language had so far been favorable. The influence of the large English immigration had not yet begun, and there were still about forty persons living in the area of New Sweden who had been born in the old country.

Initially the question of Swedish language retention did not seem to have been a major issue for the Swedish church or the Swedish ministers in the Delaware area. To them, the issue was rather the maintenance of a Swedish religious tradition. The first ministers to arrive, Björck and Rudman, preached in the English churches and allowed English ministers to conduct services in the Swedish congregations. Swedish, English, and Dutch representatives were present at Rudman's funeral in 1708. It was also common that sermons were given in Swedish and English on special occasions such as the installations of new pastors or at funerals.[47]

Swedish ministers often held services in other churches as a way of supplementing their incomes. Eventually the Swedish ministers in the Delaware area and the leadership in Sweden realized that the use of English could be dangerous for the continuance of the Swedish language. One way of counteracting this was to discourage the use of English in the congregations. However, the leadership found itself in a dilemma since growing numbers of the parishioners preferred English to Swedish and it was feared that they would leave the Swedish congregations for the English. To make matters worse, a number of other sects such as Quakers, Sabbathians, Independents, Anabaptists, and Moravians were actively recruiting members. The Swedish Lutheran ministers had to be careful.[48]

The situation was even more complex since the congregations themselves were divided over the proper language for the services. The younger members preferred English, while the older ones favored Swedish. For example, a conflict broke out when the elderly and domineering Carl Springer accused Samuel Hesselius, who was minister at Christina between 1723 and 1731, of having conducted too many services in English. Hesselius conducted one service in Swedish at Christina in the morning and then preached to an English congregation in the afternoon. This meant, his critics charged, that he was neglecting his own congregation.[49] In addition, he was married to an English woman.

The growing influence of the English language created increasingly complex problems on several levels. First, a social problem developed for the leaders of the Swedish churches in that it was necessary to maintain good relations with the English congregations. At the same time, however, it was also important to distance themselves from the more extreme denominations in the area. Second, an economic problem arose since the ministers supplemented their incomes by serving in other congregations. Third, language use was a generational issue between the older Swedish-speaking members of the congregations and the younger English-speakers. Finally, it was an issue for the Swedish church, which would only provide financial support if the Swedish language and Swedish liturgical practices were used.

The difficulties stemming from the English influence resulted in closer contacts between the Swedish and German ministers as they became allies in the struggle against the supremacy of the English language and churches. The German Lutheran church was led by the able Henry Melchior Muhlenberg, with whom Israel Acrelius and Carl Magnus Wrangel, vicar of Wicacoa, 1759 to 1768, worked closely in the organization of conferences and congregations.[50]

To meet the threat from the English language, the archdiocese of Uppsala issued an ordinance in 1758 saying that the continued existence of the Swedish mission in Delaware was predicated on the maintenance of the Swedish language. This meant, in other words, Swedish language in a Swedish mission or no mission at all.[51]

Wrangel and the other ministers in Delaware did their best to follow these instructions, even though it was often difficult. Erik Unander, who served in Christina from 1756 to 1760, described the situation: "I cannot recall that I have ever seen more than 50 persons attendance at any Swedish sermon and sometimes no more than twelve. It also happens that no one at all will come."[52] Wrangel reported that when he preached in Swedish more than three-fourths of the congregation could not understand him, especially the younger members. The archdiocese recognized these difficulties and made some concessions, although it emphasized that "as far as possible the Swedish language should be used."[53]

The generational conflict can also be seen in the discussions about funding the churches. When collections were made for the church in Christina, those who did not understand Swedish refused to contribute unless the sermons in English were given the same status as those in Swedish. Otherwise, they threatened to join the English congregation.[54]

The pattern of the language transition varied among the congregations. The situation during the second half of the eighteenth century can be seen in figure 2, which is based on the notations in the membership records about members' ability to speak Swedish. The English influence was weakest in Raccoon and Penns Neck, which were agrarian congrega-

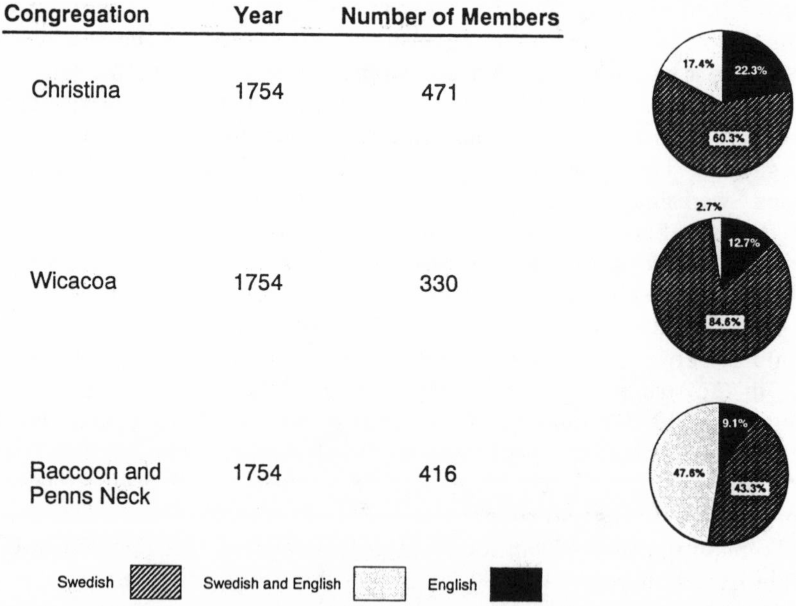

Congregation	Year	Number of Members	
Christina	1754	471	17.4% 22.3% 60.3%
Wicacoa	1754	330	2.7% 12.7% 84.6%
Raccoon and Penns Neck	1754	416	9.1% 47.6% 43.3%

Swedish ⟨hatched⟩ Swedish and English ⟨open⟩ English ⟨black⟩

Fig. 2. Knowledge of Swedish, Swedish and English, and English in the Swedish Lutheran congregations of Christina, Wicacoa, and Raccoon and Penns Neck. *Source*: S. Eilertz, 1986 (see table 2). Figures are based on information in the membership records.

tions, and strongest in Wicacoa and Kingsessing, probably due to their proximity to Philadelphia.

The transition pattern can also be seen in the number of sermons in Swedish in the different congregations during the 1780s. In Raccoon a Swedish service was held regularly every third or fourth Sunday and on major holidays. In Christina Swedish services were held only two or three times a year and on the major holidays. In Wicacoa Swedish-language services occurred only when visitors or seamen from Sweden were present. Finally, in Kingsessing, Upper Merion, and Penns Neck there were no Swedish-language services at all. In fact, Mathias Hultgren, who served in Wicacoa from 1779 to 1786, reported that many Swedish descendants were ashamed of using their ancestral language.[55]

During the 1780s the Swedish mission in America declined rapidly, particularly in Wicacoa. One of the reasons for the declining interest apparently arose from the fact that membership in the congregation was based on ownership of pews, which could be inherited. Through intermarriage many of the pews became the property of persons who felt more affiliation with other churches or who, for various reasons, showed little interest in the life of the congregations. A notation in Hultgren's diary from 2 June 1780 illustrates this point: "I traveled from Raccoon to Kingsessing which is four Swedish miles. I visited all the church councils and reminded them to be present at the meeting of the 5th of this month." Three days later he wrote that "in spite of this few persons were present at the meeting, and as usual nothing was achieved."[56]

The Swedish ministers thus met with increasing difficulties in their work, especially among the younger groups, making it understandable why the ministers, parishioners, and authorities in Sweden expressed doubts about the future of the mission.[57]

The Swedish church withdrew its support of the American ministry in several phases. By the mid-1770s there was pressure to reduce the cost of the mission. In 1775 the archdiocese of Uppsala requested an assessment of the situation from Johan Wicksell, who had recently returned to Sweden from Raccoon and Penns Neck. About the parishioners in the Delaware area Wicksell wrote that he disapproved of the fact that "this ever-wealthier growing people should henceforth continue to be an unnecessary burden on the poorer and less advantageous people here at home." Consequently King Gustav III decided to reduce the Swedish expenditures for the American ministry.[58]

The declining Swedish interest, the increased difficulties for the ministers in America, and the problems resulting from the North American colonies' War of Independence against England were all factors that contributed to the demise of the Swedish mission in America.

The end was finally reached in 1786 over the issue of calling a new minister to replace Mathias Hultgren. The two church wardens in Wicacoa, R. Keen and J. Stille, wrote to Archbishop Mennander stating "that hereafter it will be entirely unnecessary for any future appointment to take place from Sweden of a minister to serve in these Congregations ... as the Swedish Language is almost entirely extinct in Pennsylvania."[59]

Thus ended the influx of tradition-bearers who, for a long time, in spite of increasing difficulties, had contributed to the maintenance of the Swedish ethnic heritage in America.

It seems natural to make some comparisons between this seventeenth-century Swedish emigration to America and the mass emigration that took place about two hundred years later.

Many theoretical questions have been raised concerning the consequences of the nineteenth-century emigration, including the situation of the ethnic group in its new environment, often surrounded by other ethnic groups. Oscar Handlin's thesis emphasizes that emigrants who wanted to adjust quickly to a new country became "uprooted"; that is, they rapidly shed many of the traits that they had brought with them from the old country. Rudolph Vecoli, on the other hand, has maintained that the emigrants to a large extent maintained their own culture. It has also been argued that the emigrants largely lived in a "transmuted past," bringing with and maintaining substantial parts of the heritage of the old world, while at the same time adjusting to the demands of the new.[60]

An important difference between the seventeenth-century New Sweden emigration and the nineteenth-century mass emigration is that during the nineteenth century the Swedes immigrated into a society where the English language was well established. The New Sweden colonists, on the other hand, were the first cohesive European group in their area and were slowly and subsequently surrounded by members of other ethnic groups. After several decades they had become a linguistic minority.

Those people who emigrated from the Swedish realm to the Delaware area during the seventeenth century were not "uprooted" in Handlin's sense of the term. On the contrary, they were able to maintain an ethnic distinctness based on their own subjective criteria and were even referred to as "the Swedish nation." Using objective criteria, they did maintain their ethnicity for a long time, primarily in language and religion. The ministers sent over from Sweden were undoubtedly of great significance in this context as tradition-bearers, but they fought an uneven battle against an inevitable development. This meant that the descendants of the New Sweden colonists less and less found themselves living in the "transmuted past." The group was too small numerically to maintain its cultural cohesion. In addition, and as Fredrika Bremer noted in the quotation that began this article, marriages across ethnic boundaries resulted in complete integration into the dominating, English-speaking society.

NOTES

1. Fredrika Bremer, *America of the Fifties: Letters of Fredrika Bremer*, selected and ed. by Adolph B. Benson (New York: The American-Scandinavian Foundation, 1924), 157–58.
2. Richard Broberg, "Äldre invandringar från Finland i historia och tradition," *Fataburen, nordiska museets och Skansens årsbok* (Stockholm: Tryckeribolaget, Ivan Haeggstrom, 1981), 52–54.
3. Israel Helm's recruitment journey is an interesting parallel to a similar phenomenon that occurred during the Swedish mass emigration to America during the nineteenth century, when agents who were familiar with North American conditions successfully attracted emigrants from the homeland. Since emigration to New Sweden had been under way for some years, it is likely that this group had been in contact with earlier emigrants and had considered emigrating even before Helm's arrival. D'Hinojossa, who had been back to Holland himself, arranged it so that no fewer than 150 emigrants, including Finns, landed in his colony on the ship from Amsterdam.
4. Jeannette Eckman, *Crane Hook on the Delaware, 1667–1699: An Early Swedish Lutheran Church and Community, With the Historical Background of the Delaware River Valley* (Newark: Published for the Delaware Swedish Colonial Society by the Institute of Delaware History and Culture, University of Delaware, 1958), 27.
5. Ibid., 42–70.
6. K. G. Davis, *The North Atlantic World in the Seventeenth Century* (Minneapolis: University of Minnesota Press, 1974), 66; Marianne Wokeck, "The Flow and Composition of German Immigration to Philadelphia, 1727–1775," *Pennsylvania Magazine of History and Biography* 105 (1981): 249–78; D. W. Meinig, *The Shaping of America: A Geographical Perspective on 500 Years of History*, vol. 1, *Atlantic America, 1492–1800* (New Haven: Yale University Press, 1986), 131–33.
7. According to a 1697 account by one of the Swedish ministers, as many as twelve hundred people in the Delaware area were able to speak Swedish. See Sten Carlsson, *Swedes in North America, 1638–1988: Technical, Cultural and Political Achievements* (Stockholm: Streiffert, 1988), 18.
8. Claes Corlin, "Etnisk grupp," in *De mångkulturella Sverige: En handbok om etniska gruppen och minoriteter*, ed. Harald Runblom and Ingvar Svanberg (Stockholm: Gudlunds, 1988), 74–81.
9. For further discussion of the role of various factors defining ethnicity, see John G. Rice, "Patterns of Ethnicity in a Minnesota County, 1880–1905," *Geographical Reports* 4 (1973): 37–39; Hans Norman, "Swedes in North America," in *From Sweden to America: A History of the Migration*, ed. Harald Runblom and Hans Norman (Minnesota: University of Minnesota Press, 1976), 260–77; Harald Runblom, "Svenskarna i Canada: En studie i låg etnisk medvetenhet," in *Historieforskning på nya vägar: Studier tillägnade Sten Carlsson*, ed. Lars-Goran Tedebrand (Lund: Studentlitt, 1977), 213–28; Lennart Lundmark, *Protest och profetia* (Lund: Arkiv forlag, 1985), 17–22, 172–76; and Werner Sollors, *Beyond Ethnicity: Consent and Descent in American Culture* (New York: Oxford University Press, 1986), 33–39.
10. That many of the Dutch and the English in the area initially used the Swedish language is attributed to the fact that they did not have their own churches. See Adrian C. Leiby, *The Early Dutch and Swedish Settlers of*

New Jersey, New Jersey Historical Series (Princeton: Van Nostrand, 1964), 10:91–108.

11. For Queen Christina's letter, see Stellan Dahlgren, "New Sweden: The State, the Company and Johan Risingh," in *The Rise and Fall of New Sweden: Governor Johan Risingh's Journal, 1654–1655, in Its Historical Context*, ed. Stellan Dahlgren and Hans Norman (Stockholm: Almqvist & Wiksell International, 1988), 18.

12. Only nineteen of the colonists swore the loyalty oath. See Israel Acrelius, *A History of New Sweden; or, the Settlements on the Delaware River*, trans. William M. Reynolds, vol. 11 of Memoirs of the Historical Society of Pennsylvania (Philadelphia: The Society, 1874), 89.

13. The proposed areas for Swedish villages were Upland, Passayunk, Finland, Kingsessing, and Trinity Hook. See E. B. O'Callaghan and B. Fernow, eds., *Documents Relative to the Colonial History of the State of New York*, 15 vols. (Albany, 1853–87), 12:191 (hereafter *NYCD*); Eckman, *Crane Hook*, 19.

14. Acrelius, *History of New Sweden*, 19; C. A. Weslager, *The Swedes and Dutch at New Castle* (New York: Bart; Wilmington, Del.: Middle Atlantic Press, 1987), 153.

15. Eckman, *Crane Hook*, 22–24; *NYCD* 12:211–13.

16. Patricia U. Bonomi, "The Middle Colonies: Embryo of the New Political Order," in *Perspectives on Early American History: Essays in Honor of Richard B. Morris*, ed. Alden T. Vaughan and George A. Billias (New York: Harper & Row, 1973), 63–72; R. C. Simmons, *The American Colonies: From Settlement to Independence* (London: Longman, 1976), 130–34.

17. Eckman, *Crane Hook*, 119. Penn offered the Swedish colonists land at good prices further up the Schuylkill River instead of at other and better locations. Many colonists accepted, and thus Swedish settlements at, for example, Upper Merion, came into being. See Acrelius, *History of New Sweden*, 125–27, and Edward J. Gibbons, "The Swedes' Tract in Upper Merion Township, Montgomery County, Pennsylvania: Land Transaction and Settlement, 1648–1700," *American Swedish Historical Foundation Yearbook* (1968): 1–10.

18. Otto Norberg, *Svenska kyrkans mission vid Delaware i Nordamerika* (Stockholm: A. V. Carlson, 1893), 10. See also Horace Burr, ed., *The Records of Holy Trinity (Old Swedes) Church, Wilmington, Delaware, from 1697–1773*, vol. 9, Papers of the Historical Society of Delaware (Wilmington: The Society, 1890).

19. J. Thelin and L. Riddermarck to the Royal Chancellery, September 1691; J. Gezelius to King Charles XI, 20 February, 1692, in which Gezelius suggests Magister Hennigh Fulda. See Handel och Sjöfart, vol. 194, Riksarkivet, Stockholm.

20. J. Thelin and L. Riddermarck to the Royal Chancellery, September 1691, Handel och Sjöfart, vol. 194, Riksarkivet.

21. One should note that both Thelin and Riddermarck had problems with the law. Johan Thelin was born about 1651 and became postmaster in Göteborg, through his marriage with the widow of Hindrich Smidt. In 1709 he was sentenced to death following an argument with an assessor named Ström. The sentence was commuted to life imprisonment at the fortress of Marstrand, but Thelin was set free after a short time, rehabilitated to "life, honor and reputation." See E. Grape, *Postkontor och postmästare* (Stockholm: Postverkets tryckeri, 1951), 133.

Lars Perssen Wetterhamn, knighted Riddermarck in 1688, was born in 1650. He served as a financial officer at the House of Nobility, a post that he handled so poorly that he accrued a deficit of fourteen thousand daler silvermynt. In addition he was prosecuted for "insufferable litigation" and "offensive writings." He was dismissed in 1693 and was prosecuted in a process lasting until 1697. In 1701 he was sentenced to death by the Göta Court of Appeals, but the sentence was commuted to life imprisonment at Marstrand. In addition, his writings were to be burned by the executioner. He was released in 1719. See Gustaf Elgenstierna, *Den introducerade svenska adelns ättartavlor*, 9 vols. (Stockholm: P. A. Norstedt och Söners frilag, 1925–36), 6:344.

22. Acrelius, *History of New Sweden*, 200–201.

23. Ibid., 181. Sven Björnsson was a minister in Fröjdered in the province of Västergötland. See Johan W. Warholm, *Skara stifts herdaminne* (Mariestad: Berg, 1871), 2:19.

24. In this connection, one of Armegot Printz's sons, Johan Papegoja, comes to the fore. The father, also called Johan Papegoja, married Armegot in New Sweden. When Governor Johan Printz returned to Sweden, Papegoja, senior, served as vice-governor of the colony for a short while, leaving the colony after Johan Rising arrived. Johan Papegoja, Jr., was probably born around 1650, which would fit with Thelin's statement that he was in his thirties when Thelin met him. According to some accounts, Papegoja junior lived with his mother at Tinicum until 1668. In 1678 he is listed as an ensign in the Södermanland Regiment in Sweden and was later stationed at the fortress of Bohus and in Göteborg. He was forced to resign in 1681, as he was considered to be "completely inept," and in 1691 he was sentenced to two years' imprisonment and a fine of two thousand daler silvermynt for having attacked Ensign Johan Liliestielke while the latter slept. Later Papegoja junior is said to have fled to America. See Elgenstierna, *Den introducerade* 5:658.

25. J. Thelin to the Delaware Swedes, 16 November 1692, Handel och Sjöfart, vol. 194, Riksarkivet.

26. C. Springer to J. Thelin, 31 May 1693. The letter contains a list of the number of Swedish households in the area (188) and the number of persons in them (942). Thirty-nine of these people had been born in the Swedish realm. The letter is printed in Acrelius, *History of New Sweden*, 186–94.

27. Norberg, *Svenska kyrkans*, 13.

28. Ibid., 12–13.

29. Ibid., 15–19; Richard H. Hulan, "Historiska minnen i Delaware," in *Det började vid Delaware: Om svenska hembygder i Amerika*, ed. Gunilla Lindberg (Karlskrona: Riksförbundet för Hembygdsvård, 1986), 47.

30. Norberg, *Svenska kyrkans*, 21, 23.

31. Acrelius, *History of New Sweden*, 324–25, 354; Norberg, *Svenska kyrkans*, 33–34.

32. Wicksell complained in his diary for 1763 that those who wanted to put up the banns for marriage did not notify him in time. Instead, the couple would merely tell him of their intention to wed immediately before the service, and sometimes would simply come directly to the pulpit, regardless if "they were Christians, Quakers, Jews, or heathens," a practice that Wicksell never accepted. He also deplored the funeral customs, where ministers very rarely were employed, and usually only when a wealthy or old person

had died and a sermon was desired. Otherwise the parishioners buried their dead themselves, and not always in cemeteries, but sometimes in a back yard or on a hillside. In a 1783 entry in his diary, Mathias Hultgren expressed dismay over the peoples' tendency to cohabit without the benefit of matrimony. He wrote that he had been asked to marry the shipbuilder William Coats and Mary Powel when they had been living together for six or seven years and had four children. He commented that many persons in the Delaware Valley lived in such an unlawful manner.

33. Norberg, *Svenska kyrkans*, 83. It should be noted that the interest of the Swedish church in obtaining statistical information about the parishioners in Delaware coincides with the establishment of Tabellverket (the forerunner of the Central Bureau of Statistics) in Sweden in 1749. Tebellverket was founded to gather systematic population statistics.

34. The population accounts that exist before this time consist of Springer's list and two records from Wicacoa, one from 1697–98 by Andreas Rudman and one from 1743, most likely by Gabriel Nassman. The record from 1697–98 can be used for demographic calculations. See Susan Klepp, "Five Early Pennsylvania Censuses," *Pennsylvania Magazine of History and Biography* 106 (October 1982): 485–87.

35. The following extant records are kept at the Provincial Archives at Uppsala (the name in parentheses is that of the minister who kept the records): Christina: 1754 (Acrelius) and 1764 (Borell); Wicacoa: 1754 (Parlin) and 1786 (Hultgren); Manatawny: 1760 (Borell); Kingsessing and Upper Merion: 1784 (Hultgren); Raccoon and Penns Neck: 1754 (Unander), 1771 (Wicksell), and 1786 (Collin).

36. Erik Unander, vicar at Christina from 1756 to 1760, stated that the Swedish Lutheran congregations on the Delaware had a total membership of three thousand around 1760. This is probably a gross exaggeration. One explanation could be that he included persons who attended and used the services of the churches but were not registered as members. See Unander, "En sannfärdig berättelse," chap. 1, par. 1–2, Handlingar angående svenska kyrkans mission i Amerika, Uppsala domkapitels arkiv, F VIII, Landsarkivet i Uppsala, Uppsala, Sweden (hereafter ULA).

37. Martti Kerkkonen, *Peter Kalm's North American Journey: Its Ideological Background and Results* (Helsinki: Finnish Historical Society, 1959), 206; John H. Wuorinen, *The Finns on the Delaware, 1638–1655: An Essay in American Colonial History* (New York: Columbia University Press, 1938); E. A. Louhi, *The Delaware Finns* (New York: Humanity Press, 1925). Both Wuorinen and Louhi discuss the Finnish element in the New Sweden area. Louhi strongly exaggerates the role of the Finnish colonists.

38. Carl Springer (1658–1738) came from a wealthy family in Stockholm and during his studies in London had been forced to accompany a ship to Virginia, where he was forced to work in agriculture for several years before he could reach the Swedish colonists on the Delaware. He settled there in the 1680s and became one of the leading men in the Swedish ethnic group. See Eckman, *Crane Hook*, 105–21.

39. To draw sound conclusions about the natural growth of a population, one needs to know how many children were born during the women's fertile years. To calculate age-specific marital fertility, it is also necessary to know how long the women were married during their fertile years and at what ages they had their children. We cannot expect to find this kind of

detailed information about the descendants of the New Sweden colonists, but we have some means of calculating their reproduction.

40. William Penn, 6 August 1683, quoted in B. Ferris, *A History of the Original Settlements on the Delaware* (Wilmington, 1846), 137.

41. Undated letter from Peter Gunnarsson Rambo in answer to a letter from his sister in Göteborg, 16 November 1692; Lars Persson Cock to his uncle Måns Larsson in Bångstaby, Södermanland, Sweden, 31 May 1693, Svenska ecklesiastika handlingar, 1686–1694, R1100, #187, 186, Riksarkivet, Stockholm.

42. Gustav Sundbärg, *Bevölkerungsstatstik Schwedens, 1750–1900*, Skriftserie utgiven av statistiska centralbyran nr. 3 (Stockholm: Statistiska centralbyran, 1970), 4.

43. Klepp, "Five Early Pennsylvania Censuses," 491–92.

44. Kenneth A. Lockridge, "The Population of Dedham, Massachusetts, 1637–1736," *Economic History Review*, 2d ser., 19 (1966): 318–44; Philip J. Greven, Jr., *Four Generations: Population, Land and Family in Colonial Andover, Massachusetts* (Ithaca: Cornell University Press, 1970), 21–40; John Demos, *A Little Commonwealth: Family Life in Plymouth Colony* (New York: Oxford University Press, 1970), 192, tables; Jacques Henripin and Yves Peron, "The Demographic Transition of the Province of Quebec," in *Population and Social Change*, ed. D. V. Glass and Robert Revelle (London: E. Arnold, 1972), 213–29.

45. Weslager, *Swedes and Dutch at New Castle*, 144. The same pattern seems to have occurred in the pioneer phase of the Swedish mass immigration during the nineteenth century in some immigrant communities in Wisconsin. See Norman, "Swedes in North America," 277–90.

46. Klepp, "Five Early Pennsylvania Censuses," 486–87; Greven, *Four Generations*, 200–203.

47. Norberg, *Svenska kyrkans*, 22, 27, 74.

48. Ibid., 36, 50, 68.

49. Acrelius, *History of New Sweden*, 285–86.

50. Ibid., 89.

51. Ordinance of the Archdiocese of Uppsala to the Swedish Ministerium in America, 3 July 1758. Uppsala domkapitels arkiv, F VIII, ULA.

52. Unander, "En sannfärdig berättelse," chap. 2, par. 1.

53. Carl Magnus Wrangel to the Archbiship of Uppsala, 3 November 1759, Uppsala domkapitels arkiv, F VIII, ULA. Norberg, *Svenska kyrkans*, 149–50.

54. Norberg, *Svenska kyrkans*, 152–53.

55. Norberg, *Svenska kyrkans*, 202; Kerkkonen, *Peter Kalm's North American Journey*, 207. In Penns Neck services in Swedish ceased by 1742. See Amandus Johnson, ed., *The Records of the Swedish Lutheran Churches at Raccoon and Penns Neck, 1713–1776* (Elizabeth, N.J.: Colby and McGown, 1938), xi. At Christina the church records were kept in English from 1773. See Burr, *Records of Holy Trinity Church*, 8.

56. Mathias Hultgren's diary entries, 1780–86, manuscript collection, D1501: 1–7, Kingliga Biblioteket, Stockholm; Acrelius, *History of New Sweden*, 267–68.

57. On 19 March 1780 Hultgren wrote, "Early this morning I went to the church to examine the youth, but only 3 of 26 were there. This happens rather often nowadays and complaints to the parents do not help much. Many say that they cannot force their children to do something they do

not want. In this country, children can do almost anything they please."
Sometime later he added, "Went to church today, which was Sunday, but
since it rained all morning no one but the church warden was there. This
has happened many times."

58. Norberg, *Svenska kyrkans*, 193–94.
59. Letter dated Philadelphia, 16 June 1786, Handlingar angående svenska kyr-
    kans mission i Amerika. Uppsala domkapitels arkiv, F VIII, ULA.
60. Oscar Handlin, *The Uprooted: The Epic Story of the Great Migrations That
    Made the American People* (Boston: Little, Brown & Co., 1951); Rudolph J.
    Vecoli, "European Americans: From Immigrants to Ethnics," *International
    Migration Review* 6 (1972): 403–34.

Swedish Settlement in New Jersey Before 1800

PETER O. WACKER

The study of history and the study of geography go hand in hand. Peter Lindeström, in his *Geographia Americae*, put it very well.[1]

All histories inform us how high and noble this science of geography is everywhere esteemed by learned and experienced men. Yes, histories, they are based on this science, nor can anyone without a geographical delineation write a history properly and intelligently, such as is written and taught by wise and learned men.

A historical and geographic study of ethnic groups can often be pursued profitably through a regional approach.[2] New Jersey serves as an especially useful regional entity for studying the early Swedish and Finnish settlement of the New World because it exhibits great spatial diversity in its environmental endowment and settlement history. Additionally, and most helpfully, there are also systematically gathered economic data that allow comparisons to be made between the Swedes and their contemporaries. (By *Swede* I mean all those who came to intermarry with the early Swedes and Finns, adopt their language and often their Swedish Lutheran religion.)

Swedes and Finns arrived early in New Jersey, establishing Fort Elfsborg in 1643 (see map, "Swedish Settlement in Southern New Jersey"). Fort Elfsborg was established to protect the approach upriver to the major Swedish settlement on the west bank of the Delaware at Fort Christina and to neutralize the small Dutch emplacement, Fort Nassau, farther up the Delaware on the New Jersey side. As is well known, the Dutch conquered New Sweden in 1655.[3]

Accounts vary as to the establishment of Swedish settlements on the east bank after the abandonment of Fort Elfsborg in 1651. Swedish squatters are alleged to have been on the Maurice River by 1659–65.[4] Claims have also been made for a Finnish settlement in Salem County by 1660.[5] Perhaps some of the emerging early Dutch records will shed light on this question.[6]

215

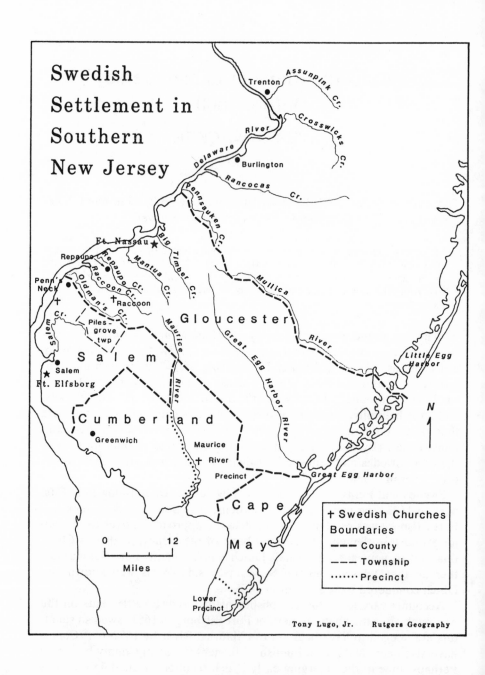

Swedish
Settlement in
Southern
New Jersey

Trenton

Assunpink Cr.

Crosswicks Cr.

Delaware River

Burlington

Rancocas Cr.

Pennsauken Cr.

Ft. Nassau ★

Repaupo

Repaupo Cr.

Mantua Cr.

Big Timber Cr.

Penn's Neck

Oldman's Cr.

Raccoon Cr.

Raccoon

Piles-grove twp

Salem Cr.

S a l e m

Salem

Ft. Elfsborg ★

Mullica River

G l o u c e s t e r

Great Egg Harbor River

Maurice River

Little Egg Harbor

C u m b e r l a n d

Greenwich

Maurice
River
Precinct

Great Egg Harbor

C a p e

M a y

N

0   12

Miles

Lower
Precinct

+ Swedish Churches
Boundaries
– – – County
– – Township
· · · · · · Precinct

Tony Lugo, Jr.   Rutgers Geography

New Netherland, including the former Swedish colony, was conquered by the English in 1664. A list of freeholders resident in New Jersey who swore loyalty to the new regime between 1665 and 1668 included 137 names. Only two, who did not have Swedish names, were listed as living on the Delaware River. All the rest were located in the northeastern portion of the province.[7] Squatters, of course, might not appear on such a list.

A permit to purchase Indian land, covering the area between Oldman's Creek and Big Timber Creek, was issued by Governor Carteret of New Jersey to three Swedes in 1668. These rights were in turn conveyed to three other Swedes, who were later certified as having been resident there since 1673.[8] The Burlington court, in 1684, heard several Swedes claim parcels of land in what later became Gloucester County (see map, "County Boundaries"). They all claimed rights under permits from Governor Carteret beginning in 1668 but did not produce the permits nor did they have the land surveyed.[9]

It is not likely that this early movement of Swedes involved large numbers. The list of tydables compiled by the Upland court (Chester, Pennsylvania) in 1677 contained 136 names. Only ten were counted on the east bank, of whom at least seven were Swedes.[10] That same year the Swedes on the New Jersey side of the river were inundated by English Quakers who were coming to settle their newly established colony of West New Jersey. The first vessel to what later became Gloucester County unloaded 230 people at the mouth of Raccoon Creek, "where the Swedes had some scattering habitations. They were too numerous to be all provided for in house: some were obliged to lay their beds and furniture in cow stalls, and apartments of that sort...."[11]

The year before the colony of West New Jersey was formally founded, John Fenwick settled Salem and Greenwich in Salem County (later divided into Salem and Cumberland counties). Fenwick apparently found Finns already settled near Salem at what later became Penns Neck[12] and subsequently sold land to several of these Finns.[13] The list of tydables for the Newcastle court, which claimed authority in New Jersey south of Oldman's Creek, contained 307 names, of which sixty-three were resident in Fenwick's colony in 1677. At least seventeen of these people were Finns or Swedes.[14]

Swedes continued to move to New Jersey from what are today the states of Pennsylvania and Delaware. In 1697 to 1698 Pastor Rudman listed the names of people associated with the Swedish church of Wicacoa (Philadelphia):[15] ninety-five people across from Philadelphia, six at Trumpeter's Creek (Repaupo),[16] two families of Steelmans consisting of nine people at Great Egg Harbor, and Eric Mullica's family of five at Takokan near Little Egg Harbor. Parishioners on the west bank (not includ-

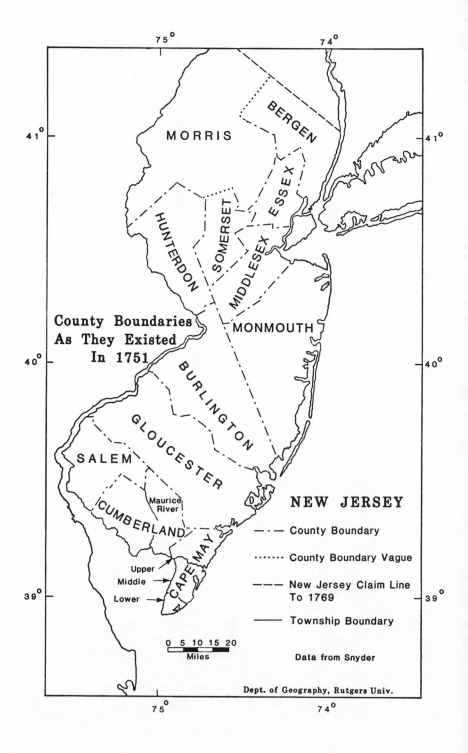

County Boundaries
As They Existed
In 1751

MORRIS

BERGEN

ESSEX

HUNTERDON

SOMERSET

MIDDLESEX

MONMOUTH

BURLINGTON

GLOUCESTER

SALEM

CUMBERLAND

Maurice River

Upper

Middle

Lower

CAPE MAY

NEW JERSEY

-·-· County Boundary

······· County Boundary Vague

--- New Jersey Claim Line To 1769

——— Township Boundary

0 5 10 15 20
Miles

Data from Snyder

Dept. of Geography, Rutgers Univ.

Table 1

Estimated Swedish Population by State, 1790

State	Hansen		Purvis	
New Jersey	6,650	(3.9%)	1,869	(1.1%)
Pennsylvania	3,325	(0.8%)	2,545	(0.6%)
Delaware	4,100	(8.9%)	1,760	(3.8%)
Maryland	900	(0.5%)	626	(0.3%)

ing Christina Parish) numbered 435. Thus the New Jersey contingent of Wicacoa Parish contained a little more than a quarter of the total. If we estimate as many as seventy or eighty Finns and Swedes in Salem County who were not on Rudman's list, the New Jersey Swedish population would have been about one-sixth of the one thousand to twelve hundred estimated Swedes resident in old New Sweden around 1690–1700.[17]

Estimates also exist of the Swedish population in the general region at the time of the first national census in 1790. A comparison at the state level can be seen on table 1.[18]

The Hansen estimate was based on the general knowledge of the settlement history of the region. Purvis used a more systematic approach, which may or may not be more accurate.[19] In any case, whether Hansen or Purvis is the more accurate, three salient facts emerge: (1) there were not very many Swedes in absolute terms; (2) the Swedes were a small percentage of the total population; and (3) New Jersey remained an important location for the descendants of the early Swedes.

For New Jersey as a whole, three sets of estimates by county exist for 1790 (see table 2).[20] All agree on one point: Gloucester County, one of the points of entry for Swedes to New Jersey, remained an important locale for their descendants. All three estimates also agree that Salem held comparatively large numbers of Swedes. Purvis believed that there were more Swedes in Salem than in Gloucester in 1790. For other counties, there are great discrepancies between the estimates. Who is closer to the truth? I believe that there is merit in Purvis's systematic approach but that he has not cast his net widely enough in identifying Swedes. Purvis used only eleven names in his analysis, several of which do not appear in New Jersey during that period and several of which appear only once in the record. Many of the Swedes of southern New Jersey were Swedes by intermarriage and acculturation, not by Swedish surname. However, I

Table 2

New Jersey: Various Estimates of
Swedes by County, 1790

	Total White Population	Nelson (1909)	Hansen	Purvis
BERGEN	10,108	505	303	0
BURLINGTON	17,270	864	1,399	86
CAPE MAY	2,416	1,208	198	0
CUMBERLAND	7,990	959	799	88
ESSEX	16,454	0	49	0
GLOUCESTER	12,830	1,283	1,796	590
HUNTERDON	18,651	0	93	149
MIDDLESEX	14,498	0	203	0
MONMOUTH	14,969	0	25	0
MORRIS	15,532	0	249	0
SALEM	9,891	692	989	781
SOMERSET	10,339	0	196	0
SUSSEX	18,996	0	95	189
STATE	169,940	4,928	6,394	1,883

think Purvis is essentially correct in not assigning numbers of Swedes to the northeastern portion of New Jersey, and I would add Hunterdon and Sussex counties to the non-Swedish area.[21]

An attempt to more accurately locate the New Jersey Swedes can be accomplished via the township (see map). Using Purvis's data and the tax lists of the period (the original census is lost), but by adding more family names known to be Swedish, one can calculate the percentage of Swedes in each township in southern New Jersey.[22]

The map of names on township tax lists clearly shows the sphere of Swedish settlement, extending from the earliest settlements on the Inner Coastal Plain in western Salem County and southern Gloucester County to the Outer Coastal Plain, with the Maurice River district being an especially important sphere of Swedish activity. (The significance of the distinction between the two major physiographic regions of southern New Jersey will be discussed later.) The map also clearly shows that even in

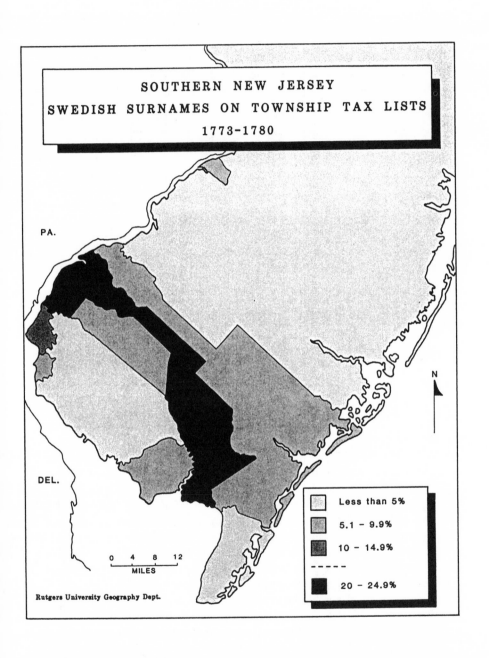

SOUTHERN NEW JERSEY
SWEDISH SURNAMES ON TOWNSHIP TAX LISTS
1773-1780

PA.

DEL.

Less than 5%

5.1 - 9.9%

10 - 14.9%

- - - - -

20 - 24.9%

0   4   8   12
MILES

Rutgers University Geography Dept.

N

Table 3

Southern New Jersey: White Population Totals
by County, 1699-1790

County	1699 Number of Freeholders	1699 Estimated White Population	1726 White Population	1738 White Population	1745 White Population	1772 White Population	1790 White Population
BURLINGTON	302	1,208	3,872	4,895	6,373	12,393	17,270
GLOUCESTER	134	536	2,125	3,145	3,304	8,438	12,830
SALEM	326	1,304	3,827	5,700	6,660	5,662	9,891
CUMBERLAND*						4,949	7,990
CAPE MAY	70	280	654	962	1,136	1,648	2,416

*Cumberland County was set off from Salem County in January 1748.

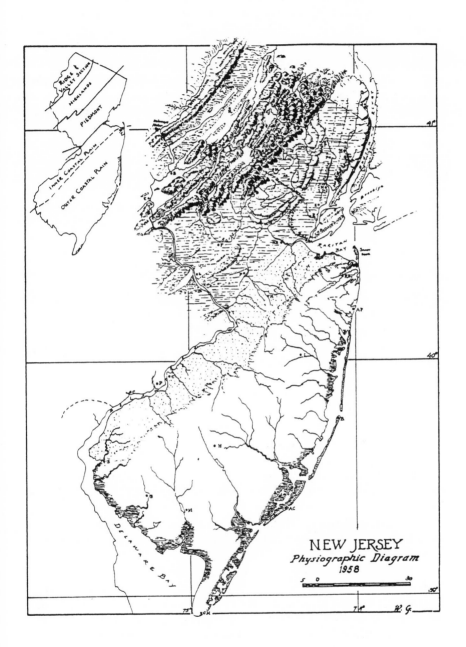

NEW JERSEY
Physiographic Diagram
1958

the areas of their greatest numbers, the Swedes never formed as much as a quarter of the population for each township. In fact, in most of the townships shown as having less than 5 percent Swedes, the true figure was less than 2 percent. The map clearly reveals that the Swedes stayed in southern New Jersey or moved south and west rather than taking advantage of the rapid settlement of areas to the north, especially the more fertile (as then perceived) Piedmont (see physiographic diagram of New Jersey).[23]

Table 3 shows how quickly the Swedes were overwhelmed numerically, especially in Gloucester County.[24] At first the in-migrants were English and Irish Quakers, but by midcentury large numbers of other English, Scots-Irish, and German settlers had arrived.[25]

SWEDISH SETTLEMENT PATTERNS

The settlement pattern established by the Swedes should be understood in light of the fact that they did not control the land system; the proprietors of West New Jersey owned and sold the land and recorded the surveys.[26] The earliest Swedes and Finns in New Jersey appear to have lived in dispersed "neighborhoods" on navigable water. Perhaps a desire to have access to church services and to the larger Swedish communities on the west bank of the Delaware River encouraged settlement on navigable waters. The early tax records of Gloucester County, for example, show clusters of Swedish names.[27] This, presumably, indicates that the tax assessor, in making his rounds, visited people in residential succession.

Pehr Kalm described the Swedish settlement pattern in New Jersey at midcentury. He lived in Raccoon, renamed Swedesboro in 1763,[28] and described the settlement pattern as "single farmhouses ... scattered in the country, and in one place only was a small village [Raccoon]. The country was yet more covered with forest than cultivated, and most of the time we were in a wood."[29]

A few days later he rode south from Raccoon to Pilesgrove Township. "Here and there appear single farms, yet they are very scarce, and large extensive pieces of ground are still covered with forests...."[30] One day he rode out to visit Nils Gustafson, a ninety-one-year-old Swede, and since he returned that night after extensive conversation with Gustafson, he presumably had not ridden more than ten miles or so from Raccoon. "Sometimes there appeared, though at a considerable distance from each other, some farms, frequently surrounded on all sides by grain fields. Almost on every field there yet remained the stumps of trees, which had been cut down, a proof that this country had not been long cultivated.... The farms did not lie together in villages, or so that several of them were near to each other in one place, but were all unconnected. Each countryman lived by himself, and had his own ground about the house separated from the property of his neighbor."[31] Kalm also rode north to Repaupo, an area "habited only by Swedes," which he described as "a very large village, whose farms, however, lie quite scattered."[32]

The village of Raccoon evolved after the Lutheran church had been built there. The location is at what was the head of sloop navigation on Raccoon Creek.[33] It lies on the King's Highway, which reached the place in 1704.[34] Later maps of the place suggest that it was a linear settlement, along the road.[35] The town's layout was dictated by church leadership because church lands were subdivided into parcels averaging about an acre and rented on a yearly basis. This method of raising revenue was also followed by the Swedish churches at Wicacoa and Christina.[36] Interestingly, surviving church records show that in the late 1760s and early 1770s six of fifteen lots rented were occupied by non-Swedes.[37]

Swedish settlements elsewhere, for example on the Maurice River[38] and at Great Egg and Little Egg harbors,[39] also appear to have been very dispersed. This pattern did not change rapidly, as can be ascertained from Pastor Nils Collin's statement about Swedish southern New Jersey in 1786: "It is to be observed that all the homesteads in this country are more or less isolated and no real villages are to be found, excepting that a few craftsmen, or laborers, may at some place live together, and that in some districts several households live in a group, without any decided admixture of other sects."[40] Mixing with other sects was especially troubling to the Swedish clergy, as it implied both intermarriage and discarding Swedish ways, including the Lutheran religion. In 1759 when Swedish pastors described Raccoon and Penns Neck parishes as "those densest settled,"[41] they were referring to the density of Swedes, which was even lighter in other areas and reflected in the rate of acculturation from place to place.

ACCULTURATION OF THE SWEDISH POPULATION

As time passed the Swedes began to take on English traits. In 1683, for example, recently arrived Thomas Paschall remarked on how quickly the Swedes were accepting English fashion in clothing.[42] By the mid-eighteenth century, according to a contemporary, Pastor Israel Acrelius, "it would expose one to ridicule to wear skins or furs. They [Swedes] talked of their forefathers who used to do so but laugh at it."[43]

Pehr Kalm spoke at great length to "the old Swede," Nils Gustafson, who recalled the coming of the first large numbers of English. From him Kalm "concluded that before the English settled here they followed wholly the customs of old Sweden; but after the English had been in the country for some time, the Swedes began gradually to follow theirs."[44] This was true for axes and cutlery, special games and foods at Christmas, and the abandonment of the bath house. At about the same time Acrelius wrote at great length describing the move from the Swedish to the prevailing English culture.[45]

Although the Swedish language and the Lutheran religion lasted longer than did material traits, the language was under stress wherever Swedes found themselves surrounded by English speakers. The religion began to die out especially where Swedish pastors were not often present. The letters of the Swedish pastors back to Sweden explicitly cover these points. Pastor Dylander, in describing the situation near Philadelphia in 1738, said that his parishioners "are Swedes neither to the language nor to habits, for the aged are dying daily, the younger can make out Swedish but slightly, but can neither read nor speak the language and are most of them married to the English."[46]

Dylander felt that the Raccoon and Penns Neck parishes "are as yet in a better state than is this one ... partly because they have always had pastors, and also partly because they do not live more than ten to twelve English miles from the church, and thereto have no English churches in their close vicinity, affording them opportunity to desert their own."[47] Petrus Tranberg, pastor of the New Jersey parishes, was less optimistic when he wrote in 1738, "I have been preaching in the Swedish and the English languages (from the reason that Swedish families have intermingled with the English)...."[48]

For 1754 we have the register of the parishes of Raccoon and Penns Neck,[49] which lists the names of the members, their general locations, ability to understand, speak, and read Swedish, as well as the occupations of adult males. Tables 4 and 5 summarize these data. The locations are an excellent indication of the most Swedish part of New Jersey, which began around Repaupo and ran south down through Penns Neck, with the eastern terminus somewhere "in the woods," presumably beyond Pilesgrove but not in the Maurice River area or farther northeast in the Outer Coastal Plain since the family names do not match those mentioned there. Of the 429 members of the Raccoon Parish, 361 (84 percent) still understood Swedish "well," 354 (82.5 percent) spoke Swedish well, and 196 (45.7 percent) could read Swedish. This is in many ways an excellent testimony to the retention of some aspects of Swedish culture by these people almost one hundred years after the fall of New Sweden to the Dutch and more than seventy years after the beginning of massive English migration to the region.

Table 4

Register of Members of Parishes of Raccoon and Penns Neck:
Language Understood and Spoken and Occupations Listed, 1754

Ward	Members	Understand Swedish	Speak Swedish	Read Swedish	Occupations Listed
REPAUPO	83	80	79	56	18 peasants, 1 peasant/brick moulder, 1 brick moulder, 1 tailor, 1 Lieutenant, 3 servant girls, 1 man servant, 3 servant boys
RACCOON KILL	77	68	68	32	10 peasants, 1 peasant/joiner, 2 day laborers, 1 man servant, 2 servant girls, 1 servant boy, 1 tailor, 1 ditcher
OLDMAN'S KILL	80	77	77	50	15 peasants, 1 joiner, 1 woman servant, 3 man servants (1 mulatto)
PILES GROVE	44	30	30	12	8 peasants, 2 tailors, 1 surveyor (English)
IN THE WOODS	64	42	37	25	10 peasants, 1 tailor, 1 servant boy, 1 man servant, 1 joiner (English), 1 shoemaker (English)
PENNS NECK, UPPER	63	53	53	16	14 peasants, 1 smith, 1 Lieutenant, 1 Ensign, 1 mail servant, 1 man servant
PENNS NECK, LOWER	18	11	10	5	6 peasants
TOTALS	429	361	354	196	81 peasants, 1 peasant/brick moulder, 1 brick moulder, 5 tailors, 2 Lieutenants, 1 Ensign, 5 servant girls, 7 man servants, 5 servant boys, 1 peasant/joiner, 2 joiners, 2 day laborers, 1 ditcher, 1 surveyor, 1 shoemaker

Table 5

Selected Wards of Parishes of Wicacoa and Christina:
Language Understood and Spoken and Occupations Listed, 1754

Understand Ward	Speak Members	Read Swedish	Swedish	Swedish	Occupations Listed
PHILADELPHIA AND WICACOA	64	39	34	26	1 portrait artist (Hesseltus), 2 master ship-builders, 1 merchant, 2 carpenters, 1 seaman, 1 smith, 1 master mason, 1 tavern owner
WILMINGTON	54	30	28	26	1 merchant, 1 joiner, 1 apprentice, 1 master mason, 2 man servants, 2 tavern keepers, 1 apprentice joiner, 1 tailor, 3 peasants, 1 weaver/peasant
AMMASLAND (PENNSYLVANIA)	39	34	26	12	9 peasants, 1 justiciary
PENNYPACK (PENNSYLVANIA)	39	36	36	14	8 peasants, 1 shoemaker
NEW CASTLE (DELAWARE)	48	18	16	11	10 peasants

Table 6

Names of Church Members of Raccoon Parish, 1786
(Neighborhood Distances Calculated From Raccoon [Swedesboro] Church)

Neighborhood	Swedes*	Others	Understand Swedish	Speak Swedish	Ethnic Association of Others
RAPAPO (4-1/2 MI./NNW)	103	13	49	32	Irish and English
CLEMELL (BORDERS RAPAPO)	7	17	3	3	English and Irish
(6-9 MI.N)	5	24	4	4	German and English
(6 MI.NE)	35	10	18	15	English
(3 MI.SE)	--	35	--	--	English and German
(6 MI.SE)	7	--	3	3	
(6 MI.S)	8	47	1	1	English, Irish, German
(9 MI.SW)	8	17	4	4	English
(4-1/2 MI.W)	47	38	14	11	German, English, Irish
3 - 4-1/2 MI.NW	66	63	18	18	English, German, Dutch, Irish
2 MI.NW	20	29	8	7	English, German
1-1/2 MI.NW	--	15	--	--	German, Irish
2 MI.NE	20	5	1	1	Irish, English
2-3 MI.S	4	4	2	2	Irish
4 MI.SW	20	14	3	3	English, German, Irish
1-1/2 MI. RADIUS	64	75	11	10	German, Irish, English, "Negroes"
TOTALS	414	406	139	114	

*As identified or by surname.

Table 7

Names of Church Members of Penns Neck Parish, 1786

Neighborhood*	Swedes**	Others	Understand Swedish	Speak Swedish	Ethnic Association of Others**
4-1/2 MI.S	30	13	--	--	English, German
1-1/2 - 2 MI. RADIUS	8	42	--	--	German, English
3-3/4 MI. NEAR DELAWARE	21	4	3	3	English
2-3 MI. FROM RIVER, 5 MI. FROM CHURCH	28	45	2	2	English
9 MI. ON THE RIVER, 12 MI. FROM RACCOON	63	47	8	7	English, Irish, German
FURTHER FROM THE RIVER TO THE EAST	23	4	--	--	English
TOTALS	173	155	13	12	

*Neighborhood distances calculated from Penns Neck Church unless otherwise indicated.
**As identified or by surname.

The greatest amount of acculturation to English seems to have occurred to the east, in "the woods," and to the south in Pilesgrove, where the lack of Swedish marriage partners was undoubtedly the major contributing factor. In Pilesgrove, for example, Johan Keen was married to Rachel Chandler, who understood only English. Their four children understood only English. Catherina Keen, possibly Johan's sister, understood, spoke, and read Swedish. Her husband was Joseph Wood, listed in the register as a "Baptist." Their oldest daughter was listed as understanding a "little" Swedish, but the other three children understood only English.

The retention of Swedish in New Jersey compares very favorably to a sampling of the wards of the parishes of Wicacoa (Philadelphia) and Christina (Wilmington). Table 5 lists these data, which were also compiled in 1754. Here too, a rural-urban discontinuity is apparent. More rural districts held onto spoken Swedish but had lost the written language. The list of occupations clearly distinguishes rural from nonrural areas in a functional sense.

An entirely different picture of the retention of Swedish emerges in 1786, when Nils Collin provided another census of the members of the Raccoon and Penns Neck congregations.[50] Since the earlier census included many people who had died in the intervening thirty-two years, Acrelius and Kalm had been correct about the diminution in the understanding of the language by the younger people. Tables 6 and 7 contain a summary of Collin's census. For Raccoon, only about one-third of those with Swedish names understood Swedish and only a little more than one-third could speak some Swedish. Significantly the church membership included as many people of non-Swedish origins as it did Swedes.[51] Repaupo appeared to remain the most Swedish place, while Swedesboro, as an "urban" entity, had the most non-Swedes and the fewest Swedes who spoke Swedish. The situation was especially dismal in Penns Neck, where less than 8 percent understood Swedish and less than 7 percent spoke the language. There too church membership included almost as many non-Swedes as Swedes. As Collin remarked, "The real so-called English people are mostly from Ireland."[52] We may surmise that the Scots-Irish constituted the largest non-Swedish church membership.

SWEDISH LAND USE

A discussion of land use can be helped by an understanding of the physical environment as it actually was and as it was perceived to be by the Swedes. Most important are the soils, as seen in the accompanying map.[53] The Greenwich soils, which immediately front the Delaware River, are very productive and are high in fine sands and silts. Areas

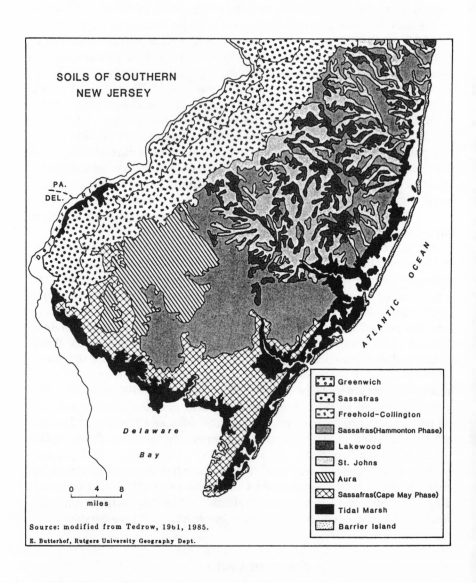

SOILS OF SOUTHERN
NEW JERSEY

PA.
DEL.

ATLANTIC OCEAN

Delaware

Bay

0   4   8
miles

Source: modified from Tedrow, 1961, 1985.

E. Butterhof, Rutgers University Geography Dept.

Greenwich

Sassafras

Freehold-Collington

Sassafras(Hammonton Phase)

Lakewood

St. Johns

Aura

Sassafras(Cape May Phase)

Tidal Marsh

Barrier Island

along streams and adjacent to tidewater tend to be wet. To the east and south are the Sassafras soils, formed on yellowish brown acid sands and silts. These are among the best soils in New Jersey. Farther to the south and east is a band of soils traditionally labeled Freehold-Collington, which also includes other series. They are generally medium-textured sands with smaller quantities of silt and clay. These soils are generally excellent for agriculture.

East of these bands of good soils, which generally lie on the Inner Coastal Plain, are the poorer soils of the Outer Coastal Plain. Wide areas are covered by the Hammonton Phase of the Sassafras. These are sandy, acid, droughty, and have a relatively low capacity to retain nutrients. Lakewood soils are even poorer and consist of dry sands. St. Johns soils are found in depressions and in poorly drained areas along water courses.

To the south are the Aura soils and the Cape May Phase of the Sassafras. Aura soils are located on well-drained, acid, loose sands and silts with a hard, sandy clay mixture lying about two feet below the surface that restricts root growth. The Cape May Phase of the Sassafras is a relatively poor acid soil also having a low retentive capacity for plant nutrients and a relatively high water table in many places.

"Natural" vegetation generally parallels the soil types. Abundant evidence exists that extensive burning especially in the Outer Coastal Plain altered species composition there.[54] On the Inner Coastal Plain, the Greenwich-Collington-Sassafras areas generally had mixed oak, beech, and maple forests. Pitch pine dominated oaks and other pines on the Lakewood soils and Hammonton Phase of the Sassafras. The St. Johns was known for its white cedars and swamp hardwoods. The Cape May Phase of the Sassafras and Aura soils harbored oaks and pines. In freshwater areas of poor drainage white cedar swamps predominated.

Swedish assessment of environmental circumstances in the Delaware Valley began with initial settlement. Peter Lindeström made an excellent record, a systematic survey of the Delaware River shoreline south of the head of deep water navigation near Trenton, New Jersey.[55] This survey, completed in the last years of the colony, is the major clue to Swedish avoidance of the east bank. Lindeström began his narrative with the area between Fort Elfsborg and Salem Creek, which he described as having a soil mixed with black earth and sand and being unhealthy due to poor drainage. From there to Oldman's Creek the soil was better and suitable for tobacco. There was fine pastureland and fruitful valleys containing an abundance of fish. This, of course, would later be a major area of Finnish and Swedish settlement.

Northeast to Repaupo Creek, later a prime sphere of Swedish settlement, the land was similar, but there were also reed flats on the shoreline containing tubers that supported hogs which were allowed to run wild until needed. From there to Big Timber Creek the land was level and suitable for cultivation but the shoreline was overgrown by brush and the water was shallow, preventing easy landing. Lindeström's account is not as clear as it was beyond this point. Apparently he found the soil from the Rancocas to the vicinity of present Burlington sandy and unsuitable for two varieties of maize but fine for tobacco, rye, oats, and other maize crops. Still further on the soil was similar. Near the Assunpink the soil was better and suitable for all maize varieties and barley.

In general the east bank is described much more favorably and was "particularly well suited for the grain of the Christians." Particularly fruitful was the area around Fort Christina. Lindeström's account was written after he returned to Sweden and after the colony had been lost, so there is no reason to doubt his veracity. Indeed, the account appears to be accurate, pointing out that the Swedes believed the New Jersey side was less fertile and not good for European grains. In any case, the Swedes later settled the areas he described most favorably.

This early Swedish perception of the relative infertility of the New Jersey side was reiterated by Pehr Kalm about a century later. When he first arrived in New Jersey he contrasted the soil with what he had seen in Pennsylvania. "The land here [opposite Philadelphia] is very different ... for here the ground is almost entirely sand, while in the other province it is mixed with a good deal of clay and this makes the soil very rich." He was surprised to find such sandy soil productive. "One might be led to think that a soil like this in New Jersey could produce nothing, because it is so dry and poor. Yet the corn which is planted on it grows extremely well, and we saw many fields covered with it." He went on to say that such soil was good for tobacco, echoing Lindeström's remarks.[56]

It was the sandy nature of the soil that apparently led the Swedes to believe that the soil was infertile. As early as 1715 Raccoon church records indicate concern that the minister "could not expect any grain crop"[57] on church land because the soil was "only sand."[58] Acrelius, roughly contemporaneous with Kalm, repeated the common attitude by calling the east side of the Delaware "a poor sandy and abominable country."[59] He also agreed with the perception of the church land in Raccoon, calling it "sandy, poor, and unsuitable for grain."[60]

The cultivation methods may have been partly responsible for the perception that the soils were poor for European grains. On 24 March 1749 Kalm described cultivation near Raccoon: "Near all the fields through which I walked today, I did not see a single ditch, though many needed them." He blamed this problem on English practices, which may or may not have been the case. He writes, "The consequence was that the late rain had in many places washed away great pieces of the grounds sown with wheat and rye."[61]

Almost contemporary with Kalm (1765) is Smith's description of agriculture and stock-raising in southern New Jersey.[62] The St. Johns and other poor soils of the Outer Coastal Plain supported cattle, for sale to graziers on bogs and meadows, and a lumber industry based especially on white cedar. On the Inner Coastal Plain Burlington County's land was "indifferent: yet interspersed with good meadow." Pork was the staple, with beef, mutton, cheese, and butter taken to Philadelphia. Gloucester County's situation opposite Philadelphia was excellent but the "uplands as to the general are poor," although meadows were improving rapidly. Products were beef, pork, mutton, butter, and cheese. Salem had rich land and meadows and produced beef, sheep, pork, butter, cheese, and grain. Cumberland's soil was "mostly poor; but they have good meadows and marshes" where cattle and sheep were raised for graziers. Cape May also had "generally poor" land, but the adjacent salt marshes were used for cattle and horses. Lumbering of red cedar and fishing provided additional livelihoods.

Smith's spatial assessment can be compared to the only reasonably contemporary systematic data source we have for New Jersey's economy, a province-wide list of tax ratables, by county, for 1751.[63] Comparisons by county allow some interesting observations to be made concerning the role of the Swedish population in the general economy. Also, since contemporary tax lists at the township level exist for Swedish and non-Swedish areas, some definitive statements can be made at the local level.

Table 8 summarizes the province-wide data.[64] The first column indicates the percentage of the total area taxed that lay in that county. The area taxed was, by legal definition, acreage on which some "improvement"[65] had been made. For example, if a person occupied one hundred acres on which ten acres had been cleared, that tract was taxed and one hundred acres were listed on the tax return. Thus the amount of taxed acreage is only one indication of the actual amount of improvement that had taken place.

The second column lists the actual percentage of the total area of the colony that lay in that county. In the case of Gloucester County only 8.3 percent of total area taxed in New Jersey lay in that county, but the county itself encompassed 13.3 percent of the total area of the province. From this we can clearly see that Gloucester was relatively unimproved, certainly lending additional credence to the statements of Kalm and others. It could be argued that the lack of improvement stemmed from the fact that much of the county lay in the Outer Coastal Plain, but this was also the case for Burlington and Monmouth. Cape May County lay entirely in the Outer Coastal Plain. Cumberland County was more recently settled than Gloucester but was similar in its relative lack of improvement.

Before the American Revolution horses and cattle were combined as a tax category. Gloucester appeared to have fewer animals in this category

Table 8

New Jersey

Percentage, by County, of General Assembly's
Estimates of Tax Revenue Potential, 1751

County	Acres of Taxed Land	Actual Area	Horses & Cattle	Sheep	Boats & Flats	Sawmills	Gristmills
MIDDLESEX	8.4	4.9	9.2	10.5	14.1	7.6	10.9
MONMOUTH	12.3	14.7	13.6	11.1	15.1	17.8	10.2
ESSEX	5.4	3.7	9.0	9.9	13.7	18.4	14.6
SOMERSET	11.1	4.9	9.9	10.7	.1	3.2	11.1
BERGEN	6.3	6.8	7.1	5.9	3.3	5.4	9.8
BURLINGTON	11.6	11.2	8.8	10.9	14.6	11.9	8.2
GLOUCESTER	8.3	13.3	5.9	5.5	18.4	9.7	4.9
SALEM	6.9	4.1	6.6	5.4	7.3	1.1	2.9
CUMBERLAND	4.2	8.7	5.1	4.1	5.2	4.3	4.1
CAPE MAY	2.9	3.0	2.9	3.4	7.5	1.1	1.6
HUNTERDON	14.5	6.9	13.7	13.6	--	5.9	15.5
MORRIS	8.2	17.8	8.3	8.9	--	13.5	6.5
PROVINCE	100.1	100.0	100.1	99.9	99.3	99.9	100.3

than the actual or taxed areas would warrant.[66] This was also true for Burlington but not for Salem or Cape May. In Cumberland there were more horses and cattle than the average for the taxed acreage; presumably some of these animals were running in the woods.

This ratable list contains the only province-wide data available on sheep since the tax law was revised to exclude sheep in 1769.[67] Here the contrast between Gloucester and the other counties is striking. Gloucester, by any measure, held relatively few sheep. Neighboring counties north and south had fewer sheep than warranted by taxed or actual area, but the disparity was not nearly as great as in the case of Gloucester. (The matter of sheep will be brought up again in comparing a Swedish and a non-Swedish township.) The data for 1751 in regard to sheep are not an aberration. A petition on the part of Gloucester County freeholders in 1768 also indicates a low presence of sheep, while tax lists from New-England-settled Lower Township in Cape May continue to show a high count of sheep.[68]

Other relevant tax categories on the 1751 list include boats and flats, gristmills and sawmills. Gloucester had no established port, unlike Burlington,[69] so the large number of vessels were related to the lumber and wood trade. The latter, especially, supplied to Philadelphia fuel wood from local landings on navigable streams.[70] Gristmills were few in all of southern New Jersey, presumably because corn was favored over wheat. The actual number of sawmills was only slightly greater than the taxed area might suggest, but this is as much due to the relatively large numbers of very small sawmills in counties such as Essex.[71] In any case, later tax lists show a tremendous increase in sawmills in Gloucester County.[72]

Two township tax lists exist for 1751, as mentioned above. These are for Lower Precinct, Cape May County, and Maurice River Precinct, Cumberland County.[73] These townships (officially "precincts" then) lay within fifteen miles of each other. Both were in the Outer Coastal Plain, lay on the same soils (Cape May Phase of the Sassafras), and had approximately the same topography. Lower Precinct had been settled earlier and included many settlers from New England.[74] In 1751 only two taxables (Johnson) of the 101 listed were possibly of Swedish origin. Maurice River Precinct was in the early years of the settlement process, having been settled perhaps only thirty years before.[75] Maurice River's sixty-two taxables included twenty-five Swedish surnames, or about 40 percent of those listed.

Lower Precinct and Maurice River Precinct contrasted greatly in land use in 1751. Undoubtedly part of the reason lay in the length of time Europeans had been living in each district and also in the fact that the Cape May residents had a long-developed orientation toward the sea. One can also argue, however, that some of the contrasts occurred because the large Swedish component in Maurice River had a very differ-

Table 9

Maurice River Precinct and Lower Precinct,
Tax Ratables, 1751

	Maurice River	Lower Precinct
ACRES TAXED (51.6%)	3,090	10,830 (2.4%)
TAXABLES	62	101
SWEDES	25 (40.3%)	2? (1.9%?)
THOSE HOLDING IMPROVED LAND AND HORSES AND CATTLE	14 (22.6%)	64 (63.4%)
THOSE HOLDING HORSES AND CATTLE ONLY	30 (48.4%)	13 (12.9%)
HORSES AND CATTLE	538	820
HORSES AND CATTLE PER TAXABLE	8.7	8.1
SHEEP	74	942
SHEEP PER TAXABLE	1.2	9.3
LIVESTOCK OWNERS HOLDING HORSES AND CATTLE BUT NO SHEEP	25 (56.8%)	10 (15.6%)
MEAN HOLDING OF HORSES AND CATTLE	11.6	10.9
MEDIAN HOLDING OF HORSES AND CATTLE	11.0	10.0
MEAN HOLDING OF SHEEP	8.1	14.6
MEDIAN HOLDING OF SHEEP	7.0	13.0
HORSES AND CATTLE TO SHEEP RATIO	3.5	.9

ent economic focus that did the population of Lower Precinct. Table 9 summarizes the comparisons between the two precincts. Not surprisingly, much more land was taxed as "improved" in Lower Precinct. In comparing the number of people who held both improved land and horses and cattle with those who held the livestock but not any land, one can see that more than twice as many people were running stock on unimproved, untaxed land in Maurice River than were paying taxes on land on which they grazed their stock. In Lower Precinct this relationship was reversed.

Table 10
Maurice River Precinct, Tax Ratables,
1751

	Swedes	Others
TAXABLES	25 (40.3%)	37 (59.7%?)
HOLDERS OF IMPROVED LAND AND HORSES AND CATTLE	7 (50.0%)	7 (50.0%)
HOLDERS OF IMPROVED LAND NOT HORSES AND CATTLE	3 (75.0%)	1 (25.0%)
HOLDERS OF HORSES AND CATTLE ONLY	11 (39.3%)	17 (50.7%)
TOTAL HOLDING HORSES AND CATTLE	18 (41.9%)	25 (58.1%)
TOTAL HOLDING SHEEP	5 (27.8%)	13 (72.2%)
MEAN IMPROVED ACREAGE	192.9	184.3
MEDIAN IMPROVED ACREAGE	180.0	150.0

Another striking contrast concerns the relative numbers of sheep being run. By any measure, whether sheep per taxable or numbers of taxables running horses and cattle but not sheep, it is quite obvious that there were far more sheep and a greater emphasis on them in Lower Precinct than in Maurice River.

Other readily perceived differences between the two precincts include the fact that Lower Precinct held seven pilot boats (for guiding vessels to Philadelphia) and no sawmills. Maurice River at that time had no locally owned vessels but did harbor four sawmills. This was half the number for the entire county.[76]

A comparison of the Swedish and non-Swedish population within Maurice River is useful at this point (see table 10). The percentage of Swedes was very high in the precinct, and they held more than half the improved land. They tended to run more horses and cattle on unimproved land in relation to their general numbers in the population. They did not differ much from other groups in the size of their landholdings or in their holding of horses and cattle. Again, the major contrast appears in the number of sheep owned. The non-Swedes had more sheep, thus the unimproved nature of the precinct was not the sole cause of low numbers of sheep. There can be no question but that the Swedish population was directly responsible for this.

Another major contrast with Lower Precinct was that Maurice River had four sawmills and Lower Precinct none. Two of the sawmills were owned by Swedes who were not taxed on land but who were taxed on horses and cattle. The other two were owned by people not taxed on horses and cattle and most likely nonresidents.

What the data strongly suggest is that the Swedes pioneered the area, were as involved in running stock in the woods as were others, and were even more involved in lumbering than was the general population. This is especially suggested by the neglect of sheep, which as we will see posed a special problem for part-time farmers that horses and cattle did not, and by the sawmill ownership. (Swedes elsewhere, generally, were not owners and entrepreneurs.)[77]

Let us turn to other data bearing on Swedish land use in the Outer Coastal Plain. Pastor Sandel visited Little Egg Harbor and Great Egg Harbor in 1704. As he describes the wilderness, "we saw the valley meadows, vaste widths ... English people and Swedes live here on the banks, for the valley meadows are lying between."[78] Stock raising on the marshes is implied but not explicit. Pastor Wrangel visited the same general area in 1764. On the way there he described the soil as being "mainly of drift sand," which produced good crops of corn and rye but was poor for wheat. Cattle grazed in the woods during the summer, and in the winter people brought their herds to the seaside at Great Egg Harbor and paid for the privilege of grazing them there. The principal activity, however, was lumbering, with the finished product being taken to Philadelphia. Shingles were made of white cedar, charcoal was produced, and some tar was extracted. Wrangel passed a landing on the Great Egg Harbor River where planks, boards, and shingles were being loaded. He visited Carl Steelman, a Swede, who lived by the side of the road and had decorated his fences with a large number of deer antlers to demonstrate his hunting prowess. In the evening they "feasted on Swedish venison."

Wrangel traveled throughout the area, apparently duplicating Sandel's route of sixty years before. He found several people who spoke Swedish and was generally welcomed by the Swedish population, who had not seen a Swedish minister for some time and who were very much intermarried with the English.[79] In general we can infer that the Swedish population lived by lumbering, some agriculture, running stock in the woods, and hunting and fishing. They do not appear to have owned any of the sawmills.

As we can see, lumbering appears to have been a major activity of the Swedish population, at least in the Outer Coastal Plain. There is evidence that this was a significant contribution of the Swedish population to the economy and material culture of the entire Delaware Bay region. Early English migrants to the area immediately perceived the Swedes as accomplished woodsmen. In a 1683 letter to an English friend, Thomas Paschall marveled at forests "full of Oakes, many very high ... about two foot through and some bigger...." He went on to note that "a Swead will fell twelve of the bigger in a day." Elsewhere in his letter he contrasted English and Swedish practices of cutting and using trees: "As for the Swedes, they use but little iron in Building, for they will build, and hardly use any other tool but an Ax; They will cut down a Tree, and cut him off when down, sooner then two [English] men can saw him, and rend into planks or what they please; only with the Ax and wooden wedges, they use no Iron...."[80]

The building of Philadelphia required a great deal of lumber. Kalm's "Old Swede," Nils Gustafson, recalled bringing a great deal of timber to Philadelphia in the first years of the city.[81] We have already seen that boats and flats continued the export of wood from Gloucester County to Philadelphia in 1751. We have also seen that there is no question about the relative lack of cleared land in Gloucester County, as established both by systematic tax records and by contemporary accounts, such as those of Pehr Kalm.

Is there another explanation for the wooded nature of Gloucester County at that time? Possibly. First, the soil was perceived to be poor. Second, evidence from an economic standpoint indicates that it made good sense to leave the area largely wooded. Wood was necessary to the urban places of that day, especially for fuel. Transportation of wood, a bulky, heavy product, was expensive. The classic Von Thunen model of land use, which was promulgated in early-nineteenth-century northern Germany, for example, placed the production of wood very near the market center for this very reason.[82]

Contemporary accounts do indicate that transportation of wood was expensive and that forested land was deliberately preserved close to Philadelphia. For example, on 24 October 1741 Pastor Joannes Dylander wrote to Sweden complaining that he lived "upon a rather costly place [Philadelphia] where it costs me ten pounds a year to keep a horse and a like amount for the transport of wood for fuel, notwithstanding the wood being my own cut upon my own land three English miles from my house."[83] In 1748 Kalm described Philadelphia as surrounded by a forest, which "Would lead one to conclude that fuel must be cheap there. But it is far from being so, because the large and high forest near the town is the property of some people of quality and fortune ... [who] leave the trees for times to come, expecting that wood will become very expensive."[84] Thus forest on nearby, perceived-to-be-poor land such as in New Jersey probably made as good economic sense as cleared cultivated land.

Where do the Swedes and sheep fit into the equation? Again, the comments of Pehr Kalm are invaluable. He describes in several places the very casual way in which stock was allowed to graze unsupervised in the woods. He also describes the very poor pasturage available due to the elimination of the native American grasses, which were annuals and not perennials like European grasses.[85] For sheep, in particular, there were dire consequences. The problem was not so much predators, since wolves were very rare,[86] although dog[87] and red fox attacks on lambs[88] were problems. The greatest danger, apparently, was poisonous vegetation, especially laurel (named by Linnaeus *Kalmia latifolia*). In early spring, when the woodland pastures were bare, this poisonous broadleaf evergreen attracted sheep.[89] The hellebore (*Veratrum album*) was another poisonous plant that was very common in local marshes.[90] Thus sheep required a great deal of supervision.

It is evident, from data derived from the tax lists, that many Swedes were not willing or able to provide the supervision that sheep required. The reasons for this could have been that the Swedes were inexperienced agriculturists and had come from Sweden and Finland at a time when agriculture there was relatively primitive.[91] Nevertheless the Swedes did bring sheep from Sweden.[92] A better explanation is that many of the Swedes were as concerned with various lumbering activities as they were with agriculture. Sheep required much more supervision than could be given. Grazing horses and cattle in the woodlands required little supervision, and hogs required much less supervision than sheep. The soil was perceived to be poor for the European grains but good for maize. In addition, the Swedes fed their cattle and hogs large amounts of corn to fatten them for the market. The hogs, especially, developed an "agreeable flavor, preferable to all other meat."[93]

Swedes and Finns pioneered settlement in southern New Jersey, especially in the Outer Coastal Plain. Even though they were inundated by people of other ethnic origins, they held on to language and religion through about the middle of the eighteenth century. In 1786, when the Swedish Lutheran church in Swedesboro became an Episcopal church,[94] there were still Swedish speakers in the congregation.

A core of Swedish settlements developed in southern Gloucester County and in adjacent townships in Salem and Cumberland counties. The Swedish settled area exhibited a different land-use pattern than could be found in other parts of New Jersey. Gloucester County, even in areas of excellent soils, was relatively undeveloped. Sheep, common elsewhere, were relatively scarce in Gloucester. Swedes had initially perceived the soil as poor because it was sandy and had introduced an economy based on the utilization of the woodlands to run their stock (horses, cattle, and hogs) and to provide lumber and fuel for Philadelphia. Corn was grown extensively as feed for the animals, which were taken to the Philadelphia market. Rather than producing wheat for export, as much of the rest of New Jersey and all of the Middle Colonies did, southwestern New Jersey relied on corn for hogs and cattle that were sent through Philadelphia to the Caribbean.[95] It is only in the context of the Swedish settlement of this area that such economic factors can be understood.[96]

NOTES

The author thanks the New Jersey Historical Commission and the Rutgers University Research Council for grants supporting his research on this project.

1. Peter Lindeström, *Geographia Americae*, trans. Amandus Johnson (Philadelphia: Swedish Colonial Society, 1925), 4.
2. For example, see Richard H. Hulan, *From Northern Shore: The Swedish and Finnish Presence in Colonial Maryland* (Rockville, Md.: Daystar Press, 1984), and Terry G. Jordan, *German Seed in Texas Soil: Immigrant Farmers in Nineteenth-Century Texas* (Austin: University of Texas Press, 1966).
3. Amandus Johnson, *The Swedish Settlements on the Delaware: Their History and Relation to the Indians, Dutch and English, 1638–1664*, 2 vols. (Philadelphia: Swedish Colonial Society, 1911), 1:169–70, 178–79, 304–5, 338–39, 439, 445. Johnson concluded that there were no Swedes on the east bank other than at Ft. Elfsborg in 1653 (526–527). For place locations and the boundaries of civil divisions, see John P. Snyder, *The Story of New Jersey's Civil Boundaries, 1606–1968* (Trenton, N.J.: Bureau of Geology and Topography, 1969).
4. Federal Writers' Project, New Jersey, *The Swedes and Finns in New Jersey* (Bayonne: Jersey Printing Co., 1938), 61.
5. Ibid., 60.
6. Acrelius said there were no residents on the east bank of the river in 1664. See Israel Acrelius, *A History of New Sweden: or, the Settlements on the Delaware River*, trans. William M. Reynolds, vol. 11 of Mem. of the Historical Society of Pennsylvania (Philadelphia: The Society, 1874), 106.
7. William A. Whitehead et al., eds., Archives of the State of New Jersey: Documents Relating to the Colonial, Revolutionary, and Post-Revolutionary History of the State of New Jersey, Newark, 1st ser., 33 vols.1:49–51. Hereafter cited as *NJA*.
8. Federal Writers' Project, *The Swedes and Finns in New Jersey*, 61.
9. John Clement, "Swedish Settlement in Gloucester County, New Jersey, Previous to 1684," *Pennsylvania Magazine of History and Biography* 17 (1893): 84.
10. Edward Armstrong, ed., *Record of Upland Court from the 14th of November, 1676 to the 14th of June, 1681* (Philadelphia: Lippincott, 1860), 80.
11. Samuel Smith, *The History of the Colony of Nova Caesaria or New Jersey* (Burlington, N.J.: James Parker, 1765), 93.
12. Robert G. Johnson, *An Historical Account of the First Settlement of Salem in West Jersey by John Fenwick, Esq.* (Philadelphia: Orrin Rogus, 1839), 34. I am indebted to Richard Hulan for calling attention to this source.

13. Salem County Historical Society, *Colonial Roof Trees and Candle Ends* (Salem, N. J.: Salem County Historical Society, 1934), 4.

14. Lewis D. Cook, "Two Assessment Lists of Settlers on the Delaware River Shores, 1677," *Genealogical Magazine of New Jersey* 51 (1938): 9.

15. "Early Swedish Records," *Pennsylvania Magazine of History and Biography* 2 (1878): 224–25. I thank Cheryl Desmond and Emily Myers for bringing this source to my attention. Apparently there were also a few Swedish squatters north of Pennsauken Creek by 1693. See John R. Stevenson, "Swedish Settlers in Burlington County, New Jersey," *Pennsylvania Magazine of History and Biography* 23 (1899): 110–11.

16. Frank H. Stewart, ed. and comp., *Gloucester County Under the Proprietors* (Woodbury, N.J.: Constitution Company, 1942), 10.

17. Thomas Campanius Holm, *Kort Beskrifning om Provincien Nya Sverige uti America* (Stockholm, 1702). Eng. ed.: *Description of the Province of New Sweden . . .*, trans. Peter S. Du Ponceau, vol. 3 of Memoirs of the Historical Society of Pennsylvania (Philadelphia: The Society, 1834), 102, 164–66.

18. Marcus L. Hansen, "The Minor Stocks in the American Population of 1790," *Annual Report of the American Historical Association for the Year 1931*, 1:122; and Thomas L. Purvis, "The European Ancestry of the United States Population," *William and Mary Quarterly* 41 (1984): 98.

19. Purvis used distinctive surnames that he took to be representative of the Swedish population. He used the Springer list of names of those resident in New Sweden in 1693 and derived eleven names from this list. From this an arithmetic coefficient was calculated which enabled the computation of that nationality within a given state. See Purvis, "The European Ancestry," 86.

20. The sources for table 2 are as follows: Hansen, "Minor Stocks," 121–22; Purvis, "The European Origins of New Jersey's Eighteenth-Century Population," *New Jersey History* 100 (1982): 16; and U. S. Bureau of the Census, *A Century of Population Growth* (Washington, D.C.: Bureau of the Census, 1909): 119–20.

21. For New Jersey at least, several criticisms can be directed toward Purvis's methodology. First, eleven names is far too small a sample to give us a clear picture of the Swedes in New Jersey. Some of these families may have migrated evenly in all directions but some surely did not. Two of the names Purvis used (Stalcop and Walraven) are not known in New Jersey at that time. Certainly, even by 1693, a great deal of intermarriage had occurred in New Sweden and many Swedish-speaking families had surnames originating elsewhere. See Acrelius, *History of New Sweden*, 190–93. Another problem with Purvis's methodology is that some of the county totals have been calculated from a very small base. In Sussex County, for example, a population of 189 Swedes is calculated from the fact that one of the eleven names used is found on a tax list for Oxford Township in 1773 and for Greenwich Township in 1774 (see n. 23 below for tax list coverage). This name, Powleson, even if it is Swedish, could have belonged to the same person, William Powleson, since the tax lists for Oxford Township do not exist after 1773 and the tax lists for Greenwich township do not exist before 1774. The population of Sussex County at that time was extremely mobile. See William C. Wright, "Newton Township 1773 Ratable," *Genealogical Magazine of New Jersey* 60 (1985): 56. Another example is that of Joseph Justice (originally Justason?) of Trenton Township, Hunterdon

County. Purvis has calculated 149 Swedes for Hunterdon on the basis of this one name. Trenton Township was the location of one of the few "urban" places in New Jersey at that time, areas that were more cosmopolitan than the surrounding rural locations and did not reflect typical ethnic distributions. Thus, without further evidence, I am not convinced of a Swedish presence in either Hunterdon or Sussex.

I also object to Purvis's findings concerning the population of Maurice River Precinct in Cumberland County. As we will see later, this was an especially Swedish area, visited regularly by Swedish ministers. Purvis's method would show no Swedes in this township. See, for example, F. W. Bowen, *History of Port Elizabeth* (Millville, N.J.: Millville Publishing Co., 1936), 9; and "Reincke's Journal of a Visit Among the Swedes of West Jersey, 1745," *Pennsylvania Magazine of History and Biography* 33 (1910): 100–101. Reincke called Gerred van Nimmen "one of the principal men among the Swedes in Penns Neck." The surname was of Dutch origin. Other good "Swedish" names can be found in Collin's register of the members of the Raccoon and Penns Neck churches in 1786. See n. 53.

22. I used contemporary tax lists to arrive at the percentages shown. Tax lists are the best systematic form of data since New Jersey's 1790 census has been lost. See Department of Education, Division of State Library, Archives and History Microfilm and Records Unit, Trenton, N.J., County Tax Ratables, 1773–1822. Not all the tax lists exist for the pre-Revolutionary period. In several cases, Revolutionary tax lists had to be used. A very useful source is Kenn Stryker-Rodda, *Revolutionary Census of New Jersey* (Lambertville, N.J.: Hunterdon House, 1986). The tax lists have been reprinted in *The Genealogical Magazine of New Jersey*. See Stryker-Rodda, *Revolutionary Census*, ix–xii. Percentages were derived by using all the names that were known to the author as "Swedish" during this period. These were derived from the lists of Springer and Rudman, as well as contemporary church registers and the statements of the Swedish pastors. Thus, Vanneman, of Dutch origin, is a typically "Swedish" name in southern New Jersey, and was considered as such in the compilation of this map.

23. John Hanson Steelman is a good example. He was living in Burlington County from 1680 to 1684. Of an entrepreneurial bent, Steelman chose to move to Elk Landing in Maryland and began a very successful career as an Indian trader. See Peter S. Craig and Henry W. Yocom, "The Yocums of Aronamock in Philadelphia, 1648–1702," *National Genealogical Society Quarterly* 71 (1983): 254–57.

24. Peter O. Wacker, *Land and People: A Cultural Geography of Pre-industrial New Jersey: Origins and Settlement Patterns* (New Brunswick, N.J.: Rutgers University Press, 1975), 131–32, 413–16.

25. Ibid., 169–91, 205–18.

26. Ibid., 275–303.

27. Lewis D. Cook, "Tax List of the Lower Division of Gloucester County, 1687," *Genealogical Magazine of New Jersey* 51 (1938): 10–12.

28. Federal Writers' Project, *The Swedes and Finns in New Jersey*, 96.

29. Adolph B. Benson, ed. and trans., *Peter Kalm's Travels in North America: The English Version of 1770*, 2 vols. (New York: Wilson-Erickson, 1937), 1:175.

30. Ibid., 185.

31. Ibid., 265.

32. Ibid., 295.

33. Thomas F. Gordon, *Gazetteer of the State of New Jersey* (Trenton, N.J.: Daniel Fenton, 1834), 249.

34. The church was built in 1704. See Amandus Johnson, ed. and trans., *The Journal and Biography of Nicholas Collin, 1746–1831* (Philadelphia: New Jersey Society of Pennsylvania, 1936), 110.

35. *Evarts and Stewart Combination Atlas Map of Salem and Gloucester Counties, New Jersey* (Philadelphia: Evarts & Stewart, 1876), 41.

36. Acrelius, *History of New Sweden*, 239–40, 289–90.

37. Amandus Johnson, trans. and comp., *The Records of the Swedish Lutheran Churches at Raccoon and Penns Neck, 1713–1786* (Elizabeth, N.J.: New Jersey Commission to Commemorate the 300th Anniversary of the Settlement by the Swedes and Finns on the Delaware, 1938), 142–54, 157–62, 165–83.

38. *Archivum Americanum. Documents Preserved in the Consistory of Upsal Relating to the Swedish Church on the Delaware*, 2 vols. (Philadelphia, 1891), 1:120, 129–33, 149.

39. Carl M. Anderson, ed. and trans., "Pastor Wrangel's Trip to the Shore," *New Jersey History* 87 (1969): 5–31.

40. Johnson, *Journal and Biography of Nicholas Collin*, 299.

41. *Archivum Americanum* 1:405.

42. "Letter of Thomas Paschall, 1683," in *Narratives of Early Pennsylvania, West New Jersey, and Delaware, 1630–1707*, ed. Albert C. Myers (New York: Charles Scribner's Sons, 1912), 251.

43. Acrelius, *History of New Sweden*, 353.

44. Benson, *Peter Kalm's Travels* 1:273.

45. Acrelius, *History of New Sweden*, 310.

46. *Archivum Americanum* 1:72–73.

47. Ibid. 1:44–45.

48. Ibid. 1:59.

49. Ibid. 1:465–92. The list of occupations of the members of the Raccoon and Penns Neck parishes reveals a population of modest economic status. This is borne out by the contemporary statements of the ministers. For example, in 1760 in a letter written to church authorities in Sweden by five pastors, they agreed that "the Raccoon and Penns Neck Parishes are although those densest populated yet the poorest" (*Archivum Americanum*, 405). Most adult males on the list are identified as bonde (peasant). Presumably this meant farmer, but would not rule out part time work in cutting wood. Specialized occupations included brick molding, specialized carpentry, ditcher (draining meadows), tailor, and the military. It may be significant that people of English origin held three of the specializations listed: surveyor, joiner, and shoemaker.

50. Johnson, *Journal and Biography of Nicholas Collin*, 300–45.

51. Collin's notes on each family indicate Swedish mothers and grandparents.

52. Ibid., 299.

53. The map is a simplification of the major soils of southern New Jersey as identified by John C. F. Tedrow, *Soils of New Jersey* (Malabar, Fla.: Robert E. Krieger Publishing Co., 1986).

54. Among Europeans, Finns were especially infamous for burning woodland, and in fact, many of the Finns transported to New Sweden had been banished from Sweden for this practice. See John H. Wuorinen, *The Finns on*

the Delaware, 1638–1655: An Essay in American Colonial History (New York: Columbia University Press, 1938), 15–20.

55. Lindeström, *Geographia*, 157–72.
56. Benson, *Peter Kalm's Travels* 1:89.
57. Federal Writers' Project, *The Swedes and Finns in New Jersey*, 7.
58. Ibid., 12.
59. Acrelius, *History of New Sweden*, 106.
60. Ibid., 323.
61. Benson, *Peter Kalm's Travels* 1:264.
62. Smith, *History of the Colony of Nova Caesaria*, 489, 494–98.
63. "Estimate of the Several Counties in the Province of New Jersey as Valued by the General Assembly, September 28, 1751," Jacob Spicer Papers, New Jersey Historical Society, Newark.
64. Peter O. Wacker, "The New Jersey Tax Ratable List of 1751," *New Jersey History* 107 (1989): 32–33.
65. *NJA*, 1st ser., 16, 301.
66. *Acts of the General Assembly of the State of New Jersey* (Trenton: Isaac Collins, 1778), 57.
67. *Votes and Proceedings of the General Assembly of the Province of New Jersey* (Woodbridge: James Parker, 1769), 50.
68. "To the Honourable House of Representatives of the Colony of New Jersey in General Assembly Convened: The Petition of the Freeholders Inhabitants of the County of Gloucester, in behalf of the said County [1768]," Stewart Collection, Savitz Library, Rowan College, Glassboro, N.J.
69. West New Jersey's official ports were Burlington, Salem, and Greenwich. For a discussion of these colonial ports and their functions in relation to Philadelphia, see Roger T. Trindell, "Historical Geography of Southern New Jersey as Related to Its Colonial Ports" (Ph.D. diss., Department of Geography and Anthropology, Louisiana State University, 1966).
70. See, for example, *NJA*, 1st ser., 25:50, 305, and Gloucester County's township tax lists for 1773 and 1774 (see n. 23).
71. See, for example, "David Camp Book A," Camp Family Papers, New Jersey Historical Society, Newark. Essex, as indicated by the 1751 tax list, was largely "improved." The Camps would occasionally saw logs as customers brought them in.
72. *Votes and Proceedings of the General Assembly*, 1769, 50.
73. "A List of the Names and Sirnames [*sic*]; and of the Estates Real and Personal of the Inhabitants and House-holders of the Lower Precinct of the County of Cape May, 1751," and "Prince Maurice's River Precinct in Cumberland County, 1751," Stewart Collection, Savitz Library, Rowan College.
74. Lewis T. Stevens, *The History of Cape May County, New Jersey from the Aboriginal Times to the Present Day* (Cape May City, N.J.: L. T. Stevens, 1897), 30.
75. Bowen, *History of Port Elizabeth*, 9. A survey made in 1714 indicates at least two dwellings on or near the Maurice River. See "John Scott Survey," Pirate House Library, Cumberland and County Historical Society, Greenwich, N.J.
76. "Estimate of the Several Counties, 1751," Jacob Spicer Papers.
77. See n. 52.
78. *Archivum Americanum*, 130–31.

79. Anderson, "Pastor Wrangel's Trip," 5–31.
80. "Letter of Thomas Paschall, 1683," in *Narratives*, ed. Myers, 250–53.
81. Benson, *Peter Kalm's Travels* 1:266.
82. Johan Heinrich von Thunen, *Von Thunen's Isolated State: An English Edition of "Der Isolierte Staat,"* trans. Carla M. Wartenberg (Elmsford, N.Y.: Pergamon Press, 1966).
83. *Archivum Americanum*, 97–98.
84. Benson, *Peter Kalm's Travels* 1:50–51.
85. Ibid. 1:97, 267, 289, 293.
86. Ibid. 1:150.
87. "Petition of the Inhabitants of Burlington County to the Legislature Requesting Redress for the damages Done to their Flocks by Dogs," 8 March 1763, Manuscripts Collection, New Jersey State Archives, Trenton.
88. Benson, *Peter Kalm's Travels* 1:149.
89. Ibid. 1:177–78.
90. Ibid. 1:256.
91. Wuorinen, *The Finns on the Delaware*, 11–12.
92. Amandus Johnson, *Swedish Settlements on the Delaware*, 1:14–15, 29–30.
93. Benson, *Peter Kalm's Travels* 1:179.
94. Federal Writers' Project, *The Swedes and Finns in New Jersey*, 99, 136.
95. For maps of the distribution of crops in New Jersey, see Peter O. Wacker, "A Preliminary View of the Possible Associations Between Cultural Background and Agriculture in New Jersey During the Latter Part of the Eighteenth Century," *Proceedings of the New York–New Jersey Division, Association of American Geographers* 4 (1974): 41–57. Gloucester County, in general, according to contemporary newspaper advertisements, grew more maize than wheat. Newspaper coverage of Gloucester was relatively good because of its proximity to Philadelphia. See Peter O. Wacker, "Historical Geographers, Newspaper Advertisements and the Bicentennial Celebration," *Professional Geographer* 26 (1974): 12. For neighboring Pennsylvania's dependence on wheat and the export of wheat from the region through the port of Philadelphia, see James T. Lemon, *The Best Poor Man's Country* (Baltimore: Johns Hopkins University Press, 1972), 27–28, 182, 185–86.
96. The cultural results of the "Swedish" settlement of the lower Delaware Valley were, of course, profound, as indicated by Terry Jordan's essay in this volume.

The Lutheran Churches and Their Pastors in New Sweden, 1638–1655

FRANK BLOMFELT

In a country with an official state church, such as Sweden, authority is divided between the secular and the spiritual governments. In seventeenth-century Sweden, the king and the council were the worldly government and the episcopate, the chapter (the body of clergy who helped a bishop to govern a diocese), and the clergy were the spiritual government, that of the Swedish Lutheran church.[1]

The essential acts of the Swedish Reformation were carried out by King Gustav I (1523–60). The major elements of the generally peaceful reform were the gradual spread of Lutheran doctrine during the 1520s and 1530s and the royal seizure of the property of the Catholic church during the 1530s and 1540s. Although some of the kings after Gustav wavered,[2] the people, the court, and the church were firmly Lutheran by midcentury.

By the end of the sixteenth century the Swedish Lutheran church was regulated in the main by two documents. The first, the Church Ordinance of 1571, was "at once a confession of faith and a piece of practical ecclesiastical legislation." It affirmed the basis of faith for Swedish Lutherans as the "'pure Word of God' as contained in the Scriptures." It left the church independent within the state and subject solely to the episcopacy. The ordinance preserved many ancient features, including the rite of exorcism, the use of vestments, chalice, and paten, the sign of the cross, the adoration and elevation of the host, and the use of Latin in the sung portions of the Mass. It included a school ordinance and provisions to enforce church discipline. The ordinance was largely the work of Laurentius Petri, the archbishop of Uppsala, but it was imposed on the country by the authority of King Johan III.[3]

The church's second significant governing document was the resolution produced by the Uppsala church assembly of 1593. The resolution grew out of a generation of theological and political strife among Swedish Lutherans; the historian Michael Roberts has called it "a great national act of faith, a declaration of religious rights, [and] the cornerstone of Swedish

Lutheranism." It incorporated most of the provisions of the ordinance of 1571 and broadened the basis of faith to include the Augsburg Confession of 1555, bringing Swedish Lutheranism into formal conformance with the "official" Continental variety. The resolution banned Catholicism and forbade public worship by "heretics," including other Protestants such as Calvinists and Zwinglians. It set forth punishments for "railers against the established religion."[4]

Lutheranism was fully established in Sweden's first written constitution, the "Form of Government" of 1634. This document incorporated the resolution of the Uppsala Assembly of 1593 and further expanded the basis of faith to include Martin Luther's Catechism. Drafted by Sweden's chancellor, Axel Oxenstierna (1584–1654, chancellor from 1611), it embodied the ideals of governmental reform of King Gustav II Adolf (Gustavus Adolphus, 1594–1632, reigned from 1611).[5]

The government intended to follow with a new administrative plan that would place church governance in the hands of a corporate body similar to those that the king and chancellor had created in the 1620s to manage Sweden's army, navy, finances, foreign affairs, and administration of justice. This "Consistorium General" was to be composed of church officials, but as a body it would be responsible only to the monarch. The plan was frustrated by the bishops, who managed, in the partial power vacuum created in 1632 when the king died and his six-year-old daughter, Christina, acceded, to retain their position as virtual monarchs of their dioceses. The archbishop of Uppsala, by virtue of precedence among his peers, not by legislation, remained the titular head of the church in both Sweden and New Sweden.[6]

Swedish religious life was also regulated by a body of law that dated from the Middle Ages. These laws included decrees against idolatry, witchcraft, superstition, blasphemy, mocking God's word and sacraments, misusing God's name, and forbidding cursing, oaths, lying, and fraud.[7]

As soon as plans were underway in 1637 to establish New Sweden, planning for the church in the colony began as well. Laurentius Paulinus Gothus, archbishop of Uppsala, was chosen to lead the planning. Gothus had written a church law for Sweden, but it was hardly written with the intent of becoming law in an American colony. New Sweden's religious life was governed by all of these homeland regulations. In addition, the church and the government both wished to convert the Indians to Christianity. The privileges of the New Sweden Company included as a goal spreading the Christian religion among the pagans.[8]

The government's concern with the religious life of the colony is clearly seen in its instructions to two of the colony's governors. The instructions carried by the colony's second governor, Peter Hollander Ridder, in 1639, contained regulations about daily prayers that included a system of fines for the neglectful.[9] The instructions for Governor Johan Printz, in 1642, ordered him to supervise the church life of New Sweden to ensure that services would be held in accordance with "Swedish church ceremonies" and that the faith be kept according to the Augsburg Confession and the Resolution of the Uppsala Assembly. This instruction was to ensure that the colony's youth would be taught in "the Christian faith" and that "all good church discipline" would be "kept and exercised." He was not, however, to disturb Dutch settlers in New Sweden in performance of their Reformed Church services.[10]

Printz's education and career had included extensive military and administrative experience and some theological training. His excellent relationship with the authorities in Stockholm is evidenced by the fact that many questions of detail were left to the "fidelity, caution and zeal of the Governor."[11]

In 1654 Printz was replaced as governor by Johan Classon Rising. Rising had been sent to New Sweden as Printz's assistant, but by the time he reached the colony Printz had returned home. Rising's instructions stated that he "together with the Governor should take such care that diligent religious service may be conducted there and that all may submit themselves to the Augsburg Confession and that all useless disputes for the excitement of the minds may be avoided and removed, so that everything in this regard might be ordered and regulated for harmony and the honor of the name of God."[12]

New Sweden's church was divided into two parishes. The first was organized at Fort Christina with the arrival in 1640 of the first minister, Torkillus Reovius. During the two previous years the spiritual life of the twenty-five soldiers at the fort may have consisted of no more than their morning and evening prayers. But since the authorities in Stockholm found it necessary to stress the importance of prayers in their official instructions to Governor Ridder, there may actually have been little praying going on.

Under church law none but a duly ordained minister was allowed to perform divine services or conduct morning and evening prayers in church. But there was no church at Fort Christina until the time of Governor Ridder. Perhaps Måns Kling, in charge of the colony from the departure of Peter Minuit in 1638 until Ridder's arrival in 1639, conducted morning and evening prayers. There may well have been no formal services for those first two years. Each soldier in Sweden's army carried a manual for individual devotion during field operations and in camps in Germany during the Thirty Years' War. The same was probably true in New Sweden.

By 1641 the tiny colony's population numbered no more than thirty-five souls. It was a very small congregation that assembled in the log cabin chapel at the fort. By 1643 half of the population consisted of soldiers and military personnel and the other half of farmers and tradesmen.

The colony's second parish was developing at New Gothenburg (Tinicum). Peter Lindeström wrote in his *Geographia Americae* that "on the island of Tenakong [Tinicum], Governor Printz had erected a church and for himself and his family a palace, named Printz Hall, very expensively built with a garden, a gazebo and more such things. At this place, the most important farmers had their houses and plantations."[13]

The members of Tinicum Parish were the officers and soldiers of Fort New Gothenburg, plantation owners on Tinicum Island, plantation owners and workers on the New Sweden Company's plantations on Uppland Island, and farmers and workers from the settlements by the Schuylkill River. On Uppland Island (modern Chester) a log blockhouse was built on a hill to protect settlers who were growing tobacco. South of Uppland another settlement was built around a blockhouse and was called Finland. In an area the Indians called Kingsessing, the blockhouse Wasa was the center of another settlement. Along the Schuylkill were two other tiny settlements, New Korsholm and Tornea.[14]

In 1647 Vicar Johannes Campanius wrote to the archbishop at Uppsala of the need for at least two or three ministers in the colony if there were to be the slightest continuation of the work of the church after his time in New Sweden (1643–48). He noted the scattered nature of settlement in the colony and made his request "for the sake of the many settlements here—five or six—on which the Swedes are living." Tinicum Parish consisted of a central village near Fort New Gothenburg and another tiny one by the church on Tinicum Island, and of a few settlements on the mainland to the southwest and the northwest. It is not clear if Campanius meant that two or three ministers were needed for all the religious life of both Christina and Tinicum parishes, or that two ministers were needed exclusively at Tinicum Parish. There the inhabitants were spread out in settlements, situated at "two miles distance from each other and, thus, [the people] could not always come to divine services because of the many inconveniences and hindrances." He especially mentioned weather conditions and the difficulties of traveling on "waterways, on foot or on horseback" in good weather and in bad. The faithful of Christina parish were more concentrated, but each parish had a similar population structure and a similar economy.[15]

In 1643 the population of the two parishes consisted of about two hundred persons, women and children included. In 1644 there were about ninety men, thirty-one of whom were occupied with planting tobacco. Others were officers, soldiers, tradesmen, sailors, and farmers. Their houses were simple Finnish cottages or small Swedish log cabins and their lifestyle was extremely simple, almost primitive.

THE CHURCHES

Six Swedish Lutheran churches and one Dutch Lutheran church were built in New Sweden during the seventeenth century. The six Swedish churches were Christina Chapel at Fort Christina, the two churches on Tinicum Island (one built in 1643, the other in 1646), Crane Hook Church (1677) at Crane Hook, south of the Christina River, the church at Wicacoa (1669) on the mainland in the area of modern Philadelphia, and Holy Trinity Church in Wilmington, which was dedicated in June 1699. The Dutch Lutheran church was the church at Swanwyck in the area of modern Wilmington. Three of the Swedish churches were built while the colony was under Swedish control (before 1655).

The Log Chapel at Fort Christina, 1641

This chapel, built in 1640 to 1641 near the ramparts of the fort, is not described in the historical record; we must try to imagine how it must have looked. Acrelius wrote much later that the church was built in the form of a block house because "the Indians were not always to be depended upon."[16] The settlers felt safer having the church built within the fort's ramparts. The ramparts had been erected in 1638 when the fort was built and had been gradually strengthened.

The chapel's foundation was of uncut stone, which was probably laid only at the corners. The chapel was rectangular, with an entrance in one side. Glassless windows were closed by wooden shutters and its walls were built of round logs sealed with clay. The logs were cut with axes, the only tools the settlers had for their building. Hand-hewn boards were used for the roof. Inside the floor was made of logs cut at the middle and lengthwise and the walls were whitewashed with white clay. The benches, the altar, the pulpit, and the baptismal font were of wood. The church lacked a bell tower but had a cemetery.[17]

There were no ornaments in the church. During his governorship Johan Rising wrote home to Sweden asking for "priestly vestments, an altar painting, and two or three bells" for the church at the fort. He had made Fort Christina his residence and wanted "his" church to be decorated according to Swedish use and custom. He was as eager to ornament the log chapel at Fort Christina as Governor Printz had been to ornament the church on Tinicum Island. However, Rising's ornaments did not arrive before the colony was taken over by the Dutch.[18]

The Log Church at Fort New Gothenburg, 1643

In the spring and summer of 1643 a simple church was built in the same manner near Fort New Gothenburg on Tinicum Island. Per Brahe, a member of the Royal Council, had instructed Governor Printz to decorate the little church after Swedish custom. Since Printz's "gracious lord and mighty patron" wanted the church decorated and since it was meant to be the main church of the colony, it was probably not as modest as the chapel at Fort Christina.[19]

The church at Fort New Gothenburg was probably built in a rectangle. It was a barnlike building, eight meters long and five meters wide. The altar stood in one of the narrow ends and was to be decorated with "beautiful scenes."

The walls were round logs, placed tightly on top of each other and secured with clay. The outside roof was probably covered with wood shingles, and the inner one was made from boards. The church foundation was, even here, probably of uncut stone. The church benches were also logs, cut lengthwise and standing on wooden legs. The altar, baptismal font, and pulpit were of wood. There were plans to decorate the church with small sculptures.

On 11 March 1644 a stone baptismal font arrived from Göteborg. The church bell also arrived at this time, and the settlers built a bell tower for it. The church was probably inaugurated at the latest in March 1644 by Vicar Campanius in the presence of the governor, his family and attendants, high officers and other military personnel, as well as local inhabitants of the three parish districts.[20]

On 25 November 1645 the church, the fort, the governor's palace, and the entire village of New Gothenburg burned down. Only the baptismal font and the bell were saved, so there was no Swedish Christmas celebration at the church that year on Tinicum Island.

Tinicum Church of 1646

In the spring of 1646 the governor's palace, the fort, and the church were rebuilt, more elegantly than before. The builders evidently meant this church to be more elaborate and churchlike than the simple log structure of 1643. This church was built of notched logs and had a roof of wood shingles. Nearby the parishoners built a new "church village," which contained "a number of small log cabins."[21]

Amandus Johnson relates that "the church was fitted somewhat in the style of the churches in Sweden."[22] To which Swedish church-building style does he refer? Was it the style of the wood churches of the Middle Ages, with their rectangular form and narrow rectangular sanctuary, as were raised in the provinces of Västergötland, Småland, and Dalsland? Was it rectangular, narrowing toward the sanctuary, as in Västergötland, Närke, and Värmland, or was it like the simple, barn-shaped churches without a sanctuary, which were found along the Baltic coast of Uppland, from whence some of the settlers had come?

What do the historians tell us? In his dissertation *The Planting of the Swedish Church in America*, Tobias Eric Björck discusses Tinicum's church. He wrote that the first church was built of wood.[23] But when he speaks of the "first church," does he mean the church built in 1646? The log churches in Christina (1641) and on Tinicum Island (1643), were "real" churches. Some kind of inauguration must have taken place, although such a ceremony is not mentioned in the records. We know that the new church on Tinicum Island was dedicated on 4 September 1646, which is one of the first sure dates we have in the church history of New Sweden.[24]

Björck was the son of Vicar Erik Björck, who came to the former colony in 1697 to minister to the Swedish and Finnish Lutherans of Delaware and eastern Pennsylvania. The son was born there and returned with his parents to Sweden, grew up in Falun, studied at Uppsala University, and wrote his dissertation on the church of New Sweden.[25] When his father arrived at Christina, the oldest log church at the fort, built in 1641, was not there anymore, having been replaced in 1667 by the wood church at Crane Hook, which was then in a state of disrepair. New churches, dedicated in 1699 and 1700 and constructed in the English brick style of building, were built in Tinicum and Christina parishes. Tinicum Island's wooden church of 1646 was still standing in 1697 but had started to disintegrate. It had been in use for about fifty years, serving as the main Swedish-Finnish church in the New World, but by then was no longer used.

When Björck talks about the oldest churches, he means the church buildings at Crane Hook and at Wicacoa. Quoting his father, he wrote that

> these sacred buildings ... were so constructed that, if the heathen, whose arms are bows and arrows, should rush the sacred buildings and assault the inhabitants, they could safely defend themselves and could easily overthrow them by shooting. I add what my dearest father wrote in regard to this matter: "Which [churches] were so built, that after a sufficient height like an ordinary house there was added an overhanging portion some courses higher, out of which they could shoot; so that if the heathen attacked them ... the Swedes could shoot down upon them without trouble, and the heathen ... could harm them very little."[26]

Other historians quote this passage, which refers to the wood churches at Crane Hook and Wicacoa; we also know that the latter had a defense tower. The description does not hold for the wooden church on Tinicum Island. The two later churches were, as in early Christian days in Sweden, defensive strongholds as well as churches. The Tinicum church was protected and defended by the fort on the island in the same way that the two earlier log churches had been protected by Fort Christina and Fort New Gothenburg.

If the 1646 church on Tinicum Island had been built in the same manner as the later churches at Crane Hook and at Wicacoa, it would not have been called the "beautiful temple." Instead it was built according to the Swedish church-building style. The two later churches were hybrids, having a kind of mixed form according to the demands of the circumstances. Their style deviated from that of a common seventeenth-century Swedish church of a larger size.

Its larger size was not the only thing that distinguished the second Tinicum church from the log churches of 1641 and 1643. It was the colony's main church, in a sense its "cathedral."[27] It was probably built of pine or oak logs cut from stands of timber on the island or from nearby woods. While the earlier churches must have measured five by eight meters, the main church must have been somewhat larger, perhaps seven by nine meters. It was probably rectangular and, presumably, in contrast to the earlier churches, it had a narrow, diagonal, three-sided sanctuary, the most common sanctuary shape in the Swedish provinces of Västergötland, Närke, and Dalsland, the homelands of many of the settlers. We can estimate the size of the church from the fact that we know that the settlers bought two thousand wood shingles from an Englishman. This gives a roof surface of about forty square meters, or a church of about five by eight meters. It is also possible that only a part of the roof was covered or that the Swedes could not then afford to buy enough shingles to cover the entire roof. The Swedish and Finnish farmers also used hand-cut shingles to roof their houses and other buildings, and they could have made more later to cover the remaining parts of the roof. The stone baptismal font, which survived from the ruined older church, was placed in the sanctuary. The altar and the pulpit were wooden, and the altar was decorated with wooden sculptures of angels.[28]

The governor's palace, "Printz Hall," had glass windows, but we do not know if the church did as well. If it did, it may not have had them until a later period. The church had wooden benches and a rough-hewn wooden floor like those in the first two log churches. The church was dedicated soon after its construction was finished, on 4 September 1646, "a day of rejoicing and thanksgiving." A month later the settlers celebrated the accession of Queen Christina in the church. The young queen had reached her majority in 1644, and the settlers only received news of her accession in 1646, brought by the first ship to arrive in the colony in two years. Te Deum was sung at this occasion.[29]

A new bell tower was erected to replace the one that had burned in 1645. Once again the bell's sound could be heard over the Delaware River, all the way to the settlers of Uppland and on the Schuylkill. The Swedish and Finnish settlers were faithful and devoted Lutherans. With diligence and seriousness, they taught their children the Lutheran faith, as both state and church desired them to do. The Bible, the Augsburg Confession, and Luther's Catechism—the great spiritual inheritance from the Reformation—were the most precious spiritual treasures in the homes of the people.[30]

CHURCH BELLS, BELL TOWERS, AND CEMETERIES

The Church Ordinance of 1571 states that "Church garbs [altar cloths] for mass or altar, pictures, sculptures, candles, candlesticks, crowns, bells, etc., can be used but only in moderation."[31] The Swedish church followed the Reformation view that these were material objects. But no one could deny that objects such as church bells had their importance for the Lutheran service. In this, as in other things, the Swedish model of orthodox Lutheranism differed from other church models of the seventeenth century.

Amandus Johnson wrote that "the belfrey was probably built by the side of the church [on Tinicum Island], a few feet away from it, a custom common in Sweden and Finland in olden times."[32] In *Swedish Wood Churches* Lundberg wrote that bell tower architecture is almost the only truly original Swedish contribution to the development of western church architecture before modern times.[33] The bell towers of 1644 and 1646 at Tinicum Church were probably of a very simple construction, consisting of four round logs, raised on end and fastened to each other, with a roof above.

The presence of bell and bell tower at Tinicum Church tells us that the church life of the colony had entered a new phase. The importance of bell ringing demanded that a special person should be in charge of it. In the Middle Ages church laws stated that the bells were to be entrusted to a sexton and that he was responsible for their safety. I will return to this matter when I discuss the office of the sexton in the colony.[34]

The first cemetery in New Sweden was founded at the log chapel at Christina in 1642. It was situated between the fort and the chapel, on a small lot, no more than a hundred meters square. Swedish settlers were buried there beginning in 1642. This cemetery was shared by the parishes of Christina and Tinicum until 1646.[35]

Tinicum Church's cemetery was founded in 1646. The first burial took place on 28 October 1646, when Campanius interred Anders Hansson's daughter, Katarina. The cemetery was most likely on the south side of the church and may have been surrounded by a fence. The first graves were probably placed near the south wall of the church.[36]

THE PARSONAGES

There may have been no parsonage at Christina from 1640 to 1643, at the time when the first ministers worked there. Vicar Reovius traveled around to the different settlements, performing services and teaching, while Reverend Hermanni (who arrived in 1641) served as garrison minister at the fort. The two ministers probably lived together in one of the houses that Governor Ridder had built in or near the fort, until Reovius married and needed a house for his family.[37]

The Tinicum Church parsonage, built in 1643–44 for Vicar Campanius, was actually on the Uppland Island, which the settlers called "Priest Island." Thomas Campanius Holm (Vicar Campanius's grandson) states in his history of New Sweden that it was situated between Fort Christina and Fort New Gothenburg, but nearer to the latter. Its allotment included both the vicarage land and some land belonging to the New Sweden Company.[38]

The vicarage's main building probably did not differ much from the other small buildings in the colony. In Sweden these buildings were usually similar to seventeenth-century farmhouses. The main room was the so-called single cottage, to which other rooms were often added. The single cottage was about five meters long and four meters wide. The fireplace was in one corner of the cottage. The next building to be added was usually a cattle shed or a barn for one or two cows. Next came a stable with barn and thereafter a storehouse and a bathhouse.[39]

A complete parsonage, according to the Church Code of the Uppland Law, had to have seven buildings. In addition to those already mentioned, there was also to be a smithy and a bakery. But it is plausible that not all of these buildings were built on Priest Island. Campanius would hardly have had use for a smithy or a bakery. Like everything else in New Sweden, the parsonage buildings were built of round logs.

Ola Ehn writes that the vicarages in seventeenth-century Uppland in Sweden were built in the same style as the larger farmhouses.[40] The main living quarters were "the gentleman's cottage" and a chamber with a bakery between. The vicarage on Priest Island in New Sweden was also probably a pair cottage. The other houses were placed around the main building and the barn. All the houses were small and rather insignificant looking. In his 1654 report, Governor Rising mentions "the small houses" of the vicarage at Uppland. Animals were kept at vicarages in Sweden at this time, and Campanius probably had a couple of cows and a horse.[41]

The vicarage was built with the help of craftsmen and carpenters whom the governor had ordered to work on the island.

The parsonage and its land on Priest Island, owned by the New Sweden Company, were placed at the vicar's disposal as his residence. Thus the Crown disposed of the company's property as a vicarage for Campanius and his successors.[42] The churches at Christina and Tinicum, on the other hand, were owned by the Swedish Crown during 1640 to 1643. In 1644 Queen Christina gave Tinicum Island to Governor Printz as his property. Tinicum Church and its cemetery, which customarily belonged to the state, came in practice to belong to Governor Printz and in reality were treated as such from that time on. Christina Church and its cemetery, on the other hand, belonged to the Swedish Crown.[43]

THE CLERGY

During 1640 to 1654 seven ministers came to New Sweden. The first was Torkillus Reovius. He was thirty-one years old and single when he left for America with the second expedition in 1639. He was born at Fassberg in Västergötland, near Göteborg. He had studied for ten years at the cathedral school in Linkoping and later at Skara. He was ordained in Göteborg in 1639; while serving there as a chaplain, he was asked by the superintendent, Anders Prytz, if he would like to become a minister in New Sweden. Reovius had received the customary education for a minister at the time; he had studied theology, first at the high school and then at the Cathedral Chapter. He probably passed his examinations at the Cathedral Chapter in Skara.[44]

Reovius worked as a minister in America at Christina Chapel. He was also garrison minister at the fort until that task was taken over by the minister Christopher Hermanni in 1641. Reovius died during the epidemic of 1643, on 7 September. Then thirty-five years old, he left his wife and one child.[45]

The second minister was Pastor Christopher Hermanni. We know little about him. Campanius Holm does not mention him, and neither does Mathias Hultgren in his "Notations." He must have arrived in New Sweden in November 1641, aboard the ship *Kalmar Nyckel*. He had, however, no appointment as minister in the colony. He performed ministerial tasks since the work at the parish had become too heavy for Reovius to do alone, especially during 1643, when many parishioners fell ill and were in need of spiritual help when dying. Amandus Johnson mentions that Hermanni took care of spiritual needs among "the free men" and servants in the different settlements. The fact was that it was probably Reovius who did that while Hermanni worked at Fort Christina as garrison minister, becoming more active throughout the colony only when Reovius fell ill.[46]

Many Finns from Värmland had arrived in 1641 on board the ship *Charitas*. Presumably Hermanni had accompanied them to New Sweden, helping as interpreter, as well as pastor on the trip and at arrival. He returned to Sweden on the *Fama* in the summer of 1643. We know little about his remaining life.[47]

The third minister was Johannes Campanius, the best-known of the ministers of New Sweden. He spent five years in the colony between 1643 and 1648. Campanius was born in 1601 in Clara Parish in Stockholm, where his father, Jonas Persson, was the bell-ringer and sexton at Saint Clara Church. He finished high school in Stockholm and was a student at Uppsala University from 1627 to 1633. Thus he arrived at Uppsala soon after the moribund university was reorganized and reinvigorated by King Gustavus Adolphus. In 1633 he received his degree in theology and was ordained at Uppsala by Professor Canuti Leneaus. On 13 March 1634 he accompanied the Swedish embassy to Russia, where he remained for about half a year. In the fall of 1634 Campanius returned to Sweden to become a teacher at the public school of Norrtälje. In spring 1635 he defended his doctoral thesis, and in the summer of the same year he married Margareta Persdotter and moved to Stockholm, where he became minister at Stora Barnhuset in the fall. He remained there for seven years.[48]

In February 1642 Campanius was offered the position of minister in New Sweden. In the fall he sailed with Governor Printz aboard the *Fama* for New Sweden. On board was another minister, Israel Holgher Fluviander, the thirty-year-old nephew of the new governor. Campanius was about forty.

Arriving in New Sweden in the spring of 1643, the governor and the ministers first lived at the Christina settlement. But in the summer the governor moved to Tinicum Island, where he built Fort New Gothenburg. Campanius accompanied him there and was in the beginning garrison minister at the fort. Later he became the vicar of Tinicum Parish and lived at the vicarage on Priest Island with his family. Several of his seven children were born there.

Campanius seems to have been the only one of New Sweden's ministers to have attempted a mission to the Indians. The Swedish government, the church, and the New Sweden Company all intended that the work of the pastors would include the effort to convert the Indians to Lutheran Christianity. We know that Campanius tried to visit the Indians regularly on his rounds through the colony. He attempted to understand Delaware Indian culture, learned a Delaware dialect, and translated Martin Luther's Catechism into that dialect. But we know little about the results of the mission. We do not know that any Indians became Lutherans as a result of it, or if any use was ever made by the Indians of Campanius's translation of the Catechism during his ministry or at any time thereafter, even during the eighteenth-century renewal of regular Swedish church contact with the descendants of the settlers living in the Delaware Valley.[49]

In 1648 Campanius and his family returned to Stockholm. For one year he was minister at the Admiralty on Skeppsholm, before being promoted to vicar at Frösthult and Härnevi parishes in Uppland. He remained there for thirty-five years, until his death on 17 September 1683. Campanius's and Governor Printz's correspondence with people in Sweden give us insight into the development of the church in New Sweden during the 1640s. I will come back to this in my description and analysis of ecclesiastical activities in the colony.

The fourth minister was Israel Holgher Fluviander, a nephew of Johan Printz. At his arrival he was apparently stationed as garrison minister at Fort Elfsborg in New Jersey, which Printz had built immediately after arriving in the colony. Fluviander served at the fort from 1643 until 1646.[50]

In September 1646 Fluviander helped Campanius to dedicate the new church on Tinicum Island. Fluviander preached the inauguration sermon, while Campanius handled the dedication.[51] Thereafter it seems that Fluviander was an assistant to Campanius and acted in this capacity mainly at Christina Chapel from the fall of 1646 to the spring of 1647, when he returned to Sweden. During his last year in New Sweden he was garrison and parish minister at Christina. Perhaps from time to time he substituted at Tinicum Church while Campanius was on gospel tours to the settlements and on missions among the Indians. In March 1647 Fluviander returned to Sweden. He was appointed vicar at Od in Västergötland, but might not have taken the position. We do not know what happened to him thereafter.[52]

The fifth minister was Lars Karlsson Lockenius (Lars Lock) who was sent to New Sweden in 1647 in response to Campanius's demand for additional ministers.[53]

"Who was Pastor Lock?" asked Professor Harjunpää in a 1975 article titled "Church Conditions at the Delaware Colony during the Seventeenth Century." We know very little about him, including where he came from. Harjunpää writes that many twentieth-century scholars maintained that Pastor Lock was either a Finn or a Finland Swede. They have pointed out that the oldest sources mention him only by name and say merely that he arrived in the colony during the time of Governor Printz.

Harjunpää wanted to solve the question of Lock's background and origin. He found nothing that threw light on Lock's origin. His name is absent from all church annals and documents from high schools or universi-

ties. From his studies, however, Harjunpää concluded that "Lars Lock
was a Swede, born and brought up in Sweden." His source for this information was the *Life Descriptions*, written by Bishop Jesper Swedberg and
first published in 1941. It contains letters from Swedish ministers in
America. In a 1721 letter, Vicar Jonas Lidman wrote that "Pastor Lock
whose birthplace was Lockered at Mariestad in Västergötland, was
eighty-four years old when he died. During his last years he was unable
to perform his duties in the parish."[54]

Harjunpää's diligence provided further information about Lock's early
years. He was probably born in 1604 on a farm called Lockeredstorp near
Mariestad. It is likely that he studied at the public school at Mariestad
and later at Skara, where he graduated in theology. But when and where
he was ordained is still a question. It may have been at Skara or at any of
several other places. We do know that in 1647 Chancellor Oxenstierna
requested that Superintendent Anders Prytz in Göteborg find a successor to Campanius in New Sweden.[55] Campanius's letter to the archbishop in spring 1647 had complained about being the sole minister in
the colony. He had complained that even when ill he had to travel between the different settlements to preach and administer the sacraments.
He did it willingly, in spite of good or bad weather, but he needed two or
three more ministers, preferably young, healthy, and unmarried, who
would be able to travel constantly to the different settlements. The authorities in Sweden had some difficulties finding ministers willing to
travel to the colony when they learned of Campanius's and Fluviander's
assessments of conditions there. In his letter to the archbishop Campanius insisted that the Indians every year threatened to kill the Swedes
and to completely extinguish them. This was too dark a picture, written
in a state of exhaustion and desperation; but the description was dark
enough to frighten away many candidates. Lockenius was, however, willing to go to New Sweden. He was forty-three when he left for America.

It is likely that Lockenius worked at Göteborg in some position in
1647, perhaps as a sexton or a chaplain (if the latter, he must already
have been ordained). If he was not ordained at that time, he became so
at the latest in the summer of 1647 and probably in Göteborg, before
Prytz became bishop in Linkoping.[56]

Leaving Göteborg on 25 September 1647, Lockenius arrived in New
Sweden early in January 1648. He was stationed initially at Christina
Chapel and moved to the vicarage on Priest Island in the middle of
May, when Campanius returned to Sweden. Thereafter Lockenius was
the only minister in the colony until 1654. He preached alternately at
Christina Chapel and Tinicum Church and had sole charge of the affairs
of both congregations. He was to live in New Sweden for the remaining
forty years of his life.[57]

The sixth minister was Mathias Nertunius, probably from Nartuna in Uppland. On 3 July 1649, Nertunius and seventy other passengers sailed for New Sweden from Göteborg aboard the *Katt*. The ship was wrecked in the West Indies and only a few passengers survived the catastrophe. Nertunius managed to get back to Stockholm via Amsterdam in 1651. For a few years he lived in Stockholm under bad circumstances until the spring of 1654, when he again tried to get over to America. He arrived in New Sweden on the ship *Örn*, on 18 May 1654, together with the new governor, Johan Classon Rising, and Peter Lindeström, the fortifications engineer, and another minister named Petrus Hjort.[58]

Nertunius became minister at Tinicum Parish and supervised the work of Hjort and Lockenius. He lived at the parsonage and glebe (land associated with or yielding revenue to a parish church) on Priest Island in the Uppland settlement. Since he now had become the head vicar he must have had extensive theological studies behind him, as had Campanius. Nertunius had probably studied theology at Uppsala University and had had five years' experience as a minister. He was ordained in 1643 and served as a pastor with the Swedish Royal Navy and at the Admiralty from 1643 to 1648. In 1648 to 1649 he and Campanius were probably together in Stockholm before Nertunius sailed for the colony. Nertunius was a bachelor and about thirty-five years old when he arrived in New Sweden. We know little about him or his work at Tinicum Parish. Rising called him "definitely the best" minister among the three in the colony during his time as governor. He took care of church affairs but did not pursue the Indian mission that Campanius had started. His stay in the colony was ended by the Dutch conquest of New Sweden in September 1655.[59]

Nertunius arrived back in Sweden in the spring of 1656 after an absence of two years. He became minister at Enånger in Hälsingland in 1658 and at Arbra in 1660. He married Anna Bruzelius, a vicar's daughter from Skog in Hälsingland. They had a son, Martin, who also became a minister. In 1680 he was promoted to vicar at Ovanåker but died before starting the appointment.[60]

The colony's seventh minister, Petrus Hjort, was born in 1627 at Vena in Småland. Hjort was ordained in 1654 at Göteborg, shortly before leaving for America. He was then twenty-seven years old. He arrived in New Sweden with Rising and Nertunius. Governor Rising stationed him at Fort Trefaldighet (modern New Castle, Delaware), where he was garrison minister for a year and a half, until the Dutch conquest. Like Nertunius he returned to Sweden in the spring of 1656. Thereafter Hjort became an assistant minister at Vena in 1656 and was later vicar at Vimmerby in 1658 and at Pelarne in 1669, where he remained until 1700. He died in 1704. Governor Rising called him "materially and spiritually a poor priest." This must mean that Hjort was not very ambitious and that he lacked a deep knowledge of theology and the experience of a clergyman.[61]

Governor Rising, who himself had considerable knowledge of theology and church affairs, seemed unimpressed by Lockenius, Nertunius, and Hjort in his *Relation* of 1654. "As to our church affairs," he wrote, "we are indeed in need of a learned priest, although we now have three of them." The governor planned to send Lockenius home to Sweden to defend himself against charges of mutiny raised when the colonists revolted against Printz in the summer of 1653. Lockenius exonerated himself. But the minister fell ill and was allowed to stay in the colony, although he was moved to Christina Parish. Amandus Johnson maintains that he was moved to Christina Church in 1654, when Rising arrived in America.[62]

Thus during Johan Rising's administration of the colony, Vicar Nertunius served at Tinicum Parish, Pastor Lockenius at Christina Parish, and Assistant Minister Hjort at Fort Trefaldighet.

The Sextons

The office of sexton was very important in Swedish church life. According to seventeenth-century Swedish church law, the sexton was in charge of the church keys and inventories, rang the church bell, and helped with the singing in the church and teaching the parish's children. The parish was to provide its sexton with a cottage, a stable, and a storehouse. The sexton's wife would care for the church vestments and keep house for the minister. The 1644 "Ordinance for Chaplains and Sextons" added duties and made more explicit the sexton's educational role. Men were to be employed as sextons "who could teach the young people the ABCs and the Catechism as well as help the ministers in church with the singing and praying."[63]

The first sexton came to the colony sometime between 1648 and 1654. In 1654 there was a "Lars Månsson Sexton" on the list of officers, soldiers, servants, and freemen in the colony. The sexton had probably arrived with Rising, Nertunius, and Hjort, and we presume he served mostly at Tinicum Church.[64]

With the arrival of Rising and the *Örn* in 1654, the colony's population reached 370, spread out in various small settlements. The colonists could now hear church bells calling them together for services and celebrations. The colony had three ministers, in accordance with the wishes of Campanius, and there was at least one sexton leading the hymns at Tinicum Church and keeping school for the children. Only in the colony's very last years, 1654 and 1655, was "the church as an institution" completely established in New Sweden in accordance with the model of the church in old Sweden.

THE ECONOMY OF THE CHURCH

What was the economic foundation of the church in New Sweden? The churches were built and paid for and the land was provided by the Crown. Their upkeep and decoration were the duty of the governor.[65] The material for their construction and maintenance was ordered from Sweden or from visiting English traders. The New Sweden Company lent additional property to the vicarage on Priest Island.

In February 1638 an "Ordinance of the rule for payment of tithes to the Church" was proclaimed in Sweden.[66] During several sessions of the Swedish parliament, the farmers complained about the uncertainty of what and how much they were obliged to give to vicars and chaplains for their keep. This ordinance stipulated the salaries of chaplains and sextons. The sexton's income, as a rule, was free living quarters at the parish house, some grain from every farmer, and payment in cash for certain church duties. The clergy received a large portion of their income from tithes and from fees, the so-called pastorals.[67]

The first ministers in New Sweden had no fixed salaries. Torkillus Reovius lived under a "deplorable situation." He wrote to the superintendent at Göteborg asking for an advance of the salary promised him.[68] From the time of Campanius the ministers had a more fixed salary. According to the New Sweden Company's "Monatgelderbuch," Campanius received 670 riksdaler as salary for sixty-seven months of service in America from 13 August 1642 to 1 April 1648. Occasionally he received payments in kind worth a total of about 120 riksdaler. In 1645 he received 147.19 riksdaler in cash from Governor Printz. At his return to Sweden he was paid the rest of his salary in three installments on 15 July, 24 July, and 7 August 1648.[69] We do not know how much Fluviander's or Lockenius's salaries were, but the latter was probably also paid ten riksdaler a month.

Governor Rising wanted the people to give freely to the church a tenth (a tithe) of their grain and cattle; half was to be used for the salaries of the ministers. He also wanted the West India Company (the reorganized New Sweden Company) to have the government property on Uppland Island, to be given as a glebe to Nertunius, as vicar of Tinicum Church. But the company never made this donation.

Campanius had used the glebe property for his own needs, as Lockenius probably did. The glebe property on Uppland Island consisted of seven acres of cultivated land that yielded twenty to thirty bushels of grain per acre. A small herb garden probably belonged to the vicarage. After the fall of the colony the land became the property of the parish.[70]

THE LITURGICAL BOOKS OF THE CHURCHES

The classic document of the Swedish Reformation was the Gustav I Bible of 1541. An improved version was published in 1618 (the Gustavus Adolphus Bible) and reprinted several times during the seventeenth century.[71]

We can be fairly certain of which versions of the Gustavus Adolphus Bible came to New Sweden because ministers generally used the latest edition available to them. Thus the Bible brought by the first four ministers to New Sweden was almost certainly the 1636 edition. Lars Lockenius probably brought with him the deluxe edition of 1646 when he arrived in 1648. And the last two ministers may have brought the 1650 edition. The 1633 and 1635 editions were small, portable (about six by nine inches) army Bibles, which were meant to be used by troops in the field, including those in New Sweden.

So we may presume that the Bibles used in New Sweden during 1640 to 1645 were the army Bibles of 1633 and 1635, as well as the Bible of 1636 that the ministers probably used as the "church Bible" at Christina and Tinicum churches. Bibles used from 1645 to 1655 were the army Bibles and the editions of 1646 and 1650. No New Sweden Bibles have been preserved.[72]

Another major religious book was the hymnbook. The Swedish hymnbook was published in nearly two dozen editions between 1530 and 1665, but the ministers and inhabitants of New Sweden "had no national Swedish hymnal with them."[73]

In her survey "Hymns Going West," Elisabeth Wentz Janacek points out that in Sweden a book known very loosely as "The Swedish Hymn Book" had existed since the Reformation. Over the years it had gone through many editions and unplanned additions.[74] The first official hymnbook was printed in 1645, the so-called New Uppsala Hymnbook. It was probably the 1622 edition of the Old Uppsala Hymnbook that was used in New Sweden from 1640 to 1647, while the New Uppsala Hymnbook of 1645 no doubt was used from 1648 to 1655, particularly since the new archbishop at Uppsala, Canuti Leneaus, had collaborated on it. Leneaus had helped plan the parishes and missions in New Sweden.[75]

In his book *House Punishments and House Catechism Meetings*, Hilding Pleijel entitles a chapter "Our Oldest National Books" in which he writes that Sweden began to have "national books" from the time of its Great Power Era (1620–1720). The hymnbook was more of a national book than was the Bible. Pleijel thinks that over time the hymnbook influenced Swedish religious life more than any other book. Readers and singers of the hymnbook in Sweden have been called "hymnbook Christians." Similar people in the homes of New Sweden were just such hymnbook Christians.[76]

In the seventeenth-century Swedish home the servants of the house were awakened early for morning prayers and hymn singing. Work began after breakfast. Work was performed indoors and outdoors during winter as well as summer. To avoid being lulled to sleep by the soothing sound of the spinning wheel, domestic workers sang hymns throughout the day. In the old religious homesteads people gathered around the open fire in the evenings, especially on Saturday evenings, to read the next day's gospel and epistle and sing hymns. The hymns were sung from memory, learned by heart in childhood. The hymns were studied at home and in church and taught by the minister and the sexton as young people prepared for their first communion. The hymns could thus be used as a sort of catechism. In 1633 Laurentius Paulinus Gothus published *Clenodium*, a hymnbook designed to be used to teach Lutheran doctrine through the texts of the hymns. The book may well have been in use in New Sweden since its author became archbishop of Uppsala in 1637.[77]

The seventeenth century has been called the classic Swedish Lutheran period of hymn writing. Its hymns displayed and mirrored the hymnbook Christians' virtues of temperance, evenness, and calmness in their religious life. But there were some contradictory features of this type of religiosity, even among the hymnbook Christians in the settlements of New Sweden. Anguish and fear are expressed in some of the evening hymns, but many display the opposite traits of trust and confidence in God.[78]

Martin Luther's Catechism was the third important book of Swedish Lutheranism. The Catechism was printed in Swedish in 1537, 1567, and 1572, and its significance for the religious life of the nation was affirmed at the Uppsala Assembly of 1593, which confirmed the Reformation in Sweden.[79] The Catechism consisted of summaries of Scripture and Luther's explanatory text. Over time the two parts became almost indistinguishable in the minds of most people, and Luther's explanations were given more and more importance. The Catechism acquired the character of a national book, and it was used to bring up the people in the right Lutheran faith.[80]

In his theological and pedagogical work *Ethicae Christianae* (1610–30), Laurentius Paulinus Gothus explained the concept of "catechism" as it was understood during the first half of the seventeenth century. The Catechism, he wrote, "is a short summary of the Holy Scriptures which through questions and answers contains everything that is useful and needed for people to know God's existence and will and a Christian life, a blessed end, and an eternal life. That is why it is rightly called the little, or common man's 'Bible and Divine Christian Rules of Ethics.'" Swedish religious authorities considered the Scriptures to be too extensive to serve as a confessional document; the Catechism was used in their stead, and among the people it acquired the same authority as the Scriptures. The Bible was also, during the seventeenth century, difficult to find and hard for most people to understand. For these reasons the Swedish church tried very hard to put the Catechism into people's hands since it summarized the "core and marrow" of the Bible. Under those circumstances it was logical, at certain times, to preach the Catechism in church and to have the Catechism printed together with the hymnbook (it was a part of the New Uppsala Hymnbook of 1645), the book most read in the home.[81]

The growing influence of the Catechism in the Swedish church as an unofficial Bible is obvious in the constitution of 1634. Mention of the Catechism in the Form of Government of 1634 is a formal assurance of the high and general esteem in which the book was held in the Swedish Lutheran church at that time.

The Catechism was also published as a part of soldiers' manuals, which were originally created to explain the content and meaning of the Bible to the Swedish, Finnish, and German soldiers in the Swedish army. Over time they also came to be used by ordinary people. These manuals were surely in use in New Sweden. We know that Campanius read the Catechism from the pulpit at Christina and Tinicum and, as we have seen, translated it into an Indian language.

The manuals were also extremely important for the practice of seventeenth-century religion. They contained some Bible stories, a hymnbook, a gospel book, a prayer book, and religious discourses, as well as excerpts from the Swedish morning service. At least seven manuals were published between 1639 and 1691. In the province of New Sweden, the manuals of 1639, 1643, 1651, and 1653 were surely used by the settlers in their devotions at home, as well as by the soldiers at the Swedish forts at morning and evening services. When prayers and divine services were held in the field, the fort minister or the parish minister took part, using the book for church services.[82]

The *Handbook for Divine Service* of 1614 was the culmination of the Swedish Reformation's liturgical work. It collected the forms for all services and ceremonies in a single volume, but it did not achieve complete uniformity. It was not until 1693 that the church created a handbook for rituals that it regarded as canonical and absolute.[83]

Other religious material commonly available included excerpts from hymn and gospel books, excerpts from manuals, and Bible editions and translations of religious works into the Finnish and Lapp languages. The rituals for the morning services were published in the diocesan constitutions, synod rules, and other regulations of a more or less official character for the different dioceses. In his dissertation on the Swedish ritual for morning services from 1614 to 1693, Gustav Lizell writes about the rules for church services in the new provinces that Sweden acquired from Denmark during the seventeenth century (Gotland, Skåne, Blekinge, Halland, and Bohuslän). But he does not speak about church practices in the European territories Sweden held during the seventeenth century in modern Germany, Poland, Estonia, Latvia, Lithuania, and the former Soviet Union.[84]

New Sweden did not have existing traditions in Christian divine services, and it could not even be compared with the new Swedish provinces or Sweden's European possessions.[85] The 1648 manual for the Lapps in Sweden contained translations from the most common manuals and hymnbooks. The rituals for morning services in the 1671 manual for Finns are similar to those in other manuals. But except for Campanius's Catechism, no such translations were ever made for Indians. Nor is there evidence that Indians ever used Campanius's translation.

Among liturgical rules for church services abroad was the "Church Agenda for the Swedish Forts."[86] The liturgical rules for services at Swedish forts show a careful distinction between the daily sermon services (including morning services), and the much less frequent Holy Communion services. Religious services in New Sweden were similar, not only for the soldiers but for the whole population. A special "Prayer and Church Ordinance for the Swedish Army" of 1637 contains many hymns and prayers for different occasions. As in the "Church Agenda for the Swedish Forts" there is a distinction between sermon services and Holy Communion services. The sermon service at the Swedish forts began with a penance prayer or some Christian hymns (from Luther's *Gesangbuch* for German soldiers), and was followed by readings from the Epistles, a collection prayer, confession, the sermon, a church prayer and the Lord's Prayer, a hymn, and benediction.[87] The Holy Communion service differed only by the addition of the hymn "God Alone in Heaven," which was sung between the collection prayer and confession, and introduction to the confession of sin at the beginning of the service, and the distribution of the Sacrament.[88]

The ritual for the morning service celebrated at Christina and Tincium churches followed the 1614 manual and had five parts. The Introduction included the Introduction to the Confession of Sin, the Confession of Sin, the Prayer at the Confession of Sin, the Kyrie ("Lord, Have Mercy"), the Gloria and Laudamus ("Blessed be God in Heaven"), and the hymn "God Alone in Heaven." The second part of the service focused on Bible reading and included the Salutation: Greetings to the Congregation;

the Invitation to Prayer and the Collection Prayer; the Reading of the Epistle; the Graduation Hymn; the Reading of the Gospel; and concluded with the Confession (Credo). Central to the third part was the sermon. This portion of the service began with hymns and a prayer, followed by a reading from the Gospels and then the sermon itself. This portion of the service concluded with another prayer, absolution of the congregation, and a church prayer. The communion portion of the service began with the Pater Noster, a Holy Communion exhortation by the priest and a response by the congregation, communion, and a prayer. The service concluded with the benediction by the priest and the singing of two hymns by the congregation.[89]

The common church life was regulated by the Church Ordinance of 1571, but the 1614 handbook was the first Swedish one accepted by the clergy, "approved and consented" to by the king, and published with a royal privilege. In it the manual and the missal were united in a single book. But it was still the Church Ordinance of 1571 that set forth liturgical rules for the church. All of this was used in New Sweden since the church there was formed "according to our Swedish fashion."[90]

THE ACTIVITIES OF THE CHURCHES AND THE MINISTERS

Amandus Johnson assumes that the rules and regulations for Swedish cities of three church services on Sundays were also followed at Tinicum Church in New Sweden.[91] In accordance with an old Swedish custom, the church bell rang three times every day before the beginning of the church service, and each evening the bell rang for peace. This Swedish custom was probably carried over to New Sweden. At the sound of the church bell at six o'clock in the evening all work stopped for the day. The bells called everyone "wherever they were, indoors or outdoors, in a Christian spirit to pray and call on God to give peace, bless the authority and by this grace give everything for their well-being and happiness."

The completion of all church activities demanded by the 1614 handbook made much work for the clergy. Their main duties were performing the church services, administering the sacraments, maintaining the church functions, and teaching. During times when there was more than one minister in the colony, each held service at his own workplace, either at church or at a fort. At the fort, divine service was according to the rules described above. At church, the sermon services were held according to the Church Ordinance of 1571. Morning service with Holy Communion was held about once each month. On days when no divine service was held, the ordinance of 1571 ordered that "in the big cities prayers should be said at church evening and morning." These rules were also kept on Tinicum Island.[92]

According to the church ordinance and older Swedish customs, sermons were to be preached at church on Wednesdays and Fridays. These days were called "station days" because they were associated with turning points in the suffering of Christ: on Wednesday he was betrayed and on Friday he was crucified. The church ordinance demanded that in a country parish with two churches a weekday sermon should be held in one on Wednesdays and on Fridays in the other. The sermon was taken from a text in the Old or New Testament according to the gospel prescribed for the coming Sunday. During Advent and Lent, the ministers offered special Catechism sermons. Both Campanius and Lockenius held alternate weekly sermons at Christina Chapel and Tinicum Church. When Campanius wrote that he often traveled around to different settlements with the Word and the Sacraments, he meant that he was performing sermon services, baptisms, and giving Holy Communion to the sick. Funerals were performed at church.[93]

Special Holy Communion services were held perhaps two or three times a year. The ministers prepared for these services held especially at Easter, on Maundy Thursday, and on Good Friday, by special teaching and examination. There was no special instruction to prepare children for Confirmation. Young people were taught the main parts of the Catechism to pass the test for admission to Communion at a more mature age. The ministers did most of their teaching after the church service and during preparations for Holy Communion, weddings, and baptisms.[94]

In their official duties the ministers were dressed in the clerical robes customary during the seventeenth century. It was important in New Sweden that the Swedish clerical robes were used to distinguish the Swedish ministers from the Dutch Calvinists and the English Puritans.[95]

The work of the Swedish ministers in New Sweden introduced Lutheranism into North America during the seventeenth century. Both the Swedish government and the Swedish Lutheran church intended church life in the colony to be as exact a replica as was possible of church life at home. As far as we can tell from the historical record that has come down to us from the period of Swedish rule (1638–55), the seven ministers who came to the colony succeeded in this replication, at least as far as formal religious observances were concerned. They were hampered somewhat in the performance of their duties by their small numbers in relation to the size of the colony. Their parishioners were spread out along the Delaware River from modern Wilmington to modern Philadelphia, and there were never more than three ministers in the colony at one time. While three ministers might have sufficed for a compact settlement of a few hundred people, we have Campanius's eloquent testimony of 1648 about the difficulties imposed on priests and people by the colony's linear distance along the river.

From the colony's beginning, the government, the church, and the New Sweden Company were united in their intention to convert the local Indians to Lutheran Christianity. Campanius went so far as to attempt to visit the Indians regularly and translated Martin Luther's Catechism into a Delaware Indian dialect. But little came of his effort. We do not know that any Indians became Christians through the efforts of the Swedish priests, nor if any ministers after Campanius attempted to continue the Lutheran mission to them.

After the colony fell to the Dutch in 1655, it was more than forty years before another group of Swedish priests came to the Delaware Valley to renew their church's mission in North America. During most of that time we assume that Reverend Lars Lock continued to minister to the Swedes and the Finns in the valley as long as his health and increasing age permitted. But in 1693 Carl Christophersson Springer, on behalf of the original colonists and their descendants, wrote to the postmaster of Göteborg, Johan Thelin, asking him to request the government to send Swedish priests, prayer books, and hymnals to the valley so that Swedish religion and culture would not disappear from North America.

In 1697 three priests arrived, Anders Rudman, Eric Björck, and Jonas Auren, who renewed the mission. They were followed by many other priests in the next century who ministered to the spiritual needs of Swedish- and Finnish-Americans in Delaware, New Jersey, and Pennsylvania. Thus the Swedish Lutheran church provided a cultural continuation of New Sweden long after Sweden had ceased to rule in the Delaware Valley.[96]

NOTES

1. Hjalmar Holmquist, *Handbok i Svensk Kyrkohistoria* (Stockholm: Svenska Kyrkans Diakonistyrelses Bokförlag, 1953), 2:63; Hilding Pleijel, *Svenska Kyrkans historia*, 6 vols. (1952), 2:7. For a brief history of the Swedish Reformation, see Michael Roberts, *The Early Vasas: A History of Sweden, 1523–1611* (New York: Cambridge University Press, 1986), esp. 59–90, 107–23, 273–95, 327–37, and 412–25. For the evolution of the church in the seventeenth century, see Roberts's essay "The Swedish Church" in *Sweden's Age of Greatness, 1632–1718*, ed. Michael Roberts (London: Macmillan & Co., 1973), 132–73.

2. Johan III (1568–92), the second son of King Gustav I, occasionally flirted with Catholicism. His son Sigismund (1592–99) actually was a Catholic, but he was mostly concerned with his other kingdom, Poland, and he left the governance of Sweden to the royal council and Gustav's youngest son, Karl (king in his own right, 1604–11, but not crowned until 1607). Karl tilted incessantly toward Calvinism. See Roberts, *The Early Vasas*, 277–89, for Johan's flirtations with Catholicism.

3. For the Church Ordinance of 1571, see ibid., 278–79.
4. For the Uppsala Assembly and the Resolution of 1593, see ibid., 331–38. The quotation is from 336.
5. Yngve Brillioth, *Svensk Kyrkokunskap* (Stockholm: Svenska Kyrkans Diakonistyrelse, 1933), 92–95. An English text of most of the articles of the Form of Government is in Michael Roberts, ed., *Sweden as a Great Power, 1611–1697: Government, Society, Foreign Policy* (London: Edward Arnold, 1968), 18–28. Article I decreed that everyone would "adhere to the pure and plain word of God, as it stands in the prophetic and apostolic Scriptures; as it is expounded in the creeds, Luther's catechism, and the unaltered Confession of Augsburg; and as it is established by the decisions of the Council of Uppsala [1593] and the resolutions of the Diet [the *riksdag*, Sweden's parliament] and the charters of the realm" (19).
6. Brillioth, *Svensk Kyrkokunskap*, 92–95.
7. Sven Kjöllerström, *Praktisk Teologi: En handbok i kyrkans organisation och verksamhets-former* (Lund: Gleerup, 1959), 146.
8. *Uthföhrlig Förklaring Öfwer Handels Contractet angåendes thet Södre Compagniet uti Konungarijket Swerige* (Stockholm, 1626).
9. Instruktionen för kommendanten Peter Hollender Ridder, 1 July 1639, Oxenstierna Collection, Riksarkivet, Stockholm. See also Jacob Blees, *Svenska Kolonien vid Delaware, 1638–1655* (Stockholm: Boktryckare W. Hedberg, 1937), 45–47.
10. Amandus Johnson, trans., *The Instruction for Johan Printz, Governor of New Sweden* (Philadelphia: Swedish Colonial Society, 1930). Only section 26 of the *Instruction* pertains to religion (94–96). The Swedish text is printed in Israel Acrelius, *Beskrifning om de Swenska Församlingarnas Forna och Närwarande Tillstånd, uti det sa Kallade Nya Swerige* (Stockholm, 1759), 55–58. Translated by William M. Reynolds, *A History of New Sweden, or, The Settlements on the Delaware River*, vol. 11 of Memoirs of the Historical Society of Pennsylvania (Philadelphia: The Society, 1874).
11. Josef Ryden, "Big Belly pa Printz Hall," in *Det började vid Delaware: Om Svenska hembygder i Amerika*, ed. Gunilla Lindberg (Karlskrona: Riksförbundet för Hembygdsvård, 1986), 59–65. The quotation is from Johnson, *Instruction for Johan Printz*, 90, 92.
12. An English translation of the instruction for Johan Rising is in Amandus Johnson, *The Swedish Settlements on the Delaware, 1638–1664*, 2 vols. (Philadelphia: Swedish Colonial Society, 1911), 2:741–46. The quotation is from section 2, p. 741.
13. Nils Jacobsson, ed., *Per Lindeströms Resa Till Nya Sverige, 1653–1655* (Stockholm: Wahlstrom & Widstrand, 1923), 122.
14. Amandus Johnson, *The Swedes on the Delaware, 1638–1664* (Philadelphia: Swedish Colonial Society, 1927), 210.
15. Campanius to Johannes Canuti Leneaus, 30 January 1647, Uppsala domkapitels arkiv, FVIII, vol. 2, Landsarkivet i Uppsala. Excerpts are quoted (in English) in Johnson, *Swedish Settlements*, 1:372–73.
16. Acrelius, *History of New Sweden*, 176. Richard H. Hulan disagrees with the common assumption that the settlers built a church within the walls of Fort Christina. See his "New Sweden and Its Churches," in *The Church in New Sweden*, ed. Oliver K. Olson (Milwaukee, Wisc.: Lutheran Quarterly, 1988), 28, n. 5.
17. On Swedish wooden architecture of the seventeenth century, see Gerda

Boethius, *Den Svenska Timmerbyggnads konsten* (Stockholm, 1927), especially the last chapter on Swedish "blockhouse" churches; Richard H. Hulan, "Historic Memories on the Delaware," in *Det började vid Delaware*, 10–15; and Jimmy Roosval, *Amerikansk Konst* (Stockholm, 1924), 25–27. For Swedish wooden churches see Erik Lundberg, "Swedish Wood Churches," in *Svenska Träkyrkor*, ed. Erik Nordin (Stockholm, 1980). The author is deeply indebted to Gunnar Zetterquist, of Falun, Sweden, for numerous consultations about Swedish vernacular architecture and construction techniques. Mr. Zetterquist's expertise informs much of the description of the churches of New Sweden in this essay.

18. Johan Rising, "Report of Governor Johan Rising, 1654," in *Narratives of Early Pennsylvania, West New Jersey and Delaware, 1630–1707*, ed. Albert Cook Myers (1912; reprint, New York: Barnes & Noble, 1967), 150.

19. Acrelius, *History of New Sweden*, 176; Per Brahe to Printz, 9 November 1643, and Printz to Brahe, 19 July 1644, in Johnson, *Instruction for Johan Printz*, 155–56, 163–64 (see also 33–34 for Johnson's brief general description of church-building techniques and the colony's religious life under Printz's governorship); Nils Jacobsson, *Svenska Öden vid Delaware, 1638–1831* (Stockholm: Svenska Kyrkans Diakonistyrelses Bokförlag, 1938), 15.

20. For Amandus Johnson's more detailed description of the colony's religious life under Printz, see *Swedish Settlements*, 1:366–74.

21. C. A. Weslager, *The Log Cabin in America* (New Brunswick: Rutgers University Press, 1969), 23; Johnson, *Instruction for Johan Printz*, 33.

22. Johnson, *Swedes on the Delaware*, 212.

23. Tobias Eric Björck, *Dissertatio gradualis de plantatione ecclesiae suecanae in America* (Uppsala, 1825); Eng. trans. by Ira Oliver Nothstein, *Planting of the Swedish Church in America*, publication no. 19 (Rock Island, Ill.: Augustana College Library, 1943), 11.

24. Johnson, *Swedes on the Delaware*, 212.

25. Björck, "Planting of the Swedish Church," 18–19.

26. Ibid., 19. See also Acrelius, *History of New Sweden*, 176.

27. Johnson, *Swedes on the Delaware*, 212.

28. Ibid. Erik Lundberg, "Swedish Wood Churches," 12–28; Jacobsson, *Svenska Öden vid Delaware*, 76.

29. Johnson, *Instruction for Johan Printz*, 36.

30. J. A. Enander, *Förenta Staternas Historia* (Chicago, 1880), 28–30.

31. *Kyrkoordningen* 1571.

32. Johnson, *Swedish Settlements*, 1:336.

33. Lundberg, "Swedish Wood Churches," 4.

34. N. A. Bringeus, *Klockringningsseden i Sverige* (Stockholm, 1968), 66.

35. Horace Burr, trans., *The Records of Holy Trinity (Old Swedes) Church, Wilmington, Delaware, from 1697 to 1773* (Wilmington: Historical Society of Delaware, 1980), 7–12.

36. Thomas Campanius Holm, *Kort Beskrifning om Provincien Nya Sverige uti America* (Stockholm, 1702). Eng. ed.: *Description of the Province of New Sweden . . .*, trans. Peter S. Du Ponceau, vol. 3 of Memoirs of the Historical Society of Pennsylvania (Philadelphia: The Society, 1834; reprinted, Millwood, N.Y.: Kraus Reprint Co., 1975), 79–80.

37. Johnson, *Swedes on the Delaware*, 134–35.

38. Holm, *Description of the Province of New Sweden*, 80.

39. Gunnar Zetterquist, "Beskrivning av en 1600—tals bondgård i Nya Sverige," unpublished manuscript, Falun, Sweden.

40. Ola Ehn, "Prästgårdar i Uppland," in *Sartryck ur Uppland* (Uppsala: Upplands Museum, 1980), 89.
41. Rising, "Report, 1654," 150; Jacobsson, *Svenska Öden vid Delaware*, 40–49.
42. Johnson, *Swedes on the Delaware*, 296–97.
43. Acrelius, *History of New Sweden*, 29–43, 85–87; Rising, "Report, 1654," 150.
44. Holm, *Description of the Province of New Sweden*, 107; Mathias Hultgren, "Anteckningar om Svenska Församlingarna och deras präster," Manuscript Collection, Kungliga Biblioteket, D1501, 1–7; Jacobsson, *Svenska Öden vid Delaware*, 53–54.
45. Holm, *Description of the Province of New Sweden*, 107; Johnson, *Swedes on the Delaware*, 134.
46. Hultgren, "Anteckningar"; Johnson, *Swedes on the Delaware*, 134.
47. Johnson, *Swedes on the Delaware*, 134.
48. Holm, *Description of the Province of New Sweden*, 107.
49. Johnson, *Swedish Settlements*, 1:371–72, 2:681. A recent treatment of Campanius's ministry and his work with the Delaware Indians is Trygve Skarsten, "Johan Campanius, Pastor in New Sweden," in *The Church in New Sweden*, ed. Olson, 47–87. The same volume reprints Isak Collijn's 1937 essay "The Swedish-Indian Catechism: Some Notes," 89–98.
50. Hultgren, "Anteckningar"; Johnson, *Swedish Settlements*, 1:371–72, 2:681.
51. Johnson, *Swedish Settlements*, 1:371–72.
52. Carl David Arfwedson, *De Colonia Nova Svecia in Americam Borealem Deducta Historiola* (Uppsala, 1825), 31.
53. Hultgren, "Anteckningar."
54. Lidman's letter is printed in Gunnar Wetterberg, ed., *Jesper Swedbergs Lefwernes Beskrifning* (Lund: Håkan Ohlssons Boktryckeri, 1941), 359.
55. Harjunpää, *Delawaren Kirkollisista*, 52.
56. Ibid., 54.
57. Ibid., 55; Acrelius, *History of New Sweden*, 85; Arfwedson, *De Colonia Nova Svecia*, 31; Enander, *Förenta Staternas Historia*, 42.
58. The story of the wreck of the *Katt* and the adventures of its passengers and crew is in Johnson, *Swedes on the Delaware*, 155–64. See also Otto Norberg, *Svenska Kyrkans Mission vid Delaware i Nord America* (Stockholm: A. V. Carlson, 1893), 4–5.
59. Norberg, *Svenska Kyrkans Mission*, 5; Rising, "Report, 1654," 150; *Uppsala Stifts Herdaminne*, pt. 2, p. 391.
60. *Uppsala Stifts Herdaminne*, pt. 2, p. 391.
61. *Lindköpings Stifts Herdaminne*, 19; Norberg, *Svenska Kyrkans Mission*, 5–6; Arfwedson, *De Colonia Nova Svecia*, 31; Carl Sprinchorn, "Kolonien Nya Sveriges Historia," *Historiskt Bibliotek*, n.s., 3 (1878): 237; Rising, "Report, 1654," 150.
62. Rising, "Report, 1654," 150; Johnson, *Swedes on the Delaware*, 297.
63. A. Warne, *Till Folkskolans förhistoria i Sverige* (Stockholm: Svenska Kyrkans Diakonistyrelses Bokförlag, 1929), 140–48.
64. Johnson, *Swedes on the Delaware*, 296–97.
65. Brahe to Printz, 9 November 1643, in Johnson, *Instruction for Johan Printz*, 156.
66. Sten Alsne, *Från prästtionde till reglerad lön* (Uppsala: Acta Universitatis Upsaliensis, 1966), 17–21.
67. Alsne, *Från prästtionde*, 23–29; Warne, *Svenska Folkskolans Historia*, 146–47.

68. Jacobsson, *Svenska Öden vid Delaware*, 54.
69. Ibid,; Monatgelderbuch, 1639–48, Handel och Sjofart, vol. 42 (Kammararkivet), Riksarkivet, Stockholm; Johnson, *Swedish Settlements*, 1:374. A *monatgeldebuch* is a "cash book," or an accounting of the colony's income and expenses.
70. Harjunpää, *Delawaren Kirkollisista*, 60.
71. Pleijel, *Svenska Kyrkans Historia* 5:37–41; Toivo Harjunpää, "Notes on the Swedish Bible of 1674 and Its Publication," *American Swedish Historical Foundation Yearbook 1969–1970*, 5–13.
72. Harjunpää, "Notes on the Swedish Bible of 1674," 5–13.
73. Allan Arwastsson, *Svensk psalm genom tiderna* (Lund: Liber Läromedel, 1975), 33–39; Elisabeth Janacek Wentz, "Hymns Going West," unpublished paper, Lund University, Lund, Sweden.
74. Wentz, "Hymns Going West."
75. Bror Olsson, *Psalmboken som folkbok* (Lund, 1942), 15–25.
76. Hilding Pleijel, *Husandakt, Husaga och Husförhör* (Stockholm: Svenska Kyrkans Diakonistyrelses Bokförlag, 1965), 124.
77. Hilding Pleijel, *Katekesen som Svensk folkbok* (Lund, 1942), 31–51.
78. Ibid., 129–40.
79. Ibid., 23–28; Pleijel, *Husandakt, Husaga och Husförhör*, 132.
80. Pleijel, *Katekesen som Svensk folkbok*, 23–28.
81. Ibid., 28–30.
82. Gustav Lizell, *Svenska Högmässoritualet, 1614–1693* (Stockholm, 1896), 108–10.
83. Kjollerstrom, *Praktisk Teologi*, 237.
84. Lizell, *Svenska Högmässoritualet*, 101–08.
85. Ibid., 144.
86. Ibid., 149–50. The *Agenda Ecclesiastica in Castris Sueticis* was published in 1631. Amandus Johnson summarized "the order of service that was followed in the colony" in *Swedish Settlements*, 1:367–68.
87. Lizell, *Svenska Högmässoritualet*, 149–50; *Bone och Kyrkoordning for den svenska haren*, 1640.
88. Lizell, *Svenska Högmässoritualet*, 151–53.
89. Ibid., 1–85.
90. Johan Printz, "Report to the Right Honorable West India Company in Old Sweden, sent from New Sweden, February 20, 1647," in *Narratives of Early Pennsylvania, West New Jersey And Delaware, 1630–1707*, ed. Myers, 122.
91. Johnson, *Swedish Settlements*, 1:367–70.
92. Ibid., 369–70, 379.
93. Ibid., 369.
94. Ibid., 371.
95. Ibid., 360; Brahe to Printz, 9 November 1643, in Johnson, *Instruction for Johan Printz*, 156.
96. A recent brief survey of the renewal of the Swedish mission in the eighteenth century is included in Richard H. Hulan, "New Sweden and Its Churches," in *The Church in New Sweden*, ed. Olson, 3–33.

Part IV
The Forest Finns and the American Frontier

Finns in Seventeenth-Century Sweden
and Their Contributions to the
New Sweden Colony

PER MARTIN TVENGSBERG

Neither cultural nor political history can be understood without considering the relationship of people to their environment, which includes soil, flora, fauna, climate, and the way they get their nourishment. Knowledge of these cycles of human activity is essential. As the Finnish people say, "Sita kuusta kuuleminen, jonka juurella asunto" (You should listen to the spruce tree, under which you are living).

For the Finns, burn-beating cultivation was an important part of life well into the twentieth century.[1] Many scholars think that this ancient method of tillage is both a more primitive and a simpler farming method than the field cultivation system. This opinion is based more on classic European cultural tradition than on scientific research. Burn-beating culture is not well understood by scholars or the ordinary Finn, whether he or she is in Finland, Scandinavia, or in the United States.[2]

Burn-beating has been of much greater historical importance than the more recent cultivation of cleared fields.[3] In fact, most grains have been grown by burn-beating for as long as humans have practiced agriculture of any kind. Through time the Finns developed a sophisticated system of burn-beating variations to account for different kinds of forests, topography, and climatic fluctuations. The size of the burned area is the most important variable in this type of cultivation. When the climate is unfavorable, for example, farmers must increase the size of the burned area to obtain a crop of the same size. In A.D. 450–550, A.D. 750–850, and A.D. 1050–1150 poor growing weather was followed by corresponding burn-beating expansions. The century A.D. 1550–1650 was another such period. The severe climate starting about A.D. 1550 encouraged Finnish expansion in Finland and throughout Scandinavia and into Russia. It was based on the *huuhta* technology—the migratory cultivation of rye and turnips in the ashes of burned spruce forest (see fig. 1).

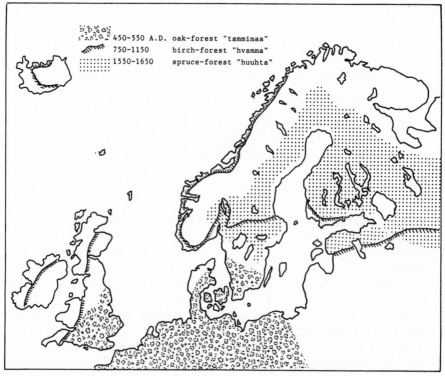

```
              450-550 A.D.  oak-forest "tammimaa"
              750-1150      birch-forest "hvamma"
              1550-1650     spruce-forest "huuhta"
```

Fig. 1. Burn-beating expansion in northern Europe, A.D. 450–1650.

THE *HUUHTA* TECHNOLOGY

The Finns who expanded their culture across Scandinavia and Russia could support themselves as long as they had axes, sickles, rye seed, fire, and forests at their disposal. By about 1600 these forest Finns (also called burn-beating or rye Finns) had expanded throughout the virgin forests of the interior of Scandinavia to the mountains of Norway.[4] Since the spruce forest stopped there, they could not adapt their cultivation technology any further.[5] Swedish authorities encouraged their expansion, since forests were abundant but food was relatively scarce. Farmers in the province of Värmland were told in 1587 to burn about an acre each year to increase food production.[6] The Finnish pioneers were aided both by the provincial authorities and by edicts of the Swedish Crown. But from the 1630s on the Swedes needed their forests for their growing mining and forging industries, so the Swedish government began attempting to regulate burn-beating closely. But even strict prohibitions and penalties against burn-beating did not stop it. A royal resolution of 1647 stated that Finns guilty of breaking a 1641 ordinance regulating the practice should be driven from their farms, have their property and crops destroyed, and be jailed or deported to New Sweden. An ordinance of 1664 provided the death penalty for the second offense.[7]

The characteristic Finnish settlement in both Sweden and Norway was in a forested area between already-populated valleys. The newcomers grew rye in burned clearings in virgin spruce forests. The crop was usually big—often yielding twelve thousand to one—but the burned land usually gave one harvest only.

Lumbermen cut or girdled the trees in early spring and let the wood dry until the midsummer of the second or third year after girdling. Then the clearing was burned by a group of men trained in the technique. "Polta kivet, polta kannot, heita mulle musta multa," the Finns say: "Burn stones, burn stumps, give to me the black earth." Immediately after the burning the farmers built a fence around the clearing and sowed rye in the ashes without plowing or hoeing. When rain and ashes had neutralized the acid soil the seed produced big clumps of rye. After two growing seasons the rye was ripe for harvesting. Grass usually started to grow on the abandoned clearing the following summer. On the best land a new generation of spruce made *huuhta* possible again after eighty to a hundred years. The abandoned field gave good hay production for some years before the forest took over again. Cultivation could continue as long as the fence remained around the clearing. The Finnish saying that expresses this is "Tanne sulle huuhan teen, tanne kartanon raken-nan" ("Up to here I make *huuhta*; up to here I build the fence"). Continuous rain could impede burning and delay cultivation or even make it impossible.

The harvest was always divided into three parts. One third was for the workers participating in the *huuhta*, one third was for the keeper of the land, and one third was for the organizer of the *huuhta* (usually the head of the family). The family or tribe often employed specialized itinerant workers in the busy seasons. These *losfinnar* had skills that were badly needed for the *huuhta*, especially when the members of a family or a tribe lacked the necessary skills themselves. The *losfinnar* formed their own social group, which the authorities did not like because as itinerants they paid no taxes, or paid them irregularly.

A family often had several *huuhtas* going at the same time, each in various stages of progress. Sometimes families specialized in different types of *huuhta* that they provided to other families or tribes. Such specializations included a type called *ylipalo* ("over-fire"), used in older forests on sloping ground, and *tulimaa* ("fire-land"), for mixed forests on flat ground.

INTERACTION

The Finnish colonists of the forests lived quite a different kind of life from the native farmers in the valleys. The tax lists from Grue, Norway, show that from 1640 on the Finns enjoyed a higher standard of living than the field farmers.[8] The Finns were less affected than the farmers by the many wars at that time, and they moved and enlarged *huuhtas* to compensate for unsettled times and a poor climate. Rye also had a 50 percent higher caloric content than other cereals. Since rye lasted longer in storage than other cereals, the government purchased it to feed its army, providing a source of cash for the Finns.

But the forest Finns conflicted with the seventeenth-century Swedish mining, forging, and timbering industries simply by the way they used the forest. *Huuhta* destroyed areas of forest that could have been used for these industries and the forest took a long time to recover from *huuhta*, which was the source of conflict with the field farmers. While a plowed field might need to lie fallow to replenish itself only a few years in a decade, it took a forest a generation—several decades—before *huuhtas* on even the richest land could be reused. The Finns and the native farmers also had different economic relationships to the state. The Finns owned no part of the forest and paid their taxes in rye. Traditional farmers were tied to their land; since the tax collectors could always find them, they paid more in taxes. However, interaction between the forest Finns and the native farmers had many forms through the centuries and was of great economic importance. For example, abandoned *huuhtas* made good pastures, so the farmers often allowed the Finns to use their forests for *huuhta*. But timber production put an end to this by about 1850, and from then on *huuhta* was used only for clearing land for new homesteads. The single excepton was in forest areas where timber transportation was very expensive. There *huuhta* continued until after 1900.

COMMUNICATION

The forest Finns communicated both with the outside world and among themselves more effectively than we usually think. Distances did not frighten them. They were accustomed to traveling widely and had accommodated their life-styles to the search for potential forests to support *huuhta*. Literacy and knowledge of foreign languages were not uncommon among tribal leaders in the sixteenth and seventeenth centuries simply because their enterprises required them. This was true in New Sweden as well. The pastors Anders Rudman and Erik Björck wrote in 1697 from America that the Finnish freemen in New Sweden knew several languages, including Swedish, Dutch, German, English, French, and even a Native American language.[9]

The range of Finnish travels in Sweden even in the nineteenth century was impressive. Elias Lönnrot wrote in 1828 that a Finn "without hesitation and long consideration" might make "journeys of forty, fifty and sixty miles, in the summertime in his boat and wintertime upon his sled.... From this enterprise which occupies a good deal of his winter, he returns with experience and knowledge about things, practices and customs from a wide area." This constant searching after new lands to farm is the characteristic feature of the *huuhta* farmer in contrast to the "stationary" farmer.[10] Migration is the normal life-style of a burn-beating population, in contrast to the farmers who cultivate the same land year after year.

NEW SWEDEN

Forest Finns from Värmland were among the first settlers in New Sweden. "These people do not take the land in proper use," the governor complained, "they do not take part in the work after clearing."[11] Their burn-beating cultivation was fully adaptable to the forests of North America, and they soon located good forest land for *huuhta*. The Finns also adapted Indian corn to their agricultural technique because it was more profitable on most of the available land than the forest-consuming European cereals. The news about the good forests in America reached the Finns in Sweden through the authorities and the colonists who wrote to relatives to encourage emigration. A few colonists also returned to Sweden and reported about the New World in person.

But the Finns did not always go willingly to New Sweden, at least not early in the colony's history. The governor of Nerike (modern Orebro) wrote to the government in 1640 that there were a great number of vagrant Finns in his district and he did not know what to do with them.[12] The government instructed him to endeavor to persuade such Finns "to migrate to New Sweden with [their] wives and children." He was instructed to explain to them the great advantages to be had in America; that there was an abundance of forest and wild animals, and that a large number of Swedes were already there. In September of the same year Måns Kling was sent about Sweden to "collect and hire a multitude of roving people ... who nowhere have a steady residence and dwelling," and was to look especially for Finns. In the spring of 1641 Kling was sent out once more, to permit all Finns who had committed illegal burn-beating to go to the colony on the fourth expedition (sailed 3 May 1641). Johan Printz and Johan Papegoja, successive governors of the colony in the 1640s, asked for more colonists, and after 1648 there were more Finns willing to go than the government could accommodate.[13]

By the late 1640s Sweden's forest Finns increasingly sought to emigrate to New Sweden. In the spring of 1648 Mats Ericksson, a Finn from Värmland, wrote twice to Axel Oxenstierna, Sweden's chancellor, on behalf of two hundred Finns who wanted to go to New Sweden.[14] He wrote to inform the chancellor "about the poor Finnish people, who after the prohibition of the forest [regulation of burn-beating by the Swedish government], now are in lack of food. And for that reason want to go to their relatives, who some years ago came to New Sweden in the West Indies." Ericksson continued with a threat of what the Finns would do if they were not permitted to go to the colony: "Many more of us will go to Norway under the Danish crown, if we do not get a positive reply soon." In the Royal Council meeting of 12 June 1649 Sweden's Queen Christina thought it strange that they should ask for such permission "as there was enough land to be had in Sweden" and they had not done anything to cause their deportation.[15] Apparently neither the queen nor the council members knew very much about *huuhta*. Finns who had committed illegal burn-beating were often sentenced to serve the Crown, but mostly they were pardoned to go to New Sweden with their wives, children, and all that they owned. Burn-beating motivated an increasing number of Finns to go to New Sweden voluntarily, which coincided with Sweden's desire to strengthen the colony.

In the autumn of 1653 colonists were to be collected for the tenth expedition to the colony, and Sven Skute was appointed to gather 250 settlers, "mostly good men, fewer women and fewest children."[16] He was also to look for farm boys who were willing to go without pay or with as little financial aid as possible. He went to Vasteras, Värmland, and Dalsland, as it was reported that "a good many of those [Finns] who dwelt in the large forests" there were willing to go. The Crown requested the governors of those provinces to assist Skute in enlisting people. Skute returned to America on the same ship that carried Per Martensson Lindeström to New Sweden. Lindeström reported that more than a hundred Finnish families had to be left behind at Göteborg because there was no room for them on the ship.[17]

Sometimes Finns initiated the journey themselves, especially after 1655, when Sweden no longer ruled the colony. In the winter of 1663 to 1664, 140 Finns—men, women, and children—intent on emigrating to America, had made their way from Sweden to Christiania (Oslo), where they hired a Dutch vessel to take them to Amsterdam.[18] At Amsterdam they were unable to get another ship to carry them to America and were fed and housed by the city officials. Rumors that the emigrants had been enticed to migrate to America by Dutch agents were reported to Sweden.

The Swedish representative in Amsterdam, Peter Trotzig, demanded that the Finns be returned to Sweden. But New Sweden (a part of New Netherland since 1655) passed into the hands of the English in 1664 and the Finns were eventually permitted to continue on to America.[19] Trotzig found that most of these people spoke Finnish, though some of the men also spoke Swedish. Friends and relatives in New Sweden had written to them about the "glories of the country." One of the emigrants carried a letter from his brother in New Sweden dated 1657.

After the Dutch took over New Sweden in 1655, they seem to have wanted their new Swedish and Finnish subjects to be settled in villages of sixteen or twenty persons or families. To regulate the size of individual holdings, the Dutch governor was to impose a tax of twelve stivers annually for each *morgen* (acre). Several times the Dutch attempted to settle the Finns in villages, but they never succeeded. The Finns spread out in the forests along the Delaware's tributary rivers and were able to maintain good relations with the Indians. They held "secret conferences" with the Indians, "who often came to the homes of the Swedes [and the Finns] and were, as usual, well received." The Finns gained the confidence of the Dutch authorities and performed many services for them as interpreters and guides.[20]

The Finns were very successful cultivators, and many of them prospered. The Dutch colonial government, always in search of immigrant farmers, was impressed with the Scandinavians and requested "not Hollanders, however, but other nations and especially Finns and Swedes, who are good farmers."[21] The Dutch encouraged the settlers to write to relatives and friends in Sweden, praising the land and inviting them to come to America. And several settlers arrived from time to time, as in the summer of 1663 and in December of the same year.

Burn-beating continued wherever the Finns were in North America. They burned a new stretch of the best forest whenever the yield fell off after several harvests. The old clearing was abandoned and grass took it over. But this practice eventually caused the Finns to leave the colony; they were not prepared to permanently occupy a piece of land, as the colonial authorities wanted them to do. In 1654 Johan Rising (New Sweden's last governor), "to avoid much trouble out here," ordered that "no donations be given or any land assigned to anyone, unless he occupies it effectively or settles it himself, or in this either serves the Crown or the Company.... I intend now to buy [land] from them [the Indians] for the Company, the improvements only being compensated for." "Unused land" was valuable, but after ten years' use the "outworn grain fields" were free.[22]

Emigration continued after England captured the colony in the autumn of 1664. Many Finns came to the area of what had been New Sweden after that time, but increasing economic and political difficulties at home and the measures taken in Sweden against emigration finally stopped them. Many Finns moved from the Delaware River Valley into Pennsylvania, New Jersey, and Maryland, as for example Peter Myer, "a subject of Sweden," who came into Maryland from New Amstel (in modern Delaware) in 1661 with his wife and children. They were granted permission to live there as "free denizens."

The colonial administration quite often misunderstood the Finns' behavior. Some observers characterized them as unsocial, lazy, stupid, and destructive, and complained that they disappeared into the forests "to avoid work for the colony." Burn-beating was also misunderstood. Johan Rising's inventory of September 1667 described Finnish farming practices as essentially ruinous of the land. "The people cleared land, used it as it was new and strong, but did not think of manuring or clearing until recent years.... Some miles up in the inland," he continued, "the stumps are still left in the fields [and] big trees are left behind ... thereby are seen many fields full of dead trees and thick grain thereunder."[23]

Largely because of their common background in burn-beating cultivation, the Finns and the Indians got on well with each other. Their cultures had many corresponding elements, such as the use of the shamanic drum, the sauna, and rituals involving singing, and they often had a common opinion of the colonial administration. The Indian culture and the Finnish burn-beating culture shared certain traits that were foreign to the Swedish and other European cultures, including their attitudes on land use and the temporally extended cultivation cycles that their agricultural methods required.

THE FINNS AS AN ETHNIC GROUP

An ethnic group can be defined as a population that is largely biologically self-perpetuating. It shares fundamental cultural values that are realized in overt unity in cultural forms; makes up a field of communication and interaction; and has a membership that identifies itself, and is identified by others, as constituting a category distinguishable from other categories of the same order.

The boundaries of ethnic groups define the group, not the cultural stuff that the boundaries enclose. The analysis of interactional and organizational features of interethnic relations is important for the study of the problems of boundary maintenance.

It is clear that ethnic boundaries are maintained in each case by a limited set of cultural features. However, most of the cultural matter that at any time is associated with a human population is not constrained by this boundary. It can vary, be learned, and change without any critical relation to the boundary maintenance of the ethnic group. So when one traces the history of an ethnic group through time, one is not simultaneously, in the same sense, tracing the history of "a culture." The elements of the present culture of that ethnic group have not sprung from the particular set that constituted the group's culture at a previous time, whereas the group has a continual organizational existence with boundaries (critieria of membership) that despite modifications have marked off a continuing unit.

The Finnish migratory cultivation method, *huuhta*, is just such a cultural feature. It maintained the ethnic boundaries between the Finns and the neighbors with whom they interacted. The search for freedom to practice *huuhta* was the main reason for the Finnish migration to the New World, and it gave the Finns the opportunity to interact both with the Indians and with the other Europeans in America. In the wooded backcountry sections of the eastern United States, Finnish cultural elements survived, even where a new ethnic stock succeeded the Finns. These first effective colonizers contributed disproportionately to forming a new culture that was built on fragments of European cultural elements with strong traits preadapted to successful pioneering.[24]

Examples of surviving Finnish elements in American culture are log buildings, the zigzag wooden fence, and the tradition of separating farmsteads by large spaces.[25] The settlers' first houses were little cottages built of round logs with doors so low that it was necessary to stoop when entering.[26] Little remains of their abandoned farmsteads but their stoves, some changes in the local vegetation, and a high ash content in the soil.

Huuhta is an agricultural method especially adapted to spruce forests and to rye cultivation. Scholars have long sought to discover its technical details to compare it with the agricultural techniques of other burn-beating cultures. Therefore I took the initiative to create a research group in 1981. Its members and their tasks are as follows: Erkki Jauhiainen, Institute of Geography, University of Joensuu, is analyzing soil types; Pertti Huttunen, Ecological Section, University of Joensuu, analyzes sediments and pollen; Christian Carpelan, Archaeological Institute, University of Helsinki, is the project's archaeologist; and as county curator in Hamar, Norway, I am the project's ethnographer.

We have made investigations in Grue Finnskog, Norway, in 1982; Sigdal and Ringsaker, Norway, in 1983; Kuusamo, Finland, in 1984; and Dalarna, Sweden, in 1985, to determine how *huuhta* has changed over time, especially how it was situated in the forest and how *huuhta* corresponded to local population density (see fig. 2). We are also planning inquiries in middle Finland. We plan to study Karelian expansion from north of Lake Ladoga toward the area of Tver in Russia. But of greatest interest to us

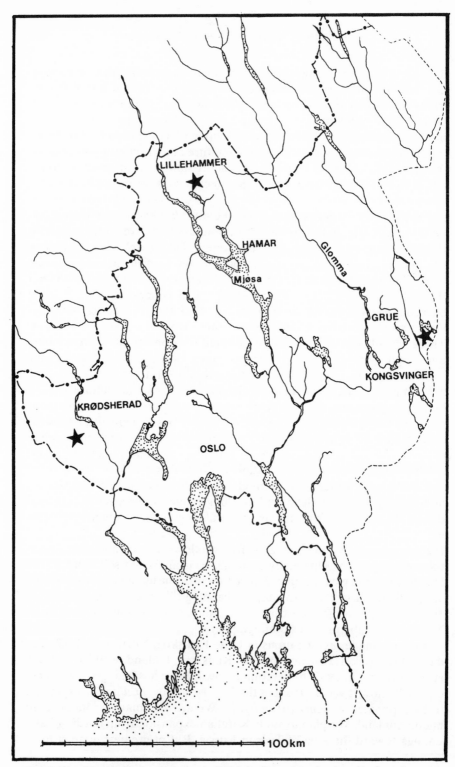

Fig. 2. Finnish population density in 1686 (indicated by broken line) and recent areas of investigation (stars).

now are the Finns from Värmland who came to New Sweden. We think that research in the United States can help us to locate factors that further changed the cultivation technique and may help us to understand the extension of *huuhta*.

We have progressed enough to be hopeful of useful results. The technical methods and the experience we have gained in these investigations will be of great value in future work. And the same sort of technical research in the United States as we have done in Norway, Sweden, and Finland would be of great value for the project. These studies have made it possible to begin to understand some of the ways in which the Finns have interacted with their neighbors, both in northern Europe and in North America.

NOTES

1. Arvo M. Soininen, "Burn-beating as the Technical Basis of Colonisation in Finland in the 16th and the 17th Centuries," *Scandinavian Economic History Review* 7 (1959): 150–66.
2. C. Schott, *Urlandschaft und Rodung* (Berlin: Zeitschrift der Gesellschaft für Erdkunde zu Berlin, 1935), 81–102; A. Dopsch, *Gesammelte Aufsätze/ Zweite Reihe, Selbstadarstellung* (Vienna: Beiträge zur Sozial-und-Wirtschaftsgeschichte, 1938), 301.
3. Olli Heikinheimo, *Kaskiviljelyksen Vaikutus Suomen Metsiin* (Helsinki: Suomen Metsähallitus, 1915), 21–47; J. G. D. Clark, *Prehistoric Europe: The Economic Basis* (London: Methuen, 1952), 91–93.
4. Isidor Sundberg, *Finnmarksräfsten i Norge år 1686* (Falun: Nya Boktryckeri, 1942), 136.
5. Per Martin Tvengsberg, *Skogsfinnene på Finnskogen: Värmlandsfinnar* (Stockholm: Kulturfonden för Sverige och Finland, 1986), 37–64.
6. Duke Carl of Värmland, to the "community," 21 September 1587, ordering "new" farmers to burn land each year to grow rye; Riksarkivet, Stockholm. See also Petrus Nordmann, *Finnarna i Mellersta Sverige* (Helsingfors: Kejserlige Alexanders Universitet, 1888), 42, and Johan Johansson, *Noraskogs arkiv*, 6 vols. (Stockholm, 1889–1928), 3:2.211.
7. Royal resolution, 22 June 1641; its prohibitions were repeated in 1647, 1664, and 1734. See Axel Oxenstierna Skrifter och Brefvexling, 1898, branch 2, vol. 9, Riksarkivet, Stockholm, 684.
8. Per Martin Tvengsberg, *Gruen suomalaismetsan Kaskiviljelysta Kalevalaseuran Vuosikirja 62* (Helsinki: SKS Finnish Literature Society, 1982), 190.
9. C. V. Jacobowsky, *Literaturen om Nya Sverige* (Stockholm: Ymer, 1937), 285.
10. Matti Klinge, *Östersjövälden* (Borgå: Askelin & Hägglund, 1985), 185. Elias Lönnrot (1802–84) was a twenty-six-year-old teacher when he went on his first journey to collect old *runa* (songs) in 1828. From his collection of these songs Lönnrot published the *Kalevala* (1835, 1849), the Finnish national epic.
11. Nordmann, *Finnarna i Mellersta Sverige*, 148.

12. Amandus Johnson, *The Swedish Settlements on the Delaware: Their History and Relation to the Indians, Dutch and English, 1638–1664*, 2 vols. (Philadelphia: Swedish Colonial Society, 1911), 1:148.
13. Ibid., 150.
14. Mats Ericksson to Axel Oxenstierna, Tido Samlingen, undated; Axel Oxenstiernas Arkiv, Riksarkivet, Stockholm.
15. Johnson, *Swedish Settlements*, 1:267; Riksradet Protocol, 1647–70, 12 June 1649, Riksarkivet, Stockholm. See also F. F. Carlson, *Sveriges historia under Carl den Tionde Gustafs Regering*, 2 vols. (Stockholm: F. G. Beiger, 1883), 1:390, note.
16. Carlson, *Sveriges historia* 1:471.
17. Nils Jacobsson, *Per Lindeströms resa till Nya Sverige, 1653–1656* (Stockholm: Wahlstrom & Widstrand, 1923), 51.
18. Johnson, *Swedish Settlements*, 2:650.
19. John H. Wuorinen, *The Finns on the Delaware, 1638–1655* (New York: Columbia University Press, 1938), 79.
20. Thomas Campanius Holm, *Kort Beskrifning om Provincien Nya Sverige uti America* (Stockholm, 1702). Eng. ed.: *Description of the Province of New Sweden . . .*, trans. Peter S. Du Ponceau, vol. 3 of Memoirs of the Historical Society of Pennsylvania (Philadelphia: The Society, 1834), 68.
21. Amandus Johnson, *The Swedes on the Delaware, 1638–1664* (Philadelphia: Swedish Colonial Society, 1927), 372.
22. Johan Rising, "Report of Governor Rising, 1654," in *Narratives of Early Pennsylvania, West New Jersey and Delaware, 1630–1707*, ed. Albert Cook Myers (1912; reprint, New York: Barnes & Noble, 1967), 148.
23. Israel Acrelius, *Beskrifning om de Swenska Församlingars Forna och Närwarande Tillstånd, uti det så Kallade Nya Sverige* (Stockholm, 1759), 162. The English translation is *A History of New Sweden; or, the Settlements on the Delaware River*, trans. William M. Reynolds, vol. 11 of Memoirs of the Historical Society of Pennsylvania (Philadelphia: Historical Society of Pennsylvania, 1874). See also Förtechningh uppå K:Maij: och Amerikha Compag Ägendohm: Nya Sverie . . . September 1667; Riksarkivet, Stockholm.
24. Terry G. Jordan and Matti Kaups, *The American Backwoods Frontier: An Ethnic and Ecological Interpretation* (Baltimore: Johns Hopkins University Press, 1989), 134.
25. Acrelius, *Beskrifning om de Swenska Fösamlingars*, 162.
26. Johnson, *Swedish Settlements*, 1:198.

The Forest Finns as Transmitters of Finnish Culture From Savo Via Central Scandinavia to Delaware

JUHA PENTIKÄINEN

FINNISH PARTICIPATION IN THE HISTORY OF NEW SWEDEN

"Nova Suecia eller the Swenskas Revier in India Occidentali" is the title of the famous map that Peter Lindeström drew for his *Geographia Americae*.[1] New Sweden is, of course, historically the correct name of the colony founded in 1638 under the auspices of the Swedish Crown. However, people of Finnish origin played a crucial role in the colony from the very beginning. The main owners of the New Sweden trading company formed in 1637 were Axel Oxenstierna of Queen Christina's court and the Finnish-born Admiral Klaus Fleming.[2]

Swedish and Finnish history are, of course, interrelated. Finland was a part of Sweden from the period of the Crusades—officially since 1216, when the pope promised Finland to the King of Sweden—until 1809, when Finland was ceded to the Russian Empire as an autonomous grand duchy. During Queen Christina's reign (1632–54) the bonds between Finland and Sweden were friendly. Per Brahe, the governor general of Finland (1637–40 and 1648–54), influenced Finnish cultural and economic life by founding the Turku Academy (now the University of Helsinki) in 1640, by establishing trade connections across the Gulf of Bothnia, and by founding several new towns along the Finnish coast. Swedish remained the official language of Finnish cultural, social, and economic life until the latter part of the nineteenth century.

The history of New Sweden has generally been written from the Swedish point of view for two reasons. First, when Amandus Johnson published his monumental work *The Swedish Settlements on the Delaware* in two volumes in 1911, he scarcely emphasized the role of the Finns on the various expeditions and gave no references for the origins of the Finnish colonists.[3] This is not surprising because Finland was not an independent country when Johnson's work appeared. Second, most of the

Finns who settled in New Sweden had not moved directly from Finland
but had spent several decades in central Scandinavia. During that time
many changed their Finnish names to Swedish or Norwegian ones, a practice that has caused considerable trouble for those studying the background of the Finnish colonists. However, in the oldest records of New
Sweden, it was usual to indicate Finnish origin by adding "the Finn" as
in "Anders Andersson the Finn," "Anders the Finn," "Evert the Finn,"
"Lasse the Finn," and so on.[4]

Thus it is difficult to identity the first Finnish colonists in New Sweden.
According to Finnish tradition canonized by Finnish author A. Järnefelt-
Rauenheimo (1861–1932), the first commander of Fort Christina, Lieutenant Måns Nilsson Kling, was a Finn.[5] It is known that he spoke Finnish
because one of his assignments was to recruit Finnish-speaking immigrants from central Scandinavia to New Sweden. Solomon Ilmonen, the
historian of the American Finns, mentions three Finns who participated
in the second expedition of the *Kalmar Nyckel*: the seaman Lars Andersson from the Åland Islands; the soldier Maunu Andersson; and Peter
Rambo, a soldier who had escaped from military service.[6] Estimates of
the number of Finns who came to Delaware vary from source to source.
According to some estimates, the majority (from 50 to 75 percent) of seventeenth-century settlers in New Sweden were Finns. Ilmonen found 295
Finns in the lists of immigrants who moved to New Sweden.[7]

While living in central Scandinavia, many Finnish people probably became bilingual. Professor Pehr Kalm (1716–79), a scientist from the
Turku Academy who lived briefly in the area of the former New Sweden
in the mid-eighteenth century, found no Finnish speakers. Because the
"official" language of the colony was Swedish, the first Finnish generation had to learn that language. Swedish retained a certain preeminence
in the Delaware Valley in the eighteenth century due to the influence of
Lutheran ministers who continued to be sent to Delaware from Sweden.[8]
Thus it can be said that colonists with Finnish origins became America-
nized via Scandinavian languages.

WHERE DID THE FOREST FINNS COME FROM?

An aspect of the yet-unwritten history of the first Scandinavian colonization of the New World concerns the Forest Finns, *metsäsuomalaiset* in
Finnish, *skogsfinnarna* in Swedish. It is, therefore, important to study
their cultural history in the Old World to understand the role they
played as part of the first Scandinavian colonization in the New World.

The term *Forest Finn* was probably coined by Swedish and Norwegian
farmers living in the river valleys of central Scandinavia to describe the

Finnish-speaking people who settled the neighboring forest areas. According to historical sources, most of these newcomers came from Savo, a Finnish district located far from the sea and isolated from the capital of Sweden.[9] From the Middle Ages until the sixteenth century Savo was the border province between Finland (that is, Sweden) and Russia. There were successive wars between the two kingdoms in 1493–95, 1555–67, 1570–95, 1609–17, 1656–61, 1700–21, 1741–43, 1788–90, and 1808–9. The boundary, first drawn in 1323 by the Treaty of Pähkinänsaari, was confusing because the treaty boundary was also designated as the boundary between two religions: the Roman Catholic and the Russian Orthodox. During the course of history the Catholics—after the Lutheran Reformation, the Protestants—were to live on the Swedish side while the Orthodox believers were to live on the Russian side of the border. Every new negotiation meant obligatory population movements across the boundary, either to the west or to the east. In some cases completely new Finnish settlements were formed far outside of Finland.

In religious terms the people in Savo belonged to the Catholic/Protestant part of the population and were obliged to move several times. During the Middle Ages the forest area of St. Michael was the center of settlement and the economy was based on local forest resources. It combined hunting, fishing, berry-picking, tar-burning, and cattle breeding. But above all, the most distinctive Finnish activity was the use of burn-beating methods for cultivating the land. When the Finns first moved to central Scandinavia, their way of life was nomadic or seminomadic because the resources they used were available in different regions during different seasons. However, even after people had settled down, the Forest Finns were obliged to move periodically because their agricultural methods depleted resources within two or three generations. Medieval sources state that Karelian peasants moved every ten or twenty years.[10] Thus an integral aspect of their life-style was the willingness to migrate when necessary.

Gustav Vasa was the first Swedish king (1523–60) to recognize the positive political effect that the Forest Finn economy might have on a centralized government. The Lutheran Reformation and the settlement of the wilderness in the Finnish regions of northern Savo, Häme, Satakunta, and Karelia, as well as Kainuu, were completed during his reign. His principle was that all wilderness belonged to the Crown and could be distributed to new settlers who would then become taxpayers. People from Savo who spoke an eastern Finnish dialect formed the majority of newcomers in what is now central and eastern Finland. Most moves across the borders of Savo Province were voluntary; nevertheless, migration was strongly encouraged by the Crown during Gustav Vasa's reign and on into the seventeenth century. These moves promised economic advantages to the immigrants. When problems arose between the new-comers and the longtime occupants of the wilderness, the solutions usually benefited the newcomers. For this reason the original residents, the Saami people and their reindeer, were pushed north beyond the cir-cumpolar zone in Finland. A similar fate befell those Finns who preferred hunting and fishing to permanent agricultural settlements.

During this same period, the Crown and the Lutheran church orga-nized local administrations in the wilderness. They built churches and founded extensive parishes like Rautalampi, where people speaking Savo dialects were in the majority. It was from this area that the primary Finnish immigration took place to the forests of Värmland and its neigh-boring provinces in central Scandinavia during the sixteenth and seven-teenth centuries.

THE IMMIGRATION FROM SAVO TO CENTRAL SCANDINAVIA

At the 1987 Nordic Symposium, Kauko Pirinen, professor emeritus of the University of Helsinki, discussed the people who formed important links between the Crown and the emigrants from Savo. Gustav Vasa had given Gustav Fincke, the commander of Savonlinna Castle, the task of engaging men from Savo to build fortresses in Sweden during the 1540s and 1550s.[11] Thus in the latter half of the sixteenth century several men from Savo worked in different capacities in Stockholm Castle. How-ever, the great immigration to the forests in Värmland did not occur by way of the capital of the country; it was a direct continuation of the pre-viously described moves.

The first document about immigration across the Gulf of Bothnia to Sweden is in an appeal to King Johan III in 1578, which stated that sev-eral soldiers and other men conscripted for the war between Sweden and Russia (1570–95) had been obliged to leave the country with their famil-ies for other areas.[12] The migration continued despite a war that lasted twenty-five years and a king who opposed it. The movement seems to have been led by Duke Carl (later King Carl IX, 1550–1611), who, for political and economic reasons, encouraged the peasants from Savo to move to the central Scandinavian forests. It is likely that his chamber sec-retary, Måns Jönson Auvinen, who came from Sulkava parish in Savo, acted as the necessary link coordinating the early waves of immigration at the end of the sixteenth century.[13]

Encouraging immigration from Savo to the uninhabited forest areas on the border of Sweden and Norway became the policy of the Crown dur-ing the reigns of Carl IX and Gustav II Adolf (1611–32). Most of this immigration took place between 1600 and 1620, and the number of the

Finnish people who came and remained in central Scandinavia exceeded ten thousand.

The once huge parish of Rautalampi in Savo is often mentioned in literary and historical sources as the main point of departure for Finnish immigrants[14] to the Swedish province of Värmland.[15] This is only partially true. As the ethnologist Richard Broberg has shown in his careful studies of the roots of the newcomers and their settlements, the immigrants originated from a much wider area of Finland and settled in many provinces. They formed an almost unified belt from Ångermanland and Jämtland to the lake area in central Sweden.[16]

THE FINN FORESTS AND THE FOREST FINNS

The districts that the Finnish newcomers inhabited are called *Finnskogen* (Finn forests) in Swedish, and, as mentioned above, the people themselves are termed *skogsfinnarna* (Forest Finns). Both names refer to a specific way of life and form of culture. To non-Finns the forest was the natural environment for the Finns and the main focus of their culture since they were thought to be perfectly adapted to the ways of forest life. When Finns from Savo, Kainuu, and central Finland came to central Scandinavia, they found surroundings that, at least ecologically, were very much like their native lake country in Finland. Both the old and new milieus included hills and slopes, lakes and streams. In the new environment these Finns could practice the same combined economy to which they were accustomed.

In the new areas were virgin forests for burn-beating cultivation, *huuhta*, and *kaski*, a woodland path cleared by cutting trees and brush and then burning the debris. These are the special slash-and-burn techniques of cultivation that the Finns brought with them first to Sweden and then to the New World, as historian Per Martin Tvengsberg, a descendant of Forest Finns, has shown in his studies.[17] This type of economy brought good harvests—many times more than what was sowed—but also meant a short-term use of the resources. It took two or three generations (sixty to eighty years) before an area could be used again in this manner.

People coming from Savo used a special technique (described by Tvengsberg), different from other Finns, when practicing *huuhta* and burning *kaski*.[18] As a result they were exceedingly efficient in utilizing the forest resources for agricultural purposes. They were not poor peasants; rather they were rich farmers who traded their harvests as far away as the coastal towns of Sweden and even abroad. They used the same wooden tools for agriculture that they had made in Finland.

Another important use of forest resources was tar burning, a cash crop for the Forest Finns. In addition they kept the same domestic animals they had in Finland: cows, horses, pigs, and sheep. Hunting, fishing, berry- and mushroom-picking were carried on much the same way as they were in Finland.

A common story is told by the Forest Finns about a Finn who migrated a long time ago:

> He had an axe and a sickle in his bag and some salt. He also had a small bag made out of a bird's skin and some barley there. He had another bag of bark when he went hunting in his forest. He immediately started to make his "huuhta," to burn it down when it was ready. He built his sauna and then the smoke house. And sometimes the Swedes came and wanted to send him back where he had come from.[19]

This story could also describe the experience of the many Finns who responded to a new appeal from the Crown to sail to the colony in America. The Finnish population had increased as rapidly in Scandinavia as it previously had in Savo. In Scandinavia the Finns and the native inhabitants had quarreled from the beginning over rights to land and its use for the Finnish type of cultivation.[20] The statute of 1647 that prohibited Finnish slash-and-burn cultivation, with the exception of making new fields, coincided with the active mission of encouraging Forest Finns to move overseas. They left in great numbers, particularly in the 1650s, when about two hundred Finns went to America in a single boat. In fact, on the twelfth expedition to New Sweden in 1655, many more than the ninety-two Finns who were accepted at the harbor of Göteborg had wanted to go. The leader of this expedition, Lieutenant J. Papegoja, felt it "both sorrowful and shameful that they could not be taken along. For these people, disappointed in their hopes, had sold their property for nothing, they had used their resources for the long journey to the coast, and now had to take up a begging staff and go on unknown ways, such a cry and weeping began as can seldom be heard."[21]

When those who had been fortunate enough to be selected finally arrived in America, they learned that the New Sweden colony already belonged to the Dutch. The Dutch permitted the immigrant members of the expedition to remain, but the crew and the soldiers had to return to Sweden. This expedition had, however, started such a great "American fever" among the Forest Finns that many of them tried to move to America during the following decade. Thirty-two people finally succeeded in arriving at Delaware in 1663, and another group of 140 arrived in 1664 via Amsterdam.[22] These people are easier to identify as Finns because they kept their original names.

Oral tradition about this first "American fever" has survived until recently among the Forest Finns of Central Sweden. Thus the Swedish priest E. G. Fryxell, who collected material on the Forest Finns from Ösmark in Värmland, reported in 1889 to Albrekt Segerstedt, writer and collector of folktales, that "perhaps the first Finns and Swedes to move to America during Queen Christina's time came from here."[23] Because of this "American fever," Finnish people from Värmland and the neighboring provinces left for America when new opportunities arose, in the process nearly emptying Forest Finn villages in Sweden and Norway.

ASPECTS OF FOREST FINN CULTURE

Two important elements in the definition of a *Forest Finn* are the ecological environment of forests and "Finnishness" itself. It is possible to reconstruct the culture and worldview of those men and women who left Savo and the neighboring provinces in Finland to move to central Scandinavia—and then after from one to three generations in Scandinavia to move on to Delaware.

Their language was Finnish. More strictly speaking, it was a dialect called "Savo," very different from western Finnish, which is the basis for the literary Finnish language. Many of its archaisms have been preserved in the central Scandinavian forests until modern times—a survival of more than ten generations. Some speakers of this dialect still live in the Finnish forests. Maintaining such a linguistic tradition in formal oral communication is quite rare anywhere in the world today.

A culture that survives in this kind of isolation, surrounded by another language, tends to be quite conservative, including its manifestations of material culture. This is especially true in the traditional set of buildings, for example, including the smoke house (*savupirtti*), threshing barn (*riihi*), tools, furniture, hunting weapons, and fishing implements. Interestingly enough, the sauna has almost disappeared from the area due to the activity of the Lutheran ministers. The clergy considered the sauna a manifestation of witchcraft; it was too barbaric for men and women to bathe naked together.

Segerstedt wrote in his 1889 report that Finns in general were religious and devout people,[24] active and faithful members of the established church. He also praised their honesty, but at the same time felt that the Finns did not care enough for religious education in their homes. In his opinion they too often practiced witchcraft because even without that mystic way of behavior, they had succeeded financially.

Early folklore collectors were able to find many other archaic elements of ancient Finnish culture among the Forest Finns. They were particularly capable in charms, incantations, and other expressions of witchcraft. They surely practiced shamanism, archaic trance techniques, during which the soul of the shaman left the body. The shaman was called *tietäjä*, a man of knowledge. He was the leader of the society and could occupy temporarily the status of healer, judge, and clergyman. Even in the twentieth century the Forest Finns can give quite thorough descriptions about the wedding of the bear—a multi-episodic drama in the course of which the bear was killed and then sent to his celestial home in the star of the Great Dipper or Otava, and then returned as the totem animal worshiped by the clan.

Segerstedt was also interested in the folk music of the Finns. They played the violin and two types of native stringed instruments, *kantele*, and had their own special melodies. Later research has shown that traditions of folk music and dance have undergone change though some Finnish songs, tunes, and dances still continue. Savo people living in central Scandinavian forests were able to sing old tunes, accompanying themselves with the *kantele*.

An important manifestation of family bonds was the ancestor cult. The relationship between the living and the dead members of a family was so intimate that the family was a whole, "one part of which lived above earth, another underground."[25] The Finns brought with them to Scandinavia the ancient custom, known only in Savo, of marking a fir tree to commemorate the deceased when his body was transported to the graveyard, "the village of the dead ones." Those members of the New Sweden churches who buried their deceased on river banks and on hillsides, according to Hans Norman, could very well have been the descendants of the Savo people.

Forest Finn society was very family-centered. The institution of extended families has survived until this century. As in Savo, Finnish families in central Scandinavia lived far from their neighbors. Village settlement is quite recent because the economy demanded migration over wide areas. As the family grew, the succeeding generations remained under the same roof or moved, as a unit, to another forest or perhaps overseas. Thus two of the early families who arrived at Grue Finnskog, Lehmoinen (cow) and Mullikka (ox), had descendants who later migrated to the Delaware River valley, as can be seen from the names preserved there. The families gradually became mixed with Norwegian and Swedish neighbors, lost their original names, but are once again now aware of their cultural roots.

It is, however, a fact that the Forest Finn language had almost disappeared before anyone became interested in preserving it. Nowadays some of the young American descendants of the Forest Finns have started studying Finnish, prolonging the linguistic connection to the Finnish forests at the last moment, just before it had almost totally disappeared as an oral tradition learned at home.

Nordic Research Project on the Culture of the Forest Finns

In May 1986 a Nordic fieldwork seminar was organized in the Finn forests between the rivers Glåma and Klara, on the boundary between Norway and Sweden. This area, studied by Carl Axel Gottlund in the 1820s and by many other ethnographers after him, seems to be a relic area where many elements of the Forest Finn culture have survived longest and where at present the Forest Finn identity seems to be strongest. Åsta Holt, the most famous author of Forest Finn origin, lives in this area, and *Finnskogsdagarna* (Finn Forest Days) are annually celebrated here.

In spite of acculturation, there are still several characteristics of the Forest Finn culture left in the speech, placenames, music and other arts, houses and utensils, habits and customs of central Scandinavia. The Finnish language is not spoken in everyday communication. Some older members of the communities, however, seem to understand Finnish questions even if they prefer to answer in Norwegian or Swedish. Some genres—for example, songs, dirty jokes, and riddles about neighboring peoples—are still told in Finnish to tease those who do not understand the message of the folklore in question. Fieldwork has disproven the formerly accepted idea that the last speaker of Finnish died in the 1960s, although this dating may well concur with the death of the last person who could speak Finnish fluently.

More interesting questions are what makes a language live so long and what are the codes and messages of communication when the language is no longer a part of a group's common knowledge.

The seminar produced many questions about the ethnicity of the Finns, their identity, and the nature and characteristics of Finnishness in the Finnish forest. The research is interdisciplinary and is trying to answer both old and new questions about the processes of their earliest Finnish immigration. The culture is being studied primarily on the following five levels: ecology and sources of livelihood; internal and external communication; origins (family roots); organizations; and worldview.[26]

The Forest Finns in the New World

Why was it so easy for the Nordic newcomers to adjust to the cultures they encountered in the New World? The native American life-style was very similar to that of the nomadic Arctic Saami or the Lapps, with whom these settlers had been in contact on the Finnish peninsula since ancient times. They had, therefore, developed skills in communicating with a culture very similar to that of the Native Americans.

During one phase New Sweden was also a target for missionaries wanting to convert the Native Americans, although they had limited success. In the later phases Swedish ministers who were sent to America were the primary tradition-bearers of the Swedish culture and the Lutheran church for the immigrants.

No one knows how Lutheran the Forest Finns really were. In respect to religion, as in other things, they probably kept alive the system they had in Scandinavia. They were members of the Lutheran church, but at the same time they kept their old customs, habits, and beliefs. Their worldview was pre-Christian in many respects. They practiced shamanism, for which they became famous, and buried their dead on hillsides and river banks because for them the realm of death was behind the river of death. In the New World as in the Old, some of them were accused of and condemned for practicing witchcraft.

One interesting topic for future study would be comparative research on shamanism: the similarities and differences between the religious concepts of the Finns, the Forest Finns, the Saami, and the Native American groups. In this respect there probably are many more similarities between the views of the Forest Finns and their Native American neighbors than between the Forest Finns and their own ministers and the officials and soldiers in the fortresses.

NOTES

1. Peter Lindeström, *Geographia Americae, With an Account of the Delaware Indians, Based on Surveys and Notes Made in 1645–1656*, trans. and ed. Amandus Johnson (Philadelphia: Swedish Colonial Society, 1925).
2. Amandus Johnson, *The Swedish Settlements on the Delaware: Their History and Relation to the Indians, Dutch and English, 1638–1664*, 2 vols. (Philadelphia: Swedish Colonial Society, 1911), 1:15–16, 79–83, 111–16.
3. Johnson, *Swedish Settlements*, 20.
4. Solomon Ilmonen, *Delawaren suomalaiset* (Hameenlinna: Karisto, 1938), 157.
5. Akseli Järnefelt-Rauanheimo, *Before William Penn* (Philadelphia: Dorrance & Co., 1929), 7–8.
6. Ilmonen, *Delawaren suomalaiset*, 26.
7. Ibid., 52.
8. Pehr Kalm, *Pehr Kalms resa till Norra Amerika*, ed. F. Elfring, 2 vols. (Helsinki: Mercators Tryckeri Aktiebolog, 1929), 2:330.
9. Ilmonon, *Delawaren suomalaiset*, 30–31.

10. Kauko Pirinen, "Förutsättningarna för savolaxarnas utflyttning," paper delivered at the Symposium on Skogsfinnarnas Kultur in Stockholm, 4 April 1987, 3.
11. Ibid., 9.
12. Ibid., 9–10.
13. Ibid., 11–12.
14. Ibid., 6.
15. Terry Jordan and Matti Kaups, "Architecture in Cultural and Ecological Context," *Geographical Review* 77 (January 1987): 69.
16. Richard Broberg, "Invandring från Finland till mellersta Skandinavien före 1700," *Svenska Landsmål och Folkliv* (1967): 65–67, 71–78.
17. Per Martin Tvengsberg, *Skogsfinnene på Finnskogen: Värmlandsfinnar* (Stockholm: Kulturfonden för Sverige och Finland, 1986), 37–64.
18. Ibid., 40–45.
19. Julius Mägiste, *Vermlannin sammuvaa savoa, Kielennäyttecta vuosilta 1947–51* (Helsinki: Suomalaisen Kirjallisuuden seura, 1960), 43.
20. Richard Broberg, "Finskt och svenskt i möte" *Karlstad stifts Julbok* (1964): 59–62.
21. Ilmonen, *Delawaren suomalaiset*, 49.
22. Ibid., 51–52, 95.
23. Albrekt Segerstedt, "Finnsbefolkningen i mellersta Sverige och sydöstra Norge" (1889), Segerstedska Samlingen (SI-II), University of Helsinki Library, 26–52.
24. Ibid., 65–67.
25. Juha Pentikäinen, *Kalevalen mytologia* (Helsinki: Gaudeamus, 1987), 260.
26. "Rapport från det förberedande fältseminarieti Finnskogen, Norge 19–25.5.1986, angäende det samnordiska forskningsprojektet om skogfinnarnas kultur," 7–8.

The Material Cultural Legacy of New Sweden on the American Frontier

TERRY G. JORDAN

The evidence I will provide concerning the legacy of New Sweden on the American backwoods frontier is necessarily out of context, since it is drawn piecemeal from the book I wrote with Professor Matti Kaups of the University of Minnesota at Duluth.[1] I am unable in the space provided here to develop adequately our theses or to present fully the evidence. As a result my remarks may seem more provocative than convincing.

In brief, our theses are as follows: first, we propose that the cultural legacy of New Sweden was greatest on the American backwoods frontier, rather than in the more durable secondary postpioneer settlement phase. Second, we are convinced that the most influential citizens of New Sweden, the ones most active in transmitting its influence to the eastern woodland frontier at large, were Savo-Karelian Finns rather than Swedes.[2] Finns of mixed Savoan and Karelian background, coming mainly from Värmland Province in interior Sweden, formed a very substantial part of the Delaware colony's population, dominating certain settlements and perhaps even forming a majority of the inhabitants following the Dutch takeover in 1655 (fig. 1).

In our book we offer a cultural ecological explanation of how the small band of Finns could have been so influential in American backwoods pioneer culture and why larger, later-arriving immigrant groups, in particular the Scotch-Irish, adopted so many Finnish practices. We suggest that the Savo-Karelian Finnish subculture of northern Europe was primed for success on the forest frontier of North America. The Savo-Karelians had been a people engaged in agricultural forest colonization for generations before their arrival in the Delaware colony and had accomplished an explosive expansion from the Lake Ladoga area that brought them even into interior Sweden by 1600 (fig. 2). They already possessed, upon arrival in America, many of the skills and techniques later associated with the backwoods pioneers—axmanship, a crude form of notched-log carpentry, hunting prowess, open-range cattle and hog

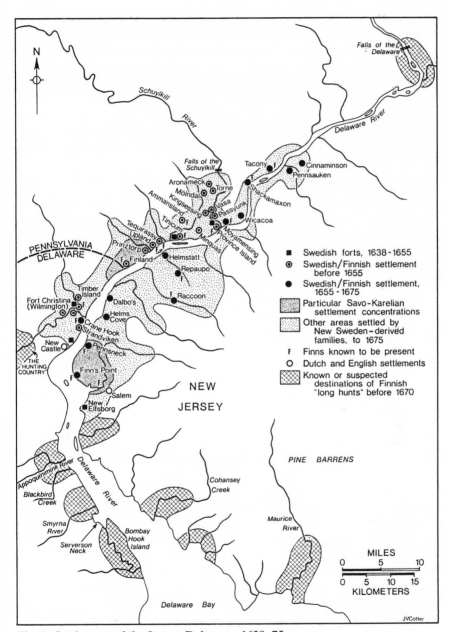

Fig. 1. Settlement of the Lower Delaware, 1638–75.

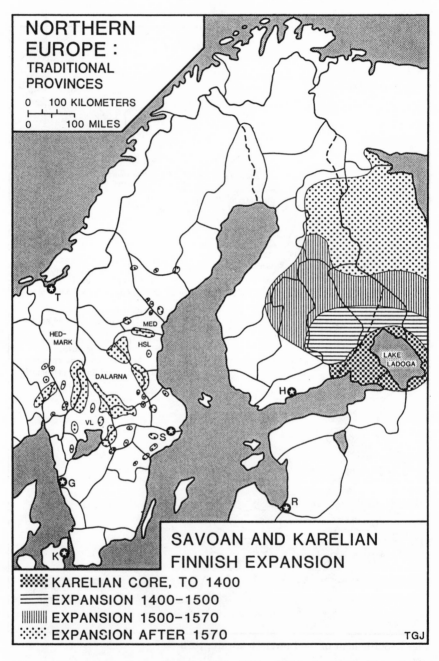

NORTHERN
EUROPE :
TRADITIONAL
PROVINCES

0   100 KILOMETERS

0   100 MILES

T

MED

HED-
MARK

HSL

DALARNA

LAKE
LADOGA

H

VL

S

G

R

SAVOAN AND KARELIAN
FINNISH EXPANSION

KARELIAN CORE, TO 1400
EXPANSION 1400–1500
EXPANSION 1500–1570
EXPANSION AFTER 1570

K

TGJ

Fig. 2. Key: *G* = Göteborg, *H* = Helsinki, *HSL* = Hälsingland, *K* = København, *MED* = Medelpad, *R* = Riga, *S* = Stockholm, *T* = Trondheim, *VL* = Värmland.

herding, and slash-and-burn grain farming. These Finns also had used split-rail fences and the long rifle; moreover they had a seemingly compulsive drive to be on the move.

We further propose that, once settled in New Sweden, the Finns freely adopted from the local Delaware Indians, a people with whom they enjoyed very cordial relations, certain other items useful in frontier colonization, most notably corn. As early as 1660 or 1670, long before the arrival of the Scotch-Irish and other groups that would help populate the frontier, a hybrid Fenno-Indian backwoods pioneering culture had already formed along the Delaware. It was a way of life splendidly adapted to the task of forest colonization, whereas the later-arriving groups lacked the requisite skills.

Five examples of American backwoods frontier material culture, we believe, constitute diagnostic evidence of Finnish influence. An appropriate point to begin is log carpentry, one of the adaptive keys to frontier occupancy.[3] One must realize, at the outset, that frontier carpentry was crude. Do not seek surviving examples of it in the well-crafted, hewn-log houses of the secondary, postpioneer settlement phase in the eastern states. Its vestiges remain largely in certain farm outbuildings, and only beyond the Mississippi, especially in the Rocky Mountains, can numerous dwellings displaying pioneer carpentry be found. Similarly, in northern Europe do not expect to find the frontier Savo-Karelian carpentry in most of the Swedish or Finnish outdoor folk museums, where fine craftsmanship is emphasized, but rather look for it in the interior rural districts.

One type of log-corner notching that especially indicates Finnish influence is that identified in the literature of folk carpentry as V notching.[4] In all of Europe, only one confined area has log structures that are V notched (fig. 3). The area straddles the Swedish-Norwegian border, coinciding in part with a major Savo-Karelian Finnish settlement district in Värmland and Hedmark provinces. The notch, apparently of Norwegian origin, evolved slowly from a medieval prototype and was eventually adopted by Finnish settlers after their arrival in Sweden (fig. 4). It occurs in both round-log and hewn-log subtypes in northern Europe as well as America. Not one shred of evidence links this notch to Germany, and our field research in all German areas of Europe where log construction occurs has failed to find a single specimen that resembles V notching. In addition, the "lower Swedish cabin," a round-log V-notched dwelling in Clifton Heights, Pennsylvania, was recently dismantled and subjected to dendrochronology, yielding a date of 1697. That is more than a decade before log-building Germans began entering Pennsylvania. Additional evidence of New Sweden's influence on log carpentry is provided by the recently published research demonstrating the northern European origin of American "diamond" notching.[5]

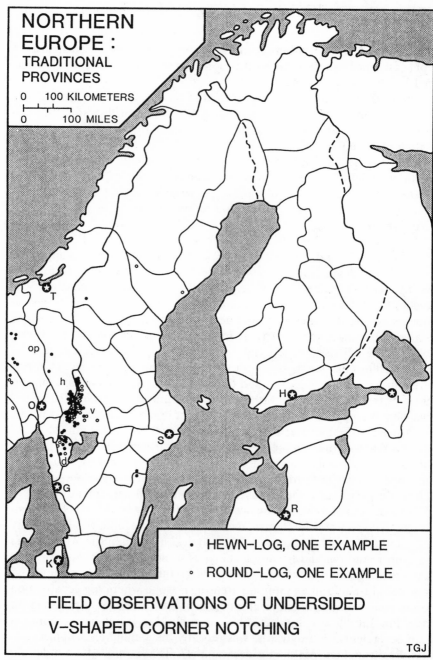

FIELD OBSERVATIONS OF UNDERSIDED
V-SHAPED CORNER NOTCHING

Fig. 3. *d* = Dalsland, *G* = Göteborg, *H* = Helsinki, *h* = Hedmark, *K* = København,
L = Leningrad, *O* = Oslo, *op* = Oppland, *R* = Riga, *S* = Stockholm, *T* = Trondheim.
For sources, see Jordan, Kaups, and Lieffort, "New Evidence," p. 28 (see n. 4).

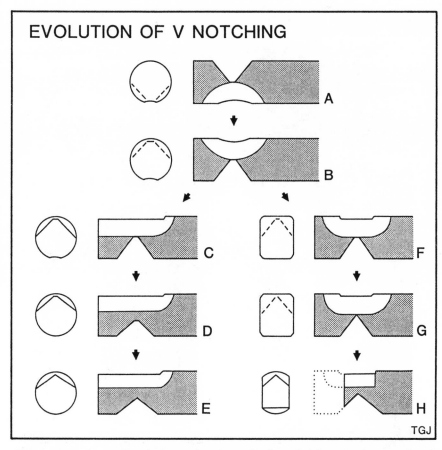

EVOLUTION OF V NOTCHING

Fig. 4. Key:. A = medieval Norwegian from Gudbrandsdalen; B = late medieval Norwegian; C = late medieval Norwegian from Hallingdalen; D = colonial Pennsylvanian, from Lower Swedish cabin at Clifton Heights; E = American, ubiquitous; F = Finnish structures in Värmland and Hedmark, eighteenth and later centuries; G = Värmland, from Eda area near Arvika; H = American, ubiquitous.

A second material example of Finnish influence in pioneer America comes from roof construction. Both backwoods American and Savo-Karelian Finnish log structures had low-pitched ridgepole-and-purlin roofs. That is, gables, in common with lower parts of the wall, consisted of logs that were notched into a ridgepole and parallel purlins, also called rib poles, that ran the length of the structures from gable to gable and bore the weight of a highly distinctive roofing material. Clapboards three to four feet long were placed loosely on the purlins. The lowest course of these boards rested against a "butting board," which was usually

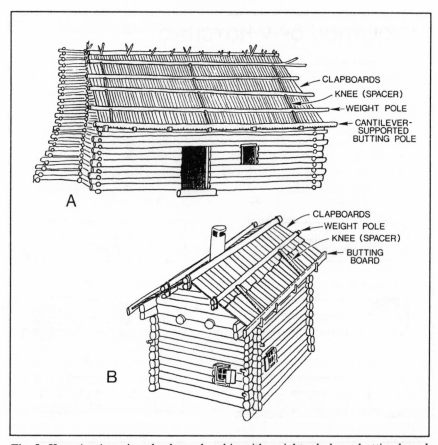

Fig. 5. Key: *A* = American backwoods cabin with weightpole-knee-butting board roof, from a 1791 sketch probably in frontier Georgia; *B* = house from Karelian isthmus, now at the Seurasaari open-air museum in Helsinki, also with a weightpole-knee-butting board roof. *Sources*: (A) John R. Swanton, *Indians of the Southeastern United States*, Bureau of American Ethnology, Bulletin No. 137 (Washington, D.C.: GPO, 1946), pl. 58; (B) Niilo Valonen, *Zur Geschichte der finnischen Wohnstuben*, no. 133 (Helsinki: Suomalais-ugrilaisen seuran toimituksia, 1963), 45.

notched into cantilevered logs projecting from the base of the gable (fig. 5). The loose clapboards were held down by log "weight poles" that lay directly above the purlins. They were kept from rolling down the roof slope by short pieces of heartwood, called "knees," that rested perpendicularly against the butting board. A second course of clapboards overlapped the first, in the manner of shingles, and a second tier of knees supported another weight pole. At the roof ridge, clapboards on the windward side projected by six inches or more beyond the crest, a practice called "capping." Such roofs, essentially identical in interior Finland and frontier America, possess the adaptive advantage of requiring no nails in construction.[6] So unusual a carpentry feature is most unlikely to have been independently invented, providing well-nigh irrefutable evidence of the cultural influence of New Sweden on the American frontier.

The next two examples of Finnish frontier influence come from folk architecture. Pioneer backwoodsmen applied log construction to a small number of interchangeable floor plans of single- and double-pen size (fig. 6). In this frontier folk architecture, houses or barns could easily be enlarged from one log unit to two, and an original house was often demoted to a barn, kitchen, or smokehouse. This interchangeability of structures minimized the number of buildings that had to be erected, an adaptive advantage on the frontier, where labor was in short supply. Expansion to double-pen size was done in such a way as to leave a roofed-over open space between the two log units, an adaptive practice that represented the most labor-efficient way to enlarge, since it avoided the problem of splicing logs and permitted the customary use of skids to raise the timbers into place.

The double-pen dwelling with open central passage is the familiar American "dogtrot" cabin of the frontier. We propose that the dogtrot plan, too, reached America with the Delaware Finns.[7] The Savo-Karelians, in common with American pioneers, possessed a small number of single- and double-unit log floor plans that were interchangeable (fig. 7). Duplicating the American pattern, the backwoods Finns of northern Europe often lived in open-passage double-pen houses that any American backwoodsman would have recognized as a dogtrot, and both groups also built double-crib barns with open runways in the center. In pioneer American and Savo-Karelian Finnish cultures alike, enlargement to dogtrot size was considered a status symbol and provided room for the abundant children of a young, forest-pioneering people. Even the methods of enlargement were identical in the two cultures, for both Finnish and American builders left the ridgepole and purlins of the original single-pen cabin projecting as cantilevered beams of seven to ten feet long on one gable end. These beams provided roof supports for the dogtrot hall after enlargement, but formed an awkward-looking protuberance as long as the cabin remained of one-room size.

In other words, the cultural, architectural, and ecological context of the dogtrot plan was very similar in backwoods America and the Savo-Karelian hinterland of northern Europe. The plan possessed adaptive value in both areas, principally through labor minimization, and in each area the dogtrot declined in post pioneer times, when the open passages were enclosed as halls. Relevant to our thesis is the fact that the oldest surviving

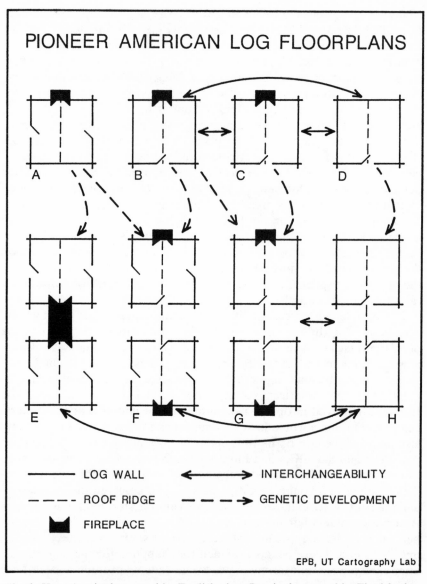

Fig. 6. Key: *A* = single-pen cabin, English plan; *B* = single-pen cabin, Finnish plan; *C* = kitchen; *D* = single-crib barn; *E* = saddlebag double-pen cabin; *F* = dogtrot double-pen cabin with British eave doors; *G* = dogtrot cabin with only Finnish doors; *H* = double-crib barn.

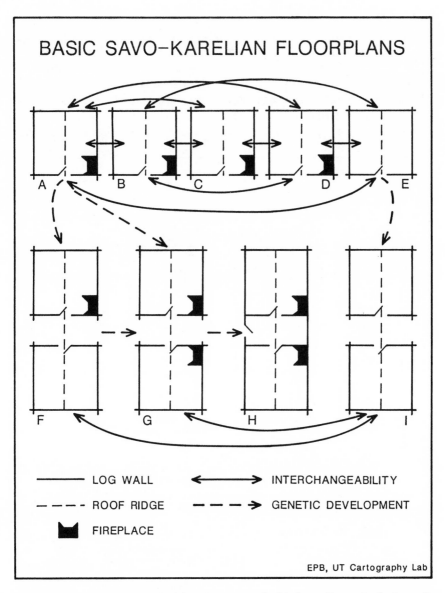

Fig. 7. Key: *A* = single-pen cabin; *B* = sauna; *C* = kitchen; *D* = grain-drying crib; *E* = single-crib granary or hayshed; *F* and *G* = double-pen house similar to "dog-trot" plan; *H* = double-pen house with enclosed hall; *I* = double-crib hayshed.

dogtrot dwelling in America, reputedly dating to 1745, is the Morton
House at Prospect Park, Pennsylvania, within the territorial bounds of
what had earlier been New Sweden. The builders of this house, originally named Mårtensson, are known to have been a Finnish family.[8]

A second element of pioneer American folk architecture that reveals
Savo-Karelian influence is the log hunter's shanty. These crude structures, none of which survive today in America, consisted of three log
walls covered by a single-pitch, lean-to roof (fig. 8). The fourth, tallest

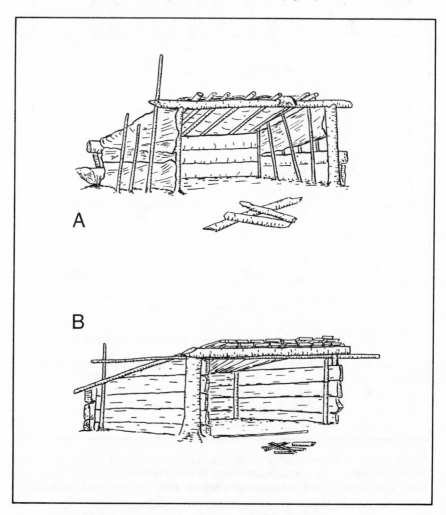

Fig. 8. Hunter's shanty, Savo-Karelian area in northern Europe. A = Repola in
Russian Karelia; B = Pielisjärvi in Finnish northern Karelia. *Source*: Sirelius,
"Über die primitiven Wohnungen," vol. 9 (1909), 19.

side of the shanty, facing the campfire, remained completely open. Variously called a "half-faced cabin," "three-faced camp," "open log cabin," or "open-faced shanty," these shelters remained surprisingly warm on winter hunts. One backwoods hunter in late-eighteenth-century western Pennsylvania described how he "cut some small trees and put up three sides of a small cabin, leaving the front open, having our fire on the outside." His shanty measured nine or ten feet square, and most were not over three or four feet tall at the rear.[9] A more detailed description of shanty-building from the Virginia backcountry frontier mentioned that the rear wall sometimes consisted of a single large log, and at a distance of eight to ten feet from it two pairs of "stakes were set in the ground a few inches apart to receive the ends of the poles for the sides of the camp." Above, "the whole slope of the roof was from the front to the back" and made of "slabs, skins, or ... the bark of hickory or ash trees." To complete the shanty, "the cracks between the logs were filled with moss."[10] In addition to serving hunters, the frontier log shanty was also used by some pioneers as a first crude dwelling at a new settlement site, which was a logical development since the backwoods people often converted their former hunting grounds into farms.

The precise prototype of the American hunter's shanty, even to the last detail, occurred among the Savo-Karelian Finns in northern Europe (see fig. 8).[11] Even the moss chinking was the same, and back country Finns used their shanties for the identical purposes as the American pioneers. An ecological analysis of the structure helps explain why, once introduced by the New Sweden settlers, the Finnish hunter's shanty would have been acceptable to the Scotch-Irish and other groups. It benefits from the principle known to physicists as the "heat-reflector oven," in which the campfire's warmth is reflected downward from the underside of the single-pitch roof and trapped. This natural heating efficiency lent it an ecological advantage on the winter hunt.

The final example of Finnish-influenced items of pioneer American material culture is a fence type. Enclosure of newly fired clearings by pioneers was essential to protect the fields from open-range livestock, and fences were built as a normal part of the clearing process. Medium-sized trees suitable for fencing material were spared in the burning of the clearing, cut into suitable lengths, and dragged to the edge of the field. There they were usually split into "rails" with wedges by using the blunt side of the ax as a mallet. Depending upon the diameter of the logs, they were split into halves, fourths, or eighths, and about eight hundred rails were needed to fence an acre. Sometimes, though, whole unsplit logs from small trees were used for fencing.

The favored and almost universal style for backwoods American field enclosures was the famous "worm" or "snake" fence, which consisted of

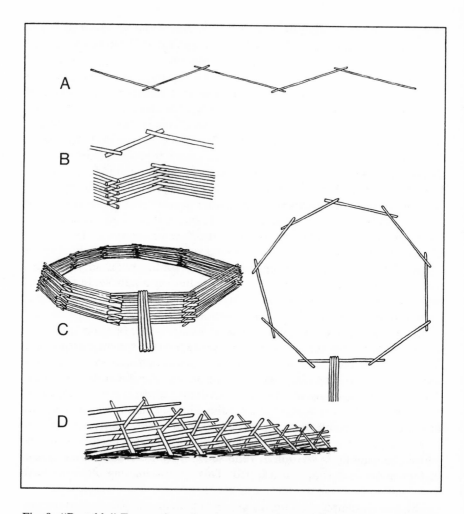

Fig. 9. "Portable" Fences, Scandinavia and North America. Key: *A* = traditional type of portable worm fence consisting of round notched logs, from Gräsmark, a Savo-Karelian Finnish parish in Värmland Province, Sweden, sketched over fifty years ago from memory; *B* = worm fence in Sweden, most common in Swedish Lappland, labeled type 20c in a Nordiska museet survey; *C* = worm fence reindeer corral, Inari area, Finnish Lapland; *D* = stake-and-ridered Savo-Karelian fence from a clearing in Pieksämäki area, Savo Province, Finland, of the slanted-rail type known in Pennsylvania as a "Swede" or "buck" fence. *Sources*: (A and B) see n. 17; (C) Itkonen item in n. 19; (D) Grotenfelt item in n. 19 and Stevenson W. Fletcher, *Pennsylvania Agriculture and Country Life* (Harrisburg: Pennsylvania Historical and Museum Commission, 1950), 85.

a zigzag stacking of rails or logs, in panels usually six to seven rails high and meeting at an angle of about 60 degrees (fig. 9).[12] No posts were required since the worm fence gained it stability from the tripod principle. The simpler type also contained no lateral supports, and depended only on gravity for survival. To add strength many pioneers placed two diagonal stakes at each joint, set against the ground at about a 45-degree angle, leaning against the top rail of the fence and crisscrossed in an X-shape. Then an additional rail or two, called "riders," were placed atop the crossed stakes to lock the joining. The resulting worm fence, called a "stake-and-rider" type, could resist the shoving pressure of animals and high wind much better than the simpler variety. If round, unsplit logs were used, a slight notching provided the needed lateral strength at the joints. Wherever the American pioneers went, the usual kind of enclosure surrounding their fields was this "rough zigzag log fence."[13]

A crude livestock corral was also built using the worm fence principle. Instead of zigzagging at each joint, the rails or logs were laid in such a way as to describe an arc, forming a circle or, more accurately, a polygonal enclosure (fig. 9C). Such log corrals—as well as round-log zigzagged worm pasture fences—can still be seen today on ranches in different parts of the Rocky Mountains, an area rich in pioneer material culture.

The adaptive advantages of worm fencing, which explained its popularity on the frontier, were several. It was made of an abundant raw material, required no mortising, hardware, or post holes, and could be erected quickly and cheaply with minimal labor in comparison to other fence types. No gates were needed since the field was entered by pulling down a corner of the fence. The rails could easily be disassembled and taken to a new clearing when a field was abandoned. Following a harvest the worm fence could be thrown down in several places to allow stock to forage on straw, husks, and weeds. Rail fences were not very durable, however, and had to be rebuilt on an average of once every twelve to fifteen years, but that hardly concerned the mobile backwoodsman.

The origin of the worm fence has long been debated. Some historians, completely without evidence, wrongly attributed it to the American Indian, overlooking the fact that the natives lacked the tools to cut tree trunks to the proper lengths or split them into rails, and ignoring early accounts describing Indian corn fields in the eastern seaboard area as unfenced on all sides. Others have fallen back on the tired, if convenient, notion that pioneer innovation explains the worm fence. Even the original regional cultural affiliation has been unclear, confused by the popular term *Virginia worm fence*.[14] In fact, documentary evidence points very clearly to a Delaware Valley origin since the earliest-known reference to a worm fence was on Alloway's Creek near Salem, New Jersey, in 1685.[15]

Alloway's Creek and Salem are located only a few scant miles from the

notable seventeenth-century concentration of Savo-Karelians in the settlement known as Finns Point (fig. 1). We propose that the worm fence,
in both its zigzag and polygon configurations, was implanted in America
by the Finns.[16] Indeed, we must now confess that the fences illustrated in
figure 9, fences that would instantly be recognized by an American pioneer, were all sketched in Finnish areas of northern Europe.

In the Savo-Karelian districts of Värmland and Hedmark, archaeological research has occasionally revealed a zigzag tracing around the peri-
meter of long-abandoned grain fields. A field survey of traditional fence
types undertaken by Nordiska Museet staff in Sweden earlier in this century yielded a respondent from a Finnish parish in Värmland who recalled that zigzag enclosures were formerly used there in cases where
the fence was frequently relocated, as in shifting cultivation and snow
baffles. The respondent's sketch leaves no doubt that a worm fence was
being described (fig. 9A), and as a result a detailed drawing of such an
enclosure appeared in the questionnaire subsequently developed by the
museum staff (fig. 9B).[17] Worm fences have been photographed in Swedish Lappland, though none apparently survive in Savo-Karelian settled
areas.[18]

The ultimate origin of the worm fence and corral is apparently to be
found among the Lapps, a people for centuries in frequent contact with
the kindred Savo-Karelian Finns. The Lapps long used the zigzag log
fence to direct game during hunts, and they still today build the polygonal corrals for their reindeer (fig. 9C). Stakes and riders, on the other
hand, appear to be of Savo-Karelian origin (fig. 9D).[19] Put briefly, every
element of the form of the American backwoods worm fence is abun-
dantly present in the Finnish tradition of northern Europe.

These five features of material culture are evidence of a Finnish contribution, by way of the New Sweden colony, to American frontier life. The
features—V notching, the weight-pole–knee-butting board roof, the dogtrot dwelling plan, the hunter's shanty, and the worm fence—may be regarded as diagnostic, since they occurred only in northern Europe and
the American frontier. One must, in viewing the evidence, either accept
the notion of Finnish influence or postulate a most unlikely series of independent inventions. If one accepts the Finnish origin of just one American feature—the weight-pole–knee-butting board roof, for example—
then the likelihood of Finnish influence in other aspects of the American
forest pioneering system cannot be dismissed. When five diagnostic material traits of northern European origin are accepted, then reason demands approval of a rather considerable Fenno-Scandian role in the
shaping of American frontier culture. A single Finnish-like trait in backwoods America could be dismissed as chance independent invention, but
complexes of multiple, interrelated, diagnostic northern European traits,

such as exist in carpentry, architecture, and fence-building, simply cannot be cast aside rationally.

How did the Finns achieve such importance? Cultural ecology provides the answer. The Finnish complex of preadapted traits diffused to a larger American population simply because it worked far better than any competing system. If a Finnish trait possessed no adaptive value that made pioneering easier, it did not survive, as was the case with the Finnish language and sauna, neither of which spread far beyond the banks of the Delaware. In such matters of taste, including speech, music, and folklore, the heritage of the British highland majority on the American frontier prevailed. Indeed, we present in our book evidence of Celtic, Dutch, English, and German influence, as well as American Indian contributions. By no means do we propose that the backwoods culture of the United States was exclusively Finnish. We do, however, feel that our evidence demands that an important Finnish contribution be acknowledged. Heretofore students of the frontier have, by and large, denied that contribution.[20]

What, in the final analysis, was the legacy of New Sweden? I say you should seek it in the outrageously successful forest pioneering culture that permitted the United States to deal in Manifest Destiny and to become a transcontinental nation rather than remaining a littoral state clinging to the Atlantic. I say seek it among Finns, not Swedes.

NOTES

1. Terry G. Jordan and Matti Kaups, *The American Backwoods Frontier: An Ethnic and Ecological Interpretation* (Baltimore: Johns Hopkins University Press, 1989).
2. Terry G. Jordan, "Evolution of American Backwoods Pioneer Culture: The Role of the Delaware Finns," in *Mississippi's Piney Woods: A Human Perspective*, ed. Noel Polk (Jackson: University Press of Mississippi, 1986), 25–39.
3. Terry G. Jordan, *American Log Buildings: An Old World Heritage* (Chapel Hill: University of North Carolina Press, 1985), 41–83.
4. For a complete treatment of this subject see Terry G. Jordan, Matti Kaups, and Richard M. Lieffort, "New Evidence on the European Origin of Pennsylvanian V Notching," *Pennsylvania Folklife* 36 (1986): 20–31.
5. Terry G. Jordan, Matti Kaups, and Richard M. Lieffort, "Diamond Notching in America and Europe," *Pennsylvania Folklife* 36 (1986): 70–78.
6. For surviving examples of the weight-pole–knee-butting board roof in Finland and America, see the Abraham Lincoln birth cabin at Hodgenville, Kentucky, and exhibit number 20, from the Karelian isthmus, in the Seurasaari outdoor folk museum in Helsinki.
7. For a much fuller discussion of the dogtrot plan in America see Terry G.

Jordan and Matti Kaups, "Folk Architecture in Cultural and Ecological Context," *Geographical Review* 77 (1987): 52–75.

8. C. A. Weslager, *The Log Cabin in America From Pioneer Days to the Present* (New Brunswick, N.J.: Rutgers University Press, 1969), 166–67; Akseli Järnefelt-Rauanheimo, "Rautalammin lahja Amerikalle," *Kansanvalistusseura kalenteri* (1921): 36–40.

9. John W. Harpster, ed., *Pen Pictures of Early Western Pennsylvania* (Pittsburgh: University of Pittsburgh Press, 1938), 223–24.

10. Joseph Doddridge, *Notes, on the Settlement and Indian Wars, of the Western Parts of Virginia and Pennsylvania* (Wellsburgh, Va.: The Gazette, 1824), 124–25.

11. U. T. Sirelius, "Über die primitiven Wohnungen der finnischen und ob-ugrischen Völker," *Finnisch-ugrische Forschungen: Zeitschrift für finnisch-ugrische Sprach- und Volkskunde* 8 (1908): 8, 12, 15–19, 28; 9 (1909): 17–19; Albert Hämäläinen, *Bostads- och byggnadsskick hos skogsfinnarna i Mellan-Skandinavien*, no. 23 (Stockholm: Nordiska museets handlingar, 1945): 25–27.

12. Mamie Meredith, "The Nomenclature of American Pioneer Fences," *Southern Folklore Quarterly* 15 (1951): 135–47; U.S. Department of Agriculture, "Statistics of Fences in the United States," *Report of the Commissioner of Agriculture for the Year 1871* (Washington, D.C.: GPO, 1872), 500, 504.

13. F. A. Michaux, *Travels to the West of the Allegheny Mountains* (London: Crosby & Co., 1805), 58; Leslie Hewes, "Early Fencing on the Western Margin of the Prairie," *Nebraska History* 63 (1982): 301–5.

14. John R. Stilgoe, *Common Landscapes of America, 1580 to 1845* (New Haven: Yale University Press, 1982), 190; Vera T. Via, "The Old Rail Fence," *Virginia Cavalcade* 12 (Summer 1962): 33–40; Wilbur Zelinsky, "Walls and Fences," *Landscape* 8 (Spring 1959): 15; Meredith, "Nomenclature of American Pioneer Fences," 144.

15. H. F. Raup, "The Fence in the Cultural Landscape," *Western Folklore* 6 (1947): 3. Raup, however, mistook Salem, New Jersey, for Salem, Massachusetts.

16. Amandus Johnson was the first to propose a northern European origin for the worm fence; see his "Sweden Gave Americans the Rail Fence," *American Swedish Monthly* 49 (June 1955): 6–7, 29.

17. "Etnologiska undersökningen" files, "Hågnader," vol. 1 (1927–45), 157; and vol. 2 (1927–37), fig. 20C preceding p. 1, Nordiska museet arkiv, Stockholm.

18. Photograph Collection, photos no. 424.K.ah. and 424.K.ak, Nordiska museet arkiv, Stockholm.

19. T. I. Itkonen, *Suomen Lappalaiset vuoteen 1945* (Porvoo and Helsinki: Werner Söderström, 1948), 2:64; Gösta Grotenfelt, *Det primitiva jordbrukets metoder i Finland under den historiska tiden* (Helsinki: Simeli, 1899), 183.

20. See, for example, Henry Glassie, "Eighteenth-Century Cultural Process in Delaware Valley Folk Building," *Winterthur Portfolio* 7 (1972): 49.

Part V
Sources and Questions for Further Study

Resources for New Sweden Studies

RICHARD WALDRON

In 1986 and 1987, the New Jersey State Museum and the New Jersey Historical Commission inventoried American and Swedish collections of manuscripts dealing with the colony of New Sweden and the Swedish Lutheran mission to the Delaware Valley. The two agencies undertook this project to provide a research base for the museum's exhibition "The New Sweden Colony," and to provide historians with a guide to further research on these two subjects.

The discussion that follows recounts briefly the history of the inventory project, summarizes some of its findings, and suggests some ways to strengthen New Sweden studies in the future.

Work began in 1986 with grants from the New Jersey Committee for the Humanities and the Pennsylvania Humanities Council, with additional funds from the Historical Commission. From the project's very beginning, we thought that to do the job properly we ought to include Finnish, Dutch, British, and German repositories in our survey. But we lacked the money and the time to do that. We still believe that an extended manuscript survey of these proportions should be done.

Our original intention was to investigate manuscript collections of the seventeenth century only. Because the project's planners thought that relevant manuscripts in Sweden would be relatively few and those in the United States almost nonexistent, we intended to describe in our published guide individual manuscripts that the survey uncovered.

We hired Richard H. Hulan of Arlington, Virginia, to survey collections in the United States and Kurt A. Larson of Rockford, Illinois, then a graduate student in history at Uppsala University, to carry out the Swedish portion of the survey.

For the United States we gathered a list of potential repositories of New Sweden material (see Appendix), and polled them by mail. Dr. Hulan telephoned or visited those which indicated possession of relevant manuscripts and completed a worksheet for each collection held by the repository. We planned the same procedure for Swedish repositories, but Kurt Larson and Professors Stellan Dahlgren and Hans Norman, of the Department of History, Uppsala University, convinced us to widen our scope to include the eighteenth century and the material left us by the Lutheran pastors who served the mission on the Delaware through the time of the American Revolution. They also persuaded us that material in Swedish repositories, especially that dealing with the mission to the Delaware, was too massive to be treated by document.

Dr. Hulan's initial fieldwork proved this assumption to be true also of material in the United States. The scope of the published guide, therefore, will include the seventeenth and the eighteenth centuries and will give general descriptions of the collections the project surveyed.

We left to Mr. Larson the decision about which repositories to survey since, aside from obvious places such as Riksarkivet (the Swedish National Archives), Kungliga Biblioteket (the Royal Library), Carolina Rediviva (Uppsala University Library), and the Landsarkivet i Uppsala (the Regional Archives at Uppsala), the project's planners at the State Museum and the Historical Commission lacked knowledge of Swedish repositories. In fact, there do not seem to be very many more Swedish repositories with relevant holdings than these four major ones. American repositories holding some manuscript material concerning New Sweden are fairly numerous, though there are few strong collections.

After an initial survey, Dr. Hulan and Mr. Larson were to prepare worksheets that Lorraine Williams of the State Museum and I, representing the Historical Commission, were to edit into inventory entries.

THE AMERICAN SURVEY

In the United States we contacted fifty-six repositories; eighteen told us that they had a relevant collection. Collections vary in richness, though most of them consist of just a few items or of genealogical material and land transfers chiefly of the eighteenth century. There are a few very large collections including Dutch and English material related to New Sweden. Several—including the Library of Congress—contain photocopies of some material in Swedish repositories. Overall, the American material contains few surprises. Our project did not unearth startling caches of hitherto unknown manuscripts.

For a flavor of what the survey did uncover about New Sweden manuscript collections in the United States, here are brief descriptions of four collections—the New York Public Library's Rare Books and Manuscripts Division; the Historical Society of Pennsylvania; the Library of Congress Manuscript Division; and the Gloucester County (New Jersey) Historical Society.

New York Public Library's Rare Books and Manuscripts Division initially reported that it held no relevant manuscripts, but Dr. Hulan noticed that Charles Gehring's *Guide to Dutch Manuscripts*[1] contains ten pages of citations from NYPL, most notably from the Hans Bontemantel Papers. Relevant items include Gehring's item 559, a memorandum about Swedish claims and activities on the South River (as the Dutch called the Delaware) from Peter Minuit's time as governor of New Sweden (spring 1638) until Johan Rising's capture of Fort Casimir in 1654; Gehring's items 564–66, documents concerning the invasion and surrender of New Sweden in 1655; Gehring's items 569, 571, and 574, relations from and about the South River to the States General in 1656–58; and Gehring's item 583, Hans Bontemantel's manuscript concerning events on the South River, presumably written in 1660. None of these had been published when Gehring's guide was published in 1978.

The Historical Society of Pennsylvania holds dozens of separate collections in which appear a few useful documents. A number of larger collections (the William Penn, James Logan, Jonathan Dickinson, and John F. Watson papers, for example) have been well analyzed and contain relevant material, especially about the continuing presence of Swedish families and churches in the Delaware Valley until late in the eighteenth century. The society holds the original manuscript "Record of Upland Court, 1676–1681." The court was established under the Duke of York's government and represented a largely Swedish population centered at present Chester.

The society also holds the Archivum Americanum,[2] two volumes of handwritten excerpts from Swedish originals made for Dr. Charles J. Stille, a descendant of New Sweden's original settlers, and a substantial collection made for Joseph J. Mickley of transcriptions of Swedish documents relating to the Delaware from Riksarkivet dating from 1636 to 1811. The collection is in Swedish, but the nineteenth-century manuscript is much easier to read than the Gothic script of the originals.

The Manuscripts Division of the Library of Congress holds copies of manuscripts on microfilm from many foreign collections, including that of the English Society for the Propagation of the Gospel in Foreign Parts. The SPG's activity in colonial North America was contemporary with the Swedish mission to the Delaware. The SPG material includes correspondence to, from, and about Swedish pastors Eric Björck, Andreas and Samuel Hesselius, Anders Rudman, and others.

Many of the SPG letters were selected and published, arranged by colonies, in William Stevens Perry's five-volume *Papers Relating to the History of the Church, in [name of Colony]*, printed during the 1870s.[3] As fine as Perry's volumes are, the original letters and transcriptions are more complete and substantially more numerous than those he published or extracted.

The manuscript collections of the Gloucester County Historical Society number about two thousand items, primarily county court documents, but also include family Bibles, church minutes, and other sources concerning Swedish-surnamed settlers of early Gloucester County. Deeds and wills include original signatures, often in the form of Nordic *bomarken.*

The American survey contains one special collection of great richness and versatility—the Amandus Johnson Papers (MSS Group 41), which are housed at the Balch Institute for Ethnic Studies in Philadelphia. Most of the voluminous Johnson material has nothing to do with New Sweden; the collection comprises for the most part Johnson's personal and business papers dealing with a variety of subjects. But the relevant material (Series 6, "Transcriptions and Translations of Research Documents, 1621–1821")—all translated into English—spans the life of New Sweden, both the political colony, 1638 to 1655, and the "cultural" colony, which lasted until the end of the eighteenth century. It includes every kind of document, from personal correspondence and diaries of seventeenth-century colonists and Lutheran pastors of the eighteenth-century mission to Swedish Regency orders (the Regency that ruled Sweden during Queen Christina's minority, 1632–44) to ships' passes and inventories to official correspondence between New Sweden's governors and the Swedish government. While this is not unknown material (it all exists in originals in Sweden, and some of it has been published extensively), it is the only American collection that gathers such variety in English and gives such a comprehensive overview of the life of the various New Swedens—political, economic, and cultural.

The fact that it is all translated is of great importance to Americans, most of whom cannot read the seventeenth-century manuscript versions of Swedish, Dutch, or German—or, in fact, Swedish in any form at all. Johnson seems to have gathered this material during the 1940s for a documentary history of the colony. This seems as good an idea today as it was over fifty years ago.

THE SWEDISH SURVEY

Perhaps because Sweden's population is so much smaller than that of the United States, there were few repositories to survey. The major ones were Carolina Rediviva, Riksarkivet, Kungliga Biblioteket, and the Landsarkivet i Uppsala. But though the repositories are few in number, their collections are large and varied. The material is often unpublished—especially in English—and is especially voluminous concerning the Lutheran mission to the Delaware. This is not surprising since the Lutheran mission lasted far longer than did New Sweden as an extension of Swedish sovereignty in the New World. The lengthy letters that the missionaries wrote home are, as we know from those that have been published in English, detailed descriptions not only of the lives of the Swedes and the Finns in the English colonies of Delaware, New Jersey, and Pennsylvania, but are in the aggregate a history of the Lutheran mission itself, which may be the most important New Sweden study of all.

Here is a sampling of material from collections held by five Swedish repositories:

The Västerås stadsbibliotek (Västerås Municipal Library) holds few related items. One, however, is of great interest for the study of the Swedish mission to the Delaware—the diary of Andreas Sandel (1671–1744), who served the congregation at Wicacoa from 1702 until 1718 (General collection, Bb 24). Sandel divided his diary into four sections and titled them "A short description of my journey to the West Indies Anno 1701"; "A diary of my work in Philadelphia between 1702 and 1718"; "Concerning my journey from America to Sweden"; and "Notations concerning the author's connections with America after his return to Sweden." Diary entries in the second section are long and detailed during the early years of Sandel's ministry, but they become shorter closer to 1718. The diary was to be published in Swedish by Pastor Frank Blomfelt of Fjärdhundra, Sweden, in cooperation with Kungliga Biblioteket, Stockholm, in 1988.[4]

Among the numerous collections of New Sweden-related material held by Carolina Rediviva (Uppsala University Library), several are of particular interest. One is the manuscript of Bishop Jesper Swedberg's description of North America and New Sweden (General collection E 382, "Svecia Nova seu America Illuminata...."), which he compiled from the writings of Lutheran priests of the mission to the Delaware, many of whom, as bishop of Skara, Swedberg had himself sent to the Delaware. Swedberg summarized New Sweden's history and described a variety of American conditions, including climate, colonial government, animal life, geography, and the lives and customs of the Indians. He also wrote brief biographies of each of the Swedish priests sent to America, from the founding of New Sweden to the early eighteenth century. Swedberg completed the work in 1729 and it was published in Swedish in 1732. Much of the manuscript—maybe all of it—is translated in the Johnson Papers at the Balch Institute for Ethnic Studies in Philadelphia.

The university's library also holds a volume of letters from the Swedish government, 1639–43, to Olof Stake, the governor of Dalarna and Värmland provinces, some of which instruct him to gather colonists for New Sweden (General collection E 391). Many are translated in the Johnson Papers.

The diary or journal of Johan Rising, New Sweden's last governor

(1654–55), is held by the library (General collection E 433; another manuscript copy is in the Palmskiöldska collection, vol. 322). Rising's journal is an invaluable source for conditions in the colony during its last eighteen months under Swedish control and for a description of the Dutch invasion and conquest in September 1655.

Rising divided his diary into two sections. The first deals primarily with his journey to the New World and the Dutch attack. The second consists of his "Reflections on how the American Company at New Sweden could receive satisfactory compensation for those damages which the Dutch of New Holland [inflicted]...." The diary is also translated in whole or in part in the Johnson Papers. It was published in Swedish and English in 1988, edited by Professors Stellan Dahlgren and Hans Norman of the Department of History, Uppsala University.[5]

The last item needing mention in Carolina Rediviva's collections is a volume of trade agreements between Sweden and England and between Sweden and the Netherlands (Nordin collection, vol. 430). Especially interesting are those from the 1650s (pages 293–313) concerning trade with New Guinea, Africa, the West Indies, and New Sweden.

The Landsarkivet i Uppsala (Regional Archives at Uppsala) contains fifty-five letters from pastors in New Sweden that describe North America and the lives of their coreligionists in the Delaware Valley (Uppsala domkapitels arkiv, EI: vols. 1–3, 11–19, and EII: 1–2). Series EI and EII are twenty-eight volumes of incoming correspondence to the Consistory of Uppsala Diocese, 1400 to 1850. The volumes include letters from New Sweden priests Israel Acrelius, Jonas Aurén, Eric Björck, Anders Borell, Johannes Campanius (two letters), Nils Collin (seven letters), Andreas Hesselius, Samuel Hesselius, Anders Lidman, Andreas Rudman, Johan Sandin, and Johan Wicksell. This collection should be of great interest to students of New Sweden and the Swedish mission to the Delaware since it has not been used in earlier studies of these subjects.

A similar and much larger collection of correspondence (Uppsala domkapitel F VIII: 1–14) to and from the Consistory of Uppsala Diocese contains material written by pastors of the mission to the Delaware, from 1647 to 1791. It concerns church life and organization in North America, and, of course, the lives of the Swedish-Americans there.

One highlight of this rich collection is an undated translation of Martin Luther's *Small Catechism into English* ("A simple explication of CATECHISM by questions and answers"). The translator was probably Mathias Hultgren, who perhaps made the translation during his years at Wicacoa (F VIII: 12).

Another is volume 14 which is a listing of all families in the Swedish congregations at Racoon and Penns Neck and a listing of English families that attended the Swedish churches but were members of the Church of England. It was probably compiled around 1773 by Johan Wicksell, dean of the Swedish congregations at Racoon and Penns Neck, 1763 to 1773. The compilation gives each member's name and address and lists whether he or she spoke Swedish, possessed a Swedish- or English-language Bible, and was capable of reciting Luther's Catechism. It also noted the number of sermons and Holy Communion services each had attended, and each person's approximate age, "mode of life," how far and by what route or means each member traveled to church.

A similar document in the same series (F VIII: 6) is a 1754 list of the members of the same congregations, probably compiled by Israel Acrelius. It gives each member's name, occupation, place of residence, and whether he or she read, wrote, spoke, or understood Swedish and/or English. There is a photostatic copy in the collections of the American Swedish Historical Museum in Philadelphia.

The subjects of these two documents were crucial matters on which the missionaries had to report, for as time passed in the eighteenth century, continued Swedish maintenance of the mission came to depend increasingly on Swedish- and Finnish-American ability and willingness to retain the use of Swedish in their liturgies and not to abandon their Swedish churches for services in English at neighboring Anglican, Methodist, and Moravian churches.

Lunds universitetsbibliotek handskriftsavdelningen (Lund University Library, Manuscript Division) does not hold very much that is related to New Sweden, but its collections include a series of letters from Nils Collin to a professor at Lund on numerous topics, including the American climate and its effect on crops, vegetation, and human health (Samlingen Agardh, C. A. vol. 4).

Krigsarkivet (the Royal Military Archives) in Stockholm holds seven manuscript lists of military personnel sent out to New Sweden as members of expeditions to the colony from 1642 to 1645 (Sjöexpeditioner Ex-kaderchefer 1642–45 [Expeditioner till Nya Sverige och till Västindien]), and forty pages of the minutes of a hearing for Johan Printz on his surrender of the city of Chemnitz (in eastern Germany) to the enemy in 1641 (Rättshandlingar, vol. 2, Dombok för 1641, pp. 2–42).

RECOMMENDATIONS FOR THE FUTURE OF NEW SWEDEN STUDIES

The State Museum/Historical Commission manuscript inventory has shown us, if we did not suspect it before, that there is a great deal of information about New Sweden—colony and mission—undigested by students of early American history and of Swedish history of the seventeenth century. We fear, though, that this material will remain unassimilated into the historiography of these two subjects unless three major problems are solved fairly soon. The problems are of popularization, language, and accessibility.

A major problem in promoting the study of New Sweden as a way to a better understanding of early American history is that in the United States there is little "mass" to scholarship about New Sweden: only a few historians, anthropologists, and students of material culture study the colony. A partial remedy for this situation might be to follow through with Amandus Johnson's plan for a documentary history of the colony, including the Swedish mission to the Delaware. This is a project that should not be difficult to do, since Johnson's and Johan Liljiencrants's translations of relevant documents, now already held by the Balch Institute, provide the essential body of the work. Such a volume might stimulate interest in New Sweden below the graduate level and help to interest a new generation of scholars for whom New Sweden would be their major object of study.

But there is a more significant problem. One of the weaknesses of American scholarship on New Sweden is the inability of Americans to read Swedish—either in print or in manuscript. We need to stimulate training in Swedish and the seventeenth-century manuscript versions of Swedish, Dutch, and German. But while that long-term goal is being pursued, some shorter-term activities could make the material for the study of New Sweden and the Swedish mission to the Delaware more accessible to graduate students, academic and avocational scholars, and the general public—activities that will place New Sweden studies on a firm foundation and enable us to continue to broaden and deepen our knowledge of early American history by having access to the records of the colony and the mission.

The first of these activities is to expand the scope of the State Museum/ Historical Commission manuscript inventory far beyond its original boundaries of repositories in the United States and Sweden. A larger-scale project would survey collections in the Netherlands, France, Great Britain, Finland, and Germany. New Sweden was a multinational enterprise and Sweden's status as a Great Power in the seventeenth century made nearly all of its activities interesting—at least—to most of Europe. It is not unreasonable to expect that some material in repositories in these countries will expand our knowledge of the economic and commercial underpinnings of both Sweden and its colony and help us to understand better the New Sweden Company's commercial goals for its colony and the odd relationship between the New Sweden Company, the Swedish Crown, and the company's Dutch investors.

Second, since we have such difficulty reading the seventeenth-century manuscript hand, whether in Swedish or other languages, we need to transcribe carefully these documents into a typescript easily read by those fluent in Swedish. Then of course we need to translate into English those documents and publish them in some form, as Charles Gehring's New Netherland Project has been doing for the records of New Netherlands.

While all of this expensive and time-consuming activity is going on we will have stimulated at least one generation of New Sweden specialists (taking New Sweden in its widest application, from the foundation of the colony to the end of the Swedish mission with the death of Nils Collin, 1638 to 1831) to expand our knowledge of both early American and seventeenth-century Swedish history. This will surely be a worthy legacy to pass on to those who will plan the four-hundredth anniversary of the colony's foundation in 2038.

NOTES

1. Charles Gehring, ed., *A Guide to Dutch Manuscripts Relating to New Netherland in United States Repositories* (Albany: University of the State of New York, State Education Department, New York State Library, 1978).
2. Published as *Archivum Americanum. Documents Preserved in the Consistory of Upsal Relating to the Swedish Church on the Delaware*, 2 vols. (Philadelphia, 1891).
3. William Stevens Perry, ed., *Papers Relating to The History of the Church . . .*, 5 vols. (Privately printed, 1870–78).
4. Frank Blomfelt, ed., *Andreas Sandels Dagbok, 1701–1743* (Stockholm: Norstedts Tryckeri, 1988).
5. Stellan Dahlgren and Hans Norman, eds., *The Rise and Fall of New Sweden: Governor Johan Risingh's Journal, 1654–1655, in Its Historical Context*, trans. Maire Clark Nelson (Stockholm: Almqvist & Wicksell International, 1988).

Appendix
American Repositories Surveyed
New Jersey State Museum/New Jersey
Historical Commission
Manuscript Inventory Project

(*Indicates relevant holdings)

Connecticut

Connecticut Historical Society, Hartford

Connecticut State Library, Hartford

Historical Manuscripts Collection, Sterling Memorial Library, Yale University, New Haven

Rare Book Room, Sterling Memorial Library, New Haven

Delaware

*Delaware Division of Historical and Cultural Affairs, Bureau of Archives and Records, Dover

Department of Special Collections, University of Delaware Library, Newark

*Historical Society of Delaware, Wilmington

Illinois

Chicago Historical Society, Chicago

Newberry Library, Chicago

Department of Special Collections, University of Chicago Library, Chicago

Lutheran Church in America Archives, Lutheran School of Theology, Chicago

Special Collections Department, Augustana College Library, Rock Island

Manuscripts Division, University of Illinois Library, Urbana

Maryland

*Maryland Historical Society, Baltimore

Massachusetts

Boston Atheneum, Boston

*Massachusetts Historical Society, Boston

Massachusetts Secretary of State, Archives Division, Boston

Massachusetts State Library, Boston

Houghton Library, Harvard University, Cambridge

American Antiquarian Society, Worcester

Michigan

*Finnish American Historical Archives, Suomi College, Hancock

Minnesota

American Swedish Institute, Minneapolis

Augsburg Archive Society, Augsburg College and Theological Seminary, Minneapolis

James Ford Bell Library, University of Minnesota, Minneapolis

Special Collections Department, University of Minnesota Libraries, Minneapolis

Minnesota Historical Society, St. Paul

University of Minnesota Library, St. Paul

Gustavus Adolphus College/Minnesota Synod of the Lutheran Church in America Archives, St. Peter

New Jersey

Camden County Historical Society, Camden

Upsala College Library, East Orange

*Cumberland County Historical Society, Greenwich

New Jersey Historical Society, Newark

Department of Archives and Special Collections, Rutgers University Libraries, New Brunswick

*Salem County Historical Society, Salem

*Division of Archives and Records Management, Department of State, Trenton

New Jersey State Library, Trenton

*Gloucester County Historical Society, Woodbury

New York

*New York State Archives, Albany

*New York State Library, Albany

Holland Society of New York, New York

*New-York Historical Society, New York

Arents Collections, New York Public Library, New York

*Manuscripts and Archives Division, New York Public Library, New York

Pierpont Morgan Library, New York

Archives of the Lutheran Church in America, Metropolitan New York Synod

Wagner College, Staten Island

Pennsylvania

Pennsylvania State Archives, Harrisburg

Pennsylvania State Library, Harrisburg

*American Philosophical Society, Philadelphia

*American Swedish Historical Museum, Philadelphia

*Balch Institute for Ethnic Studies, Philadelphia

*Historical Society of Pennsylvania, Philadelphia

Library Company of Philadelphia, Philadelphia

University of Pennsylvania Library, Philadelphia

Washington, D.C.

*Manuscript Division, Library of Congress

Geography and Map Division, Library of Congress

Microform Section, Library of Congress

Pursuing the Study of New Sweden in the Swedish National Library and in the Swedish National Archives:

A Survey of Documents on the Swedish Colony in Delaware

BÖRJE WESTLUND

One good way of presenting documents concerning New Sweden would be to emphasize sources overlooked by past research. However, that would require a great deal of knowledge about that very research—which I do not possess. Instead I have judged it suitable to survey the kinds of material and collections that can be found in the Swedish National Library and the Swedish National Archives and then to exemplify them with representative and interesting documents. Even though the chosen collections may be already listed in existing bibliographies, I want to draw attention to material that provides much more information than has hitherto been exploited.[1]

The official name of the national library is Kungliga Biblioteket (the Royal Library), so named because it belonged to the sovereigns of Sweden. It was not until 1877 that the library was moved from the Royal Palace in Stockholm to its present building. At the same time it received the status of a government authority and its activities and tasks were then controlled by government regulations. The head librarian's title was changed from Konglig Bibliotekarie (Royal Librarian) to Riksbibliotekarie (National Librarian).

Since 1661 a law has prescribed that one copy of everything printed in the country be delivered to the Royal Library, thus making it an archive for Swedish printed matter. The original acquisition policy for manuscripts was to collect anything that was considered valuable. As a result, quite a collection of European illuminated manuscripts from the Middle Ages exists, including one of the most precious manuscripts to be found anywhere: the Canterbury Golden Gospels from eighth-century England, also known as the Codex Aureus (The Golden Book).

The government regulation of 1877, however, prescribed that the Royal Library limit its manuscript acquisitions to those of Swedish interest, meaning those written in Swedish, by Swedes, or concerning Sweden. Apart from this, there is no guideline to direct the library's acquisition of manuscripts. Consequently the growth of the collection today is rather haphazard, depending on what may turn up in terms of donations or offerings on the open market. (In the latter case, the growth of the collection is to a large extent determined by the library's budget, which, I am sorry to say, is low.)

The Riksarkivet (the National Archives) was, like the Royal Library, once accommodated in the Royal Palace. But it has very rarely, if ever, been called Kungliga Arkivet (although Amandus Johnson used the term *Royal Archives* as an equivalent of *Riksarkivet* in the bibliography that concludes his standard work, *The Swedish Settlements on the Delaware*). By the end of the Middle Ages, the archives were known as Riksens Archivum (Archives of the Realm). Ever since then, this has been the official name.

The principal difference between the manuscript collections of the National Archives and the Royal Library is that the growth of the former is partly regulated by law. The main task of the National Archives has been and continues to be receiving and keeping the archives of the Swedish government and its various authorities. (On private collections in the National Archives, see below.) Consequently, when looking for documents concerning New Sweden issued or received by any authority, do not address the Royal Library but rather the National Archives (or possibly a few other official institutions such as Krigsarkivet, the Military Archives).

NEW SWEDEN MATERIAL IN THE ROYAL LIBRARY

The items in the Royal Library are divided into handwritten and printed matter; the material in the National Archives consists only of handwritten documents.

There is no need to devote much time to the inventory of printed books concerning New Sweden. The works in question are listed in several bibliographies, such as the one by Amandus Johnson. Furthermore, the need for these works is not likely to bring any researcher to the Royal Library since no item from this corpus of literature is unique; everything can be found elsewhere, whether in original edition or in facsimile. Nevertheless, it is worth remembering that everything ever printed in Sweden can be found here. Even if there are a few exceptions, the statement should be valid for the works concerning New Sweden.

The library's holographic material on New Sweden is very scanty. In his bibliography Amandus Johnson has only one entry under the heading "Collections of Letters and Documents: *Rålambska Samlingen*," or the collection of Baron Gustaf Claesson Rålamb (1675–1750), consisting mostly of copies of letters and other documents. It also has originals, including Johannes Campanius's records of his voyages to and from America in 1642 and 1648,[2] and the military engineer Peter Lindeström's map and description of Virginia Florida (1654 and 1655).[3]

More can be mentioned from the collection after 1664, the year the English occupied the area that had been New Sweden. Thus, from the year 1727 there is one of the two existing original manuscripts of Bishop Jesper Swedberg's *Svecia Nova seu America Illuminata, thet är Nyja Swerige eller America* (published in 1732).[4]

One of Swedberg's sources for his description of New Sweden was the diary and other notes of his relative Andreas Hesselius,[5] who was pastor of the Swedish parish in Christina between 1711 and 1724. The collection contains a copy of Hesselius's diary written by another hand in 1751, eighteen years after Hesselius died. It is worth mentioning that the leaves of Hesselius's original diary have been scattered, but two of them have been preserved in the Royal Library's collection of autographs.

One of Hesselius's successors in New Sweden was Matthias Hultgren, pastor in Wicacoa from 1779 to 1787. The Royal Library has his extensive notes on the Swedish parishes in America.[6]

Finally I mention a booklet called "Leaves from New Sweden in Pennsylvania & Delaware,"[7] which contains a few clippings from newspapers (such as the *Philadelphia Sunday Times* and the *Sunday Dispatch*) and some notes by the Reverend Nicholas (Nils) Collin (who died in 1831), the last priest to be sent out from Sweden to the former colony in America. The notes concern burials in "the Burial Ground of the Swedes" but do not say where the cemetery is, although we know it is not in Philadelphia.

NEW SWEDEN MATERIAL IN THE NATIONAL ARCHIVES

The collections held by the National Archives consist of official and private papers. In the former belong documents issued or received by any official authority, such as the government, in the past called Kunglig Majestät (The Royal Majesty), or the Four Estates (the nobility, the clergy, the burghers, and the peasantry). An important collection of private papers is the large Oxenstierna Collection, to which I shall return below.

HANDEL OCH SJÖFART (COMMERCE AND SHIPPING COLLECTION)

This collection is of special value for research on New Sweden since it has several of the fundamental documents from 1636 and 1637 that relate to the creation of the Swedish colony. For example, there is the letter that could be said to have started it all: the proposal of Peter Minuit to Chancellor Axel Oxenstierna, dated 15 June 1636.[7] Minuit, former governor of the Dutch colony of New Netherland, argues in his letter that Sweden should undertake the enterprise of founding a colony in America. Minuit is willing to take the task upon himself and to call the colony Nova Svecia.

The collection also contains a number of documents that chronicle most of the central events in New Sweden's history, although there are few official papers concerning the first Swedish voyages to America. (A number of documents such as ships' passports and rolls of crew are preserved in the Military Archives, mentioned above.)

There are also some documents that illustrate the first "America Fever" in Sweden such as a letter to Axel Oxenstierna dated Göteborg, 11 October 1655, from Admiral Mårten Anckarhielm,[8] the captain of the *Mercurius*, the ship used for the last expedition in 1655, saying that he had 119 colonists on board but that another one hundred had crowded on the quay hoping to join them.

Other documents concern such great losses to the colony as the wreck of the ship *Kattan* in the spring of 1649 off Puerto Rico. The French and Spanish inhabitants of the local islands plundered the ship and subjected the people on board to such treatment that most of them died and only nineteen managed to get back to Sweden. There is also a roll of *Kattan*'s crew and a list of its cargo,[9] as well as a roll of the people[10] ready to set out on *Kattan* for New Sweden on 3 July 1649.

An interesting document is a description of New Sweden's natural resources by Johan Claesson Rising,[11] the colony's last governor, appointed on 12 December 1653.

When the ruin of the colony had come by the Dutch siege of Fort Christina in August and September 1655, followed by its surrender on 14 September, Rising wrote an account of the conquest that is also in the collection.[12]

Among the documents concerning the economy of New Sweden is the colony's budget for the year 1642.[13] A list contains the monthly salary payments in Swedish riksdaler for various officials of the colony: the governor and his lieutenant, a number of military men, one chaplain, one scribe, one barber-surgeon, one military policeman, and one executioner. (It may be noted that the executioner earned the same as a private soldier, the lowest rank on the budget.)

Other documents show how tobacco was used as payment in 1643.[14] Tobacco was, in fact, the colony's most important source of income.

There are some interesting documents on the Indians. I will discuss the most important ones later, but in the Handel och Sjöfart Collection there are some remarkable purchase-deeds,[15] drawn up by the Swedes but formally issued by five Indian chiefs, mentioned by name, who by their marks confirmed Swedish purchases of land.

Closely associated with New Sweden is the name of Peter Lindeström. This engineer's most important works are not in the Handel och Sjöfart Collection, but there is an interesting letter from him dated Fort Christiana, 9 July 1654, in which he informs the Swedish Board of Trade about his plans for a town to be named Christina.[16]

The population of New Sweden is profiled in the collection by lists of colonists and workers,[17] one for the years 1643 to 1644, the other dated 1 March 1648.[18] The lists account for seventy-nine persons, all of them male, who had emigrated to New Sweden between 1639 and 1648 and who were alive in 1648.

KAMMARARKIVET (THE ARCHIVES OF THE EXCHEQUER)

Today these archives are a section of the National Archives, but in the past they were a separate institution, listed as such in Amandus Johnson's bibliography. This collection contains documents of a decidedly but not exclusively economic character. The borderline between the documents in the Handel och Sjöfart Collection and the corresponding ones in the Archives of the Exchequer is vague as far as the contents are concerned.

These archives contain one of the most important legal documents on New Sweden, a contemporary German translation of the testimony given to the notary of Amsterdam in December 1638 by some of Peter Minuit's men on the *Kalmar Nyckel*, after returning from the first visit to the recently founded colony.[19] (Remember that Minuit himself had died a few months earlier in a storm in the West Indies from which the *Kalmar Nyckel* barely escaped.) The returning Swedes report on the first Swedish purchase of land from the Indians. To our knowledge, no deed was drawn up to confirm the business, so this document has to be regarded as the legal basis of the Swedish possession of the territory.

One of the first international protests concerning the Swedish claim is also in this collection. In a note of 18 March 1642,[20] the English governor of Virginia maintains that, by virtue of the discovery of the South River (the Delaware), the English are the rightful possessors of the land; he demands that the Swedish colony submit to English rule.

Three documents concerning the third governor of New Sweden, Johan

Printz, are his original commission,[21] issued by the regency council for Queen Christina in 1642, an evaluation of his estates in New Sweden (consisting of three tobacco plantations),[22] and his genealogical table.[23]

PRÄSTESTÅNDETS ARKIV (THE ARCHIVE OF THE CLERGY)

This collection has a few important documents concerning certain colonists of New Sweden and the colony's church life. The items mentioned here are all from the last decade of the seventeenth century. Two letters are appeals for pastors and religious books, one dated 1 October 1691, in which Lars Riddermark and Johan Thelin ask for Bibles and hymnbooks.[24] They want seventy Bibles, fifty Swedish and twenty Finnish ones, which may reflect the size of the Finnish population at that time.

The second is an undated letter written by one of the most prominent of all the Swedish colonists in America, the first ancestor of a widely spread American family, Petter Gunnarsson Rambo.[25] The letter is addressed to his sister in Sweden and tells about his marriage to Britta Matsdotter from Vasa, Finland (then belonging to Sweden), and of their eight children and thirty-seven grandchildren. He ends the letter by saying that they live in "a mighty wonderful fertile country" and "in peace with the Indians." Considering the number of Rambo's offspring at the time, one is inclined to believe that at least twenty-five years have elapsed since his marriage (1648) and that the letter was written in the 1670s at the earliest.

One of the most amazing careers of all the Swedes in seventeenth-century America is that of Karl Christoffersson Springer, at least as far as can be judged from a letter to his mother dated 1 June 1693.[26] According to this letter, he first went to London, where he was taken captive and forcibly brought over the Atlantic. In America he had to work as a slave until, after some years, he managed to escape and reach New Sweden, where he served as a lay preacher during the two last decades of the century.

MANUSKRIPTSAMLINGEN OCH KARTOR OCH RITNINGAR (THE MANUSCRIPT COLLECTION AND THE COLLECTION OF MAPS AND DRAWINGS)

These collections have a few of the most important of all documents concerning New Sweden during its existence, namely the journals and maps of Peter Lindeström.[27] Among these are his famous work *Geographia Americae*, completed in 1691, many years after his return to Sweden.

There are also a number of maps, the most famous of which is his original map of the Delaware and the settlements along the river.[28]

Oxenstiernska Samlingen (The Oxenstierna Collection)

I will end this brief survey of the collections of the National Archives by mentioning a few documents that it received during the nineteenth century. This collection has been of the utmost importance for the study of New Sweden's early history. The first scholar to recognize its significance in this context was Claes Theodor Odhner in his work *Sveriges inre historia under drottning Christina förmyndare* (Stockholm, 1865).

For the most part the collection consists of letters, of which I shall give three examples. The first is a letter of 20 June 1644 in which Governor Printz communicates that he had 2,143 beaver pelts to be sent to Sweden.[29] The second item consists of several accounts of the fate of the *Kattan* expedition, delivered to Axel Oxenstierna by Johan Johansson Rudd, one of the few who came back.[30] The last is another letter from Governor Printz to Axel Oxenstierna dated 1 August 1651.[31] The governor's military force consisted of only thirty men, and he demands two ships and six or seven hundred soldiers to be able to confront the threats of the Dutch and English.

Rules and Regulations of the Institutions

One should keep a few things in mind when using the Royal Library and the National Archives. The policies of Swedish official libraries and archives are very liberal. Everything as old as the items dealt with by the New Sweden conference is accessible without special formalities. As a rule, letters of introduction will not be required.

I should also mention that in Sweden there are no copyright regulations regarding original documents as old as those of New Sweden. The Swedish copyright legislation decrees that a work is protected by copyright for fifty years after the death of the originator. Furthermore, the copyright is a matter entirely between the user and the originator, not between the user and the lending institution, whether the institution is the owner of the object or not. This means that a user of a document from a public collection in Sweden will never need permission to publish from the institution in question. (On the other hand, should less than fifty years have elapsed since the death of the originator, there is a possibility that the item in question may be protected by copyright and, in that case, a permission to publish may be required and should be obtained from the originator or, in case of this person's death, from the legal heirs).

Both the Royal Library and the National Archives provide complete reproduction services although the Royal Library does not provide microfiche copies.

NOTES

1. For information about the Swedish National Archives I am greatly indebted to Dr. Kari Tarkiainen of that institution. My account of the collections of the National Archives is based entirely on Dr. Tarkiainen's inventory for an exhibition on New Sweden presented by the National Archives in 1988. Without access to the manuscript of Dr. Tarkiainen's exhibition catalogue, this task would have exceeded my ability.
2. Rålamb Folio 201, Manuscript Collection, Kungliga Biblioteket (hereafter cited as KB), Stockholm.
3. Ibid.
4. A 1021, Manuscript Collection, KB.
5. A 248, Manuscript Collection, KB.
6. D 1501, Manuscript Collection, KB.
7. D 1502, Manuscript Collection, KB.
8. Handel och Sjöfart, vol. 194, Riksarkivet (hereafter cited as RA), Stockholm.
9. Ibid.
10. Ibid.
11. Ibid., vol. 196.
12. Ibid., vol. 194.
13. Ibid.
14. Ibid.
15. Ibid., vols. 44–50.
16. Ibid., vol. 194.
17. Ibid.
18. Ibid.
19. Ibid.
20. Kammararkivet, Handel och Sjöfart, vol. 42, RA.
21. Ibid.
22. Kammararkivet, Likvidationer, Försträckningar och leveranser 94:221, RA.
23. Kammararkivet, Handel och Sjöfart, vol. 42, RA.
24. Kammararkivet, Likvidationer, Försträckningar och leveranser 94:221, RA.
25. Prästeståndets arkiv R. 1100.
26. Ibid.
27. Ibid.
28. Manuskriptsamlingen 62, RA.
29. Ibid.
30. Oxenstiernska samlingen E691, RA.
31. Ibid., E700, RA.
32. Ibid., E691, RA.

Sources and Questions in the Study of Finnish Migration to Delaware

OLAVI KOIVUKANGAS

FINNS IN DELAWARE

During the seventeenth century about five hundred Finns settled on the banks of the Delaware River. Considering that the total number of emigrants to New Sweden numbered about one thousand, the proportion of Finns was considerable. According to many scholars, the majority of the permanent settlers were Finns, possibly because many Swedes returned to their native land after the Dutch invasion in 1655. Another reason may be that the most important governor of the colony, Johan Printz, had lived in Finland before his departure for Delaware in 1642 and had recruited quite a number of settlers from Ostrobothnia.

The Finnish settlements in Delaware were widely scattered, especially after the English invasion of 1664, when many Finns moved further north to what is now Pennsylvania. The most significant settlement, Finland, which was about ten miles north of Wilmington, is now known as Marcus Hook. There were also major Finnish settlements along the Schuylkill River. Finns also settled on the eastern side of the Delaware River, in present-day New Jersey. Their settlements, Finns Point and Mullica, are still known by these names.

There is little left of the original Finnish settlements. In addition to a few log cabins, only half a dozen stone churches, built jointly with the Swedes, remain as permanent monuments. Gravestones with Finnish names can be found in the churchyards. When Professor Pehr Kalm from the University of Turku visited the former colony of New Sweden in 1748 to 1751, he found that Finnish was no longer spoken. By the early nineteenth century Swedish, too, had died out.[1]

The most renowned descendant of the Finnish settlers in Delaware was John Morton, who, as of the Pennsylvania Assembly, was a signer of the Declaration of Independence in 1776. According to the church register of Wicacoa, his great-grandfather, Marten Martenson, Sr., who died in 1706 at the age of about one hundred years, was born in Finland.

Sources of Finnish Emigration to Delaware

The identification of the Finnish settlers and their descendants in Delaware is a difficult, if not an impossible, task. The major sources of information for the migration of Finns to Delaware are in the Swedish National Archives (Fyrverkarbacken 13–17, 10026 Stockholm):

1. Rolls and registers of passenger lists from the ships that brought the settlers over, as well as the colonial surveys, notably the catalogue of original Swedish and Finnish settlers drawn up by the colonists themselves in 1693.

2. The accounts of the New Sweden Company, especially the Great Book for 1637–57, where all economic transactions are recorded.

3. The National Archives in Stockholm has other valuable primary sources such as letters and reports that contain information about the colonists. The most important of these is a letter from Lars Riddermark and Johan Thelin, dated Stockholm, 1 October 1691. The letter, based on information from Anders Printz in Delaware, requested, in addition to pastors, twenty Finnish Bibles, two hundred Finnish hymnbooks, fifty Swedish Bibles, and three to four hundred Swedish hymnbooks. Another important document is a list of 971 Swedish and Finnish colonists living in the former colony of New Sweden in 1693.

These valuable sources require careful critical reading since they were written for various motives.[2] For example, the numbers of Finnish and Swedish religious books do not give the right proportions of the Swedish and Finnish segments in the colony since Swedish was the official language of the colony and was used by the church and in the schools. Also, in the list of 971 settlers sent to Sweden in 1693, it is impossible to tell who is a Swede or a Finn. It can also be argued that not all the colonists were included, especially the Finns who often lived in the outback while the Swedes preferred to live in towns.

4. The next most important source for New Sweden documents is Provincial Archives in Sweden. As far as the Delaware emigration and settlement are concerned, the most important sources are the parish registers (Uppsala domkapitel F VIII) kept by the Swedish pastors sent to the colony. Unfortunately the earliest of these are lost, although Pehr Kalm's valuable notes do survive. This material, located in the Provincial Archives of Uppsala, is also on microcards and can be ordered from the Swedish Archives Information, Box 160,88040, Ramsele, Sweden.

In the period of the colonization of Delaware, Finland was an integral part of Sweden and was administered from Stockholm. Consequently the major sources can be found there, but additional information can be traced in other parts of Sweden and Finland, notably at the archives of the Lutheran church in Uppsala and in the provinces of central Sweden,

the home of most of the Forest Finns who later sailed to Delaware. Perhaps the most important source will be various archives in Värmland, notably the Provincial Archives, which include local church, parish, and
court records. Similar sources may be in existence on the Norwegian
side of the border, where Finnish settlement had expanded in the early
seventeenth century.

No one has as yet investigated sources in Finland, nor has any Finnish
scholar taken up the study of the Finns in Delaware. Only a few articles
have been written from published sources. Professor Martti Kerkkonen
believes that little additional material is to be found in Finland; I am not
that pessimistic, however.

At the National Archives (Rauhankatu 17, 00170 Helsinki), I found
two contemporary documents relating, at least indirectly, to the Delaware emigration. Governor Johan Printz's name appears in a payroll for
the Province of Ostrobothnia in 1644 (VA Läänintilit 9114, pp. 64–65).

In another document, a roll of officers and soldiers in 1641, the name of
Lieutenant Sven Skute was discovered (VA Läänintilit 9109, pp. 264–65).
Skute had served for many years on the battlefields of Europe under Major Johan Printz, and it is not surprising that Skute followed his master
when Printz was appointed governor. Skute, from the parish of Kronoby
in northern Ostrobothnia, was second in command during most of the
period of the colony. He was sent back to Sweden to make an oral report
to the queen and the Council of the State. Skute also played a key role
when the colony fell into the hands of the Dutch in 1655.[3]

People from Ostrobothnia had left for Delaware even before Printz's
governorship. In the history of Korsholm, it is recorded that Marten
Knutson left for Sweden and in 1641 sailed in one of the first ships, the
Charitas, to Delaware.[4] He was probably recruited by Måns Kling. In
Delaware there were Finnish settlements known as New Korsholm and
New Vasa. The old church records of the Vaasa region, located in the
parishes, the provincial archives, and the National Archives should be investigated. Probably there would not be many, if any, direct references to
the Delaware emigration, but since we know the names of emigrants from
the Swedish and American sources, it would be interesting to try to find
the places these people came from. As indicated by Karl-Gustav Olin's
study, more emigrants to Delaware obviously came from the Swedish-
speaking coastal area of Ostrobothnia than has previously been thought.

Other places of Finnish origin were Savolaz and northern Tavastland in
central Finland. Some twelve thousand ethnic Finns had moved from
here to central Sweden between 1580 and 1630, and a few hundred of
these later moved on to Delaware. Did this group include the friends
and relatives of the burn-beating Finns who moved directly from Savolaz
to Delaware? So far there has been no attempt to trace the family names

found in Delaware on the map of central Finland. Although many Finnish names were Swedicized, and later Anglicized, it might be possible to find some clusters of places of origin by using old parish and taxation records. The nucleus of the Savo emigration, via Finnish burn-beating settlements in Sweden, was the large Rautalampi parish.

Although the Finnish emigration to Delaware stands on two legs, one in Ostrobothnia and the other in Savolax (mainly via central Sweden), a few settlers originated from southern Finland and even from Karelia. (There is also a possibility that some Finns emigrated from northern Finland. This supposition is based on the names of two early settlements: Tornea and Lapland.) The Finnish-born director of the New Sweden Company, Admiral Klaus Fleming, suggested that some minor criminals from Turku (Åbo) should be transported to Delaware.[5] Unfortunately the early court proceedings of Turku were destroyed in the fire of 1827. Perhaps in the archives of other major towns' courts, or in the correspondence with Stockholm officials, some supplementary information might be found. The best place to start would be the National Archives in Helsinki. Here, as well as in the Provincial Archives of Turku and the local church and other archives in Maarianhamina on the Åland Island, some material could perhaps be found. It is recorded that there was at least one transported seaman from Åland as early as in the second expedition that arrived in 1640.

One very important source of information is the original diary of Professor Pehr Kalm, who visited North America from 1748 to 1751, a century after the Delaware colonization. The diary is kept in the Helsinki University Library (Unioninkatu 36, 00170 Helsinki). Kalm frequently copied old church records and interviewed old people. His famous diary has been published in many languages, but for a real scholar, only the original will do since editors may have left something out or misunderstood the handwriting. Kalm's diary for December 1748 has an interesting entry; he had heard that the English, and especially William Penn, were in the habit of collecting old Swedish church records and other early documents in Delaware.[6] Presumably Penn took these papers back with him to England. It would be marvelous if these valuable documents could be found somewhere in England.

PREVIOUS STUDIES

In the seventeenth century the Finnish presence in Delaware was well recognized; after that, until the twentieth century, the Finns were more or less forgotten. Even the great Amandus Johnson in his 1911 magnum opus did not give the Finns fair treatment. As Richard H. Hulan points out, Johnson was not especially interested in the Finns, although evidence of their numerical significance can be found in the lists that he published.[7] In a way it is a pity that Johnson immediately became such an authority because his seemingly exhaustive study has perhaps discouraged later American, Swedish, or Finnish scholars from taking an interest in the topic and tackling the original archival sources of the Delaware migration.

Similarly, only a few American historians of Finnish origin have studied the Delaware Finns. The Reverend Salomon Ilmonen spent years studying the history of Finns in North America, and in 1916 published a book on the Finns in Delaware. His book was published in Finland in 1938.[8] He was a good scholar, although he did not give detailed information concerning the sources of his data. Then, in England and New York in 1925, E. A. Louhi published an extremely pro-Finnish book on the Finns in Pennsylvania and adjoining colonies.[9] In conjunction with the tercentenary celebration of New Sweden in 1938, Professor John O. Wuorinen wrote a small book, which was, however, to a great extent based on the works of Amandus Johnson.[10]

In addition to the above-mentioned histories are a few literary works, such as Akesli Jarnefelt-Fauanheimo's novel *Before William Penn*, published in 1921 in Finnish and in English in 1929.

QUESTIONS FOR INVESTIGATION

As appears from the above account, there is no systematic and methodologically sound investigation of the Nordic Delaware immigration from the Finnish perspective. A major target in the future should be a comprehensive history of the Finnish factor in the migration to and settlement of the Delaware River valley. Naturally this study should be placed in the correct historical context and background.

As chapters of a comprehensive study, or as separate topics, I would suggest the following themes:

Place of origin

The Finnish settlers in Delaware were an extension of the expansion of the burn-beating settlers, first to the unpopulated areas of central Finland, then the hilly forest of western central Sweden, and finally to the fertile Delaware River valley. This emigration of some twelve thousand persons from Finland to Värmland and other Swedish provinces has been studied to some extent. Dr. Kari Tarkianinen from the National Archives in Stockholm has recently launched a project to write a history of the Finns in Sweden before World War II. An interesting problem concerns how long the Delaware Finns lived in Sweden before their departure for America and to what degree they had become acculturated to Swedish life and language. Much of this settlement took place in the 1620s and 1630s, including some on Norwegian territory. Because the Finns were quite isolated in the great forests, they were able to maintain their language and traditions for decades.

The large number of Finns migrating from Sweden to Delaware may have contributed to the fact that those who moved directly from Finland have received less attention. It now seems likely that more Finnish immigrants than had previously been thought came to Delaware either from Finland directly or left Sweden after only a short stay. Many Finnish men, especially those from Ostrobothnia, were in the habit of going to Sweden to work during the winter months. As mentioned earlier, Governor Johan Printz lived in Korsholm near Vaasa before his departure for America. He recruited emigrants to travel with him, and during his ten years in Delaware had contacts with Ostrobothnia. At present Ostrobothnia is quite interested in the genealogical background of the emigrants to Delaware.

The number of Finns who went to Delaware

The number of Finns who went to Delaware can only be estimated and varies considerably depending whether the definition includes (1) the period under Swedish rule, 1638–55; (2) the period under Dutch rule as well, 1655–64; or (3) the whole seventeenth century. S. Ilmonen counted 295 Finns in Delaware from 1638 to 1664. Considering that many Swedes left the colony after the Dutch occupation, he estimated the number of permanent Swedish settlers to be somewhat over one hundred.[11]

In 1983 the Swedish scholar Ivan Bill estimated that during the Swedish and Dutch periods, from 1638 to 1664, about one thousand colonists arrived in New Sweden. These were mainly burn-beater Finns from Sweden who made up some 75 percent of all the settlers.[12] Until more accurate information becomes available, we can therefore estimate the number of Finns moving to Delaware in the seventeenth century to be about five hundred to six hundred persons.[13]

Settlements, adjustment, and acculturation

The Finns often settled in the outlying areas, apart from the Swedes and at peace with the Indians. In the extensive forests of Delaware they continued their ancient form of agriculture by burn-beating. Quite early the Finns started to disperse to Maryland,[14] as well as to the other adjoining colonies. In addition to better economic opportunities, their migration was caused by the harsh rule of Governor Printz. The Finns also settled early in New Amsterdam, later New York. Mans Stack from Turku was a founder of Harlem and his three sons, Peter, Matthew, and Israel, settled there permanently, under the name of Stock.[15] How far north and west this internal migration reached might be another interesting topic.

The second generation adopted the Swedish language, mainly because the Lutheran church and the schools operated in that language. An open question is whether the Reverend Mr. Lars Lock, regarded as the pastor to the Finns, conducted Divine Services in Finnish. By the third generation, both the Swedes and the Finns had adopted English. How this transition took place would make a topic for a separate study. Did the colonial Finnish language disappear completely in America, as this reading of the evidence indicates?[16] A scholar with a command of the Finnish and Swedish languages might well find some interesting new information.

Genealogical research

Almost all the Finns who migrated remained in the New World, although a few returned. According to Ilmonen, Lieutenant Måns Kling, who arrived in the first expedition in 1638 and was left in command of Fort Christina, was a Finn. He returned to Sweden in 1640 and was sent to recruit Finns from central Sweden to Delaware. In 1641 he set out again for New Sweden with a number of colonists but then returned permanently to Sweden with his family in 1648.[17] Was he really a Finn? There are good reasons to believe so. He was a good friend of Klaus Fleming, and since he was sent to recruit Finns to Delaware, he must have spoken Finnish. Peter Hollander Ridder, who was the second governor of the colony from 1640 to 1643, was the son of the Dutch merchant Hans Hollander Ridder and his wife, Anne Robertsdotter from Tammisaari (Ekenas). Thus there are many interesting Finnish characters to be studied. This group would include both those who returned and the descendants of the Finnish colonists who became the early builders of the future nation.

To promote the New Sweden research in general, I make the following two proposals:

(1) An up-to-date bibliography of the New Sweden immigration and settlement in the Delaware River valley is needed, including information on research in progress.
(2) A list of original material in various archives and libraries in Europe and America that could be the basis for plans to have the most important sources translated from Swedish and Dutch to English would be invaluable.

Most especially, I hope that a Finnish historian will take up the study of the Finns in Delaware and their contribution to their new home country.

This would serve not only as a history of the Finnish people but also as part of the history of the redistribution of European population overseas in search of better opportunities for themselves and for their unborn children.

Notes

1. This summary of the Finns in Delaware is based on Olavi Koivukangas, *Delaware 350: The Beginning of Finnish Migration to the New World* (Turku: Institute of Migration, 1988); and "The First Finnish Settlement, Delaware," *Look at Finland* 1 (1988): 12–13.
2. Kari Tarkiainen, "The Emigration of Swedish-Finnish Burnbeaters to Delaware," *Siirtolaisuus-Migration* 2 (1989): 4–10.
3. Karl-Gustav Olin, "Delaware 350—A Finnish View," *Siirtolaisuus-Migration* 2 (1989): 19. See also Olin, *Våra första amerikafarare: Historien om finlandssvenskarna i Nya Sverige* (Jakobstad: Ab Olimex Oy, 1988).
4. K. V. Akerblom, *Korsholms historia I* (Vaasa: Korsholms kommuns forlag, n.d.), 236–38.
5. Amandus Johnson, *The Swedish Settlements on the Delaware: Their History and Relation to the Indians, Dutch and English, 1638–1664*, 2 vols. (Philadelphia: Swedish Colonial Society, 1911), 239.
6. Martti Kerkkonen, "Delawaren siirtokunta ja Pietari Kalm," *Historiallinen aikakauskirja* 2 (1938): 4.
7. Richard H. Hulan, "New Sweden Bibliography," unpublished manuscript, 1985, copy at the Institute of Migration, Turku, Finland.
8. S. Ilmonen, *Amerikan ensimäiset suomalaiset eli Delawaren siirtokunnan historia* (Hancock, Mich.: Suomalais-Luteerilaisen Kustannusliikkeen Kirjapaino, 1916).
9. E. A. Louhi, *The Delaware Finns, or the First Permanent Settlements in Pennsylvania, Delaware, West New Jersey and the Eastern Part of Maryland* (New York: Humanity Press, 1925).
10. John O. Wuorinen, *The Finns on the Delaware* (New York: Columbia University Press, 1938).
11. S. Ilmonen, *Delawaren suomalaiset* (Hameenlinna: Karisto Oy, 1938), 52.
12. Ivan Bill, "Svedjefinnar koloniserade Delaware," *Folkets Historia* 11, no. 1 (1938): 37.
13. Koivukangas, *Delaware 350*, 1988.
14. George Ely Russell, "The Swedish Settlement in Maryland, 1654," *American Genealogist* 54 (1978): 203, 210.
15. John O. Evjen, *Scandinavian Immigrants in New York, 1630–1674* (Baltimore: Genealogical Publishing Co., 1972), 342; Louhi, *The Delaware Finns*, 188.
16. A. R. Dunlap and E. J. Moyne, "The Finnish Language on the Delaware," *American Speech* 27, no. 2 (1952): 86.
17. Ilmonen, *Delaware suomalaiset*, 176–78.

Summary, Criticism, and Comments on Future Directions in the Study of New Sweden

C. A. WESLAGER

We have reached the end of what certainly will be rated as an unusual and highly constructive conference. We have had what in the American academic world are known as twenty-three "preparations," which can be translated to mean that if the program were undertaken by one teacher that he or she would be called upon to do the research for twenty-three lectures on different topics and then deliver them to a class of students with diverse interests in a period of less than three days. Since that task would be impossible conferences and symposia become necessary so that scholars in a variety of disciplines can present their individual views to an interested audience, including the other speakers.

If everything has worked out as it should, the audience, as well as the speakers, should all leave better informed than they were before and be stimulated to continue their research. As one of the participants, I can say that this certainly applies to me; in fact, I consider the New Sweden conference a unique intellectual experience.

Those who planned this conference selected useful categories to constitute the agenda of papers:

1. Colonists and Native Americans
2. The Swedish Colonial Adventure
3. Life and Culture of the Swedish Colony
4. Comparative Material Culture: Sweden and England and Their Colonies in the Seventeenth Century
5. Long-term Effects of the Swedish Colony in America
6. Historiographical Sources and New Directions in the Study of New Sweden

---

At the opening dinner of the conference on 3 March 1988, Dr. Weslager was presented with the University of Delaware Medal of Distinction by President Russel C. Jones and J. Bruce Bredin, chairman of the Board of Trustees, in recognition of his books and papers dealing with early Delaware Valley history.

Other topics might have been included, but I am not aware that any of the participants felt that this listing was too restrictive. The listeners may have wished for more opportunity for audience participation, but the large number of registrants necessitated the time restrictions imposed by the moderators. Moreover, conferences like this one are not academic seminars and the thirty-minute presentations are not intended to provoke exhaustive discussions.

We Americans are indebted to those speakers whose native tongues are Swedish or Finnish because we were able to meet and communicate with them in our language. I can't imagine trying to attack the twenty-three topics covered in this conference through interpreters.

Certainly this conference is proof of the usefulness of the English language to the humanities. As an American I do not say this boastfully because we can take no credit for the proficiency of our foreign guests in our language. It is you Swedes and Finns who have undergone the linguistic pains, and what a fine job you have done. We are grateful and we thank you.

The uniqueness of the conference lies in the fact that no international symposium on New Sweden has ever been held before. One should not infer that there have not been cultural contacts between the United States and Sweden, even though historians, anthropologists, geographers, folklorists, and other scholars have not previously met as a body to exchange views. For example, so far as I can determine the first Swedish-American celebration was held in Minneapolis on 14 September 1888. It was conceived by Colonel Hans Mattson, who presided over the festivities intended to commemorate the two hundred and fiftieth anniversary of the first Swedish settlement in America. A heavy rain that started early in the day caused the scheduled parade to be abandoned, but fifteen thousand people gathered in the Exposition Building for a three-hour program of speeches, band playing, and choral music. Colonel Mattson sent a cablegram to King Oscar II in Stockholm, and the king's chamberlain wired back his majesty's best wishes for the prosperity of the Scandinavian colony in Minneapolis.[1]

This was not, however, an exclusively midwestern celebration that lacked moral support from the East. The mayor of Wilmington, Delaware, sent a congratulatory letter to Colonel Mattson, and the Wilmington City Council passed a resolution expressing cordial greetings. Accompanying the resolution was a letter containing brief historical notes by Horace Burr, who had just completed translating into English the records of Wilmington's Old Swedes Church (Holy Trinity), then awaiting publication.[2] Apparently no celebration was held in any of the three states in the Delaware Valley that cradled the colony—Delaware, New Jersey, and Pennsylvania.

Almost forty years later, Crown Prince Gustaf Adolph (later Gustaf VI Adolph) and Crown Princess Louise, visited Washington, D.C., for the unveiling of the John Ericsson Memorial on 29 May 1926. Congress appropriated thirty-five thousand dollars for this memorial, which was built next to the Lincoln Memorial, and twenty-five thousand dollars was contributed by American citizens of Swedish birth or parentage.[3] The royal guests also made a fast visit to Old Swedes Church in Wilmington on 31 May, and during this stay the Crown Prince laid the cornerstone of the American Swedish Historical Museum in Philadelphia.

Although 1926 was not a memorial year, one relevant historical publication appeared, written by Henry D. Paxson, vice president of the Swedish Colonial Society of Pennsylvania, to commemorate the visit of their Royal Highnesses.[4]

I was present in another driving rain in Wilmington twelve years later during the celebration of the Swedish-American Tercentenary in 1938. On the morning of 27 June, as the rain continued, Prince Bertil presented the monument sculpted by Carl Milles to President Franklin D. Roosevelt at Fort Christina Park on behalf of the Swedish people. His father, the same crown prince who visited in 1926, was confined to a sick bed on the *Kungsholm*, anchored in the Delaware River, and was unable to make the presentation as planned. The Swedish people contributed 226,500 kronor to the monument fund, more than was needed, and the surplus of 1,656 kronor and 96 öre was turned over to the American Swedish Museum in Philadelphia.

I witnessed the parade and pageantry that followed in downtown Wilmington that afternoon, as the rain continued unabated. There was no academic forum to attend, rain or shine. Some of us may then have foolishly thought that Dr. Amandus Johnson had said everything that could be said in 879 pages of his hefty two-volume work, *Swedish Settlements on the Delaware*, published in Philadelphia in 1911, followed by two briefer books, *The Swedes in America 1638–1900* (1914) and *The Swedes on the Delaware 1638–1664* (1927), which are identical to each other in content and pagination.

Nevertheless, the occasion was not devoid of new publications. Christopher Ward, chairman of the executive committee of the Delaware Tercentenary Commission, authorized two small books to be published in conjunction with the celebration.[5]

I have since read that English-speaking lecturers from Sweden made 270 appearances on a number of American college and university campuses in 1937 and 1938 to discuss New Sweden, although I have not been able to locate a schedule of their appearances.[6] I have not found any evidence that American universities reciprocated by sending faculty members to Sweden to lecture at Swedish institutions, which is not surprising. American scholars who were well informed about the history of New Sweden were less numerous fifty years ago than they are today.

Another twenty-five years passed. and in the spring of 1963, special programs were held in Wilmington, Philadelphia, southern New Jersey, and Sweden to commemorate the three hundred and twenty-fifth anniversary of the founding of New Sweden. On 29 March Prince Bertil made his second visit to Wilmington. I well remember the occasion, but I have no recollection of the issuance of any historical publications or books. The two issues of *Delaware History* in 1963 contain nothing relevant to New Sweden, which suggests no contributions were submitted.

As we critically examine the present conference, it is obvious that it would be presumptive of one auditor to attempt to make judgments on the medley of papers presented in three days. I would prefer to call constructive attention to topics that I believe could have received more careful examination; the first is Swedish-Lenape relations in the seventeenth century. A myth has grown, and this applies especially to hyperbolic popular accounts published in Sweden, that the Lenape and the early Swedes and Finns were always the best of friends.

Those who are familiar with the dialogue in the Lenape dialect that Johan Campanius Holm recorded in his notes between the Lenape chief, Matta Horn, and his son, Agga Horn, during Governor Johan Printz's administration are aware that the Lenape purportedly debated whether or not to kill all the Swedes. Their reason was, "They have no cloth, red, blue or brown. They have not kettles, no brass, no lead, no guns, no powder; they have nothing to sell us; but the English and Dutch have got all sorts of good merchandise." The final decision made by the chiefs was that they would not kill the Swedes because the Indians were promised that a ship would soon arrive from Sweden with a large supply of trade goods.[7]

When ships with trade goods did not arrive to barter for their furs, the Indians were angered that Printz had broken his promise. In an official report Printz wrote that as a consequence, "they murdered a man and wife on their bed, and a few days afterwards they killed two soldiers and a workman."[8]

Because of these deaths, Printz summoned the Lenape chiefs to a treaty conference, where he warned them that

in case they thereafter practiced the smallest hostility against our people we would not let a soul of them live upon which they gave their writing and all their sachems signed their names to it (according to their custom) gave us 20 beaver [pelts] and some sewant [shell beads], and we presented them with a piece of cloth in return. But they do not trust us, and we trust them still less.[9]

Printz's successor, Governor Johan Rising, also ran into problems with the Lenape. In a report dated 14 June 1655 he complained that

> Our neighbours the Renappi [Lenape] threaten not only to kill our people in the land and ruin them, before we can become stronger and prevent such things, but also to destroy even the trade, both with the Minques and the other savage nations, as well as with the Christians. We must daily buy their friendship with presents, for they are and continue to be hostile, and worse than they have been hitherto.[10]

Without belaboring the question by adding further citations, I believe that an uneasy friendship existed between Swedes and Lenape at certain times, and at other times the relationship was hostile. Neither this ambivalence nor its effects on the daily life of the families settled in New Sweden were brought out during the conference.

I observed that both American and Swedish scholars gave undue importance to a book by Thomas Campanius Holm, published in Stockholm in 1702. Holm based his book on Peter Lindeström's manuscript journal and the notes of his grandfather, Johan Campanius, who was a Lutheran pastor in New Sweden from 1643 to 1648.[11] There has been only one English version of this work, which Amandus Johnson characterized as "poorly translated" by "one unequal to the task."[12] Future studies of New Sweden should by all means include a new English translation of this work, suitably annotated.

Thomas Campanius Holm was never in America and his book contains obvious errors in general history. An engraver, he capitalized on the interest in American Indians in Sweden by including illustrations in his book which allegedly depicted Lenape life. Actually he never saw a Lenape Indian in the native habitat. Dr. Herbert Kraft has shown that Holm's drawings of a fortified Indian village and Indians traveling in canoes were copied from embellishments on early Dutch maps and do not apply to the Lenape. Furthermore, Holm's imaginative frontispiece, which illustrates Lenape Indians bartering with Swedish traders, is inaccurate in regard to Lenape dress, houses, and the battle and burial scenes superimposed on the engraving.[13] Unfortunately these illustrations have been reprinted in historical volumes published in both Sweden and America, but they do not accurately portray Lenape culture.

Among the outstanding papers read at the symposium were several dealing with the early Finns, another area that deserves more research. Confusion still exits as to whether certain individuals who played an active part in the colony were Swedes or Finns. What contributions were made by Finns, compared to the Swedes? As we are aware, many Finnish and Swedish names and the majority of Finns who arrived on the early voyages were from Sweden, not Finland. Amandus Johnson did not ignore the Finns in his monumental volume, but neither did he treat them in depth. Only two books published in America deal with the Finns in the colony; one, written by a competent historian, contains only 179 pages and leaves much unsaid.[14] Ironically the second, with 331 pages, has no documentation and is factually untrustworthy.[15] The topic is worthy of high priority among Finnish historians and sociologists.

By design the focus of the conference was on New Sweden, but how about the influence of the American colony on the culture in Sweden and Finland? We have seen that letters were written by Peter Gunnarson Rambo and Lars Persson Cock to relatives in Sweden, and Timen Stiddem wrote a touching letter about the death of his wife and three small children when the *Katt*, enroute to New Sweden, was wrecked in Puerto Rico. Did this and other correspondence play any part in shaping attitudes in Sweden toward the New World? How about the officers, soldiers, and company employees who returned to Sweden with Governor Printz in 1653 and with Governor Rising in 1656? They must have talked or written about their experiences in America. Was interest aroused in Sweden to come to America, or did their reports have an opposite effect?

It is well known how the demand for European trade goods in the fur trade changed the material culture of the eastern Indians, but how did the thousands of animal pelts and the tons of American tobacco affect the Swedish market and Scandinavian economic history? Does this not hold an important direction for future study?

Of paramount importance in mapping out directions for future study, it seems to me, is the task of making available English translations of documentary material in Swedish archival collections. Ways must be found to make known the unpublished and untranslated letters written by Peter Spiring, who represented Sweden in Amsterdam when the New Sweden venture was being planned. Johnson wrote that there were six large bundles of his letters in the Royal Archives, mostly written in German, but many in Dutch.[16] Peter Hollander Ridder also had extensive correspondence relating to the colony that likewise awaits translation.[17]

Hendrick von Elswick's journal and letters also remain to be translated into English. Since he was the factor in New Sweden in 1654, when Rising surrendered to Stuyvesant, one might expect his papers to contain useful historical information.[18]

Many other untranslated manuscripts unquestionably contain valuable historical data. I learned with great pleasure that two of the Swedish participants in the conference have been working on the unpublished journal of Johan Rising, the publication of which will be a significant contribution to the history of New Sweden.[19]

Some means should also be found to make available to scholars in Sweden and Finland papers and books, or photocopies of them, published in

America that deal with the New Sweden colony. The absence of relevant books well known to American scholars is conspicuous in the bibliographies of some of the papers presented at this symposium because of the unavailability of the references in Swedish or Finnish institutions. By the same token, American historians should be kept appraised of pertinent works published in the Scandinavian countries pertaining to New Sweden. There is no easy answer to the problem, but if human beings can walk on the moon, they should be able to set up a clearing house between an American and a Swedish university library so that scholars' needs will be fulfilled.

Finally, the gratifying question has been raised several times during this conference about the date of the next one. If history repeats itself, some kind of celebration will be held somewhere in A.D. 2038 for the four-hundredth anniversary of the New Sweden colony. I'm afraid I will have to pass that one up. I can't wait that long and others of us will also miss it. This has been a wonderful conference and the presentations have spurred my interest, as I hope they have stimulated yours. Let's continue to research, publish, and exchange views, and to those of you who are crossing over the same ocean that brought Swedes, Finns, Dutch, and others to our shores 350 years ago, we wish you good luck, good health, and bon voyage.

NOTES

1. Hans Mattson, *250th Anniversary of the First Swedish Settlement in America* (Minneapolis, 1889), 43.
2. Ibid., 49–51. The translation was subsequently published by the Historical Society of Delaware, *The Records of Holy Trinity (Old Swedes) Church*, Papers 3, 1890.
3. Jehu Curtis Clay, *Annals of the Swedes on the Delaware*, 4th ed., John Ericsson Memorial Committee (Chicago: The Committee, 1938), 212.
4. Henry D. Paxson, *Where Pennsylvania History Began* (Philadelphia: Swedish Colonial Society, 1926).
5. Christopher Ward, *New Sweden on the Delaware* (Philadelphia: University of Pennsylvania Press, 1938); *Delaware Tercentenary Almanac & Historical Repository* (Wilmington: Delaware Tercentenary Committee, 1938).
6. *Sweden's Participation in the U.S. Celebration of the New Sweden Tercentenary*, comp. Fritz Henriksson, trans. Gosta E. Sandstrom (Stockholm, 1939), 67–68.
7. Thomas Campanius Holm, *Kort Beskrifning om Provincien Nya Sverige uti America* (Stockholm, 1702). Eng. ed.: *A Short Description of the Province of New Sweden*, trans. Peter S. Du Ponceau, Vol. 3 of the Memoirs of the Historical Society of Pennsylvania (Philadelphia: The Society, 1834), 153–56.

8. *The Instruction for Johan Printz*, trans. Amandus Johnson (Philadelphia: The Swedish Colonial Society, 1930), 116.
9. Ibid., 117.
10. Johan Rising, "Report for 1655," in *Narratives of Early Pennsylvania, West New Jersey, and Delaware, 1630–1707*, ed. Albert Cook Myers (1912; reprint, New York: Barnes & Noble, 1967), 156–57.
11. See Holm, *A Short Description of New Sweden*, 153–56.
12. *Instruction for Printz*, 23–24.
13. Herbert C. Kraft, "The Northern Lenape," in *The Lenape Indian: A Symposium* (South Orange, N.J.: Archaeological Research Center, Seton Hall University, 1984), map, 4; *The Lenape: Archaeology, History, and Ethnography*, vol. 21, collections of the New Jersey Historical Society (Newark: The Society, 1986), 9.
14. John H. Wuorinen, *The Finns on the Delaware 1638–1655* (New York: Columbia University Press, 1938).
15. E. A. Louhi, *The Delaware Finns* (New York: Humanity Press, 1925).
16. Johnson, *Swedish Settlements*, 2:696.
17. Ibid., 692.
18. Ibid., 680.
19. The English translation and a Swedish transcript has since been published; see Stellan Dahlgren and Hans Norman, *The Rise and Fall of New Sweden: Governor Johan Risingh's Journal, 1654–1655, in Its Historical Context* (Stockholm: Almqvist & Wicksell International, 1988), 130–287.

Contributors

MARSHALL JOSEPH BECKER is professor of anthropology at West Chester University. He is the author of "The Stature of a Susquehannock Population of the Mid-16th Century Based on Skeletal Remains from 46HM73," *Pennsylvania Archaeologist* 61 (1991): 73–88, and "Lenape Clothing of the Early 16th Century as Indicated by Artifacts in the Ethnographic Collections of the Historical Museum of the University of Lund, Sweden," *Meddelanden från Lunds universitets historiska museum*, n.s., 9 (1991–92): 1–24.

BARBARA E. BENSON is Director of the Historical Society of Delaware and adjunct professor of history at the University of Delaware. She is the author of *Logs and Lumber: The Development of the Lumber Industry in Michigan's Lower Peninsula (1837–1870)* (1989).

FRANK BLOMFELT is an independent scholar living in Fjardhundra, Sweden. He is the editor of *Andreas Sandels Dagbok 1701–1743* (Stockholm: Norstedts Tryckeri, 1988).

STAFFAN BRUNIUS is Curator of the Americas at Folkens Museum-Etnografiska, Stockholm, Sweden. He is the author of "North American Indian Collections at the Folkens Museum-Etnografiska, Stockholm," *European Review of Native American Studies* 4 (1990).

STEN CARL OSCAR CARLSSON. The late Sten Carlsson was a professor of history at Uppsala University and a noted authority on Swedish history in the seventeenth century. He was the author of *Swedes in North America, 1638–1988: Technical, Cultural, and Political Achievements* (Stockholm: Streiffert, 1988).

STELLAN DAHLGREN is associate professor of history at the University of Uppsala. He published (with Hans Norman) *The Rise and Fall of New Sweden: Governor Johan Risingh's Journal 1654–1655 in Its Historical Context* (Stockholm: Almqvist & Wiksell Int., 1988). He is also the coauthor of *Från feodalism till kapitalism* (Uppsala: Uppsala University, 1990) and *Kungar och Krigare* (Stockholm: Atlantis, 1992).

CHARLES T. GEHRING is director of the New Netherland Project at the New York State Library in Albany, New York. His recent publications include *Laws and Writs of Appeal, 1647–1663* and *Fort Orange Court Minutes, 1652–1660*, New Netherland Documents Series (Syracuse, N.Y.: Syracuse University Press, 1991 and 1990, respectively).

IVES GODDARD is curator, department of anthropology, National Museum of Natural History and National Museum of Man, Smithsonian Institution, Washington, D.C. He is most recently the coauthor (with Kathleen J. Bragdon) of *Native Writings in Massachusetts*, 2 vols., no. 185 of Memoirs of the American Philosophical Society (Philadelphia: The Society, 1988).

CAROL E. HOFFECKER, Richards Professor of History and Associate Provost for Graduate Studies, University of Delaware, is the author of numerous works on the history of Wilmington and Delaware including: *Wilmington Delaware: Portrait of an Industrial City* (University of Virginia, 1974); *Delaware: A Bicentennial History* (Norton, 1977); and *Corporate Capital: Wilmington in the Twentieth Century* (Temple, 1984).

TERRY G. JORDAN is Walter Prescott Webb Professor of Geography at the University of Texas at Austin. He is the coauthor (with Matti Kaups) of *The American Backwoods Frontier: An Ethnic and Ecological Interpretation* (Baltimore: Johns Hopkins University Press, 1989) and *North American Cattle Ranching Frontiers* (Albuquerque: University of New Mexico Press, 1993).

OLAVI KOIVUKANGAS is the director of the Institute of Migration in Turku, Finland. He is the author of *Delaware 350: The Beginning of Finnish Migration to the New World* (Turku: Institute of Migration, 1988), and *Sea, Gold, and Sugarcane: Attraction vs. Distance, Finns in Australia, 1851–1947* (Turku: Institute of Migration, 1986).

KAREN ORDAHL KUPPERMAN is professor of history at the University of Connecticut. She is the editor of *Major Problems in Colonial American History* (New York: D. C. Heath, 1993) and the author of *Providence Island, 1630–1641: The Other Puritan Colony* (Cambridge: Cambridge University Press, 1993).

HANS NORMAN is associate professor and head of the Department of History at Uppsala University. He is the coauthor (with Harold Runblom) of *Nordic Transatlantic Connections: Nordic Migration to the New World After 1800* (Norwegian University Press, 1988) and (with Stellan Dahlgren) *The Rise and Fall of New Sweden: Governor Johan Risingh's Journal 1654–1655 in Its Historical Context* (Stockholm: Almqvist & Wiksell Int., 1988).

JUHA Y. PENTIKÄINEN is chairman of the Department of Comparative Religion, University of Helsinki. His books include *Cultural Minorities in Finland: An Overview Towards Cultural Policy* (Helsinki, 1985), and *Kalevala Mythology* (Bloomington: Indiana University Press, 1989).

MARGARETA REVERA is associate professor of history at the University of Uppsala. Her publications include *Gods och gård 1650–1680* (Uppsala, 1975) and several articles including "1600—talsbönderna och deras herrar," *Rättshistoriska studier*, Ser. 2, vol. 9 (Stockholm, 1984), and "En barock historia" in *Tre Karlar* (Stockholm, 1984).

PER MARTIN TVENGSBERG, a free-lance scientist, studies the cultivation of Finnish forest rye. He is the author of *Weather-Prophesier and Healer in Solor-Värmland Finnforest* (Estonian Academy of Sciences, 1990).

PETER WACKER, professor of geography at Rutgers University, is the author of *Land and People: A Cultural Geography of Preindustrial New Jersey, Origins and Settlement Patterns* (New Brunswick: Rutgers University Press, 1975).

RICHARD WALDRON is executive director of the New Jersey Historical Commission.

CLINTON A. WESLAGER. The late Clinton A. Weslager, retired professor of history at Brandywine College, was the author of many works on Delaware's early history and the history of Indians in the mid-Atlantic region. Among his books are *The Delaware Indians: A History* (New Brunswick: Rutgers University Press, 1972), *The Log Cabin in America: From Pioneer Days to the Present* (New Brunswick: Rutgers University Press, 1969), and *New Sweden on the Delaware: 1638–1655* (Wilmington, Del.: Middle Atlantic Press, 1988).

BORJE WESTLUND is head of the Manuscripts Department of the Swedish Royal Library in Stockholm, Sweden.

LORRAINE E. WILLIAMS. is curator of Archaeology and Ethnology at the New Jersey State Museum. Her publications include (with Karen A. Flinn) *Trade Wampum: New Jersey to the Plains* (Trenton: New Jersey State Museum, 1990).

Index